HIGH TIDE IN THE KOREAN WAR

★ ★ ★

How an Outnumbered American Regiment
Defeated the Chinese at the Battle of Chipyong–ni

Leo Barron

STACKPOLE
BOOKS

Published by
STACKPOLE BOOKS
5067 Ritter Road
Mechanicsburg, PA 17055
www.stackpolebooks.com

Printed in the United States of America

10 9 8 7 6 5 4 3 2 1

Library of Congress Cataloging-in-Publication Data

Barron, Leo, author.
  High tide in the Korean War : how an outnumbered American regiment defeated the Chinese at the Battle of Chipyong-ni / Leo Barron.
    pages cm
  Includes bibliographical references and index.
  ISBN 978-0-8117-1561-4
1. Chipyong-ni, Battle of, Chip'yong-ni, Korea, 1951. 2. Twin Tunnels, Battle of, Korea, 1951. 3. Korean War, 1950-1953—Regimental histories—United States. 4. United States. Army. Infantry Regiment, 23rd (1866-1957) I. Title.
  DS918.2.C37B37 2015
  951.904'242—dc23
                           2015024361

CONTENTS

PREFACE

"We're going to have to get to the top of that hill! The Chinese are coming up from the other side! This is our only chance!"

—1st Lt. Harold P. Mueller, Fox Company, 21st Infantry Regiment

MONDAY, JANUARY 29, 1951, 1215 HOURS: CHARLIE COMPANY, 23RD INFANTRY REGIMENT, 2ND INFANTRY DIVISION, SOUTH OF CHIPYONG-NI, SOUTH KOREA

"Let's get out of here!" the platoon leader shouted.

For Pvt. Richard C. Fockler, the lieutenant yelling was the second indication that the patrol was in trouble. The first was the exploding mortar round that cut short his chow time. Fockler had been with the platoon for only five days; in fact, he had been on active duty for less than three months. Prior to that, he had worked in a Chevy plant near Flint, Michigan. Now, he was wondering why he was in Korea in the first place.

The previous night, his platoon leader, 1st Lt. James P. Mitchell, had summoned his entire unit into his hut. For the few veterans left in the platoon, a meeting this late was out of the ordinary, and anything out of the ordinary was a bad thing. Their nervousness was evident, and even the newbies could tell that something was up. Finally, Mitchell revealed the purpose behind the late-night get-together: They were heading out on a mounted patrol to find the Chinese, who were hiding somewhere north of the Han River, near the town of Chipyong-ni.

Like many young men, the Army had recalled Private Fockler from the Inactive Reserve in November 1950. November had been a bad month for the U.N. forces. The Chinese People's Volunteer Force (CPVF) had invaded North Korea, sending the American forces and their allies retreating pell-mell until they were below the 38th Parallel, like panicked refugees fleeing a flash flood.

For several months, the various Army and Marine units fought a running battle southward against the inexorable communist onslaught. Finally, the Chinese armies reached the end of their supply lines. Commissar Peng Dehuai, the commander of the Chinese and North Korean forces, then ordered his armies to stop and reorganize before the next big push. Bruised and battered, the U.N. forces broke contact and withdrew south of the Han River. For several days, the front lines were quiet. As a result, no one really knew where the Chinese and North Korean forces had halted, hence the reason for the patrols.

On January 28, twenty-four hours prior to Mitchell's reconnaissance, Maj. Gen. Clark L. Ruffner, commander of the 2nd Infantry Division, had ordered the 23rd Infantry Regiment to send out a patrol to the Chipyong-ni area. Ruffner chose Chipyong-ni because of its strategic location as a road hub. Other than that, he had no inkling as to the whereabouts of the Chinese forces. Col. Paul L. Freeman, the regiment's commanding officer, was not too pleased with the assignment. Chipyong-ni was over twenty miles by air and nearly forty miles by road from friendly lines. If the patrol ran into trouble, it would be hard-pressed to escape, let alone defend itself. However, he had his orders, and he sent out a patrol to investigate the situation. Amazingly, the patrol from 1st Battalion found nothing and returned later that day.

Ruffner's boss, Maj. Gen. Edward Almond, the X Corps commander, desperately needed to know the whereabouts of the CPVF, so Ruffner ordered another reconnaissance of the same area, using the same route. Freeman knew using the same avenue of approach for an infiltration mission was a recipe for disaster, but it was the only way any unit could reach Chipyong-ni, since only one north–south highway existed in his immediate area. Hence, he issued an order to 1st Battalion to repeat the operation. Maj. George Russell, the commander of 1st Battalion, selected his Charlie Company to carry out the operation. At 2300 hours, Lieutenant Mitchell received his first warning order, and several minutes later he was in a hut, briefing his platoon about the upcoming reconnaissance mission.

Since the route skirted the boundary between X Corps and IX Corps, General Almond requested additional combat power for the patrol from the 24th Infantry Division, which shared the boundary line with the 2nd Infantry Division. The 24th Infantry Division headquarters delegated the mission to Fox Company, 21st Infantry Regiment. First Lt. Harold P. Mueller would lead the understrength platoon of only fourteen men. The rendezvous point would be the town of Iho-ri, the only hamlet in the vicinity, located along the east bank of the Han River, which served as the boundary line between the two divisions.

At 0600 hours the next morning, Lieutenant Mitchell walked into the S3 Operations tent to receive the complete order. His mission was to lead his platoon and its attachments to the Twin Tunnels area, several miles south of Chipyong-ni. Along the way, he would link up with the other platoon from the 24th Infantry Division at approximately 1030 hours. Because the roads were in poor condition and no bridges spanned the Han River in this sector, they would cross the Han at a fording site. This meant cumbersome tanks and unwieldy trucks were out of the question; the patrol would have to use mainly jeeps to reach its objective. Moreover, Colonel Russell wanted Mitchell to find the enemy, but he did not want the small patrol to become decisively engaged with them.

Mitchell had a hodgepodge force to accomplish his mission, including forty-four officers and men, with two $^3/_4$-ton weapons carriers and nine jeeps. To beef up his platoon, Russell allocated a section from Dog Company, which provided 75mm and 57mm recoilless rifles. In addition to those weapons, the patrol was armed with a 3.5-inch bazooka, a 60mm mortar, two .50-caliber and three .30-caliber machine guns mounted on pintles on their jeeps, and two .30-caliber machine guns on tripods that could be dismounted if the mission required. Scattered throughout his force were several Browning Automatic riflemen. Everyone else carried carbines or M1 Garands. For radio coverage, the patrol had two SCR-300 radios, the standard company-level FM radios. Mitchell also had two SCR-619 radios, allowing him to communicate with the single-engine L-5 Sentinel prop plane that would fly ahead of the patrol to provide over-the-horizon coverage. The pilot could also direct air support, if required.

Accompanying Mitchell was Capt. Melvin R. Stai, one of the assistant S3s, whose job was to coordinate the linkup between the two division patrols. Once he had completed that mission, he was to return to base. To ensure better command and control, Stai would ride along in the jeep that had the SCR-619 radios.

At 0950 hours, the patrol left its assembly area to link up with the platoon from the 21st Infantry Regiment. In terms of military value, the Twin Tunnels had little to offer. The area had earned its name because it was a railroad burrowed underneath two separate ridges. Tucked away in a small valley to the north was the village of Chipyong-ni. The otherwise-unimportant town was a road net, and thus decisive terrain. In order for the Chinese to conduct further offensive operations to the south, they would want to flank the U.N. forces occupying the other major road hub at Wonju to the east; to do so, they would need to control Chipyong-ni.

Of course, Private Fockler did not know any of this. He was just a rifleman, riding along on the back of a jeep and trailing behind the lead vehicle in the column. To him, Korea looked like a Martian wasteland from an H. G. Wells novel. Most of the snow-covered hills were devoid of trees, save for the occasional Lombardy poplar. Dotting the valleys were terraced rice paddies, many of which were iced over and looked like sheets of frosted glass. Thankfully, the patrol was on a paved road, but it was icy, forcing the column to slow down. Everything around Fockler was still, save the sounds of the plane, buzzing overhead like a flying lawn mower, and his own jeep engine, gurgling like someone using mouth-wash. Fockler wondered if his squad leader knew something he didn't, as he did not depart with the platoon. As it turned out, the officer had attended company sick call earlier that morning before the patrol left, leaving Fockler with a squad of rookies. It was a team without a leader, and since everyone was brand new, none of the team members knew how to play well with each other. To the young soldier from Michigan, it was not an auspicious start to one of his first combat patrols. He hoped the enemy would not test his inexperienced squad.

Initially, it was a smooth ride. Around 1115 hours, the two patrols met up near Iho-ri. Since Lieutenant Mueller's platoon from Fox Company, 21st Infantry, was on foot, the soldiers of Charlie Company provided them with five jeeps brought along for that purpose. Together, the two groups continued their trek north toward the Twin Tunnels. Suddenly, the lead jeep blew a tire, and its crew traded places with Fockler in his jeep, leaving the young private and several other soldiers with the stricken vehicle. Lieutenant Mitchell ordered them to fix the flat tire and then catch up with the patrol as it continued farther up the road.

The men struggled to replace the flat. They had a spare, but soon discovered they did not have a lug wrench. Luckily, they found another crescent wrench, allowing them to remove the lug nuts from the flat tire, but it required some finagling. Finally, they mounted the new tire and quickly hopped into their jeep to catch up with their platoon. The whole episode took an hour. Fortunately, thought Fockler, the Chinese had left them alone during those vulnerable minutes.

Meanwhile, Lieutenant Mitchell continued with his reconnaissance. When they reached a ford site south of the tiny village of Sinchon, Mitchell halted the patrol. He looked at his watch and calculated that he was running out time. He did not want to be cruising around enemy territory after dark, especially when half of his forces—around twenty men—were rookies like Fockler. Mitchell scanned the area. To his southwest was a large hill, which the cartographers had designated as Hill 453. Because it overlooked the surrounding hills, Point 453 was key terrain. Whoever controlled it would then control the road that wound past and onto Chipyong-ni.

While Mitchell waited at the ford, Lieutenant Mueller and Captain Stai approached him, and the three officers discussed the various options. To save time, Stai proposed that he and his driver proceed alone to Sinchon in their jeep and conduct a short search of the area while Mitchell and Mueller continued on to the railroad tracks at the Twin Tunnels.

Mitchell nodded in agreement. It was not the ideal solution, but the clock was ticking. Captain Stai returned to his jeep and drove north toward Sinchon, taking the SCR-619 radios with him. As his vehicle closed in on the village, Stai decided to investigate on foot, leaving his driver behind to wait in the vehicle. It was now 1215 hours. That was the last known sighting of Captain Stai, who was never heard from again.

The main body continued to push north. When it reached the railroad, the men dismounted, and the platoon from Fox Company conducted the rest of the patrol on foot. Simultaneously, Fockler and the other grunts from Dog and Charlie Companies started to reposition the column so that the jeeps were facing south instead of their original northerly direction, enabling the patrol to make a quick exfiltration if the need arose. After completing their task, the soldiers from 23rd Infantry began to eat their meager lunch of canned meat and hard chocolate from their C rations.

Suddenly, the foot patrol from Fox Company noticed some figures on a hill north of the railroad (Hill 333). Within seconds, the men realized the figures were roughly fifteen to twenty Chinese infantry running toward them. In response, Mueller's platoon opened fire. As if on cue, Fockler heard the *crumping* sound of mortars leaving their tubes. The rounds started to detonate among the column like exploding hailstones, most landing near the two jeeps closest to the Twin Tunnels.

The Chinese infantry on Hill 333 were not the only new arrivals to the party. Flying above the column in the L-5 Sentinel was Maj. Millard O. Engen, the executive officer for 1st Battalion, 23rd Infantry Regiment. From his perch, he could make out the Chinese infantry on Hill 333. But what alarmed him the most were the enemy soldiers on Hill 453, south and behind the mounted patrol. Engen counted the men and estimated that a company of Reds was atop the dominant terrain feature. From their current location, the Chinese rifle company could easily cut off the escape route for Mitchell's force. Engen grabbed the handset from the SCR-619 and radioed Mitchell's platoon to warn them. Unfortunately, there was no one to answer the call because the radios were with Captain Stai, who had wandered alone off into Sinchon.

Back with the column, Cpl. Leroy Gibbons, a Charlie Company soldier, opened fire with his jeep's .50-caliber machine gun; the M2 started to chug away at the onrushing Chinese, sounding like a slow-moving locomotive. Within minutes, the corporal had emptied his entire ammo can at the enemy infantry, but the big gun failed to make any impact. The Chinese kept swarming down the hill like an unstoppable human avalanche. At this point, the entire column was under direct fire from unseen enemy machine guns.

To keep the men from panicking, 2nd Lt. William G. Penrod, the single officer with Dog Company, exposed himself as he moved about the row of vehicles, exhorting the men while he tried to find one of the pesky Chinese machine guns. "Penrod was walking up and down our column as cool as he could be," Fockler recalled.

Lieutenant Mitchell realized how precarious their situation had become. Since his platoon combat team was too far from the tactical assembly area, the 300-series radios were useless. In fact, the atmospheric

conditions and the high hills prevented him from even contacting anyone within the column on the radio. Even worse, he had lost communication with Captain Stai, the only one who could communicate with
the liaison plane circling above.

As his mind raced for solutions, Mitchell saw Chinese infantry barreling down Hill 453 to capture the ford site and seal off the only avenue
of escape for the patrol. At that moment, the Charlie Company platoon
leader realized he had led his reconnaissance unit into a preplanned
ambush. Colonel Freeman's misgivings about a patrol using the same
route twice were justified.

"Let's get out of here!" Mitchell shouted to his men.

Like firefighters hearing an alarm, everyone started to scramble onto
the jeeps and weapons carriers. After several minutes, the column began
to roll southward.

According to Private Fockler, who wrote about the incident in postwar correspondence, and other sources, Chinese machine gunners and
riflemen were hammering the convoy hard. Fockler recalled "the driver
in the lead jeep panicked as soon as his vehicle was hit and he jammed
on his brakes, bailed out, and stalled the column."

Like a car accident in a tunnel, the entire column screeched to a halt
with nowhere to go in the narrow valley. The men bounded out of their
jeeps and dove into the ditches that lined the road. Most of them
remained calm and began to return fire at their attackers. One of the soldiers, Pvt. Allan G. Anderson, had left his rifle back at his jeep. Corporal
Gibbons ordered him to go back and find it. Heeding the command, the
obedient soldier got up and dashed back toward the abandoned vehicles.
"The man never came back," Fockler remarked matter of factly.

Private Anderson failed to reach the jeep the first time, so he tried
again. As he crept away from the platoon the second time, several Chinese soldiers saw him. They rushed forward to grab him; according to
witnesses, Anderson "engaged them in hand-to-hand combat until he
was killed." For his bravery, the Army awarded Anderson a posthumous
Silver Star.[1]

As the soldiers lay in the roadside ditches, firing into the hills, the
Chinese commanders directed the machine guns to neutralize the now-
empty jeeps. "We heard a burst of machine gun fire and then silence,"
Fockler recalled. "Then came another burst of machine gun fire and the

sound of coolant draining from a radiator. They had effectively stopped us from leaving on the motor vehicles."

The private was scared, but he was still in the fight. As he crouched in the ditch, he noticed a solitary figure approaching the convoy. For a moment, Fockler hesitated. The man wore a pale white, quilted uniform; he looked like a bastardized version of the Michelin Man. He was the enemy. Still, Fockler could not engage.

Suddenly, the Chinese soldier noticed the American soldier staring him and swung around to shoot him. The abrupt jerk shattered the rookie's reluctance, and he opened fire with his M1 Garand, peppering the human target, who collapsed to the ground. To ensure his adversary was dead, the private then emptied all eight rounds into the man's body.

Elsewhere, the officers were scrambling to extricate themselves and their men from the trap. Seeing the roadblock to the south, Lieutenant Penrod grabbed the 75mm recoilless rifle crew and ordered them to open fire on the Chinese forces blocking the ford site. After a few rounds downrange, he quickly realized that the recoilless rifle would not save them, as the Chinese infantry continued to climb the hill that hugged the ford's east bank. He assessed that if the Chinese reached the top of the hill, they would have excellent plunging fire on the Charlie Company platoon—it would be like shooting fish in a barrel.

Nearby, Lieutenant Mueller from Fox Company had reached the same conclusion. He began to clamber up the closest ridgeline, with the rest of his platoon following behind him. The platoon leader from the 21st Infantry determined that survival depended on reaching the high ground, which would provide defensible terrain and excellent fields of fire. Unfortunately, the slippery slopes, covered in wet snow, made the trek even more arduous. After several minutes, Mueller paused to catch his breath. Between his wheezing and panting, he lifted his binoculars and scanned the hills for the Chinese infantry. Looking down the eastern slope and opposite his own location, Mueller spied scores of men in quilted uniforms scaling the same hill.

"We're going to have to get to the top of that hill! The Chinese are coming up from the other side! This is our only chance!" he shouted to Lieutenant Mitchell while pointing to the closest knoll.

The Charlie Company platoon leader, still down by the road, immediately grasped the urgency of the situation. He urged his men to climb the ridge and join Mueller's group, while Lieutenant Penrod collected the few crew-served weapons they could hump up the slope. In the end, it was only one .30-caliber light machine gun and the 3.5-inch bazooka. They abandoned everything else: the 60mm mortar, the recoilless rifles, and the jeep-mounted machine guns.

Lieutenant Mitchell had accomplished his mission. He had found the Chinese Army, but it would be to no avail if no one in his platoon survived to report the news back to headquarters. The only thing that mattered to Mitchell now was the race. Who would reach the top of the hill first? If the Americans did, then they had a chance. If the communist Chinese beat them to the top, it would be the end for the survivors of Charlie Company.[2]

INTRODUCTION

Most Americans have never heard of the Battle of Chipyong-ni. I would argue that many of those who consider themselves knowledgeable about U.S. military history are also unaware of one of the most crucial engagements of the Korean War. I was one of those people. I had written numerous articles and two books about battles in World War II, and yet, despite my extensive background in military history, I had never heard of Chipyong-ni. One day, while channel surfing, I came upon a one-hour documentary on the Korean War. One of the battles mentioned in the program was Chipyong-ni.

Immediately, I was intrigued. The central elements of the story were right out of a Hollywood blockbuster: a single U.S. Army infantry regiment found itself trapped behind enemy lines, facing several Chinese Army divisions. Despite the long odds, the 23rd Infantry, together with its attached French Battalion, whipped the Chinese divisions and altered the course of the Korean War. The story was tailor-made for a great movie. After reading more about the engagement, I asked myself, why I had never heard of the Battle of Chipyong-ni?

Visit any major bookstore and you will find an entire shelf devoted to World War II. Seventy years after it ended, filmmakers still produce profitable movies about the Second World War. For decades, stories about Vietnam were moneymakers, too. In terms of cinema, the eighties and nineties saw an explosion of Vietnam-themed movies in which the war in Southeast Asia served as the central backdrop. During this era, Vietnam War movies earned Academy Awards for Best Picture and Best Director while actors cemented their careers starring in them.

On the other hand, the Korean War holds little interest for most Americans. Other than the television show *M*A*S*H*, the Korean War has few anchors in popular culture. Sandwiched between World War II and Vietnam, the war neither divided the nation nor united it. As a result, historians have called it the Forgotten War. Still, it was a war, and a bloody one. Roughly 30,000 Americans died in the Korean War and over 109,000 were wounded or missing in action, making it the fifth bloodiest war in U.S. history.

For the Korean people, both North and South, the war was the watershed event of the twentieth century. Even the Koreans who want to move on and put the war behind them cannot ignore its lasting impact. An ugly scar of concertina wire, buried minefields, concrete blockhouses, and watchtowers crisscrosses the peninsula, as if someone performed makeshift surgery on the country and botched the stitches to close the wound. The Demilitarized Zone (DMZ) serves as a constant, painful reminder that a state of war still exists between the two countries.

In addition to the fortified border, both Koreas suffered grievous casualties during the war. Statisticians estimate the Republic of Korea suffered over 800,000 casualties (416,000 dead and 428,000 wounded) from an overall population of 20 million people: 4 percent of the total population. For the Democratic People's Republic of Korea, the war was even bloodier. Though the communist regime suffered fewer casualties (approximately 500,000), it had a smaller overall population of only 9.6 million; as a result, it lost over 5 percent of its population.

Korea (both North and South) and the United States were not the only countries to leave behind a mountain of dead. In the late autumn of 1950, the Chinese government decided to enter the war in Korea against the United States and the United Nations. Several years later, over 115,000 Chinese lay dead, while another 221,000 were wounded and a further 29,000 were missing.[1]

After battling for three years, the two sides signed an armistice on July 27, 1953, and a new border was established only a few miles from the original 1950 border. Despite all the bloodshed, the war ended in a draw, and both sides agreed to return to the *status quo ante bellum*.

Consequently, the Korean War did not end in a total victory for the United States. Instead, both sides settled for an uneasy peace that still exists to this day.

Was the Korean War America's first defeat? Foreign policy experts have been asking the question since the negotiators signed the armistice. This book is written from the position that the Korean War was not a defeat. To the contrary, I believe it was a victory. The United States entered the war in response to the North Korean invasion, and the original goals were the restoration of the international border along the 38th Parallel and the ejection of North Korean forces from South Korean territory. Using that as a benchmark, the war was a victory for the United States and the United Nations.

However, the war was more than a restoration of boundaries and sovereignty. For South Korea, it allowed for the rebirth of the Korean nation. Since the cessation of hostilities, South Korea has grown into a vibrant and powerful republic. People all over the world buy Korean-manufactured products, and its capital of Seoul has become an international center of commerce and industry. Moreover, South Koreans enjoy one of the highest standards living in the world.

None of this would have happened had the North Koreans been successful in their invasion of the South. If the communists had pushed U.N. forces into the Sea of Japan, then South Korea would have ended up like its brother to the north—a decaying and decrepit state.

North Korea is the best example of communism's failure. According to the United Nations, the North Korean economy is ranked 120th in Gross Domestic Product, while the South Korean economy is 15th in the world. With a stagnant economy, the North Korean government cannot even feed its own people, who suffer from malnutrition and famine. As North Koreans starve, South Koreans are thriving. Businesses like Daewoo, Hyundai, LG, and Samsung are some of the largest business conglomerates in the world and have become household names in U.S. family rooms, garages, and offices.[2]

But the future was far from certain in February 1951. Around the world, the evil forces of communism were on the march. In Europe, Comrade Joseph Stalin, the leader of the Soviet Union, tightened his grip over countries such as Bulgaria, Czechoslovakia, East Germany, Hungary, Poland, and Romania. In those hapless nations, a fanatical Nazi master was replaced by a ruthless communist leader. In the United States, the Venona Project, the top-secret decryption of Soviet diplomatic cables, led to the arrest and sentencing of Julius and Ethel Rosenberg for espionage and revealed the frightening level of communist infiltration in the U.S. State Department and other federal agencies. In China, the communists won the civil war against the American-backed Nationalist government. Even worse, the victorious communists of the newly constituted People's Republic of China followed up their success by signing a defense treaty with the Soviet Union. As a result, the two most populous countries in Asia and Europe were under the communist yoke. Alas, Stalin and his new allies were far from finished. They wanted to conquer the rest of Europe and Asia, and eventually they wanted to crush the United States.

In Korea, the surprise invasion of nearly 300,000 Chinese soldiers the previous November had changed the course of the war. Prior to the Chinese intervention, the U.N. forces were routing the North Koreans, who were falling back to the Yalu River after the Marines successfully invaded Inchon in September 1950. For the United Nations, the North Korean invasion was its first test as an international peacekeeping body. The members of the U.N. Security Council were cognizant that its predecessor, the League of Nations, had failed to stop World War II because it lacked the mechanisms to stop a land-grabbing Hitler. Leading the way, President Harry S. Truman decided that Korea was the arena to show the world that the young United Nations was not a paper tiger.

On the other hand, Mao Zedong, the leader of Communist China, did not want a U.S. presence so close to his border. In October 1950, he ordered his armies to push the American-led forces off the Korean peninsula. The U.N. coalition was in retreat. Even worse, the Chinese seemed unstoppable. Despite technological advantages and overwhelming firepower, the American-led U.N. Eighth Army seemed incapable of defeating the Chinese People's Volunteer Army, which swamped successive defensive positions with wave after wave of endless infantry. As a result, the rank and file believed South Korea was lost. Some even thought Korea was only the first step. They believed Stalin's appetite, like Hitler's, would grow more insatiable if Korea fell to the communists. And if Korea fell, it would only be a matter of time before the rest of the Far East came under communist domination.

Lt. Gen. Matthew Ridgway, famed former commander of the 82nd Airborne Division and the XVIII Airborne Corps in World War II, was in charge of the Eighth Army. Though he had been on the job for less than two months, he could not wait any longer to learn the ropes. He realized he had to stop the Chinese somewhere—anywhere. His men could not endure another retreat. Many of the divisions were under-strength, and morale had suffered after several weeks of retreating. He ordered a single regiment, the 23rd Infantry, under the command of Col. Paul Freeman, to hold Chipyong-ni to buy time for the rest of the U.N. forces. At the time, the small town was a vital road hub. If the Chinese seized it, they would have unfettered access to much of central Korea. Arrayed against this one regiment of 4,500 soldiers were several Chinese divisions, totaling nearly 25,000 men. The communists outnumbered the U.N. forces five to one.

Despite the odds, Freeman's victory at Chipyong-ni turned the tide of the war. If he had lost and the Chinese had destroyed his entire regiment, it would have been one of the worst defeats in U.S. military history. Furthermore, it would have led to the fall of South Korea.

The stakes could not have been any higher.

CHAPTER 1

Why Korea?

"We were laying our baby Republic [South Korea] naked on the altar."

—Lt. Gen. Matthew B. Ridgway, commander, U.S. Eighth Army

SUNDAY, JUNE 25, 1950: KOREAN PENINSULA

Korea was an odd place for the Cold War's first major conflict. In the summer of 1950, seven months before the ambush near the Twin Tunnels, most Americans—including most of the soldiers in 1st Lt. James P. Mitchell's platoon—couldn't find South Korea on a map. North Korea's dictator, Kim Il-Sung, counted on America's geographic illiteracy when he made the decision to invade South Korea, ostensibly an ally of the United States. In 1950, the dividing line that cleaved the Korean Peninsula into North and South Korea was an afterthought between the two dominant powers at the end of the Second World War: the United States and the Union of Soviet Socialist Republics (USSR). Kim Il-Sung sought to end the artificial separation and control all of Korea. Comrade Joseph Stalin, his benefactor, supported the ambitious dictator, arming his military with Soviet weapons and sending Soviet advisors to train his armies. On the morning of June 25, 1950, Kim Il-Sung's communist-trained and -equipped armies invaded South Korea.

Prior to the invasion, few policymakers in the West thought that anyone would come to the aid of South Korea if North Korea attacked it. They had good reason to feel that way. For the last hundred years, Korea had been the plaything of empires. Culturally, Korea looked to China as its protector and progenitor. As a result, when Chinese power and influence began to wane under the last emperors of the Qing

Dynasty in the latter half of the nineteenth century, Korea was ripe for exploitation. This was evident when Western traders and navies arrived to sign and enforce unfair trade agreements with Korea.

Leading the way was Japan. Unlike the Chinese, who tried to resist Western influence, the Japanese embraced it after Commodore Matthew C. Perry's fleet made landfall in Tokyo Bay in 1854. The samurai rulers of Japan believed the only way their country could survive was by becoming a colonizing nation with a modern, industrialized army and navy. However, like Germany, Great Britain, and even the United States, Japan's growing industry needed raw materials, and Japan had little mineral wealth or other natural resources within its own boundaries. On the other hand, their neighbor across the Sea of Japan did, and so—just like their European counterparts had done in Africa, Asia, and elsewhere—Japan sought to control Korea, bringing them into conflict with China. In 1894, Japan and China decided diplomacy was useless and went to war for control of the Korean Peninsula. The Imperial Japanese Army and Navy, with their modern weapons and European-trained soldiers and sailors, were too much for China. In 1895, the governments of China and Japan signed the Treaty of Shimonoseki, in which China ceded all territorial and political rights in Korea to Japan.

Obviously, no one had bothered to consult the Koreans about their new landlords. In response, King Kojong, Korea's monarch, sought assistance from another nearby power: Russia. Czar Nicholas II was thrilled, and within a few years, Russian businessmen and military advisors were operating inside Korea. The Japanese had traded one competitor for an even more powerful one. Unlike China, Russia had a modern army and navy. Despite this deterrent, Japan's government pressed ahead with its goal of conquering the Korean Peninsula; the country's growing industrial economy demanded it. In February 1904, Japan surprised and defeated the Russian Pacific Fleet based inside Port Arthur on the Liaodong Peninsula; after a protracted siege, the port fell. Even worse for the czar, Japan defeated the Russian Baltic Fleet at the battle of Tsushima and crushed the remaining land forces in the battle of Mukden in 1905. It was the first time an Asian nation had defeated a modern European country.

After the belligerents signed the Treaty of Portsmouth in September 1905, Japan found itself sharing a table with the other Western colonial powers: its new colony was the entire Hermit Kingdom, another name for Korea. The United States and Great Britain even recognized Japan's control of Korea as part of the treaty. With this new conquest, the former samurais decided to extract as much wealth and resources as they could from their neighbor. The Japanese were far worse landlords than the Russians or the Chinese. In effect, the Koreans were now slaves, and outside of the peninsula, no one in America or Europe cared. For the next forty years, the "Land of the Morning Calm" was under the yoke of the emperor of Japan.

During that time, Japan used Korea as a stepping-stone to invade Manchuria in September 1931. With little effort, the Imperial Japanese Army conquered the mineral-rich territory and added it to their growing empire. The Chinese never forgot, nor forgave, the Japanese. More importantly, the Chinese remembered the role Korea played in Manchuria's conquest. If the Japanese had not been in Korea, then they would have been hard-pressed to take the Chinese territory. In July 1937, the Japanese attacked China proper. The descendants of the samurai seemed unstoppable.

Then, the Japanese bombed Pearl Harbor on December 7, 1941. The surprise attack changed everything in the Pacific. For several years, the Japanese battled the Americans on the land, sea, and in the air, but it was a losing proposition. The United States was a far more powerful adversary than Czarist Russia. By July 1945, Japan's empire lay in ruins. Thanks to American bombers, Japanese cities were rubble, and among the smashed stones and smoldering embers lay the ruins of Japan's manufacturing base.

Across the globe, President Harry S. Truman and Comrade Stalin were making plans for the rest of the world. Germany had surrendered, leaving Japan as the sole Axis power. The great colonial powers like Great Britain were shadows of their former selves, and as a result, the United States and the USSR were calling all the shots. Both governments met in Potsdam, Germany, to discuss the postwar world. One of the many topics was Korea.

Without much thought or foresight, the American government decided that the best way to deal with Korea was to divide it in half, just as the Allies had done with Germany. Truman received a promise from Stalin that the Soviets—once they had shuttled their armies from Europe to eastern Asia—would attack the Japanese Kwantung Army to liberate

Manchuria. Stalin promised Truman that the operation would commence within a few weeks of the Potsdam Conference. For the communists, the U.S. decision to leave the northern half of Korea to the
advancing Soviet armies made it an easy conquest for Stalin. Even
though Russia had replaced the czars with communist premiers, the
importance of the Korean Peninsula remained. Stalin wanted an ally
south of the strategic port city of Vladivostok, Russia.

On August 6, a B-29 dropped a single atomic bomb on the city of
Hiroshima, Japan. On August 9, another B-29 dropped another atomic
bomb on the city of Nagasaki, Japan. Yet, Americans tend to overlook the
Soviet invasion of Manchuria, which began a minute after midnight on
the same day the city of Nagasaki vanished under a mushroom cloud.
The Japanese Kwantung Army had over a million men in Manchuria,
and it had been preparing for a Soviet invasion since it had lost the battles of Nomonhan in 1939.

As it turned out, the Russians had also learned a thing or two from
fighting the Germans during the intervening years. When the Russian
attack began, it was a disaster for the Imperial Japanese Army. Despite the
dogged resistance on the part of isolated Kwantung units, the Russians
crushed the Japanese forces in Manchuria. Within days, Soviet tanks and
infantry crossed into northern Korea. Stunned by the rapid Soviet
advance, the Americans quickly agreed to the 38th Parallel as an
armistice line on August 17, 1945.[1] The Russians reached it on August
26. The American Army, on the other hand, would not arrive for another
two weeks.

On September 2, 1945, Japanese delegates signed the articles of surrender onboard the battleship USS *Missouri*. For the Koreans, the long
occupation was over. On September 9, 1945, amid the celebrations, Lt.
Gen. John R. Hodge, commander of XXIV Corps, finally arrived and
accepted the surrender of the Japanese army in Seoul. For the Americans, the goal was the establishment of a free and democratic Korea so
that the GIs could go home. Alas, the Soviets had other ideas.

Stalin's concept of a free and democratic Korea had only one
party—the Communist Party—and he chose Kim Il-Sung to be its
leader. Born in 1912, Kim Il-Sung had been a communist since the
1920s when he joined the nascent Chinese Communist Party. He also
was a seasoned warrior; prior to World War II, he had been a guerrilla,

fighting against the Japanese occupation in Manchuria. By the end of 1940, the Japanese targeted his unit for destruction, and he escaped with his guerrillas to the USSR. There, his Soviet handlers trained his soldiers, and Kim Il-Sung became an officer in the Russian Army. After the war, he returned home, determined to make a name for himself. In December 1945, the head of the NKVD (People's Commissariat for Internal Affairs), Lavrentiy Beria, met with Kim Il-Sung and recommended him to Stalin, who then appointed him as chairman of the Korean Communist Party (North Korean branch).[2]

During that same period, the Americans, British, Chinese (Chiang Kai-shek still controlled China), and the Russians met in Moscow to discuss the future of the Korean peninsula. Delegates from each nation decided that their four nations would run Korea for a period of five years as part of a trusteeship. In the meantime, the Koreans would form a provisional government. In March 1946, the Soviets, Americans, and Koreans assembled in Seoul to hammer out the agreement. To the chagrin of the American and Russian delegates, the Koreans did not want a trusteeship. All political parties wanted instant independence, save one: the Korean Communist Party. Adding to the turmoil, the Soviet delegates recognized the Korean Communist Party as the only legitimate party. Naturally, the U.S. officials balked, and the conference ended with no tangible progress toward unification or independence. After the conference, the Korean communists established a provisional government for North Korea. Kim Il-Sung became the de facto leader north of the 38th Parallel.

Unlike the northern provisional regime, with one party in charge, the southern counterpart included compromise. In December 1946, the U.S. authorities created an assembly comprised of half elected leaders and half appointed leaders. The elected legislators were supporters of Syngman Rhee, a hard right-wing politician. To balance out the assembly, General Hodge selected liberal and moderate politicians for the appointed half. As a result, the assembly was divided and lacked any real authority over the South Korean people.

Born in 1875, Syngman Rhee was much older than his future adversary, Kim Il-Sung. Even at an early age, Rhee was an ardent nationalist and political agitator. As a result, the Korean monarchy imprisoned him for several years. At the end of the Russo-Japanese War, the monarchy released him and sent him to the United States as part of a delegation to represent Korea's interests at the peace conference in Portsmouth, New Hampshire. (Rhee spoke fluent English thanks to Methodist missionaries.) Though the delegation was unsuccessful in securing Korean independence, the trip provided Rhee with a chance to see America. After the conference ended, Rhee decided to stay in the United States, where he earned his bachelor's degree from George Washington University, his master's from Harvard, and a PhD from Princeton.

Whereas Kim Il-Sung was a soldier, Rhee was a politician. In 1919, he became president of the Korean Provisional Government in Exile and served in that role for the next twenty years. During that time, Rhee lived in the United States and married an Austrian woman, Franziska Donner. After the Japanese bombing of Pearl Harbor, Rhee assisted the Office of Strategic Services (OSS) in their efforts to defeat Japan while lobbying for an independent Korea.[3]

With the war over, Syngman Rhee did not want to wait any longer. He had lived long enough to remember the bickering between the Russians and the Japanese over the future of Korea at the beginning of the century. When the dust settled from that standoff, Korea had ended up a colony. He did not want history to repeat itself with Korea as a colony of the United States or, even worse, the Soviet Union.

With the establishment of the South Korean provisional government, Rhee departed for the United States and directly lobbied President Truman and the U.S. Government to recognize an independent Korea. Meanwhile, the supervising U.S. and USSR powers tried to reach a solution. The U.S. representatives proposed nationwide free elections, which the Soviets rejected. Realizing they had reached an impasse, the U.S. delegation referred the issue to the United Nations. In early 1948, the United Nations arrived in Korea to kick-start the election process, but the Soviets refused to allow the U.N. delegation access to North Korea. Undeterred, the South Koreans held their own elections in May 10, 1948, and on August 15 of the same year, Rhee was sworn in as the president of South Korea.

At the same time, on the other side of the globe, the Western powers learned that the Soviets were using a different dictionary to define freedom. Stalin rigged the election in Poland in 1947, with only Soviet-sponsored parties on the ballot. As a result, the communists gained control of Poland. In Czechoslovakia, the Soviet-backed communists overthrew the elected government in February 1948. Simultaneously, the communists overthrew the monarchy in Romania, establishing the People's Republic of Romania on April 13, 1948. Meanwhile, communists were also eliminating other political parties in countries like Hungary, which succumbed to Soviet rule in 1949. In East Germany, Stalin commenced the Berlin Blockade on June 24, 1948, in an attempt to starve the West Berliners. He hoped the Americans and British would cede West Berlin to Soviet control instead of risking war. Closer to Korea, the Nationalists under Chiang Kai-shek were losing the Chinese Civil War to the communists under Mao Zedong. (The war ended on October 1, 1949, with Mao's communists in complete control of mainland China.) Amid this turmoil, Western leaders came to the harsh realization that they had defeated several totalitarian governments during World War II only to replace them with a single totalitarian regime more powerful than any of the previous ones combined.

Back in "The Land of the Morning Calm," it was far from calm. As planned, General Hodge and the U.S. Army began to close up shop in September 1948. The U.S. government left South Korea with no offensive weapons, and therefore no tanks, few large-caliber artillery pieces, and virtually no air force. In effect, the Republic of Korea's army (ROK) was little more than a border constabulary. This was on purpose: The U.S. government did not want Rhee to invade North Korea and start a war with the Soviet Union. Many back in Washington, D.C., believed Rhee might have been crazy enough to do so, and they denied the Korean president the tools to conduct offensive operations.[4]

As the soldiers of the XXIV Corps started to pack their bags to return to the United States or Japan, the North Koreans instigated an insurgency in the south, using communist sympathizers and guerrillas to infiltrate from the north. Replacing XXIV Corps was the Korean Military Assistance Group (KMAG), which numbered around 500 men and was tasked with training the ROK Army. Alas, the growing insurgency meant training had to wait, and many units spent much of their time patrolling the South Korean countryside, searching for communist guerrillas, instead of learning how to shoot straight or defend a fixed position.[5]

Despite the obvious attempt by Kim Il-Sung to destabilize the ROK government, President Truman did not intend to include South Korea within the U.S. defensive zone. In a top-secret document dated April 2,

1948, the National Security Council (NSC) presented an approved policy paper to President Truman, which stated, "The U.S. should not
become so irrevocably involved in the Korean situation that any action
taken by any faction in Korea or by any other power in Korea be considered a casus belli for the U.S."6

In the same document, the Joint Chiefs of Staff argued "the U.S. has
little strategic interest in maintaining its present troops and bases in
Korea." The NSC added: "Moreover, in the event of hostilities in the Far
East, these troops would constitute a military liability. U.S. troops could
be maintained there without substantial reinforcement prior to the initiation of hostilities, but this would be militarily inadvisable since any land
operations would, in all probability, bypass the Korea Peninsula."7

This hands-off policy in Korea continued into 1949. The American
people had enjoyed the postwar economic boom, and if they were concerned with any international news, Europe was usually the topic. In
response to the Berlin Blockade, Truman ordered the Berlin Airlift to
feed the citizens of West Berlin. Meanwhile, diplomats on both sides of
the Atlantic worked on a mutual defense treaty, and on April 4, 1949, the
North Atlantic Treaty Organization (NATO) was born. On October 1,
China finally fell to the communists, but that was not the worst news of
1949. On the morning of August 29, 1949, the Soviets detonated an
atomic bomb. Truman's announcement of the act shocked the world
because it was so unexpected. The U.S. military no longer had a nuclear
monopoly. For the Pentagon and the State Department, the strategy of
nuclear deterrence was now in jeopardy.

Back in the Hermit Kingdom, KMAG had their hands full. The U.S.
advisors had to train several Korean divisions while assisting them in
conducting counterinsurgency operations. In addition, several more
divisions remained stationed along the 38th Parallel to block North
Korean infiltrators from sneaking into the South. The divisions along the
border lacked truck transports, spare parts for the vehicles they did have,
and other items essential for a modern, motorized army. Thanks to a
postwar austerity program that affected everyone in the U.S. armed services, as well as nations that received weapons from the United States, the
shortages in the ROK Army were not likely to improve in the near
future. The KMAG officers knew the ROK Army was ill equipped and
ill prepared for a communist invasion.8

It was a different story in the north. Thanks to Kim Il-Sung's persistent pestering of Stalin, the North Korean Peoples' Army (NKPA) had become a well-oiled machine. Whereas the United States government did not want Syngman Rhee to have the capability to conduct offensive operations, Stalin trusted Kim Il-Sung and provided him with modern T-34/85 tanks and SU-76 self-propelled assault guns. In the air, Soviet advisors trained North Korean pilots to fly the modern Yak-9 fighters and Il-10 ground-attack aircraft. In addition to the modern weapons, the NKPA had a large cadre of trained officers who had served either in the Soviet Army or in the Chinese People's Liberation Army during World War II. Finally, unlike the ROK Army, which had to conduct pacification operations, the NKPA did not face an insurgency; therefore, it could devote all its time for training.[9]

Throughout 1949 and into early 1950, Kim Il-Sung readied his forces for an invasion of the south. Back in Washington, D.C., the analysts at the newly established Central Intelligence Agency (CIA) had missed some of the signs of what was coming. Though they detected the Soviet effort to modernize the NKPA, they assessed that it was far from ready for action. On January 13, 1950, the CIA issued the following statement in a report: "Despite this increase in North Korean military strength, the possibility of an invasion of South Korea is unlikely unless North Korean forces can develop a clear-cut superiority over the increasingly efficient South Korean Army."[10] This perception of North Korea dominated the bureaucracies inside the U.S. military and intelligence establishments for the next five months. In Seoul, however, the officers and soldiers of KMAG saw it differently. To KMAG, it was question of *when*—not if—North Korea would invade.

No one on MacArthur's staff in Tokyo or Truman's staff in Washington heeded Seoul's warnings. The major players in the intelligence establishment thought only Stalin could make the decision to go to war in Korea or anywhere else in the world. They did not think Stalin would opt for a small, short war. To the analysts and policymakers working along the Potomac River, the next war would be all or nothing. Unbeknownst to them, Stalin had already given the green light to Kim Il-Sung, who promised the Soviet leader that the war in the Hermit Kingdom would be over before the U.S. military could intervene.[11]

★ ★ ★

On Sunday morning, June 25, 1950, the U.S. ambassador to the Republic of Korea, John J. Muccio, received a call from his deputy ambassador, Everett Francis Drumright. Apparently, the KMAG was reporting to Drumright that there was "an onslaught across the 38th Parallel." Muccio had heard reports like this before and wanted to get more information before he sent a cable to Washington. He looked at his watch and saw it was 0830 hours, local Korean time. He left for the Chancery to get more information about the border incursions. As he walked out of the official residence, he ran into William James of the *United Press*.

Startled to see the ambassador so early on Sunday morning, James asked Muccio, "What are you doing stirring at this time of the morning?"

Muccio replied, "Oh, we've had some disturbing reports from activities on the 38th Parallel. You might want to look into them."

James did look into the reports. It was all-out war. Within hours of Muccio's run-in with the reporter, the U.S. ambassador had reported to Washington that the communists of North Korea had invaded the South. That evening, Syngman Rhee told Muccio that he and the ROK Cabinet were debating when to evacuate Seoul to escape the advancing NKPA. Meanwhile, MacArthur's Far East Command reported to Washington that at least three divisions and several constabulary brigades had crossed the 38th Parallel and were advancing south with roughly forty tanks. To Muccio, the last twenty-four hours had been a disaster for American interests in the region.[12]

Lt. Gen. Matthew B. Ridgway, who would later command the U.S. Eighth Army in Korea, said of the U.S. policy for South Korea prior to the invasion, "we were laying our baby Republic [South Korea] naked on the altar."[13]

The question now facing President Truman was whether the United States would sacrifice South Korea to keep the peace. Truman answered it. Once again, the United States was going to war.[14]

CHAPTER 2

The 23rd Infantry Regiment
Goes to War

"The regiment was not sufficiently trained for combat. It was a skeleton organization with partially trained leaders and specialists."

—Lt. Col. Frank Meszar

SUNDAY AFTERNOON, JUNE 25, 1950: WILDWOOD, NEW JERSEY

The invasion of South Korea caught most Americans by surprise. Bob Beeby, a soldier in the Inactive Ready Reserve (IRR), heard the news while sunbathing on a beach in New Jersey. War seemed far away for Beeby and for most Americans. World War II had ended less than five years ago, and many thought that large-scale conventional wars were an anachronism in the age of the atomic bomb. It was summer, and most Americans wanted to enjoy the postwar economic boom, a time of prosperity that many were experiencing for the first time in their lives. Like other young men of the time, Beeby was enjoying his youth. He recently had returned from serving a couple of years in Korea as an army welder. While there, he had been attached to a combat engineer unit stationed near Kimpo Airfield.

When Beeby heard the news, his friends jokingly said to him, "You'll be the first to go back in the army because you've had experience in Korea." The twenty-four-year-old veteran laughed. He did not want to go back there. Beeby later wrote, "My time in Korea did help me to appreciate what a lousy duty station [it] was. I had never seen weather that was so cold . . . and I remember one of my buddies saying, 'I sure would hate to be here fighting a war.'"

Several weeks later, Beeby received a telegram in the mail calling him back to active duty to serve in Korea with the 23rd Infantry Regiment, 2nd Infantry Division. He would not be the only soldier returning to the Army and to the 23rd Infantry. Despite the many warnings of a North Korean invasion, most of the units in the ROK Army were overwhelmed in the first few days of fighting. If Truman wanted to make a stand in Korea, he would need the U.S. military to do it.[1]

TUESDAY, JUNE 27, 0826 HOURS: PENTAGON, ARLINGTON, VIRGINIA

North Korea's naked aggression angered the president of the United States. Though he loathed the idea of going to war, he despised appeasement even more. Memories of Munich were still fresh in everyone's minds. Truman felt that if the British and the French had stood up to Hitler over the annexation of the Sudetenland in 1938, World War II could have been avoided. He would not repeat Neville Chamberlain's mistake. He also wanted the involvement of the international community. It was time for the United Nations to show the world it was not like the powerless League of Nations that had preceded it.

Less than twenty-fours after receiving the news from Korea, the Security Council stood up to Truman's challenge and passed Resolution 82, which required "the authorities in North Korea to withdraw forthwith their armed forces to the 38th Parallel." The vote was almost unanimous, with only Yugoslavia abstaining.[2]

For the next forty-eight hours, the president collected more information. He wanted to know if the invasion was the first part of a larger communist operation. When he was convinced that the Soviets were behind it, but not actively participating, he decided to act. (Stalin forbade Soviet advisors from traveling south of the 38th Parallel with the invading North Korean Army). On the morning of June 27, Truman authorized Gen. Douglas MacArthur to use force to stop the North Korean invasion. At 0826 hours, the teletypes in the Pentagon started to click and tap. The message was coded TOP SECRET and read:

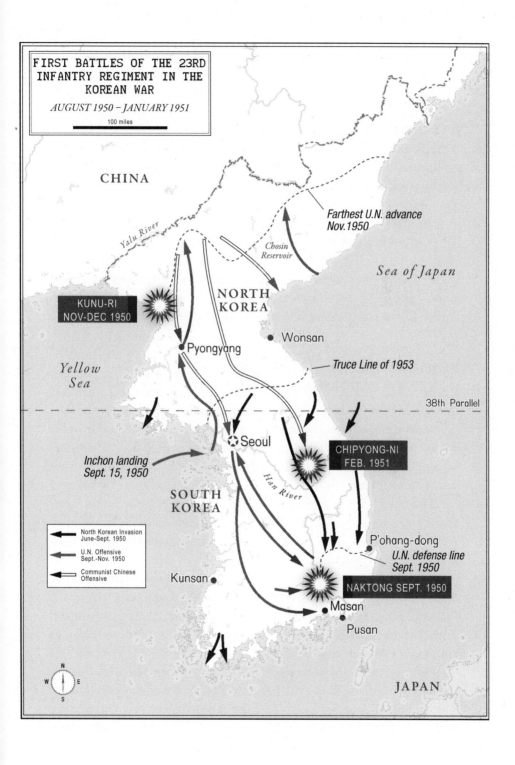

FIRST BATTLES OF THE 23RD
INFANTRY REGIMENT IN THE
KOREAN WAR

AUGUST 1950 – JANUARY 1951

100 miles

CHINA

Yalu River

KUNU-RI
NOV-DEC 1950

*Farthest U.N. advance
Nov. 1950*

*Chosin
Reservoir*

NORTH
KOREA

Sea of Japan

Wonsan

Pyongyang

*Yellow
Sea*

Truce Line of 1953

38th Parallel

Seoul

*Inchon landing
Sept. 15, 1950*

CHIPYONG-NI
FEB. 1951

Han River

SOUTH
KOREA

P'ohang-dong

*U.N. defense line
Sept. 1950*

North Korean Invasion
June-Sept. 1950

U.N. Offensive
Sept.-Nov. 1950

Communist Chinese
Offensive

Kunsan

NAKTONG SEPT. 1950

Masan

Pusan

N
W   E
S

JAPAN

President has directed that instructions be issued as follows: . . .
All restrictions which have previously prevented the full utiliza-
tion of the U.S. Far East Air Forces to support and assist the
defense of the South Korean territory are lifted for operations
below the 38th Parallel. All North Korean tanks, guns, military
columns and other military targets south of the 38th Parallel are
cleared for attack by U.S. Air Forces. The purpose is to clear
South Korea of North Korean military forces. Similarly naval
forces may be used without restriction in coastal waters and sea
approaches of Korea south of [the] 38th Parallel against forces
engaged in aggression against South Korea.[3]

Truman hoped it would be enough to staunch the flow of North
Korean troops heading south. However, events on the ground dashed his
aspirations within hours of his cable to the Pentagon.

FRIDAY, JUNE 30, 0131 HOURS:
STATE DEPARTMENT, WASHINGTON, D.C.

While much of the Federal City slept, the lights were on at Foggy Bottom. Teletype machines chattered as cable after cable arrived from Japan,
where Ambassador William J. Sebald was collecting and forwarding
reports from General MacArthur and Ambassador John Muccio, both
still in South Korea.

The news was not good. Despite commencing air interdiction operations and a naval blockade, nothing could stop the NKPA steamroller.
Adding to the bad news, scores of brave ROK junior officers had been
killed in the fighting north of Seoul. The ROK Army would feel the
leadership loss later on when they needed to rebuild the shattered force
in July and August and were bereft of those trained officers. On June 27,
President Rhee abandoned Seoul, along with much of the government.
They became refugees, just like the citizens of Seoul, and retreated to
Suwon, 30 kilometers south of the capital.

However, signs of hope appeared. To the surprise of Kim Il-Sung
and almost everyone in the Far East, Rhee reestablished the government.
Kim and Stalin had both expected the Rhee regime to collapse once
Seoul fell. Much to their chagrin, that did not happen. Even more

worrisome for the aggressors was the lack of prisoners. Large numbers of prisoners indicated a defeated army, but according to the NKPA reports, the communists had rounded up only a few ROK soldiers. Though reeling and retreating, the ROK Army was still fighting hard.[4]

The South Koreans did not have the proper weapons or the expertise to fight a conventional war. If help did not arrive quickly, their sacrifices would be in vain. The latest teletype report from Sebald was stark. Ambassador Muccio spoke plainly in the communique, which Sebald relayed directly to Secretary of State Dean Acheson. Muccio told Sebald: "It is absolutely essential that we adopt the bold plan without further delay. It is essential that a master stroke be carried out, the sooner the better." It was 0136 hours in Washington. Time was of the essence in the Far East.

Acheson read the note. Even though Truman had authorized the Army to conduct limited operations to protect the port of Pusan (the only major port still under ROK control) and other airbases, it was not enough for MacArthur. According to Muccio, "an all-out effort is necessary if the situation is to be saved." Acheson knew the president would have to make another decision, and soon. To Muccio and MacArthur, a few soldiers on a guard detail were not going to cut it in Korea. If Truman wanted to save the fledgling democracy, he would have to commit American GIs and Marines to do so.[5]

JUNE 30, 0500–0700 HOURS: BLAIR HOUSE, WASHINGTON, D.C.

President Truman stared at the green walls in his makeshift office. Since 1948, he had called the Blair House his home while the White House underwent a major renovation. He had chosen a small room to be his office. Behind him was a fireplace, and in front of him were portraits of Francis Preston Blair and his wife, Eliza, who had owned the Federal-style house in the early nineteenth century. Truman had not thought the room he now called his office would be a witness to major historic events. The North Korean invasion proved him wrong.[6]

At 0500 hours, Truman received a phone call from the secretary of the Army, Frank Pace. As he listened to Pace, he wiped the last bits of shaving cream from his smooth face. MacArthur had sent a message to

Pace from Korea, his request straightforward: the general wanted two infantry divisions to buttress the ROK Army and secure the port of Pusan, and he wanted a regimental combat team that he could use at his own discretion.

For the next two hours, the president thought about MacArthur's appeal. At 0700 hours, he telephoned Pace and Secretary of Defense Louis A. Johnson and told them he was authorizing MacArthur's request for additional troops. Truman also suggested that they consider using Chinese Nationalists from Formosa, offered by Chiang Kai-shek when he heard about the invasion, to augment the ROK forces. After the calls, Truman jotted down a few notes from his phone conversations on some White House stationery. Writing his thoughts helped him work through complex issues. On the same stationery note, he wrote, "Must be careful not to start to a general Asiatic war."

Truman felt that the Korea Incident, as the Joint Chiefs and the State Department were calling it, might be a distraction. He then scribbled, "Russia is figuring on an attack in the Black Sea and toward the Persian Gulf. Both prizes Moscow has wanted since Ivan the Terrible who is now their hero with Stalin and Russia." If the United Nations could stop the communists in Korea, maybe then they would think twice about attacking somewhere else.

That afternoon, the rest of the country learned what Truman had decided that morning. Even though Congress had not declared it as such, the United States was certainly going to war. The White House's press release read:

> In keeping with the United Nations Security Council's request for support to the Republic of Korea in repelling the North Korean invaders and restoring peace in Korea, the President announced that he had authorized the United States Air Force to conduct missions on specific military targets in Northern Korea wherever militarily necessary, and had ordered a Naval blockade of the entire Korean coast. General MacArthur has been authorized to use certain supporting ground units.

One of those units that MacArthur later requested was the 2nd Infantry Division and all of its regiments, including the 23rd Infantry.[7]

SUNDAY, JULY 9, 0700 HOURS:
HEADQUARTERS, 23RD INFANTRY REGIMENT,
NORTH FORT, FORT LEWIS, WASHINGTON

After the White House press release on June 30, rumors swirled on all Army posts as to who was going to get the call to go to South Korea. On Fort Lewis, it was no different. So far, it had been an uneventful and lazy summer. The soldiers and officers of the 2nd Infantry Division had been training the soldiers of the 41st National Guard Division, and key personnel had been teaching officer cadets at the newly opened Reserve Officer Training Corps Camp (still in operation today). Since it was near the end of the fiscal year, many soldiers were on leave, as most of the units had spent their annual training dollars and were back in the barracks.

Then North Korea invaded South Korea. Everyone tried to maintain a business-as-usual attitude, but the soldiers and their families were on edge, concerned that they or their spouses were going off to war again. The buzz went into overdrive when the division commander, Maj. Gen. Laurence B. Keiser, called a meeting with all the major commanders of the division on July 4. The topic of the conference was top secret.

Afterward, no one heard anything from anyone who had attended the hush-hush session. For three days, nothing happened. The tension began to dissipate as personnel thought that maybe some other division would get the call. Regardless of who was going, Korea was the topic at the various restaurants and homes around post. July 9, 1950, dashed their hopes.[8]

On Saturday evening, July 8, General Keiser gathered his staff together once more and told the officers that the division was heading to Korea by the end of the month. The following morning, at 0700 hours, the various regimental headquarters received the official notification that they were deploying to the Far East, which meant Korea, and that the 23rd Infantry Regiment was one of them. At 0830 hours, the acting regimental commander, Lt. Col. Edwin J. Messinger, summoned the regimental staff and all of the battalion commanders for a meeting at his headquarters at 1000 hours. In the same telephonic alert, he canceled all leaves. The 23rd was heading off to war, and no one was going to be left behind.[9]

Even before the Korean War, the 23rd Infantry Regiment was a unit with a long and impressive history. Its nickname was the "Tomahawks," and its motto was "We Serve." The regiment was formed in 1861 as 1st and then 2nd Battalion, 14th Infantry, and participated in several Civil War battles, including the Peninsula Campaign, Second Manassas, Antietam, Fredericksburg, Chancellorsville, Gettysburg, the Wilderness, Spotsylvania, Cold Harbor, and Petersburg. After the Civil War, it became the 23rd Infantry. Throughout the latter half of the nineteenth century, the regiment earned several more campaign credits fighting in the Indian Wars. In 1898, it went to the Far East for the first time as part of the force that liberated Manila in the Spanish-American War. Afterward, it remained in the Philippines for several years and conducted counterinsurgency operations against Emilio Aguinaldo and his band of Filipino rebels. Fifteen years later, the 23rd Infantry Regiment left for France to fight in the First World War as part of the 2nd Infantry Division, where it saw action at the battles of Aisne, Aisne-Marne, Saint Mihiel, and the Meuse-Argonne Offensive.

More than twenty-five years later, the 23rd returned to northern France, once again as part of the 2nd Infantry Division, and landed in Normandy on June 8, 1944, with the rest of the division. For two months, it slogged through hedgerow country until the German defenses broke in mid-August. In September, the men of the 23rd Infantry defeated the German defenders of Brest, France, after several weeks of nasty street fighting. That December, the regiment was resting on the German border when the Battle of the Bulge began. Despite intense pressure, the Germans could not penetrate the 23rd's defensive lines. After the Bulge, the regiment crossed the Rhine River in March 1945. When the war ended, the 23rd Infantry returned with the 2nd Infantry Division and moved to Fort Lewis, Washington, in 1946.[10]

Even though World War II had ended less than five years before, the 23rd Infantry was not ready for war. The parsimonious secretary of defense, Louis Johnson, had cut the Army and the other services to the bone. Hindsight has shown this was a bad decision, but at the time, the majority of Americans, including the president, supported him. After World War II ended, no one saw the need for a large, conventional military. America had the Bomb. Consequently, Army units did not have enough radios, weapons, or, most of all, men. Lt. Col. Frank Meszar, the regiment's executive officer in July 1950, wrote, "The regiment was not sufficiently trained for combat. It was a skeleton organization with partially trained leaders and specialists."[11]

In fact, the entire division was ill prepared. When he visited the 2nd Infantry Division in June, Chief of Army Field Forces Gen. Mark W. Clark declared it would take several months for the 2nd to train for combat. Even worse, the Indianhead Division, (a nickname for the 2nd Infantry Division, after its unit patch) was short 5,000 trigger pullers.[12]

Contrary to popular belief, soldiers in a professional army want to fight. To fill gaps in the ranks, a call went out for volunteers. One soldier who answered the call was Cpl. Donald W. Hoffman, who belonged to the 633rd Light Equipment Company, also located on Fort Lewis. On an early July morning, the company commander stood in front of the formation and asked if anyone was interested in joining the 2nd Infantry Division, which was shipping out to Korea. His company had over 250 men, and approximately 200 of them fell out of the formation to volunteer for overseas combat. Hoffman later wrote, "I think in this case it was duty and that's it."[13]

Other soldiers were on leave when the division issued the recall alert. PFC Morris V. Evans was on a thirty-day authorized absence, visiting his family in Bangor, Pennsylvania, when he got the call. As a private, he did not have lot of money, so the only way he could return to Fort Lewis was by Greyhound bus. Evans wrote: "I phoned my company commander Captain William Payne and advised him I would leave immediately on the first bus out, which I did. On my return to 'H' Company, 2nd Battalion, 23rd Regiment, we started packing and getting ready to go to Korea."[14]

The twenty-year-old private from the Lehigh Valley region of Pennsylvania was not the only one rushing to get to the West Coast. The 23rd Infantry Regiment did not have its commander; Messinger was only the acting commander. The actual commanding officer was still driving across the country from Washington, D.C. His name was Col. Paul L. Freeman, Jr.

The new commander was an army brat, born in 1907 in the Philippines. His father had been an army surgeon and was stationed in the Philippines three times before his son had reached the age of seven. Later on, young Paul Freeman secured an appointment to attend the United States Military Academy, but he did not stand out among his peers at West Point. In his own words, he "led a very undistinguished cadet life."

After earning his commission as a second lieutenant in the infantry in 1929, Paul shipped out to Texas to serve in the 9th Infantry Regiment, 2nd Infantry Division, at Fort Sam Houston, Texas. Capt. Lawrence Keiser was his first company commander when Freeman was a platoon leader, and would be his commanding officer again when Freeman took command of the 23rd Infantry, over twenty years later.

In the summer of 1932, Paul married his wife, Mary Anne Fishburn from Roanoke, Virginia. After attending the infantry company officers course at Fort Benning, Georgia, the Freemans left for Tientsin, China, in July 1933, when Paul was assigned to serve in the 15th Infantry Regiment, part of a force known as the International Mission that had been in China since the Boxer Rebellion. For the next three years, Freeman traveled all over China and much of Southeast Asia before returning to the United States in 1936. He attended the Tank Course at Fort Benning, Georgia, where he stayed until December 1939. In January 1940, he left to join the diplomatic mission in China, which was at war with Japan at the time, and remained in the Far East until July 1943. During the intervening years, Paul learned to speak fluent Mandarin and immersed himself in Chinese culture, which helped him in his later years as the commander of the 23rd Infantry. In addition, he worked under Lt. Gen. Joseph W. Stilwell, the commander of the Chinese Burma India (CBI) Theater Command.

After his stint in the CBI, Freeman transferred back to D.C. as an assistant to the Combined Chiefs of Staff, where he served as an advisor to Gen. George C. Marshall on Asian affairs. In November 1944, Marshall released him, and Freeman landed a job on the staff of the U.S. Sixth Army, which had just landed in the Philippines. While there, he was the acting chief of staff for the 77th Infantry Division, serving in that role as a task force commander during the operations on the island of Leyte. Prior to his command of the 23rd Infantry, this was his only combat command.

In 1945, the War Department and the General Staff recalled him, and he served in the Joint War Plans division until November 1945. When the war ended, Paul's career aspirations seemed dim. He had little command time in a postwar Army, which was awash with commanders with combat experience. Luckily for the Army, he chose to remain in the service. For the next two years, the now-Colonel Freeman was a member of the Joint United States–Brazil Military Commission. While serving in that post, he met Lt. Gen. Matthew Ridgway, who would later be his army commander in Korea. Freeman later remarked that Ridgway was "my number one combat commander." After Brazil, he returned to D.C. to serve in the Plans Division of the General Staff.

In the spring of 1950, Paul learned he would take command of the 23rd Infantry Regiment at Fort Lewis, Washington. Once again, he would be in the 2nd Infantry Division. He and his wife had just sold their house in D.C. on June 25 when they heard the news about Korea. Soon after, they learned that the 23rd was shipping out. Like Private Evans and many other soldiers of the Tomahawk Regiment, Paul Freeman left his wife and headed to Fort Lewis.[15]

THURSDAY, JULY 20, 1515 HOURS: HEADQUARTERS, 23RD INFANTRY REGIMENT, NORTH FORT, FORT LEWIS

General Keiser arrived at the regimental command post on the afternoon of July 20 with a full-bird colonel standing behind him. The room of junior and field grade officers came to attention, and Keiser introduced them to their new commanding officer. Colonel Freeman was a mystery to them, and he was taking over their regiment right before it embarked for Korea. In an ideal situation, a new regimental commander would have taken the unit out to the field to train before heading off to war, so that both the commander and his command could get a measure of each other. However, with deployment only days away, the regiment did not have that opportunity. The 23rd Infantry would conduct their first major exercise in combat. It was like a new coach taking over a team before a championship game.

After the introductions, Colonel Freeman met with his staff and his subordinate commanders. The first group of soldiers was going to leave for Tacoma in less than forty-eight hours. The new boss wanted to know if his soldiers were ready for combat. His executive officer, Lieutenant Colonel Meszar, and the rest of staff tried to put on a good face, but the regiment's operational rating was far from ideal.[16]

Because of the shortened timeline, the regiment had spent the last ten days packing and preparing for departure instead of training. The men had fired their assigned personal weapons, but few had fired or even tested the various crew-served weapons like the 57mm and 75mm recoilless rifles. Moreover, the supporting units had not conducted any realistic close air support training. Fortunately, the regiment had conducted some field exercises earlier in the year, which meant they were more trained than the garrison units in Japan. Unfortunately, the garrison units in Japan were the first sent into combat.[17]

SATURDAY, JULY 22, 1325 HOURS: 23RD INFANTRY REGIMENT BARRACKS AREA, NORTH FORT, FORT LEWIS, TO THE PORT OF TACOMA, WASHINGTON

For many men in the 23rd Infantry, July 22, 1950, was the last time they saw their loved ones. At 1325 hours, the first Greyhound buses arrived in the parking lot to carry the soldiers and officers to the port of Tacoma, Washington, where they would board the awaiting transport, the USS *General H. B. Freeman* (named after Henry Blanchard Freeman, a Union general in the Civil War, but not an ancestor of Col. Paul Freeman). The previous two weeks had been a whirlwind of activity. Suddenly, the wait was over.

Wives, girlfriends, mothers, and fathers hugged their husbands, boyfriends, and sons good-bye. Some sobbed or fought back tears. Others were too busy tidying up last-minute jobs to worry about sentiment or the future.

The 23rd Infantry Regiment had accomplished the monumental task of preparing for a wartime deployment in less than two weeks. The first units to embark for Korea were the two headquarters companies from 1st and 2nd Battalion, the regiment's heavy mortar company, and the tank companies, totaling 82 officers and 1,267 enlisted men.[18]

One of the soldiers walking up the gangplank that afternoon was Sgt. Frank C. Butler, a young tank commander in the heavy tank company, a post–World War II addition to the infantry regiment's table of organization. The Department of the Army (DA) assessed that the towed antitank guns had been a failure in the last war and replaced the regimental antitank company with one composed of Sherman tanks. The company was considered a heavy company because it had four platoons of tanks instead of the standard three; the designation had nothing to do with the size of the tanks, as the army considered the Sherman to be a medium tank. The platoon composition had not changed from World War II, so each platoon had five tanks when at full strength.[19]

Like many soldiers in the 23rd Infantry, Butler wondered what fate awaited him as he stepped onto the deck of the *General Freeman*. Like Bob Beeby, Butler had been to Korea before, having enlisted in the Army in 1946 and served in the 1st Infantry Regiment, 6th Infantry Division, which was stationed in South Korea for two years. The tanker had then left for China as part of a clandestine mission to deliver Shermans to the Nationalists. When the Chinese civil war ended, Butler went back to the United States, where he was assigned to the 23rd Infantry Regiment in December 1949.[20]

After his return to the States, Butler met a woman, and within a few months they were engaged. Kim Il-Sung interrupted his marriage plans by invading South Korea. Several days later, Butler learned he was deploying to Korea. Undeterred, the tanker requested that his Catholic chaplain marry them before he shipped out. His chaplain responded that, "in spite of the urgency, it was not his policy to perform 'gang-plank weddings' and that he would not do it."

Butler was crushed. His fiancée was someone he had known for months, and the two already had announced their plans to marry before the invasion. Seeking assistance, Butler moved up the chain of command to his company commander, Capt. William M. Westfall. Realizing that he could not order the regimental chaplain to change his mind, Westfall raised the issue with the new regimental commander, Colonel Freeman.

Even though Freeman was a newcomer, Butler had seen him around the barracks because the colonel had wanted to visit every company in his regiment and speak directly to his soldiers. In a postwar letter, Butler wrote: "He came to Tank Company one evening and stood on the mess hall steps. He spoke quietly, in a very informal manner. Not a bombastic speech, but one in which you could sense his sincerity. I don't remember all that he said, but one thing stands out. He promised each man would get three days off before we left to take care of his personal affairs. Considering all that had to be done, this was a large order, but he did it. Every man did get his full three days off."

The tank commander described his new boss: "He was tall, his hair was graying and his voice was soft. I know he wore rank insignia, but somehow it did not stand out. No flashing lights, siren or eagle-numberplate on his jeep, no flags at the Regimental CP." Perhaps this meeting gave Butler the notion he had a chance with the new commander.

When Westfall presented his sergeant's case to Freeman, the 23rd's new commanding officer rang up the division chaplain and requested that he marry Butler and his fiancée. Later that night, while the Tomahawks packed up the last few things for war, Butler and his bride were married at the regimental chapel. The experience made a profound impression on Butler, who later remarked that "Paul Freeman cared."[21] Now, the newly married sergeant was boarding an Army transport, bound for the Far East.

Unlike his executive officer, who felt the regiment was ill prepared for war, Butler sensed there was something about the 23rd that gave it an edge over other Army units. First, the 2nd Infantry Division was one of the few Table of Organization and Equipment (TO&E) units, meaning it was eligible for combat. All of the other divisions were divisions in name only. The Army had labeled them as "training" divisions, which meant that the cadre in those units had the sole mission of molding new recruits into soldiers; consequently, they were focused on individual soldier training, not collective training. On the other hand, the 2nd Infantry Division, including the 23rd Infantry, had previously conducted some collective training in Hawaii, and thus was far more prepared than the other units in the U.S. Army.[22]

However, there was more. Sergeant Butler believed not only that the 2nd Infantry Division was better than any other Army division, but also that the 23rd Infantry was the best regiment in the division. The young tank commander felt the Tomahawks had esprit de corps. "The 23rd was unique in that it was separated from the rest of the Division," he wrote. "We were located on the North Fort, in World War II mobilization-type barracks and not under the direct eye of Division Headquarters, which was at Fort Lewis proper, in fine brick buildings, several miles away. Being apart as we were, we were able to do things 'our way' without too much interference. This certainly helped to build espirit [sic]. The various elements of the Division were in fierce competition in all aspects of training and all kinds of athletics events. The 23rd Infantry excelled in all."

Freeman's unit had other advantages, too. According to Butler, many of the NCOs were veterans from World War II, including one who had earned the Medal of Honor while serving with the division in Europe.

Despite its lack of readiness, the 23rd had the essential tools to become a great unit. Butler argued that "the 23d was not just another regiment of infantry, it was 'Family.'"[23]

This *family* was departing for Korea, where it would learn how to fight in combat. Over the next few months, the bitter and hard-fought battles in the Hermit Kingdom would sharpen the Tomahawk Regiment into a lethal weapon capable of tremendous feats. At a place called Chipyong-ni, it would need those skills and swagger to survive.

AUGUST–DECEMBER 1950: 23RD INFANTRY REGIMENT, SOUTH KOREA TO NORTH KOREA, THEN BACK TO SOUTH KOREA

When the 23rd Infantry Regiment arrived in the Far East, many of the officers felt it would be several more months before MacArthur committed them and the rest of the 2nd Infantry Division to combat. The enlisted men thought otherwise. Even though they were not privy to a lot of the information their commanders had, the grunts sensed the situation on the Korean Peninsula was far worse than what the news was reporting back home. As it turned out, the soldiers were right.

Several weeks before the 23rd Infantry arrived, MacArthur deployed the first regimental combat team to Korea. Many in the U.S. defense establishment thought the peasant conscripts from North Korea would run at the first sight of American GIs. They expected great things from a battalion task force known as Task Force Smith, named after its commander, Lt. Col. Charles B. Smith.

The events of July 4 proved to be a wake-up call. The peasants nearly wiped out Smith's tiny force near the town of Osan, where NKPA tanks and infantry enveloped the ill-fated battalion, inflicting over 150 casualties on a force that numbered a little over 500 men.[24] For the rest of the month, the communists pushed farther south, despite the steady infusion of U.S. troops and materiel. As a result, by the beginning of August, the NKPA had cornered the U.S.-led United Nations force into a small area around the port of Pusan, which later became known as the Pusan Perimeter.

Lt. Gen. Walton H. Walker, commander of the U.S. Eighth Army, was the senior commander on the ground in Korea and responsible for holding the perimeter while MacArthur assembled a sizeable offensive force to wrest the initiative from the communists. Since the divisions from the United States and Japan did not arrive as entire units, Walker had to dispatch the battalions and regiments as they arrived, one by one. It was far from an ideal situation, but given the circumstances, he had little choice. He needed to stop the NKPA or face the prospect of a Dunkirk-style evacuation from the peninsula. The 2nd Infantry Division was one of the units that Walker fed piecemeal into the Korean cauldron; the first regiment to arrive from 2nd Infantry was the 9th Infantry Regiment.

On August 8, 1950, the 9th Infantry engaged the NKPA along the Naktong River. Several days later, the 23rd Infantry Regiment established defensive positions near the town of Taegu, South Korea, where it fought its first battles since the Second World War. By the end of August, the entire 2nd Infantry Division was in South Korea, fighting for its life as the communists squeezed the perimeter tighter, like a boa constrictor.[25]

For the first two weeks of September, the 23rd Infantry Regiment battled the NKPA between the Naktong River and the town of Changnyeong. The communists assaulted the 23rd Infantry's positions several times on September 1, 6, 8, 9, and 15, but each time Freeman's Tomahawks threw them back, inflicting crippling losses on the attackers. It became a test of wills between the two opposing armies.[26] However, time was running out for the NKPA. As the communists hurled themselves at the Pusan Perimeter, General MacArthur was planning a trap for them. He wanted to land the U.S. Army X Corps and its 1st Marine Division at the port of Inchon on the Yellow Sea, far behind the front lines. Inchon serviced the city of Seoul, 20 miles to the east. If the amphibious landing succeeded, MacArthur could then march on Seoul with ease and trap most of the NKPA south of the 38th Parallel.

Korea's particular geography aided the general's plan. Because of the Taebaek Mountain Range and the various rivers that crisscrossed the peninsula, most of the major highways in South Korea ran west of the mountains and ended up in Seoul. Thus, Seoul was not only the capital but also the central communications hub for the entire southern half of the peninsula. If the U.N. forces could recapture the city, then the NKPA would have to retreat or face total annihilation.

MacArthur also would have the advantage of surprise. No one—including many in the Joint Chiefs of Staff (JCS)—believed Inchon was an ideal spot for an amphibious landing. First, it was a city, which meant it would be hard to capture. The bloody battle of Stalingrad had proven that fact. Second, the tides were treacherous in the bay, which meant the landings would have to occur at two different times; the initial invaders would have to wait several hours before reinforcements could arrive with the next tide. The JCS thought this was a bad idea, as did the North Korean Army, which left few soldiers to defend the port.

Despite the misgivings of the JCS, MacArthur got his way. On September 10, 1950, the 1st Marine Division landed at Inchon. It was a smashing success. As the general predicted, the NKPA did not expect a landing, and within days the Marines had brushed aside the few scattered communist units and advanced toward the outskirts of Seoul with the rest of X Corps. The news of the invasion sent shockwaves throughout the communist ranks. Coinciding with the landings, General Walker ordered his U.S. Eighth Army to conduct a general assault on the besieging NKPA armies outside of Pusan on September 16.

Within hours, the communists began to withdraw from the perimeter. Once out in the open, the retreating NKPA forces were easy pickings for the U.S. Air Force. In a matter of days, the retrograde had become a rout as the North Korean soldiers struggled to make it back to the illusory safety north of the 38th Parallel.

Hounding them were the forces of Eighth Army and the 2nd Infantry Division. As part of the 2nd Infantry Division, the 23rd Infantry played a major role in the counteroffensive. By the afternoon of September 16, enemy resistance slackened in front of the Tomahawks, and Freeman's lead elements closed in on the east bank of the Naktong River. On September 20, the regiment crossed the waterway with assault boats, and by September 22, it had secured a bridgehead along the west bank. The next day, the 2nd Battalion reached the town of Changnyu, while the 3rd Battalion captured the town of Hyopchon. For several days, the regiment conducted clearance operations to destroy any remnants of the NKPA trapped behind friendly lines. On September 26, the regiment resumed its advance and reached the town of Kochang.[27]

Elsewhere on September 26, X Corps and the Eighth Army linked up near the city of Osan. Simultaneously, the Marines had captured most of Seoul, and a sizeable portion of the NKPA was in the final stages of disintegration south of the capital. MacArthur had his victory, but he was intent on finishing off the communist regime of Kim Il-Sung.

To complete his quest, MacArthur needed to advance north of the 38th Parallel, but as of September 10, the United Nations did not have the authority to conduct operations north of the line. Despite this restriction, officers and politicians were discussing the possibility of reunifying Korea after the U.N. forces defeated the NKPA south of the international border. In a position paper dated September 1, 1950, the National Security Council debated whether to pursue the communists into North Korea and reunify the country. "The United States has strongly supported this political objective [reunification]," wrote Executive Secretary James S. Lay. "If the present United Nations action in Korea can accomplish this political objective without substantial risk of general war with the Soviet Union or Communist China, it would be in our interest to advocate the pressing of the United Nations action to this conclusion."[28]

Within weeks of this memorandum, the situation on the ground in Korea changed dramatically. By the end of September, the U.N. forces were poised to cross into North Korea and pursue the retreating remnants of the NKPA. On September 27, 1950, Truman received a recommendation from the JCS, current Secretary of State Dean Acheson, and former secretary of state George C. Marshall to grant MacArthur the authorization "to conduct military operations, including amphibious and airborne landings or ground operations north of the 38th Parallel in Korea, provided that at the time of such operation there has been no entry into North Korea by major Soviet or Chinese Communist forces." Truman agreed and signed the authorization. The war entered a new phase.[29]

The president's directive meant that the 23rd Infantry Regiment and the rest of the 2nd Infantry Division would continue north toward the 38th Parallel and beyond it. On October 2, Colonel Freeman established his regimental command post at Chungju, South Korea, where it remained for several weeks, conducting patrols to root out communist stragglers cut off by the U.N. forces during the counteroffensive. On October 11, the soldiers of the regiment folded up their tents and headed northwest to the town of Kwach'on, a suburb of Seoul, remaining there until October 20. During that time, the regiment received supplies, new vehicles, and replacements for the casualties sustained up until that point. On October 21, the regiment received the mission to head across the 38th Parallel and to occupy the town of Haeju, North Korea, where it stayed through the end of the month. In five weeks, the Tomahawks had travelled over 330 miles.[30]

While the 23rd Infantry conducted a security mission around Haeju, troubling indicators started to pop up north of its location near the town of Unsan. There, the 8th Cavalry Regiment was advancing toward the Yalu River. On the night of November 1, the isolated regiment came under heavy attack. Amid blaring bugles, a well-trained enemy force swarmed through the gaps between the spread-out battalions of 8th Cavalry. By the morning of November 2, everyone in the 8th Cavalry knew that the attackers were Chinese soldiers and, more importantly, that the Chinese units had surrounded them, cutting off their escape to the south. In response, the cavalry troopers from 1st and 2nd Battalion broke into small groups and infiltrated through the Chinese cordon to fight another day. The men from 3rd Battalion were not as lucky, and the unit ceased to be a fighting force. By November 3, the 8th Cavalry Regiment reported that it had been reduced to 45-percent strength. Much to the bewilderment of the U.N. high command, the Chinese forces disappeared into the hills after the battle.[31]

Understandably, the introduction of Red Chinese army units alarmed Washington, D.C., power circles. To assuage their concerns, General MacArthur sent a telegram to the JCS on November 4. In it he wrote, "I recommend against hasty conclusions which might be premature and believe that a final appraisement should await a more complete accumulation of military facts." MacArthur believed that the Chinese would not "openly" attack the U.N. forces south of the Yalu and that the Chinese would continue to send "volunteers" and supplies into Korea. His initial theory was that the Chinese were attempting to maintain some sort of foothold in North Korea to provide the NKPA with a place to rebuild and refit.[32]

Two days later, on November 6, MacArthur requested permission to bomb the bridges that spanned the Yalu River, since military intelligence indicated that the Chinese forces were using them to supply the NKPA. Several hours later, the JCS approved MacArthur's request. On the same day, the National Security Council (NSC) reiterated that MacArthur, as Commander in Chief, Far East Command, still had the authorization to conduct "appropriate air and naval action outside of Korea against Communist China."[33]

As of November 9, the Joint Chiefs did not have clear idea as to what the Chinese hoped to achieve in Korea, but they still supported MacArthur's decision to continue with his planned offensive, slated to start on November 24. Elsewhere in Washington, concerns grew that things were beginning to unravel. The NSC recommended that the president order the intelligence and defense establishment to "intensify covert actions to determine Chinese Communist intentions." Despite lacking knowledge of the Chinese objectives, the NSC would not recommend any curtailment of current military operations in the Far East. No one wanted to overrule MacArthur.[34]

On November 21, the Joint Chiefs held a meeting with Secretary of State Acheson and other members of the State Department at the Pentagon. With the exception of the president and vice president, all the other key players attended, including General Marshall, who was now the secretary of defense. The subject was Korea. The debate centered on how to achieve a victory without antagonizing the Chinese or the Russians. The meeting concluded, and other than discussing a potential demilitarized zone along the Yalu and the possibility of a Third World War, it solved nothing.[35]

On November 25, the Chinese military settled the issue. Contrary to MacArthur's assertions that the Chinese were only interested in sending "volunteers" into the Korean maelstrom, Mao Zedong had decided to enter into the war in early October, after the U.N. forces crossed the 38th Parallel, and had appointed Peng Dehuai to lead the Chinese People's Volunteer Force (CPVF). Peng was one of Mao's most trusted subordinates and convinced him that the CPVF could defeat a modern, Western army with proven Chinese tactics honed against the Nationalists and the Japanese. Mao thought a U.S.-backed ally on his border was unacceptable. Korea was a stepping-stone for the Imperial Japanese Army when it invaded Manchuria in the early thirties, and Mao was not going to allow the United States to have that same advantage in the fifties.[36]

When the Chinese tempest struck the U.N. forces, the 23rd Infantry Regiment traveled north to the Ch'ongch'on River and established several battle positions near the town of Kujang, North Korea. The 2nd Infantry Division, like the 8th Cavalry Regiment, was isolated, so Peng chose it as one of his key targets in the upcoming offensive, which later became known as the Second Phase Offensive. The 1st Marine Division and the ROK II Corps were the other major targets.

At 2230 hours on the night of November 25, the CPVF attacked the 23rd Infantry. For several days, the battle seesawed back and forth. At one point, the CPVF even overran the regimental command post, but Freeman later recaptured it. The Chinese communist soldiers had stunned the American defenders, but in the end, the 23rd Infantry held its position. Alas, that was not the case for all the units.

One of the soldiers, Sgt. Martin Lee from Easy Company, recalled the initial Chinese attacks. "When the gooks hit the riverside, it was just black with people. I mean you couldn't even see the ground [through] the people. That's how many Chinese came across the river. And we'd done everything we could to stop them and they [the commanders] told us to pull back."[37]

On the night of November 27, Peng Dehuai achieved one of his goals: the ROK II Corps, which was covering the eastern flank of the Eighth Army, buckled and shattered. It had the effect of falling dominos. The next unit in line was the 2nd Infantry Division's 38th Infantry Regiment, but with their eastern flank exposed, the men of the 38th had no choice but to fall back or risk encirclement by the rapidly advancing Chinese forces. Sweeping past their lines were two CPVF armies: the 38th and the 42nd. Meanwhile, the 40th Army had the mission of fixing the 2nd Infantry Division so that the 38th and the 42nd could envelop it from the east and destroy it. Major General Keiser, the 2nd Infantry Division's commanding officer, realized it was time to go because of these threats, and he ordered Colonel Freeman and the 23rd Infantry to cover the division's withdrawal from the Ch'ongch'on River region. Throughout the entire peninsula, it was the same story. Peng Dehuai's offensive had caught MacArthur flat-footed, and everyone retreated south.[38]

Following orders, Freeman repositioned his regiment north of Kujang. From there, it was a running battle as the Tomahawks parried each blow the Chinese hurled at them. To ensure fresh troops, Freeman rotated the rearguard among his infantry battalions as they marched farther south. At Kunu-ri, 1st Battalion occupied a battle position east of the road junction so that the entire division could escape. From this position, 1st Battalion blocked elements from the CPVF's 38th Army.

Meanwhile, the battered units of the 2nd Infantry Division streamed through the 23rd's positions and stumbled southward toward safety. West of Kunu-ri, L Company fought off an entire battalion from the CPVF's 40th Army.[39]

Elsewhere, things got worse for the rest of the 2nd Infantry Division. South of Kunu-ri, the CPVF established a blocking position on the highway between Kunu-ri and Sunch'on. To escape, the soldiers of the 2nd Infantry Division would have to destroy the Chinese blocking position. The CPVF had five divisions in the area occupying the high ground that lined both sides of the road. Throughout the day on November 30, the 2nd Infantry Division fought off attack after attack, attempting to punch its way through the gauntlet. Meanwhile, the 23rd Infantry secured the rear of the division column. The decision to select the 23rd Infantry as the rearguard probably saved the regiment.

The Kunu-ri–Sunch'on highway was a deathtrap. Along its length lay the detritus of a wrecked division: abandoned vehicles and, among them, the bodies of American GIs. By the end of the day, the division had few working trucks. The commanders decided that instead of leaving behind the wounded, they would leave the dead. Despite this decision, there were not enough resources to transport all the seriously injured soldiers.

Douglas Graney was a radio operator for Easy Company, 23rd Infantry Regiment. "As we hiked south to relieve the 1st Battalion, we passed the 2nd Battalion's medical aid station," he wrote. "Serious wounded lay huddled on the frozen ground that surrounded the aid tent. I couldn't see any trucks or medical vehicles in the area." Puzzled, he asked his company commander, "What's going to happen to those wounded? We're the last troops passing here."

His commanding officer replied, "I hate to tell you but I heard from Battalion the Doctor said he'd surrender and continue taking care of the wounded. There's no trucks or ambulances available to move them. They're all about to become prisoners."

The officer's answer stunned him. Graney wrote, "I couldn't respond to what he said except to feel disgust for our not being able to help move them."[40] When the G1 compiled the numbers, the division had sustained over 5,000 casualties, most of which were from the 9th and 38th Infantry Regiments.

By the evening of November 30, it was obvious to the U.N. commanders that the Chinese 38th Army had blocked the road between Kunu-ri and Sunch'on. The 2nd Infantry Division's assistant division commander, Brig. Gen. Joseph S. Bradley, authorized Freeman to march west toward the town of Anju and then south to Sukchon, bypassing the main highway. Late on the thirtieth, the 23rd Infantry withdrew from its position around Kunu-ri, heading west. With Chinese forces concentrated along the main route, the Tomahawks avoided ambushes along the main highway by using this alternate route. After the long, meandering march around the enemy, Freeman's soldiers emerged unscathed at the division area. They had survived a harrowing ordeal. The 23rd Infantry was the only regiment fit for combat in the Indianhead Division after the disasters of late November.[41]

For much of December, the 23rd Infantry Regiment was behind the lines, recovering with the rest of the 2nd Infantry Division. Dozens of countries were a part of the war effort in Korea, some contributing ships, planes, and service units, while others offered entire combat units. In the case of France, it was an infantry battalion. Since battalions did not operate independently, General Walker attached it to a U.S. infantry regiment, and in mid-December the French Battalion became part of the 23rd Infantry Regiment, linking up while the Tomahawks refitted near the town of Angyong-Ni, South Korea.[42]

The U.N. French Battalion, known formally as the *Bataillon français de l'ONU*, was not an official battalion under the French Army Order of Battle, but rather a hodgepodge unit specifically created to deploy and fight in Korea. Despite its ad hoc nature, it was a fully manned infantry battalion, receiving some of the best soldiers France had to offer, with 42 officers, over 170 noncommissioned officers, and more than 800 enlisted men. It had three line companies, one headquarters company, and one command company, and was an all-volunteer force.

The French numbered their companies, unlike the U.S. Army, which still uses letters to name line companies. Accordingly, 1st Company was composed of French Marines; 2nd Company was made up of soldiers from the Metropolitan Infantry units, while paratroopers and legionnaires from the French Foreign Legion filled the ranks of 3rd Company. The Headquarters Company received specially trained soldiers and artillery personnel. The C.B., or *Compagnie de commandement de Bataillon*, a staff company, was comprised of soldiers who could "operate their jobs independently."[43]

The French Battalion's best asset was its commander, Raoul Charles Magrin-Vernerey, who fought under the nom de guerre Ralph Monclar. In 1950, Monclar was a lieutenant general in the French Army. Instead of riding his final years into retirement, Monclar wanted to see more action. Moreover, like many professional French soldiers, he wanted to expunge the shame the French Army had suffered at the beginning of World War II. Therefore, he requested to lead the battalion to Korea. To do so required a demotion, which he gladly accepted. He was now Lt. Col. Ralph Monclar.

Korea was not Monclar's first wartime experience. He had served in World War I as an infantry officer and was wounded seven times. He earned eleven citations, including the Légion d'Honneur. In 1924, he left for Morocco to serve in the French Foreign Legion. By 1928, he was a battalion commander in the Legion and remained in that role for most of the next decade. When the Second World War broke out, Monclar was appointed to lead two battalions of legionnaires as part of the ill-fated invasion of Narvik, Norway. He joined the Free French forces in the summer of 1940, after France fell. By December 1941, he had attained the rank of brigadier general, and from December 1942 to 1943, he was in charge of French land forces in Great Britain. He was transferred to the Middle East in 1944, where he oversaw administering French colonial territories. After the war, he became inspector of the French Foreign Legion and spent some time in French Indochina. But in Korea, he was a battalion commander once again.[44]

William R. Guthrie, the Dog Company commander when the French Battalion arrived, said of Monclar, "We all knew his background and felt that he was the titular head of the French contingent, but [he] provided a backdrop to the Battalion in courage, sacrifice and experience." Describing the French soldiers, Guthrie remarked, "The French troops were sloppy by US standards, but there was an air of professionalism that stood out—we were glad to have them."[45]

Albert C. Metts, the commander of M Company during the Battle of Chipyong-ni, held Monclar and the French soldiers in high esteem. He wrote, "This brave French General reduced his own rank to Lieutenant Colonel so he could come to Korea and command the French battalion. The unit was comprised of brave men, volunteers who were real fighters."[46]

Some of the enlisted men shared Guthrie's and Metts's opinions of Monclar. "Saw enough of him that one had to admire his style," wrote Douglas Graney from Easy Company. "Whenever the French were going into the attack he would walk with the attacking column until the attack actually began. His men appeared to admire him as well . . . always cheering and waving whenever he was near them."[47]

The French soldiers and officers who served under Monclar believed he was fearless. According to François DeCastries, commander of 1st Company, an American officer once asked another officer in the French Battalion how one could cure the colonel of hiccups. The French officer replied it was impossible, as no one could ever frighten Colonel Monclar.[48]

The addition of the French Battalion was not the only major change for the 23rd Infantry Regiment: Colonel Freeman had a new boss. The fiasco at Kunu-ri claimed its last casualty when General Walker relieved General Keiser. The stated reason was medical, but more than likely the Army relieved him of his command because of his failure. His replacement was Maj. Gen. Robert B. McClure, who assumed command on December 7.[49]

However, the biggest change came at the top. On December 23, Lt. Gen. Walton Walker was killed in a traffic accident north of Seoul. MacArthur already had selected someone to succeed Walker if something happened, and now it had. Lt. Gen. Matthew B. Ridgway was at a friend's house, celebrating the upcoming Christmas holiday, when the host told him that Gen. J. Lawton Collins was on the phone and wanted to speak with him. Collins informed Ridgway that he was to leave for Korea at once and assume command of the U.S. Eighth Army.

MacArthur had picked a winner. Ridgway already was something of legend. Like MacArthur and Freeman, he was a West Point graduate. He had missed action in World War I, but served in a variety of roles between the world wars. In 1942, he took over the 82nd Airborne Division, becoming the first airborne division commander in the U.S. Army. In 1943, he led the 82nd in Sicily and during the Salerno landings. He led the All American Division into combat again in 1944, when he dropped into Normandy as part of the D-Day landings. Later that summer, Eisenhower elevated Ridgway to command the XVIII Airborne Corps for Operation Market Garden. Ridgway commanded the same corps during the Battle of the Bulge. After sustaining wounds from a grenade attack in March 1945 when he jumped in with the 17th Airborne Division, Ridgway returned to the United States. From there, he headed to the Pacific, where he served under General MacArthur until the end of the war.

In 1949, Ridgway became the Army deputy chief of staff. He was serving in that capacity when he got the phone call from General Collins. Within hours of the summons, he was on a plane, flying west to Japan. When he arrived, his first stop was to see his new boss, Gen. Douglas MacArthur.[50]

TUESDAY, DECEMBER 26, 0930 HOURS: HEADQUARTERS, FAR EAST COMMAND, DAI-ICHI BUILDING, TOKYO

The new commander of the U.S. Eighth Army arrived at MacArthur's office the morning after Christmas. Aides led the paratrooper general into a room where he found MacArthur and his deputy chief of staff, Maj. Gen. Doyle Hickey, seated alone at a table. MacArthur was no stranger to Ridgway—they had known each other since 1918 when Ridgway was an instructor at West Point.

Still, despite the familiarity, Ridgway remarked, "I was again deeply impressed by the force of his personality. To confer with him was an experience that could happen with few others. He was a great actor too, with an actor's instinct for the dramatic—in tone and gesture."

MacArthur briefed Ridgway on the situation in Korea. He told the incoming Eighth Army commander that he had to defend Seoul for as long as possible, but cautioned him not turn it into a "citadel." Moreover, he had to prepare for a withdrawal back to the Pusan area, as Walker had done the previous summer.

MacArthur then added, "A military success will strengthen our diplomacy." He was right. In December 1950, China was in the driver's seat. The supposedly third-world nation had driven the U.S.-led U.N. forces back to the 38th Parallel, and it looked like the communists would recapture Seoul. A victory would show the rest of the planet that the "Free World" was far from finished.

At the end of his briefing, MacArthur said to Ridgway, "Form your own opinions. Use your own judgment. I will support you. You have my complete confidence."

MacArthur answered several questions from Ridgway, and then the new commander asked one more: "If I find the situation to my liking, would you have any objections to my attacking?"

MacArthur stared back at him and said with the conviction of a senior officer who had the utmost confidence in his subordinate, "The Eighth Army is yours, Matt. Do what you think best."

Ridgway nodded. He now had the authority to run the war the way he saw it. Ridgway was a paratrooper, and paratroopers liked to attack. The question now was *when?*[51]

JANUARY 1951: 23RD INFANTRY REGIMENT, AREA AROUND WONJU

Changes at the top had an almost immediate impact on the soldiers of the 23rd Infantry. Captain Guthrie later recalled Ridgway's rumored statement to his staff, "I don't to want to hear your withdrawal plans—I want to hear your Attack plans."

This was good news for Guthrie. "This statement permeated all elements of the Command within hours," he wrote. "It changed the course of the war. We were tired of retreating and needed that kind of leadership. All hands were excited and vowed to take the fight to the enemy."[52] Guthrie's fellow company commander, Albert Metts, agreed with his assessment of the new Eighth Army general. Metts added that when Ridgway took the reins, "order came out of chaos in Korea."[53]

Many of the enlisted men also grew to like Ridgway. Doug Graney recalled an incident when Ridgway visited the 23rd Infantry shortly after he took over the Eighth Army. He wanted to see the condition of the soldiers along the front lines, where the soldiers of Easy Company were freezing in their foxholes. "Ridgway stood over my foxhole (I was standing in my foxhole) and asked to see what I was eating," Graney wrote. "I handed him my knife and ration. He asked why it wasn't hot and I explained [to him there were] no fires on the forward slope. He said, 'I know that but hasn't [sic] the cooks heated it before we got it?' I explained that we've been eating like this for quite sometime [sic] and we hadn't seen our cooks for about the same time."

Hearing this, the general was furious. Graney wrote, "He [Ridgway] got angry and shouted some orders to one of his staff. Then he said, 'Tonight you'll have a nice, hot steak!' Everyday [sic] after that each squad would go behind the hill for a complete hot meal." For Graney and the other soldiers, the addition of hot chow was a boon to morale. To them, Ridgway was a fighter, but he was also a commander who cared about his soldiers.[54]

Alas, Ridgway was not the only new boss. On January 2, the 2nd Infantry Division would join X Corps, which was under the command of Maj. Gen. Edward M. Almond. However, unlike the almost universally admired Ridgway and Monclar, Almond did not engender the same feelings of respect or warmth in his subordinates.[55]

Glenn C. MacGuyer commanded Able Company during the Battle of Chipyong-ni and recalled, "I didn't like him [Almond] and never talked to anyone in the 2nd Division who did like him. He was a martinet who enjoyed instilling fear in subordinates. He was also very unreasonable at times."[56] Sgt. Frank Butler from the regimental tank company was even more succinct describing his opinion of Almond: "I saw him [Almond] only once, and that was enough," he wrote.[57]

In July 1950, Colonel Freeman was an unknown entity, but by the end of the year, that was no longer the case. Lt. Ralph H. Krueger, a platoon leader in Easy Company, served under the colonel for only four months before he was captured at Kunu-ri, yet Freeman left an indelible impression on him. Of Freeman, Krueger wrote, "The greatest officer I ever had the pleasure of serving under. . . . My men tried [sic] to copy him in every respect. Trying to grow a mustache, not wearing a helmet and wearing a scarf because that's what the Colonel did." This observation was affirmed by a story told to Krueger by a member of the graves registration unit. "You can always tell a body was [in the] 23rd Infantry," the soldier said, "because he is usually shot through the head, no helmet, trying to grow a mustache and wearing a red, or white, or blue scarf like your regimental commander." Kruger added, "We loved our colonel."[58]

Like the officers, the 23rd Infantry's enlisted men felt deep admiration for Colonel Freeman. Donald E. Hoffman was a volunteer who joined Fox Company, 23rd Infantry, after the call went out for volunteers at Fort Lewis. He left the United States as a corporal, but was now a seasoned, grizzled sergeant in charge of a rifle squad. He had survived the ordeal of Kunu-ri and believed Colonel Freeman was the reason. "I would follow him through the gates of hell," he wrote. "He was a man that stood on his own two feet. I think he gave us that kind of pride that made us 'stand-to' at the Naktong, at Kunu-ri, and at Chipyong-ni. He made the 23rd a proud outfit that lived up to its tradition."[59]

Douglas Graney from Easy Company credited Colonel Freeman with saving the regiment at Kunu-ri by directing the Tomahawks to use the western avenue approach instead of the southern one. Because of this order, the 23rd Infantry remained intact while the CPVF ravaged the 9th and 38th Infantry Regiments.[60]

Pvt. Morris Evans from How Company summed up the sentiment about Freeman best: "I along with many others would have followed that man anywhere as he was a true leader of men, and he really cared about his men," he wrote.[61]

With all of these men counting on him, Colonel Freeman would face his greatest test as a commander at Chipyong-ni and the Twin Tunnels.

With a new commander, the New Year brought hope and a change of attitude to the Eighth Army. However, before Ridgway could order an attack, he first had to defend the Han River line. Intelligence indicated that the Chinese were preparing for another massive offensive, similar to the one they had launched the previous November. At this point, the 2nd Infantry Division was east of Seoul. It entered the area around the town of Chungju on January 1, and then proceeded north to Wonju the next day. The terrain around Wonju was more defensible than Chungju, and Ridgway wanted the 2nd Infantry Division in place before the Chinese attacked.

Meanwhile, the 23rd Infantry Regiment was north of the division command post, operating along the Hoengseong–Hongcheon highway. While advancing north, the regiment discovered several NKPA units occupying a roadblock, which it destroyed on the afternoon of January 2. At that point, General McClure ordered Freeman to go on the defensive.

As the division prepared for the inevitable communist attack, General Ridgway visited the Indianhead command post in Wonju. Ridgway viewed Wonju as key terrain because it was a road hub, and the Chinese would need to seize it if they wanted to flank the ROK III Corps. After Ridgway left, the Eighth Army commander officially transferred the Indianhead Division to General Almond's X Corps at 1800 hours on January 2.

In the meantime, Commissar Peng Dehuai's armies were marching south as part of his Third Phase Offensive, which had begun twenty-four hours earlier. Elements of the NKPA's II Corps were attempting to flank the ROK II and III Corps. Once again, in most locations, the Eighth Army was withdrawing. Much to his chagrin, but as expected, Ridgway ordered the evacuation of Seoul on January 3.

For the Tomahawks, the Chinese offensive meant another holding action. First, the 23rd Infantry secured the Hoengseong–Hongcheon highway so that the ROK II Corps could withdraw through their lines. By January 5, the ROK II Corps had passed. On the sixth, NKPA units streamed past Wonju to the east. As a result, General McClure ordered the 23rd Infantry to withdraw south of Wonju so that the NKPA could not flank it. The Tomahawks then occupied the high ground that ringed the town's southern edges.

On January 9, General McClure reversed his order, ordering Colonel Freeman to recapture Wonju. For the next few days, the battalions of the 23rd Infantry battered themselves against the communist defenses. One piece of key terrain was Hill 247, overlooking the town. Both sides recognized its importance and fought hard for it, trading control of the hill back and forth several times, but despite their best efforts, the Tomahawks could not retake Wonju.

In the end, McClure's decision to yield the town cost the new division commander his career. Capt. Bickford E. Sawyer, the mortar platoon leader for 2nd Battalion and future Easy Company commander, recalled seeing General Almond visit the regiment a few days after McClure ceded the vital road hub to the communists. With the corps commander was General McClure. Sawyer recalled, "I ran up to them to report, but

General Almond waved me off and with his entourage walked up the rise toward Wonju . . . General Almond then proceeded to give General McClure a vigorous dressing down for sanctioning the withdrawal from Wonju."[62]

On January 14, a few days after the confrontation Sawyer witnessed, Almond officially relieved McClure after only five weeks as division commander. His replacement was Maj. Gen. Clark L. Ruffner. Prior to his assumption of command of the 2nd Infantry Division, Ruffner had been Almond's chief of staff for X Corps; this would be his first major command. Over the previous decade, he had served mainly in staff roles and had not seen much front-line action during World War II. His service in Korea would provide him with many opportunities to see some fighting.

Ruffner's assumption of command had little impact on the daily lives of the men on the front lines. This was in part because the 23rd Infantry had assumed a defensive mission. For the next eleven days, the soldiers conducted training while absorbing new replacements to fill their depleted ranks. During this period, Easy Company, 9th Infantry Regiment, moved into an empty Wonju on January 17. The CPVF and the NKPA had vanished, and the generals and colonels wanted to know where they had gone.

With Wonju back under U.N. control, IX Corps and I Corps kicked off Operation Thunderbolt in the west, Ridgway's first operational offensive. It began on January 25 and lasted a week. By the end of January, the two corps had pushed the Chinese 15 miles north of the line of departure. It was a modest success, but a victory nonetheless. Not to be outdone, General Almond's X Corps began its own reconnaissance in force to find the Chinese in their own sector.

On the same day that Thunderbolt commenced, General Ruffner ordered Colonel Freeman to send patrols from Wonju to the Han River. The patrols came back and reported that the CPVF were gone. Ruffner then forwarded the news to Almond at X Corps. By the end of January, 2nd Infantry Division patrols had made contact with several NKPA units north of Wonju. One patrol was ambushed on January 28 north of the Wonju–Yoju highway near the town of Mannangpo, but to the northwest and west, information about the enemy remained elusive. The X Corps G2 section assessed that the CPVF 42nd Army was near

Chipyong-ni, but it was only a hypothesis, not a fact. On the twenty-eighth, Ruffner ordered Freeman to send a patrol northwest to Chipyong-ni to find the Chinese, and on the morning of the twenty-ninth, Lieutenant Mitchell set out to locate them. Unfortunately for Mitchell and his platoon, the communists found them first.[63]

CHAPTER 3

Ambush at the Twin Tunnels

"Who won the Rose Bowl game?"

—Unknown soldier, trapped patrol

MONDAY, JANUARY 29, 1951, 1245–1500 HOURS: CHARLIE COMPANY, 23RD INFANTRY REGIMENT, 2ND INFANTRY DIVISION, SOUTH OF CHIPYONG-NI

The sudden blaring of bugles and the rushing onslaught of Chinese soldiers unnerved many of the men in Charlie Company. A deadly ambush had trapped them in a narrow valley with little chance of survival.

"We didn't have any idea we were so close to the Gooks until they opened up on us," said PFC Billy B. Blizzard, a rifleman. "They waited until we got into their trap and then cut us off."[1]

The only refuge was atop a ridge that ran along the eastern side of the road. The three remaining officers—2nd Lt. Harold P. Mueller from Fox Company, 21st Infantry; 1st Lt. James P. Mitchell from Charlie Company, 23rd Infantry; and 2nd Lt. William G. Penrod, from Dog Company, 23rd Infantry—ordered the survivors to destroy what they could not carry with them and climb the hill to establish a defensive perimeter on the high ground.

Blizzard recalled the mad dash. "We left our vehicles and ran up a hill. We didn't have any tools or time to dig in, if we had [*sic*]. We just hid behind anything we could find—bushes mostly. All we could carry with us were rifles, carbines, one automatic rifle and one 30-caliber machinegun [*sic*]."

Cpl. John Hinkel and Pvt. Donald Hinkel, two brothers, also participated in the mad scramble. John Hinkel described the desperate determination of the men to survive. "There was about a foot of snow on the hill and it was pretty steep. We ran and crawled and climbed any way we could to get up there. There must have been hundreds of them firing at us. We had at least six men hit before we got to the top."[2]

Bobby G. Hensley had a harder time than most of the men. Other soldiers carried carbines or rifles, but he was lugging the M1919 30-caliber machine gun and its tripod. Cold, sweaty, and sore, he stumbled because of the weight dragging him down. It was as if he were lifting a set of barbells up the steep hill. He could only take so much, then slipped and fell, breaking several ribs in the process.

His section leader, Sgt. Alfred Buchanan, saw him fall and rushed over to him, shoving some snow in his face to revive him. Buchanan did not want to leave anyone behind, especially the machine gunner. The cold snow worked, and Hensley came to his senses. Exhausted and in excruciating pain, Henley swore he could not finish the climb.

Nearby, Lieutenant Penrod from Dog Company heard Hensley's protests. Like any good officer would, Penrod simply ordered him to continue. "You've got to make it, son. Just keep climbing." To lighten his load, Penrod ordered Hensley to break down the machine gun and leave it on the hill, instructing the private to toss the bolt away from the gun so the Chinese could not find it in the snow and reassemble the machine gun to use against its former owners.[3]

Not far from Hensley and Penrod, Lieutenant Mitchell was falling behind. His legs had gone numb because of a spinal injury he had sustained during World War II. With little feeling in his calves and thighs, the exhausted lieutenant sat down in the snow to catch his breath. One of the jeep drivers saw him and told him to keep moving. Mitchell replied that he couldn't due to his injury, so the driver decided to stay with the stricken lieutenant. The driver's arrival was fortuitous because three Chinese soldiers suddenly appeared from behind a ridge. According to Mitchell, they were only 15 feet away. The driver opened fire with his M1 Garand but failed to score a single hit. Mitchell raised his carbine and squeezed off a round. Instead, he heard a *thunk*—his carbine had jammed. Frantic, the lieutenant grabbed his bayonet and wedged it into the chamber to pry out the spent brass. As Mitchell struggled with his weapon, the Chinese soldiers fired back. One of the bullets slammed into the driver's hand and shattered his rifle stock, causing him to reel back in pain. Luckily, the Chinese soldier who had fired at the driver had his own troubles when his rifle jammed. Mitchell saw his chance. He finally freed the stuck cartridge and opened fire on the three communist soldiers, killing them.

Realizing the vulnerability of their current location, Mitchell spied a nearby gully and ordered the driver to hide there with him until he was strong enough to climb the rest of the way up the hill. The two slid down the slope, only to find Private Hensley already there. For thirty minutes, the three soldiers hid in the gully before attempting to finish their climb to the top.[4]

While Mitchell recovered in the gully, Lieutenant Mueller was atop the ridge, trying to bring order to the chaos. The twenty-something officer from Milwaukee, Wisconsin, saw that the platoon's position was far from ideal. From the south and north, Chinese soldiers could pour plunging fire on the exposed ridge. Two narrow saddles linked the summit, and Mueller decided the saddle to the south was the more likely enemy avenue of approach, since it afforded the Chinese some defilade. Moreover, the Chinese had already set up a machine gun on the southern hill to provide suppressive fire. Fortunately for Mueller and his men, the path along the southern saddle tapered off as it neared the American lines. The restrictive terrain would allow the Chinese to send only one or two men at a time up the trail. To exploit this advantage, Mueller decided to place his one remaining machine gun to cover the approach, then took stock of what he had left in this polyglot force. Besides the M1919 machine gun, he had eight Browning Automatic Rifles and one 3.5-inch bazooka. Everyone else had Garands or carbine rifles.

Once the rest of the survivors arrived, it became obvious to Mueller and 2nd Lieutenant Penrod that the hilltop could not accommodate everyone. The two officers opted to send some of the men to occupy the northern saddle. A small group moved out to the north and lay down behind whatever cover they could find. Shortly after the small group had occupied the northern saddle, the Chinese attacked it from the south. The initial assault began with a short but intense mortar barrage. While the GIs hugged the earth, the communists opened fire with machine guns and rifles. Mueller ordered the lone machine-gun team to return fire while the other men began to toss hand grenades at the onrushing Chinese. The ferocity of the American response stunned the Chinese soldiers. After several minutes, twenty communists lay dead in the snow. Chastened, the CPVF soldiers withdrew to lick their wounds. A hush fell over the battlefield, but Mueller and Penrod knew the stillness would not last long before the Chinese tried again.[5]

JANUARY 29, 1245–1455 HOURS:
23RD INFANTRY REGIMENT COMMAND POST,
2ND INFANTRY DIVISION, MOKKYEDONG

"Red patrol in a firefight," the voice chirped over the radio. The time was 1245 hours.

Red was the call sign for 1st Battalion. Colonel Freeman knew it was the combined patrol from C and D Companies in contact. On the squawk box was Maj. Millard O. Engen, 1st Battalion's executive officer.

Fifteen minutes later, the regiment received another call from Major Engen: "Red patrol cut off after reaching objective. Hit from three sides from coordinates Charlie Sugar 8 . . . 3 . . . 9 . . . 4 . . . 4 . . . 9 to 0 . . . 8 . . . 3 . . . 4 . . . 2 . . . 5 and from high ground in rear of objective."[6]

Colonel Freeman had to act fast to save the trapped platoons. First, he requested air support to give the platoons some firepower. He also reasoned that the encircled soldiers would need supplies, namely ammunition, so he requested an airdrop. The platoon would be unable to break out on its own—Freeman needed to scrounge together a relief force.

To save time, he decided that the force had to be mounted, which was a problem. "There was a definite limit to the number of light vehicles that could negotiate the nearly demolished bridge at Munmang-ni to transport forces," he later wrote. "By rounding up all available jeeps and weapons carriers in the vicinity, F (Fox) Company, reinforced, hurriedly was sent on its second rescue mission within two days."[7]

At 1320 hours, only twenty minutes after Colonel Freeman received the news, 2nd Battalion headquarters alerted the soldiers of Fox Company of their new mission. Freeman wanted an infantry company that could fight its way through any potential roadblock, so he ordered Lt. Col. James W. Edwards, the 2nd Battalion commander, to reinforce it before departure. Edwards allocated a section of 81mm mortars and a section of heavy machine guns to the relief column.[8]

As they set out, Fox Company was under the command of Capt. Stanley C. Tyrrell. Like many officers, Tyrrell was a World War II veteran who also had been an NCO before earning a commission. Born in 1910, he grew up in Lackawanna, Pennsylvania, and joined the National Guard in 1941. By the end of the Second World War, Tyrrell had reached the rank of staff sergeant. When he left for Korea, he was forty, older than most Army captains who were usually in their twenties. Edwards had chosen Tyrrell because the Fox Company commander had some experience when it came to relief operations. The day before, Tyrrell had led his company north of the Wonju–Yoju highway to rescue an ambushed patrol from 3rd Battalion's K Company near the village of Mannangpo. Because of this, Freeman was confident that Tyrrell would succeed in his mission.[9]

At 1415 hours, Tyrrell reported to his battalion command post to receive any final orders from Colonel Edwards. According to Major Engen, the surrounded patrol had dug in on top of a ridge several hundred meters north of the village of Sinchon. Engen also reported that abandoned vehicles lined the road west of the patrol's current location. After forty minutes of discussing his plan with his battalion commander, Tyrrell and his column rolled out at 1455 hours. No one knew how long the beleaguered platoon would last, but help was on the way.[10]

JANUARY 29, 1500–2030 HOURS: CHARLIE COMPANY, 23RD INFANTRY REGIMENT, 2ND INFANTRY DIVISION, SOUTH OF CHIPYONG-NI

While Fox Company was on its way, the CPVF soldiers tightened their vise on the makeshift American patrol base on the ridgeline. Soon after the attack from the south petered out, the communist forces opened fire from the northern hill. As bullets peppered the hillside, many of the men sought cover on the ground, lying motionless like prostrate statues.

Cpl. Leroy Gibbons, a Charlie Company squad leader from Illinois, refused to let the Chinese beat him into submission. He stood up and began to walk over to Lieutenant Mitchell, who had arrived a few minutes after 1500 hours. The other soldiers shouted at Gibbons, telling him to get down. The eighteen-year-old corporal assured them, "Aw, hell, they couldn't hit the broad side of a barn." Much to the amazement of everyone watching, Gibbons continued his march over to the lieutenant, making it safely to the platoon leader's location.

Another soldier, Sgt. Everett Lee, saw Gibbons and decided that he could do something about the offending machine gun. "I'm going to get that son of bitch," Lee announced to those near him on the north side of the platoon position. After making his declaration, he crawled several feet and then zeroed his M1 Garand by firing two rounds. Satisfied with his aim, Lee raised his weapon and, staring down the barrel, squeezed off a couple of rounds at the machine-gun team. His aim was true—he killed both the gunner and assistant gunner within seconds. In the meantime, other soldiers in the immediate area found the courage to take up arms and began to pop at the Chinese soldiers with their own rifles and carbines. Thanks to Lee's decisive action, the Chinese never again attempted to attack from the north side of the perimeter.[11]

It was a different story along the southern side. The Chinese repeatedly hurled themselves at the lone machine-gun team that Lieutenant Mueller had established to overwatch the southern saddle. Seven times, Mueller had to replace the gunner, and each time he dragged a soldier back from the gun, he noticed they had a head wound.

Meanwhile, Private Blizzard was on the M1919, chugging away at the endless stream of Chinese soldiers advancing like frenzied, mindless berserkers. Mueller watched as Blizzard's head suddenly shuddered and recoiled, as if someone had slapped him with an invisible two-by-four piece of lumber. Looking closer, he noticed a telltale hole in Blizzard's helmet. Miraculously, Blizzard kept firing.

Mueller shouted at the young private, as if he were a coach assuring a stunned quarterback attempting to stand up after a sack: "You aren't hurt, son. That was a ricochet."

Blizzard then turned his head to face Mueller. A crimson rivulet was streaming down his forehead. The private growled, "Like hell it's a ricochet."

The platoon leader shook his head and then pleaded, "For God's sake, we've got to keep this gun going."[12]

Elsewhere along the perimeter, soldiers were keeping the enemy at bay. Pvt. Bill Horton was a Charlie Company rifleman from Texas. During the constant storm of Chinese assaults, he went where the action was, braving enemy fire to save his comrades. In the course of one attack, a communist machine-gun team had pinned down the flank of Horton's platoon. He dashed through the maelstrom to where the action was thickest, rushed toward the machine gun, and silenced it as he slew one man and chased off others. When the Texan attempted to return to American lines, however, another hidden Chinese machine-gun team opened fire, killing him instantly. For his selfless courage, the Army posthumously awarded Horton the Silver Star.[13]

The three lieutenants on the hill knew time was not their ally. The Chinese had surrounded them on all sides with overwhelming numbers. One unit had occupied Hill 333, north of their embattled location, while another communist company had set up its position on Hill 453 to the southwest. Directly to the west was another detachment of CPVF on Hill 279, while the main assault force was south of their battle position on the unnamed hill above the village of Sinchon. It was a large force, numbering in the hundreds. Worse, the Chinese had isolated them. Any relief column from the 23rd Infantry would have to clear out the Chinese defenders on Hill 453 if they wanted to rescue the trapped patrol. The GIs were running on low on ammunition. Yet, despite the grim outlook, the men continued to fight and fight hard.[14]

Sometime between 1630 and 1715 hours, the beleaguered patrol got its first break. The droning sound of a prop-engine plane heralded the arrival of air support. Major Engen's plane, which had been circling above the patrol earlier that afternoon, had returned to base because it was running low on fuel, but when Engen got back at 1548 hours, he had requested air support. A T-6 Mosquito was now on station to provide that much-needed assistance.[15]

The Mosquito was a larger airplane than Engen's Sentinel and sported a much more rugged airframe than the L-5, which was little more than an olive-drab crop duster. The young U.S. Air Force had chosen the T-6 as its forward air controller aircraft for several reasons, but primarily because of its hardy fuselage, which meant pilots could fly from small, short, unimproved runaways (typical of the airfields in Korea). However, according to Mosquito pilot John Collins, the fighter jockeys who flew the newer jet planes discovered an unforeseen issue in the skies over Korea: "blinded by their own speed and rushed by their tremendous thirst for fuel, the jet bombers [and fighters] could not pick out ground targets," he explained. "So the heavy, slow T-6 Mosquitos preceded them in flak-heavy-enemy-territory, dropped down to tree-top level to spot the gun emplacements and tanks and pinpointed them with smoke markers for the kill."[16] For the soldiers on the ground, the improvised system worked with gratifying results.

The Mosquito the platoon heard was not alone. Several minutes after the plane appeared, the men heard the shrill, distinctive whooshing and whining of jets in the distance. Seconds later, a sleek aircraft screamed over the ridgeline and rocketed past the platoon's position. The first planes strafed and shot rockets at Hills 453 and 279. Not long after the first jets, another pair roared over the mountains. The soldiers watched in hushed anticipation as several metal cylinders fell from the jets' wings and floated and tumbled to the earth. The canisters contained napalm, and the effect on the Chinese soldiers huddled atop the barren summits of 453 and 279 was immediate as the two hillsides erupted in flame. It was as if each peak were a volcano.

Cpl. John Hinkel vividly remembered the impact: "We'd been fighting about two hours when eight jets showed up and shot the Gooks up. That took some pressure off."[17] In all, six flights of four planes each provided close air support for the trapped soldiers of Charlie Company and its attachments. Without the jets, the Chinese would have easily overrun the surrounded American patrol. Instead, the fighter-bombers turned the two hills into charred Golgothas and left the pair of peaks littered with Chinese dead.[18]

The appearance of the jets brought a needed respite for the men. They could finally stand up after lying in the wet snow for several hours. The break also allowed the officers to shift men around the perimeter while the medics tended to the wounded. As the men shuffled around the hill, another L-5 Sentinel showed up, carrying Major Engen. The 1st Battalion executive officer returned with Maj. George Russell, the commander for 1st Battalion. From their airborne perch, the two officers could direct the resupply operation. The pilot of the L-5 made several passes, each time airdropping supplies on top of the mountain. Unfortunately, many of the bundles landed behind enemy lines. Once all of the drops were completed, the trapped soldiers had secured only one can of machine-gun ammunition. Still, one can was better than no cans at all.

On the final pass, one of the L-5 crewmembers tossed out an envelope tied to a yellow streamer. Without a working a radio, the platoon members knew that the airdropped message was the only way the out-side world could communicate with them. Without any prompting, a few soldiers ran out to find the message. One grabbed the streamer, returned to the perimeter, and handed the envelope to Lieutenant Mitchell, the senior officer on site. Mitchell opened the envelope and read the message. It said, "Friendly column approaching from the south. Will be with you shortly."

The officer knew it would be a boon to morale, so he decided to show it to all the men on perimeter. The Chinese had recovered from the aerial shellacking and had begun to fire back, so Mitchell crawled to each man's position to tell him the news, feeling it was worth the risk to assure them that help was on the way. With the sun rapidly descending behind Hills 453 and 279, the lieutenant predicted that the Chinese attacks would intensify with the onset of darkness. Higher morale was crucial if he wanted the soldiers to keep fighting. Knowing that help was on the way would bolster their sagging spirits.[19]

A few minutes after the letter arrived, the men thought they saw mortar rounds impact on Hill 453, southwest of their location. They concluded that the mortar rounds could only have come from the relief column, and as a result, morale further skyrocketed. However, they knew that the column still had to clear the Chinese from the hill. It was hours away from linking up with the men of Charlie Company.

The night enveloped them. Mitchell and the other officers knew the next few hours would be the toughest. The Chinese opened up with their mortars, and rounds exploded among the men inside the patrol base.

Four soldiers then slithered southward to see if anyone was approaching. Sgt. Donald H. Larsen saw figures skulking along the saddle from the south. "Here they come! Here they come!" he shouted to the others. The four men let loose with their Garands and carbines, and the Chinese replied with their own rifles. In the brief melee, all four Ameri-cans sustained injuries, so instead of skirmishing with a Chinese force of unknown composition, they slinked back to their lines. "That's enough for me," remarked Larsen to Lieutenant Mitchell as he crawled back to his place on the perimeter.[20]

Not long after Larsen returned, the Chinese struck the southern perimeter again. This time, they were so close that they were within hand-grenade range of American lines. During one of many banzai charges, CPVF hand grenades landed near Corporal Gibbon's position. Twice, he picked up the live grenades and tossed them back to their former owners.[21]

Cpl. Manuel Alonzo from Rockford, Illinois, remembered how a CPVF soldier crept up to his position under the cover of darkness and wounded him. "The guy who got me was not more than 10 feet away at the time, but I never saw him," Alonzo recalled. "I just saw flashes from his gun when he opened up. They came right in among us as we lay in the bushes." Alonzo then described how one of the BAR gunners defended his position: "Our automatic rifle man played dead as a couple of them walked right over him—then he opened fire and killed both [of them]. We could hardly ever see them, but we could hear their feet crunching in the snow and we fired at their gun flashes."[22]

The fighting was up close and personal. No one was safe inside the patrol base. Lieutenant Mueller, who constantly exposed himself to enemy fire, suffered a gunshot wound above his left eye. It was his second wound that day. The resultant injury caused him to see flashes and black out intermittently. Despite the pain, Mueller continued to lead his small platoon from Fox Company, 21st Infantry.[23]

During a lull in the action, Corporal Gibbons approached Lieutenant Mitchell and the other leaders. Since it was dark, Gibbons figured he could infiltrate through the enemy lines and reach the relief column that was somewhere south of Hill 453. Mitchell knew it was a dangerous mission. Others had already tried and failed. But, despite the slim chance of success, Gibbons felt he had to try. Someone had to let the relief column know that the trapped soldiers were still fighting. Mitchell agreed, and minutes later the intrepid corporal disappeared. No one knew if he would make it through the Chinese lines.[24]

JANUARY 29, AFTERNOON TO EVENING: CUT-OFF SURVIVORS FROM CHARLIE COMPANY, 23RD INFANTRY REGIMENT, 2ND INFANTRY DIVISION, NEAR SINCHON

Pvt. Richard Fockler wondered where everyone had gone. One second, everyone and everything was shooting. The next, he and a few survivors from his squad were alone. When the Chinese ambush erupted, Fockler and his squad were near the southern end of the column, on the out-skirts of Sinchon. At one point during the battle, the fighting was heavi-est north of their position, but then it died down. Afterward, the squad realized they could no longer hear gunfire coming from the east end of the village. They decided to check it out. Fockler and his friends found nothing, and the horrible truth then dawned on him: "There was no one there. We had been left behind."

The squad went to ground and waited. Late in the afternoon, the men watched jets and Major Russell's liaison plane fly overhead. When they saw the parachute bundles fall from the sky, the group decided to climb the hill to reach the spot where the packages had landed.

Alas, when they stood up and started to ascend the slope, Chinese soldiers opened fire. As Fockler described it, "I could see the snow kick-ing up from the bullets and then I was hit in the right shin. I saw one of my friends going down at the same time and the others kept on going. I called to my friend and found out that he was unhurt."

Fockler's comrade was twenty-two-year-old PFC Clement L. Pietrasiewicz from Erie, Pennsylvania. For several minutes, the two sol-diers lay on the ground in the damp snow. Zipping above them were bullets from an unseen machine gun. Fockler figured that by lying on the ground, the Chinese gunner could not hit him or Clement.

Then the gunfire stopped. "I soon heard the crunch of snow as someone walked up on me and my weapon was taken from my hand," Fockler later wrote. "I rolled over and put my hands in the air. The Chi-nese soldier thrust his weapon toward me but to my immense good for-tune, he did not fire. I then called to my friend and he stood up."

Fockler noticed that his captor was only five feet tall. Even though Fockler could not speak Chinese, he understood that the CPVF soldier was wondering what to do with the wounded American. Then, motion-ing with his rifle, the communist ordered Fockler to wrap his arm around Pietrasiewicz's neck. The prisoners quickly understood that Pietrasiewicz had the task of assisting the wounded Fockler down the side of the hill.

Fockler remarked, "I hung on and was hauled down the slope with my broken leg bumping along the ground as he stumbled downhill with me hanging on. When we got to the road, he [Pietrasiewicz] was marched away immediately."

Fockler wondered would happen next. He was alone on the road. He did not know if anyone else from his squad had survived, and now his only friend was gone. Occasionally, a CPVF soldier would come by and check Fockler's wrist to see if he was wearing a watch. This happened several times, and each time it was someone new.

Finally, after several hours, the communists set fire to the abandoned American vehicles along the road. Without warning, they left the wounded American lying on the side of the road as if he were a discarded, broken toy. Fockler could not believe his luck. But he was not going to remain by the column of smoldering jeeps and burning carriers should the Chinese return; instead, he dragged himself to a nearby hut to wait out the night. Lying hidden under a straw blanket, he later remarked, "I spent a restless night in the hut wondering if the enemy would return. They did not."[25]

JANUARY 29, 1730–2100 HOURS: FOX COMPANY RELIEF COLUMN FROM THE 23RD INFANTRY REGIMENT, 2ND INFANTRY DIVISION, NEAR HILL 453

While the survivors from the Charlie Company patrol battled for their lives on the ridges atop the Twin Tunnels, help was closing in from the south. By 1730 hours, Captain Tyrrell's relief column arrived at the fork in the road where one road went northeast to Sinchon and the other continued north to Chipyong-ni. Up ahead, the Fox Company soldiers could see and hear the jets pummeling the hillsides around the besieged patrol. Shortly after the jets disappeared over the ridgeline, one of the liaison planes flew over their column and tossed down a message. One of the soldiers grabbed the parcel and brought it back to Captain Tyrrell, who opened it and read it. The message gave the current location of the encircled patrol. Tyrrell then looked at a map. They were close.

The Chinese force atop Hill 453 forced him to make a decision about the next course of action. Several enemy machine guns opened fire on the lead pair of jeeps in the column from the hill summit. Tyrrell, in the third jeep, stepped out of his vehicle and walked back toward the column as if no one was shooting at them.

"You'd better get in the ditch, Captain. The Chinks will get you," his driver called out to him.

Tyrrell smirked and said, "To hell with the Chinks."

The hidden enemy machine gunners on Hill 453 began to chip away at the vehicles and soldiers lined up along the road. In one instance, PFC James E. Robinson was huddled behind some cover when he noticed that the Chinese defenders had shot up his radio. The only way he could send messages back to the rear of the column was by braving the hail of bullets whizzing through the cold air. The young private from Indiana stood up and ran to the back of the convoy as tracers pelted the ground behind him. He survived the harrowing ordeal and continued to pass messages between the various elements of Fox Company throughout the course of the operation.[26]

The relief column commander had to clear Hill 453 before his rescue force could travel any farther up the road. He chose his 2nd Platoon to occupy a support-by-fire position, while his other two platoons were tasked with seizing the key terrain. To provide indirect fire support, Tyrrell ordered his 81mm mortar team to lay down a barrage atop the hill while the two platoons approached the summit.

The combination of heavy machine guns and accurate mortar fire was too much for the Chinese, and they withdrew from the hill without further fighting. Meanwhile, 1st and 3rd Platoons continued their slow ascent to the top of the 453. In the dark, the progress was slow, and Tyrrell did not declare the hill secured until 2030 hours. Once the two platoons linked up, the Fox Company commander ordered them to set up a hasty defense on top of Hill 453 while he planned the next course of action. Throughout the operation, Private Robinson continued to run between the platoons and squads to pass various messages. In many cases, he was alone, creeping through enemy territory. In recognition of his bravery and determination during the rescue operation, the Army awarded him the Silver Star.[27]

Sometime between 2030 and 2100 hours, Tyrrell noticed that the constant thumping of explosions and chattering of machine guns near the trapped patrol's location had ceased. He wondered what that meant. A voice emanated from the darkness, interrupting his thoughts.

"Hey, are you GIs?"

The voice sounded to Tyrrell like someone from the States. He replied to the question with one of his own: "Who are you?"

The commander soon learned that the voice belonged to one of three survivors from the trapped platoon, all of whom were wounded and had escaped during the last attack. They had climbed down the southeastern side and followed the railroad tracks past the back side of Sinchon. According to the trio, the Chinese had finally overwhelmed the trapped Charlie Company patrol. Even more troubling, they claimed they were the only survivors. With this news, Tyrrell decided to establish a patrol base for the night and wait until the following morning to investigate the area where Mitchell's platoon had its last stand. He issued the new orders to his platoon leaders. He knew why the firing had stopped.[28]

JANUARY 29, 2100–2230 HOURS: CHARLIE COMPANY, 23RD INFANTRY REGIMENT, 2ND INFANTRY DIVISION, SOUTH OF CHIPYONG-NI

Unbeknownst to Tyrrell, the three survivors were mistaken: Charlie Company was still alive and fighting. The last attack, which ended around 2100 hours, was a close-run thing, but the GIs won in the end. Cpl. Jesus A. Sanchez from Fox Company, 21st Infantry, blunted the assault singlehandedly when he killed several charging communists with his BAR. Despite the small victory, the survivors from the 23rd and 21st Infantries were barely hanging on. The majority were wounded—some severely. South of their position at Hill 453, the shivering soldiers heard only silence and wondered if the relief column had failed in its mission. No one knew the status of the messengers trying to infiltrate through the Chinese lines to link up with the soldiers from Tyrrell's column. All they could do now was wait . . . and fight.[29]

As they assessed the situation, not all the news was bad. Thanks to Lieutenant Mueller, the one machine gun anchored on the south side of the perimeter was still operating. After several tries, over a span of twelve hours, the Chinese commanders finally decided that the southern approach was no longer a viable option because of Mueller's machine gun. The CPVF soldiers' last effort would attempt to assault the American perimeter from the west side instead.

According to survivors, the Chinese force numbered between ten and fifteen men. Mitchell had only five riflemen at the site where the Chinese planned to attack. When they saw the Chinese approach, the small group opened fire and kept firing for a full minute. Despite the fusillade, three Chinese soldiers penetrated the perimeter.

One of the GIs cried out, "Get the son of a bitch!"

Seconds later, a Chinese soldier slumped over as the American riflemen poured several rounds into him. Another communist emerged from the darkness and opened fire with a "burp" gun, a type of submachine gun. SFC Odvin A. Martinson, Mueller's platoon sergeant, saw the burp gunner and fired back at him with his pistol. Despite the point-blank range, both missed.[30]

Without warning, a single soldier from Dog Company charged into the surging Chinese assault. With a fixed bayonet, he slew the attacking Chinese soldier and chased off the survivors. The lone soldier was PFC Thomas J. Mortimer from Iowa. He survived his suicide charge and returned to the perimeter. For his bravery, the Army later awarded Mortimer the Silver Star.[31]

With the latest assault over, the survivors took stock of their situation. Inside the American perimeter were the bodies of the enemy, including the bayoneted corpse from Mortimer's one-man counterattack. Seeing the skewered remains, Sergeant Martinson grabbed the body and tossed it outside of the patrol base. As he flung it, he growled, "I don't want them in here. Dead or alive."

The trapped patrol was still kicking—barely. It was 2230 hours. Most of the men were wounded. Some could not even hold a rifle. Even more troubling was the ammunition situation: They had no ammunition. Most of the men were down to their last few clips. Without help, the besieged soldiers had only hours left to live.[32]

JANUARY 29, 2100–2330 HOURS: FOX COMPANY RELIEF COLUMN FROM THE 23RD INFANTRY REGIMENT, 2ND INFANTRY DIVISION, SINCHON

"If you had talked with a man who just came into my position," the voice over the radio reported to Captain Tyrrell, "you wouldn't believe the patrol was wiped out."

The voice was Lt. Leonard Napier, Tyrrell's officer in 1st Platoon. Only fifteen minutes earlier, Tyrrell had lost all hope when three wounded soldiers claimed to be the sole survivors from Charlie Company.

It was good news on the radio. Napier's platoon had found a medic from Charlie Company's trapped patrol who had snuck out of the perimeter at night to search for medical supplies left behind in the abandoned vehicles along the road. In the dark, the medic lost his way and continued south, where he stumbled upon Napier's platoon.

Hearing the medic's story, Tyrrell immediately changed his plan. He was not going to wait until morning to ascend the hill. He ordered 2nd Platoon, under the command of Lt. Albert E. Jones, to move out, directing the platoon leader to approach the besieged patrol from the south, using the ridgeline that ran from Sinchon to Hill 333. Not long after 2nd Platoon left, Tyrrell received additional reports from his men that they had found more survivors from Charlie Company. One of them was Cpl. Leroy Gibbons. Like the medic, he told them that the men were still alive and full of fight.[33]

Jones's platoon pushed north. As he neared the reported location of the trapped patrol, the platoon leader decided to take a squad to investigate the area. He was concerned that he was marching into an ambush, so he kept the rest of his platoon behind and approached the hilltop with a smaller element.

Suddenly, the single squad came under fire. Muzzle bursts punctuated the darkness like flashbulbs. Fortunately, no one was hit. Could the incoming fire be from the besieged patrol?

One his men cried out, "GIs! Don't shoot! GIs!"

A voice from the darkness demanded answers. "Who won the Rose Bowl game?"

Jones knew they had found the patrol. Someone in his squad then answered, "Fox Company, 23rd Infantry, by God!"

The lieutenant stood up and followed the trail that led directly to the southern edge of Mitchell's perimeter. Waiting to greet them was Corporal Sanchez from the 21st Infantry. When Jones's squad emerged from the blackness, the corporal shouted, "We're relieved, fellows! We're relieved!"[34]

The time was between 2330 hours and midnight. It took several more hours for the men from Tyrrell's command to carry the wounded off the hill. The relief column then drove back to the 2nd Battalion's area of operation, arriving at the command post at 0835 hours. The final tally was sobering: Fox Company recovered thirty wounded and left five of the dead. Amazingly, Fox Company had not sustained a single casualty in the operation.[35]

"The Fighting Foxes, who had earned this sobriquet in the battle in the Taegu 'Bowling Alley,' on this occasion fought one of the most brilliant small unit actions in the Korean campaign," Colonel Freeman remarked of Captain Tyrrell and Fox Company, 23rd Infantry Regiment. It was high praise. As for Mitchell's platoon, Freeman said, "The cut-off patrol had itself made a brilliant stand against overwhelming attempts to annihilate it and had made the enemy pay dearly for his ambush."

Freeman recounted that the survivors from Charlie and Dog Companies presented a banner to Captain Tyrrell. On it, they had inscribed, "When in peril, send for Tyrrell."[36]

Unbeknownst to Freeman and the 23rd Infantry, the events surrounding the ambushed patrol were only the beginning of a much larger battle.

The regimental adjutant compiled statistics after the battle. Charlie Company had sustained seventeen casualties from one platoon: six enlisted men had been killed in action, another three were missing, and eight were wounded in action. Lieutenant Penrod's platoon from Dog Company had sustained four casualties: one enlisted soldier was killed in action, one was missing in action, and two enlisted soldiers had been wounded in action. Baker Company had one soldier killed in action. Headquarters Company had incurred two casualties: one enlisted soldier was killed in action, and one officer, Capt. Melvin R. Stai, was still missing in action. In total, the battalion had suffered twenty-four casualties.

According to reports, the trapped patrol had inflicted 175 casualties on the Chinese. It was a heavy price to pay for what was ostensibly a reconnaissance mission. Still, despite the losses, the patrol had accomplished its mission. The question for General Almond, the X Corps commander, was what to do next?[37]

CHAPTER 4

Battle at the Twin Tunnels

"We had a feeling we were going to get it."

—Cpl. Herman Seabolt, L Company

TUESDAY, JANUARY 30, 1951, 1840 HOURS: HEADQUARTERS, 23RD INFANTRY REGIMENT, 2ND INFANTRY DIVISION, TOKSAN-NI

At 1840 hours on January 30, Col. Paul Freeman delivered the next mission to his regiment over the radio: "[Regiment] will leave assembly area [at] 0630 and cross line of departure at 0900. Objective is high ground north of Two Tunnels. Estimated two battalions of enemy. Formation will be French on the left, 3rd on the right. 1st Battalion reserve. 2nd Battalion will patrol with reinforced infantry rifle company along axis Nine . . . . Six . . . Five . . . Three . . . Five . . . Five. [Then] Northwest to Charlie Sugar Nine . . . One . . . Four . . . Zero. 38 Infantry to occupy Wonju. Boundary is Tonguon Charlie Sugar Nine . . . Seven . . . Three . . . Zero. Line of Departure is roughly along grid line 34."[1]

Minutes after the message, commanders in 3rd Battalion and the French Battalion began troop-leading procedures. For the men of the 23rd Infantry, January 30 already had been a busy day. At 0925 hours that morning, Lt. Col. James W. Edwards, the commander of 2nd Battalion, had reported to Colonel Freeman that his Fox Company relief column had run into two companies of Reds on Hill 453 as they pushed north to rescue the trapped Charlie Company patrol. His report sent shockwaves up the chain of command. Consequently, General Almond, the X Corps commander, ordered 2nd Infantry Division to flush out the

Chinese forces and destroy them. General Ruffner, the new commander of 2nd Infantry Division, passed the order down to 23rd Infantry, since it was inside the Tomahawks' area of operations.

In less than twenty minutes, the intelligence report from 2nd Battalion triggered a new mission for the regiment. At 0945 hours, Maj. John B. Dumaine, the regimental S3 operations officer, issued a warning order to the regiment to be prepared to move out for a clearance operation near the Twin Tunnels. The official order from division supposedly came down at 1200 hours.[2]

Freeman and Dumaine organized their regimental combat team for battle with all the necessary combined arms. For indirect fire support, Freeman had the 37th Field Artillery Battalion, minus one battery that was supporting 2nd Battalion. For general support, the regiment had B Battery with M16 half-tracks from the 82nd Antiaircraft Artillery Automatic Weapons Battalion. The U.N. forces had little to fear from the Chinese Air Force, so the regiment planned to utilize the quad .50-caliber machine guns on the M16s in a direct fire role. The 1st Battalion was to occupy a patrol base with the artillery and secure the line of communication between the forward elements of the regiment and the rest of division. Finally, 2nd Battalion would remain behind with the rest of the division under the division commander's control.[3]

Freeman recalled the marching conditions on that day. "Third Battalion moved initially, the men floundering down from positions on the rough, snow-covered mountains, and carrying loads of extra ammunition and supplies that had been stocked for defensive action," he wrote. "The French battalion followed. Extra transportation was not available and again the riflemen walked."[4]

The Tomahawks' commander was not comfortable with the operation. But orders were orders. His regiment would be far out in front of the rest of the division, with no one on his flanks other than the mountains and the Chinese. Unbeknownst to many of the Tomahawks, the isolated regiment was part of a much larger plan General Ridgway had initiated on January 25. Ruffner called it a "limited objective attack." The commander of the Eighth Army was a fighter. Just like during his days as a paratrooper in the 82nd Airborne, Ridgway wanted to attack. With the end of the Chinese Third Phase Offensive, he saw his chance to get his army moving forward again.[5]

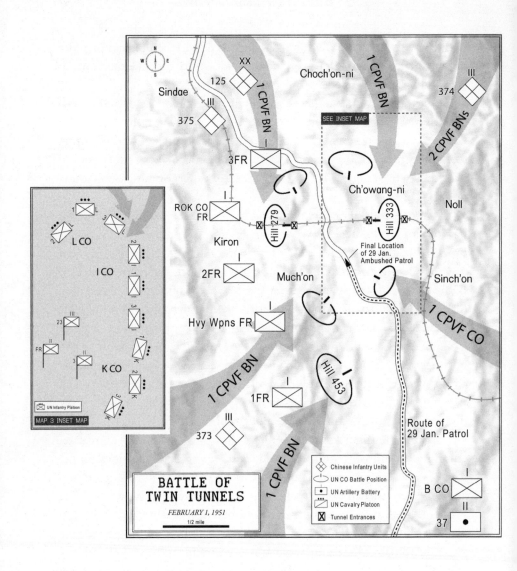

Inset Map

L CO

1 L
2 3

I CO
1 2 3

K CO
23 III
FR 3
1 3 2 K K K

UN Infantry Platoon

MAP 3 INSET MAP

Main Map

N
W E
S

Sindae

125 XX

Choch'on-ni

1 CPVF BN

374 III

375 III

1 CPVF BN

3FR

2 CPVF BNs

SEE INSET MAP

ROK CO FR

Hill 279

Ch'owang-ni

Noll

Kiron

2FR

Hill 333

Final Location
of 29 Jan.
Ambushed Patrol

Much'on

Sinch'on

Hvy Wpns FR

1 CPVF CO

Hill 453

1 CPVF BN

1FR

Route of
29 Jan. Patrol

373 III

BATTLE OF
TWIN TUNNELS

FEBRUARY 1, 1951

1/2 mile

1 CPVF BN

◇ Chinese Infantry Units
◯ UN CO Battle Position
• UN Artillery Battery
▱ UN Cavalry Platoon
☒ Tunnel Entrances

B CO

37 •

However, the commanding officer of the Eighth Army also had other reasons for an offensive. Ridgway sensed that something had to change in the Eighth Army. Shortly after the Third Phase Offensive petered out, his staff presented him with the operational plan for the upcoming spring of 1951; it called for a withdrawal to the Pusan Perimeter before the onset of monsoon season that summer. Ridgway believed defeatism hovered over the proposed operation. His instinct was correct. The paratrooper rejected the plan outright and ordered his divisions to start pushing north to find the Chinese. He needed a victory over the communists to show the rest of the U.N. forces and his own staff that the Reds were not supermen.

Thanks to the Charlie Company patrol, the U.N. forces had found the Chinese. General Almond wanted to fulfill Ridgway's wish to find the enemy and destroy them. Now he had a chance to do just that, and Freeman's regiment would be Almond's agent of destruction.[6]

The CPVF had other ideas. For starters, Captain Tyrrell was wrong: The CPVF did not have two battalions around the Twin Tunnels and Chipyong-ni. They had three entire regiments—the 373rd, 374th, and 375th—all of which belonged to the 125th Division, part of the 42nd Army. The Chinese outnumbered the approaching U.N. forces over three to one. It was a recipe for disaster.[7]

Commissar Peng Dehuai had identified the Twin Tunnels and Chipyong-ni areas as key terrain and was prepared to throw his forces into the meat grinder to control the vital locations. By now, he had been planning for his Fourth Phase Offensive to begin in the spring of 1951. His first three phases had been somewhat successful but ultimately failed to push the U.N. forces off the Korean Peninsula. The Second Phase began on the Yalu River in November 1950 and was the most successful of the offensives to date. However, since the CPVF lacked adequate motor transport, they were unable to keep up with the U.N. forces when they broke contact and withdrew southward toward the 38th Parallel. The Third Phase Offensive began shortly after the Second ended and resulted in another Chinese advance, which ended along the Taedong River near Pyongyang. The Third Phase Offensive, like the Second Phase, was a tactical victory but failed in its strategic objective to defeat and destroy the U.N. forces. Still, by the middle of January, the CPVF were on the Han River and had recaptured Seoul.[8]

Dehuai felt that the Fourth Phase would be the coup de grâce for the U.N. forces. Unfortunately, Ridgway's aggressive posture of combat patrols forced Dehuai to change his plans, and he accelerated the timetable for the next offensive to commence in early February. He could not allow the U.N. forces to push his armies north of the 38th Parallel. His offensive would be two-pronged, with one force advancing south along the Chipyong-ni axis while the other headed southeast toward Wonju. The initial objective was the destruction of the 8th ROK Division and a significant portion of the U.S. 2nd Infantry Division.

However, if the 23rd Infantry occupied the Twin Tunnels area before the offensive kicked off, then the Tomahawks would be in a position to disrupt and delay the CPVF 42nd Army at a critical point in the operation. Thus, Dehuai most likely wanted the 42nd Army to prevent the Twin Tunnels from falling into U.N. hands, to avoid having to recapture the area immediately before the Fourth Offensive commenced. As was often the case in war, both sides were unaware of the impending collision.[9]

WEDNESDAY, JANUARY 31, 0900–1730 HOURS: 3RD BATTALION, 23RD INFANTRY REGIMENT, 2ND INFANTRY DIVISION, MARCHING TO THE TWIN TUNNELS

At 0900 hours, the two battalions stepped off from their assembly area located 6 kilometers south of the Twin Tunnels. Freeman was not going to take any chances. He had been in country now for over six months, and he had seen how the Chinese had trapped U.N. units that had refused to leave the narrow valley roads. According to their tactics, the Chinese would envelop the road-bound U.N. columns by using mountain trails to get behind the encircled units, and then destroy the forces as they attempted to retreat through the communist gauntlet. It had worked with deadly consequences at Kunu-ri, where the CPVF nearly destroyed the 2nd Infantry Division.

Instead of using the road, Freeman directed his infantry battalions to march over the ridges that bordered the road on both sides. The French Battalion moved along the west side, while the 3rd Battalion approached the objective from the east side. Meanwhile, in the center, the accompanying tanks and gun trucks provided overwatch from the road, rumbling along at the same pace as the infantry.[10]

The commander of the 3rd Battalion, Lt. Col. Charles F. Kane, understood Freeman's intent and designated three successive objectives: Able, Baker, and Charlie. Each objective was a piece of key terrain. Kane assigned King Company, under the command of Capt. Charles M. Thompson, to occupy Objective Able, a piece of high ground labeled Hill 404. Once King occupied Able, then Item Company, under the command of Capt. Leander O'Neill, would leapfrog past King and clear Objective Baker, the village of Kudun and Hill 333, not far from where the platoon from Charlie Company had established its patrol base after escaping the ambush on January 29. After Item completed its mission, Love Company, under the command of Capt. Chester T. Jackson, would assume the vanguard and occupy Objective Charlie, the western spur of Hill 333.[11]

Lieutenant Colonel Kane had an accomplished record. Prior to assuming command of the 3rd Battalion, he had been its S3. On September 27, 1950, NKPA artillery and mortars had unleashed a barrage on the battalion command group. Almost immediately, bursting shrapnel injured Kane. Instead of seeking cover, the officer from Illinois continued to conduct operations, exposing himself to deadly explosions while dashing across an open area near the village of Anui, South Korea. His coolness under fire had bolstered the flagging confidence of the soldiers around him. When the medics asked the wounded Kane if he wanted to be evacuated, the brave officer refused and demanded that the medics treat and evacuate the other wounded soldiers before him. The Army later awarded Kane a Silver Star for his actions.[12]

Capt. Albert C. Metts, the Mike Company commander, liked Colonel Kane. "Conscientious, quiet, serious, capable, considerate, friendly, experienced and well liked," Metts wrote in a letter after the war. "Lieutenant Colonel Kane performed well. All the time that I knew him we were in constant combat, so I was never able to develop any kind of personal relationship, but I admired the man. . . . His exercise of command was effective. I never heard an unpleasant word from him."[13]

His soldiers admired him, too. John Kamperschroer, a medic attached to 2nd Platoon, Love Company, described Colonel Kane as "a very tall, sort of stately individual, who looked like he was born to be a leader."[14]

Like Freeman, Kane understood the importance of high ground in the Korean War. Hence, no one would move to the next hill until someone had secured the first one. At 0900 hours, Kane's men marched out from the assembly area, crossing the line of departure an hour later. At 1230 hours, Captain Thompson's King Company reached the summit of Hill 404 and did not find any evidence of communist forces. With Hill 404 secured, Item Company moved ahead to Objective Baker. Meanwhile, the French were following a parallel course on the west side of the P'yongch'on–Chipyong-ni road. In the middle were tanks from the regimental tank company and flak wagons from the antiaircraft battalion to provide fire support.[15]

The march was slow going. Yet despite the arduous trek, the men understood why they had to climb over ridges and then stagger into valleys, only to repeat the process again and again. Freeman wrote, "But our troops had learned—learned months ago—that the enemy seldom appeared in daylight in conventional formations and positions where he would be at the mercy of our artillery and air . . . he would pull back and remain hidden in darkness, or until we walked into a trap. We weren't walking into traps these days."[16]

Freeman knew high ground meant survival. Thus, he wanted his regiment to control the skyline. After surviving several battles, the soldiers of the 23rd Infantry had grasped the same concept. "That was why there were no grumbles from the men when they were ordered to the painful task of climbing the slippery, snow-covered hills, rather than to march up the peaceful looking road," Freeman later commented. "That was why many were willing to forego [sic] a can of rations that they might load themselves down with all the cartridges and grenades that they could possibly carry. That was why no thought was given to leaving behind coats and blankets though they knew it meant a bitter cold night—at least, it was insurance against survival if not against temporary misery."[17]

At approximately 1300 hours, Item Company moved past King Company on its way to the village of Kudun. As the men marched northward, 1st. Lt. Charles H. Roberts, the Item Company 3rd Platoon leader, noticed a pair of figures on the ridgeline to the southeast. One of the figures had binoculars. He immediately radioed the battalion, and shortly after, an L5 Sentinel plane buzzed overhead on its way to the suspected location. Roberts never learned if the pilots saw anything or anyone.[18]

News of the ominous sighting spread throughout the company, but despite the report, the men of Item continued their advance. First they cleared the village of Kudun, where they found the detritus of the ambushed patrol from January 29. After the company commander declared the hamlet secure, he ordered the 60mm mortar team to set up their tubes, while three tanks provided a base of fire. Meanwhile, the infantry began their climb up Hill 333. The peak was steep, and according to 1st. Lt. John Mewha, the Eighth Army historian, "In some places the men had to pull themselves up the slope."

After reaching the top, the officers and men saw four hills, each one "higher than the other—'like a ladder,'" Mewha recorded. A sea of pine trees and underbrush covered the hills. Snow blanketed the entire ridge. In some places, the drifts were over a meter deep. For the defender, it was good ground. Anyone who attempted to attack Hill 333 would have a difficult time negotiating the drifts while avoiding rifle and machine-gun fire.

The Item Company commander, Captain O'Neill, tasked his 2nd Platoon with occupying the northernmost point along the ridge; its position would be known as the "knob." In the center, Hill 333's summit, were 1st Platoon and the company command post. Lastly, 3rd Platoon occupied a smaller hill to the south of Hill 333. In addition, 3rd Platoon dispatched one squad to secure the rear of the company on a "small finger" that jutted out from Hill 333 to the west. For several hours, the men prepared their fighting positions, while signalmen strung communication wire between the various command posts. Early that evening, the platoon leaders notified their commander that they were in position.

Captain O'Neill was a fine officer according to the men who served under him. Leo Dobbs, the company mail clerk, said of O'Neill, "He was a good old company commander. . . . I liked him." Sgt. Earl Becker, a Weapons (4th) Squad leader in Item Company, described him as "a tough captain. He was a World War II guy, too." George Collingsworth, a jeep driver in Item Company, remembered his commander fondly. "He was a great, great guy," said Collingsworth. "And he was a good man."[19]

The feelings were mutual. "That's the fightingest outfit I've ever seen," O'Neill supposedly said of his men. "They ain't afraid of nothing."[20]

Even though they were ready and in their positions, and trusted their commander, the men were nervous. "The rumor that started when Lieutenant Roberts spotted the two gooks kept us on edge," SFC James Jones, the leader of 2nd Squad, later remarked.[21]

While Item Company dug in atop Hill 333, Love Company clambered up and stumbled past them. At 1730 hours, Captain Jackson established his command post in the village of Chowang-ni while his platoons occupied the high ground north of his location. He arrayed his three rifle platoons, with 2nd Platoon on the western end of the ridge and closest to the road that led north to Chipyong-ni. For additional firepower, Lieutenant Colonel Kane allocated three tanks and a flak wagon from the 82nd Antiaircraft Artillery Battalion to Love Company. Jackson used the vehicles to secure 2nd Platoon's western flank by placing them in the valley, west of Chowang-ni. Directly east of 2nd Platoon was 1st Platoon, occupying a saddle on the ridge that extended west from Hill 333. Finally, on the eastern end was 3rd Platoon, which overlooked the northeast slope of Hill 333 and was the link between Love and Item Companies.[22]

Many of Jackson's soldiers thought he was a good commander. One later said, "He was good. . . . He thought a lot of the men, and he tried to protect them, you might say. There wasn't too much you can do when you have to shove people in the way he did, but he was good. I liked him."[23]

JANUARY 31, 0900–1730 HOURS: FRENCH BATTALION, 23RD INFANTRY REGIMENT, 2ND INFANTRY DIVISION, MARCHING TO THE TWIN TUNNELS

For most of the afternoon, King Company remained at Hill 404, unable to join the other companies near Hill 333 until the French had secured the western ridgeline. For the French, that was easier said than done. These hills were far steeper and more treacherous than the ones that lined the American side of the Chipyong-ni highway.[24]

François DeCastries, the commander of the French Battalion's 1st Company, described his company's ascent of Hill 453 as constant cycle of "walk, slip, walk, slip."[25] Gérard Journet, a machine gunner in 1st Company, added, "The progression proved to be exhausting by the succession of rugged peaks to cross, with drop-offs of several hundred meters."

Journet and the soldiers of 1st Company were not alone in their odyssey of exhaustion and toil. Sharing their burden was Colonel

Monclar. Journet fondly recalled Monclar's presence: "We appreciated the endurance of the General [Monclar], despite his fifty-eight years and his numerous wounds; he made a proud figure, and in front of such an example, no one complained, as they usually did." By 1300 hours, 1st Company had secured Hill 453.[26]

By late afternoon, the rest of the French units were approaching their final locations. At the northernmost point was 3rd Company, under the command of Capt. Léon Serre. His forces hooked around the northern slope of Hill 279, while on his southern flank an attached company of ROK soldiers guarded the western slope. In the middle of the French line was 2nd Company, under the command of a Captain Huschard. His unit controlled the southern slope of Hill 279, oriented to the west. At the southern end of the French line was Hill 453, which 1st Company had occupied. Between the 1st and 2nd Companies was the Muchon Valley. Monclar could not leave the gap undefended, so he positioned the majority of his heavy weapons in the valley. Even so, he and Freeman agreed that it was a possible infiltration route between the companies. But Freeman did not want to cede Hill 453, the highest point in the area, to the enemy, and the two commanders calculated it was a worthwhile risk.[27]

JANUARY 31, 1600 HOURS TO EARLY EVENING: K COMPANY, 3RD BATTALION, 23RD INFANTRY REGIMENT, 2ND INFANTRY DIVISION, MARCHING TO THE TWIN TUNNELS

With the French finally getting into place, Kane ordered King Company to resume their march northward at 1600 hours. Their destination was the spur that overlooked the village of Kudun from the north. At 1645 hours, the tired soldiers of K Company staggered into the town and began their final ascent for the day. Captain Thompson realized that the southern side of the perimeter was wide open. Colonel Freeman had to assume risk somewhere because of the size of the objective and the terrain. That somewhere was King Company's southern flank.

To boost the firepower of Thompson's company, Kane attached a platoon of four tanks and a section of heavy machine guns from Mike Company. Thompson positioned one tank section and the heavy machine-gun section along the northeast edge of the village. From there, the machine guns and main guns on the Sherman tanks could mow down any approaching force from the village of Noll, directly north of Kudun. Thompson directed the tankers from the other section to move to the northwest side of the village so they could engage targets coming from Chipyong-ni.

Thompson knew it was a gamble. If the CPVF penetrated the maelstrom of lead from the Sherman tanks, it could be a catastrophe, as Thompson had few trigger pullers to spare who could pull close security for the M4s. Like Freeman, Thompson had to assume risk somewhere.

Because the CPVF would likely attack from the direction of Chipyong-ni, all of Thompson's platoons were up on the hills. The 1st Platoon was the farthest north, the link between K Company and I Company. In the middle of Thompson's line was 2nd Platoon, facing east toward Noll, while 3rd Platoon was the farthest south, closest to Kudun and the tanks. The K Company commander set up his command post inside one of the village homes. With everything in place, the men waited for the inevitable CPVF attack.[28]

JANUARY 31, EARLY EVENING: HEADQUARTERS, 23RD INFANTRY REGIMENT, 2ND INFANTRY DIVISION, MARCHING TO THE TWIN TUNNELS

Traveling with the regiment on January 31 was the assistant division commander, Brig. Gen. George C. Stewart, who had joined the division the previous month. Since he was new, he wanted to get to know all the commanders, and he chose to accompany Colonel Freeman on the Twin Tunnels expedition to do just that.

As the regimental column approached the tunnels, Freeman decided to halt for the night and dig in. Since Freeman seemed to know what he was doing and had more experience in country, Stewart did not question the colonel's decision. However, that would soon change.

Shortly after they stopped, General Almond suddenly showed up to see how the operation was progressing. Stewart informed Almond of the halt, and the corps commander did not like what he heard from his subordinate. Stewart recalled the incident in a postwar interview: "I explained it was near dark and that the security of the unit required preparations for the night. He [Almond] reluctantly agreed but ordered me to personally see that the village was fired upon." It was an odd order that made little sense tactically.

Even though it was a strange command, Stewart did not want to irritate his new boss, who already had a reputation for firing subordinates. He had sacked the previous division commander just a few weeks before. Instead of confronting him, Stewart climbed aboard a nearby M4 tank and directed the driver to head north toward Chipyong-ni. The assistant division commander described what happened next:

> . . . I had the village in full view. No people could be seen. I disliked the idea of shooting into the village huts which possibly could be holding women and children. So, I took the 50 cal. machine gun and fired several bursts over and on each side of the village. I followed the same procedure with the tank cannon; then I returned to the south and reported by radio that I had personally sent fire upon the village.

When Freeman learned about the general's foray, he was furious, predicting that the action would provoke the Chinese to attack. Later, Stewart explained that he regretted the confrontational gesture: "My action, while well motivated, was probably wrong, considering the next morning's attack by the Chinese."[29]

★ ★ ★

General Stewart's stunt had one unexpected benefit. When his tanks opened fire, the blasts woke Pvt. Richard Fockler, who had been sleeping near the road. Fockler was one of the few survivors from the ambushed C Company patrol. Despite his injuries, Fockler was still alive, though the only way he could move was by crawling. The last forty-eight hours had been an odyssey for the young soldier from Michigan who had escaped death on several occasions. (A U.S. Air Force fighter-bomber pilot had shot several rockets at the prone GI, almost killing him; luckily, they missed.) Fockler described what happened next:

> A jeep pulled up and a man with field glasses got out to observe the effect of the cannon fire. This was my opportunity to get rescued if it was going to happen. I rolled on to the road with my hands in the air. The jeep pulled forward and the man who

had been observing got out with a carbine pointing at me. He shouted and asked who I was. I shouted back that I was from C Company from a patrol that was lost Monday. The jeep came all the way up to me and the driver, a corporal, got out and lifted me into the front passenger seat and put my injured leg out on the fender. . . . I was driven back to the battalion aid station to have my wound dressed.

When word reached General Stewart that the 23rd Infantry had found more survivors from the ambushed patrol, he went to see Fockler in the aid station. He asked the private about the Chinese, and Fockler assured him that a large number of communists had attacked his patrol. Fockler later remarked, "I guess they doubted my estimate of enemy strength because the 23rd was led into Chipyong and the rest is history."[30]

THURSDAY, FEBRUARY 1, 0430 HOURS: L COMPANY, 3RD BATTALION, 23RD INFANTRY REGIMENT, 2ND INFANTRY DIVISION, WEST OF HILL 333

Shivering in their foxholes, the U.N. soldiers had no illusions about what the next twenty-four hours would hold. Had they heard Fockler's prediction, they would have believed him. "We had a feeling we were going to get it," remarked Cpl. Herman Seabolt from Love Company. "It was just too damn quiet," said another soldier from the same company.

Lieutenant Mewha, the Eighth Army historian, described what happened shortly after midnight. "After dark until shortly prior to the enemy's attack in the morning, small lights similar to a pencil flashlight or tips of white phosphorous were seen flickering on and off on the high ground to the right front of the 3d platoon."

One of the forward observers called for a mortar fire mission, but after firing several rounds, the observer calculated that the lights were too far away to hit. The 3rd Platoon leader, 1st Lt. Malcolm Aldrich, and M/Sgt. Henry C. Bagley even went to investigate, but nothing came of it.[31]

But as Freeman later wrote, "At 4:30 in the morning (February 1st) the manure hit the fan."[32]

FEBRUARY 1, 0430–0815 HOURS: K COMPANY, 3RD BATTALION, 23RD INFANTRY REGIMENT, 2ND INFANTRY DIVISION, HILLTOP NORTHWEST OF KUDUN

That morning, a thick, dense fog covered the hillside like a blanket and cloaked enemy movement. Even though Capt. Charles Thompson could not see anything, he sensed something was wrong. He had awoken at 0430 hours for no apparent purpose other than his gut instinct. For Thompson, that was a good enough reason to send two squads from his 2nd Platoon and one of his machine-gun sections to reinforce his other platoons and, more importantly, to defend the hill northwest of his command post. To provide indirect fire support, Thompson ordered his mortar men to move out and emplace their tubes behind the hill west of their current location. Mewha later asked Thompson to explain why he had done so and jotted the captain's reply in his notes: "He just had a hunch he should—he didn't know exactly why he did." Fortunately, Thompson's hunch was spot on.

Thirty minutes later, at 0500 hours, a cacophony of bugles burst forth 600 meters in front of K Company. Thompson ran out of his command post to see what was going on; according to him, the Chinese unleashed a furious fusillade of .51- and .30-caliber machine-gun fire, aimed at the tanks laagering along the road to the southeast. Thompson noticed that the tracers emanated from the hill opposite his location and east of Kudun. In addition to the tracers, the King Company commander observed green and red flares crisscrossing the eastern skyline like fireworks, arcing in the sky. Shortly after the initial barrage, a countless number of CPVF soldiers ran down the same hill toward him and his company.

Thompson knew he needed to prepare his unit for the impending assault. Unfortunately, his command post was between his platoons and the onrushing Chinese attackers. Moreover, surrounding the old Korean house that served as his headquarters were four trucks from his company and two trucks from Mike Company. Determining that the vehicles were soft targets, he directed Chief Willis P. Brooks, the company adjutant, to move the convoy north to link up with Colonel Kane's battalion command post. Brooks gathered the drivers and drove toward the 3rd Battalion's command post. As they rounded the bend, "the French could be observed fighting to the west on HILL 453. . . . They could be observed firing machine guns and small arms, and enemy tracers could be seen coming into the hill. As the column proceeded one-half mile further along the road, both enemy and French tracers could be seen going into valley," Brooks later recounted. Despite the turmoil all around them, he and the rest of the column arrived safely at Colonel Kane's command post around 0515 hours.[33]

Meanwhile, standing out in the open, Captain Thompson realized he was not in an ideal place to control his company. He took off west toward the newly emplaced 2nd Platoon "with bullets kicking up at his heels." Not far behind Thompson were the Chinese, who had entered Kudun only moments before the commander's escape. Luckily, four tanks from the regimental tank company were covering the captain. Their initial burst shredded the lead Chinese platoon with high-explosive shells from the 76mm cannons and slugs from the .50-caliber machine guns.[34]

When Thompson arrived at 2nd Platoon's makeshift command post, he realized his platoon battle positions were shrouded in the early morning fog. It was even worse for 1st and 3rd Platoons. Sgt. Edward L. Green, a BAR gunner in 3rd Platoon, recalled the beginning of the communist onslaught and confirmed Thompson's account:

> About 0500, bugles could be heard to the extreme left rear, and a little later, firing was heard in the same sector. Small arms and machine gun fire was heard near 1st Platoon. Bugles to the left and direct fronts then started blowing, and the tanks immediately opened fire in the general direction of the bugles. An enemy 51 caliber machine gun opened fire, from a ridge to the direct front on a 2½ ton truck coming toward the Company's positions from the south.

Despite all this activity, "3rd platoon never saw the enemy and did not return fire. The platoon remained in position all day and night with no further enemy contact," Green later said.[35]

Farther north, 1st Platoon's M/Sgt. George Chamberlain ordered his men not to fire, reasoning that because he could not see where the enemy was, the communists could not see *his* men. He did not want to give away the platoon's position until the last possible minute. His decision was the right one.[36]

At the same time, Thompson was with 2nd Platoon, waiting to see where the CPVF soldiers would strike next. Around sunrise, at 0630 hours, the haze began to evaporate, revealing fifteen to twenty Chinese soldiers marching from the Kudun Valley toward the base of the hill. The GIs opened fire, but to their dismay, they quickly discovered they were overshooting their targets because the sloping hill provided defilade to the Chinese attackers.

Even though they were safe from American rifle and machine-gun fire, the Chinese commanders pulled their forces back to the railroad, which ran along the ridge of Hill 318 and was opposite the American positions. By doing so, they sky-lined themselves. Captain Thompson requested 81mm mortar fire on their location. The first round of white phosphorus detonated on top of the Chinese line. Seeing the impact, Thompson ordered the mortars to fire for effect on the Chinese. He later said that he could not determine the effectiveness of the barrage at the time. However, the Chinese did not attack the King Company positions for the rest of the operation. At 0815 hours, Thompson reported to his battalion that K Company had successfully defeated an enemy attack. It was a different story everywhere else.[37]

FEBRUARY 1, 0430–0700 HOURS: L COMPANY, 3RD BATTALION, 23RD INFANTRY REGIMENT, 2ND INFANTRY DIVISION, WEST OF HILL 333

Sgt. William A. Sanford's squad was the first unit from Love Company to make contact with the enemy. Sanford, a squad leader in 1st Platoon, had positioned a BAR gunner out in front of his squad in an observation post early in the morning of February 1. At 0430 hours, Sanford's BAR gunner spotted approximately 500 soldiers climbing up the draw from Chochon-ni. Initially, the BAR gunner believed they were refugees, since they approached so lackadaisically, marching toward him in two columns. Still, he alerted the rest of his platoon, including Sanford.

The BAR gunner issued a challenge to the men. No one answered. Not wanting to take chances, Sergeant Sanford ordered the BAR gunner to open fire. The man emptied his entire magazine at the group. Still, the shadows advanced. That was enough for Sanford to know they were the enemy. In response, the whole platoon let loose and, according to Sanford, each rifleman expended six or seven clips of rifle ammunition. The platoon's three other BAR gunners joined the fracas, but this time the enemy responded with their own automatic weapons. The curtain of darkness and fog had concealed them, and the CPVF had closed within 300 meters of 1st Platoon's foxholes. Elsewhere, the Chinese were even closer to American lines.[38]

Sometime between 0430 and 0450 hours, the tankers attached to 2nd Platoon spotted another column of roughly 500 men marching down the road from Chochon-ni. During this same time frame, soldiers from other units reported hearing a bugle sounding the adjutant's call. In the distance, other bugles responded like howling wolves. Leading the advancing column were three men. Cpl. Nicholas Sperandio, who was guarding the tanks, immediately challenged the three strangers. No one replied. The ominous column continued to approach, so one of the tanks shot three high-explosive rounds at the group.

Suddenly, one of the three men tossed a hand grenade at the flak wagon, wounding several men inside the half-track and leading Sperandio and the tankers to believe the men were Chinese. The tank commander immediately ordered the tanks and the flak wagon to roll back toward the battalion command post, located in Chowang-ni, while Sperandio and another infantry soldier took off toward 2nd Platoon's battle position atop the hill. As he scrambled up the rocks, Sperandio kept shouting to his comrades, "Don't shoot, it's me the Greek with the new guy."

When the tanks opened fire, the blasts jolted 1st Platoon leader Lt. David Mock awake. He asked his platoon sergeant, SFC Joseph Talotta what was going on. Mock was new, and Talotta thought his platoon leader had the jitters, so he assured his lieutenant, "Aw, it's nothing; go back to sleep."

Shortly after the tanks withdrew, 2nd Platoon came under intense mortar and machine-gun fire. The leader of 2nd Platoon, 1st Lt. Richard A. Palmer, recalled that six to eight mortar rounds exploded on top of his platoon's battle position. He noticed the flashes emanating from a draw northwest of his platoon's location. William Tuttle, a rifleman in

2nd Platoon that night, recalled the effectiveness and accuracy of the Chinese mortars. "Those bastards could drop a 60mm mortar on a dime and get change," he said in a postwar interview.[39]

In response to the incoming fire, Lieutenant Palmer called on Lt. Avery Nance, the forward observer for the company mortars, to place fires on the draw. Minutes later, Palmer heard Love Company's 60mm mortars *thunk-thunk* as several rounds were outbound. Nance's calculations were on target, and the enemy mortar fire from the draw tapered off.[40]

But Palmer soon had other problems. A single soldier from the platoon's forward outpost suddenly emerged from the darkness. It was Pvt. Jack N. Smith. According to John Kamperschroer, the platoon medic, Smith kept babbling to his platoon leader, "They're all dead. They're all dead." Palmer asked the medic, "John, would you like to go down there and confirm that?"

Kamperschroer immediately thought it was a bad idea. He shot back, "If Smith says they're dead, they are dead."

Hearing his medic's argument, Palmer quickly recognized that sending an unarmed aid man was unwise. Instead, he sent a rifleman to find out what had happened to the outpost. Minutes later, the rifleman returned and reported, "Yep, Smith's right. They're all dead."[41]

By 0453 hours, the regiment had received the first report that L Company was under attack. In reality, it was far worse: everyone was under attack. Chinese units were assaulting almost the entire perimeter. At 0505 hours, the regiment learned that the tanks and flak wagon attached to 2nd Platoon, L Company, were withdrawing and carrying wounded back to Colonel Kane's command post.[42] According to Lieutenant Palmer and Sergeant Sanford, the Chinese forces had swung east toward 3rd Platoon, L Company, because the slopes around 3rd Platoon's battle position were not as steep, giving the attackers an easier approach to the American lines at that location.[43]

For men of the 3rd Platoon, the next hour was filled with confusion and terror. Pvt. Larry Hauck was a BAR gunner in 1st Squad, 3rd Platoon; his squad was the link between his platoon and Item Company, located south of his position. He vividly recalled the morning attack on February 1. His squad leader, Eliseo Garcia, had ordered Hauck and his battle buddies to dig a foxhole between 1st Squad and I Company the night before. Once there, Hauck discovered "nothing but rocks under the snow where we were." However, he recalled that the trees provided "good concealment."

The companies were at 50-percent security, meaning every two-man foxhole had one man up at all times. At midnight, Hauck's battle buddy took over guard duty. Hauck fell asleep, but his slumber was short-lived. His partner in the foxhole woke a startled Hauck to tell him that he was hearing Chinese voices.

Hauck listened. "Sure enough," he later wrote, "I heard Chinese voices between us and the rest of the squad. I figured it to be point men. No one was firing and it was very quiet. I strained my eyes but couldn't see a thing. Experience told me not to fire until I had a target, and I told my assistant to keep quiet."

For several minutes, the two soldiers waited. Suddenly, the Chinese attacked. "Just then the Chinese started yelling from off down in front of us, and bugles started blowing, and heavy firing started close to us on our left, and some behind us," Hauck recalled. "I knew right away what had happened. Somehow the Chinese had got up to us and a few had got through behind us right where 'L' Company was. I was afraid to fire into where the sound was because that was where my squad was supposed to be. . . . We saw artillery flashes in the valley in front of us, and on the hills across the valley. It was still dark, and very cold."[44]

According to later reports, the entire Chinese 374th Regiment had struck 3rd Battalion that morning. Near Hauck's position, a battalion of infantry slammed into 3rd Platoon, Love Company. The Chinese out-numbered the Americans at the point of contact at least nine to one. It was only a matter of time before 3rd Platoon broke under the weight of the Chinese assault.[45]

Along the outpost line, the lookouts could see the situation spiraling out of control. PFC Arthur Kenolio was in one of the L Company observation posts. He watched the Chinese assault sweep toward him, as if he were standing in front of a tsunami. Some of the men panicked and froze, but Kenolio opened fire, forcing the Chinese units to deploy. This bought precious time for the men manning the main line of defense behind him. He told the men in his squad to fall back to the main defensive line, and said that he would cover them. In response, Kenolio's squad scrambled out of their foxholes while he tossed hand grenades at the surging Chinese. When the Hawaiian ran out of grenades and went to get more, the Chinese gunned him down. The Army later posthumously awarded him the Silver Star for his bravery.[46]

Elsewhere along the outpost line, the Chinese assault was also met with bravery. PFC Phillip Nakamura and Cpl. Alessandrino Buluran manned an observation post 50 yards in front of 3rd Platoon. When they saw the enemy figures emerge from the inky darkness, the two soldiers tossed hand grenades at the charging communists, then scampered back toward their lines. When they reached their comrades, they exclaimed that "bunches of Chinks were coming up the hill."

One soldier from 3rd Platoon called out to the observation post, thinking that Nakamura and Buluran were still there: "Hey Phillip [Nakamura], what's wrong?"

One of the Chinese soldiers imitated an American voice and responded, "Yes, this is Phillip."

Nakamura overheard the exchange and shouted to the unaware American soldier, "That's not me. I'm right here."

After Nakamura's warning, the Chinese resumed their assault. The communists were everywhere. Because of the terrain, 3rd Platoon was spread out over 600 meters. Consequently, there were gaps of over 100 meters between some of the squads. The Chinese infantry exploited these gaps, and within minutes they had infiltrated the American battle position.

M/Sgt. Henry Bagley, 3rd Platoon's sergeant, believed that company mortar support might tip the balance. He tried to phone the 81mm mortar section from M Company. No one answered. He switched channels on the radio and tried again on Channel 37, the fires net. Once again, he heard only static. Bagley wondered if the soldiers in the mortar section had taken the night off. However, the mortar men were busy performing fire missions for 2nd Platoon, so the telephone lines were tied up with that platoon's soldiers and the company command post. Captain Jackson could not know that 3rd Platoon was in dire straits.

First Lieutenant Aldrich, the platoon leader, decided to act. He ordered his 3rd Squad to shift from their position on the western side of the platoon to a new location in the middle of the battle position, behind his platoon command post, and to the one platoon machine gun. Aldrich directed his other two squads, 1st and 2nd, to hold their ground east of the platoon command post.

Then disaster struck: Aldrich's only machine gun jammed. At this point, one of the soldiers remarked that the platoon leader "lost his head." He ordered the machine-gun section and 3rd Squad to withdraw to the reverse slope and get into prone positions. The soldiers did as they were told, but according to Sergeant Bagley, they "showed outwards signs of nervousness knowing the lieutenant was inexperienced."

For some unknown reason, Aldrich stood up and opened fire on the Chinese, as if he alone could stop them. A sergeant joined him. Both men plugged away with their carbines, but their foolhardy courage only resulted in sky-lining their silhouettes. A Chinese soldier fired a submachine gun at them, wounding the sergeant in the stomach and hitting Aldrich in the leg. The sergeant crumpled forward while Aldrich stumbled backward.

With 3rd Platoon's machine gun down, the Chinese wave flooded forward. Within minutes, the tide pushed past Aldrich's remaining 1st and 2nd Squads. Around 0630 hours, the soldiers in Aldrich's two intact squads realized that the communists were behind them.

One GI from Aldrich's platoon shouted, "Let's get the fuck out of here," and the survivors scrambled out of their holes and scurried west toward 1st Platoon. As they stampeded through the tempest, a soldier saw Aldrich and helped the stricken lieutenant limp back to friendly lines. As they ran, they yelled, "Don't shoot, it's us, 3rd Platoon!" The distance between the squads and the swarming enemy all around them forced the soldiers from 2nd Squad to head west toward 1st Platoon, while the soldiers from 1st Squad, including Private Hauck, the BAR gunner, sprinted south toward 2nd Platoon, Item Company.[47]

The 1st Platoon leader, 2nd Lt. David Mock, saw unidentified men streaming behind his platoon's battle position shortly after 3rd Platoon disintegrated. He telephoned Captain Jackson back at the company command post to ask if 3rd Platoon had withdrawn. Cpl. Carl Myers answered the phone and radioed 3rd Platoon over the SCR-300; someone told the corporal that 3rd Platoon was still in position. Myers reported the information back to Mock.

When Mock told Sergeant Sanford, his 1st Platoon squad leader, that 3rd Platoon was still in position, Sanford vehemently disagreed. The NCO believed 3rd Platoon was gone. In fact, Sanford argued that the unidentified men scrambling past their own platoon position were Chinese soldiers.[48]

Five minutes later, the lieutenant called the company command post again to report that he was still seeing soldiers from 3rd Platoon retreating from their battle position. Meanwhile, signal NCO SFC George Bammert was on the radio, speaking with someone from 3rd Platoon. The voice on the other end insisted that 3rd Platoon was still on top of the hill.

Bammert recalled the conversation in an interview shortly after the battle. "It was a normal voice speaking excellent English, and he said, 'No we're still in position.' They [the Chinese] were using our Company call signs, too."[49]

While Lieutenant Mock debated with the soldiers at the company command post, Sergeant Sanford returned to 1st Squad and his foxhole, where he saw over 100 CPVF soldiers near 3rd Platoon's former location. To provide early warning for his platoon, Sanford dispatched a BAR gunner to occupy a forward outpost a hundred meters in front.

At 0600 hours, Sanford and the other soldiers in his squad detected a group of seven CPVF soldiers attempting to infiltrate past his squad from the south. Since Sanford did not have telephone communication with the sentry, he yelled at the BAR gunner to be on the lookout for the infiltrators. Instead of warning the sentry, Sanford's shouting alerted the communist soldiers, who immediately engaged 1st Squad. The rest of 1st Platoon replied with a fusillade of rifle and automatic weapons fire. The resulting din drowned out Sanford, who tried to order his sentry to return to the platoon lines. Since the single BAR gunner did not hear the withdrawal order, Lieutenant Mock ordered Sanford to bring him back to the platoon.

However, Sanford already had his hands full. Before his platoon leader had commanded him to retrieve the sentry, the NCO had been calling fire missions on the advancing Chinese soldiers. His accurate coordinates resulted in fifteen enemy dead. To follow Mock's orders, he had to put down the telephone and race through enemy fire to find the isolated sentry. Sanford did not flinch.

"He [Sanford] went down the ridgeline to the east approximately 200 yards and ran face to face with two Chinese carrying burp guns," Sanford's interviewer wrote in an after-action report. "The underbrush was so thick that it had been impossible to see them. The enemy opened fire, wounding Sanford in the arm and knocking him off the hill. The Chinese then started toward the 1st platoon CP. The wounded man struggled back to the top of the hill, found his M1 rifle, and shot both of the enemy soldiers through the head. He then went forward to a little knoll where the sentry had been outposted, but there he observed the man lying at the base of the hill."

The Chinese had killed the sentry Sanford had been sent to retrieve. Injured, Sanford scurried back to the platoon command post. Once there, Mock ordered him to report to the battalion aid station. The Army later awarded him the Silver Star for his actions.[50]

A little after 0700 hours, Captain Jackson finally learned what had happened to his 3rd Platoon when the remaining men staggered into his command post. According to the survivors, Jackson "blew his top" and immediately ordered the senior leader, Sergeant Bagley, to gather up the few remaining uninjured soldiers and retake 3rd Platoon's position.

With a new task and purpose, the platoon sergeant collected fourteen soldiers and led them back toward their foxholes. Waiting for them, however, were twenty Chinese soldiers who opened fire on the advancing Americans. Realizing that his force was not strong enough to recapture the position, Bagley fell back behind the hill and shifted his men toward 1st Platoon's location. With 3rd Platoon, L Company, in tatters, Colonel Kane had lost control of the northeast edge of his perimeter. The Chinese achieved a breakthrough.[51]

FEBRUARY 1, 0430–0700 HOURS:
3RD COMPANY, FRENCH BATTALION,
23RD INFANTRY REGIMENT, 2ND INFANTRY
DIVISION, NORTH OF HILL 279

While Love Company battled several battalions of CPVF, another communist unit struck Colonel Monclar's 3rd Company on the northwest side of the perimeter. According to interrogations conducted after the battle, the perpetrators were another battalion from the 374th Regiment. The initial assault briefly stunned the legionnaires and paratroopers of 3rd Company. "The enemy, which had advanced silently, due to the snow and fog which muffled all sounds, moved to an assault position held by 1st section," reported one account written in 1952.

At 0430 hours, the communists initiated a blistering fusillade on 1st Section's battle position. Shortly after, CPVF elements breached the perimeter. In reply, the section commander, Lt. Ange Nicolai, ordered his single machine gun to open fire on the breach. The Chinese sappers quickly identified him as a leader and responded with grenades. One of the potato mashers landed in the hapless lieutenant's foxhole. It exploded before he could react, and the resulting shrapnel injured him. Still, he kept fighting.

Within minutes, 1st Section had incurred six casualties, including the lieutenant and three NCOs. Seeing that his position was in danger of collapse, the wounded Nicolai directed his men to withdraw to a position farther up the hill and closer to the rest of 3rd Company. At that moment, another grenade detonated near Nicolai. This time, the deadly concussion sent the section leader to the ground and lethal grenade fragments shredded his body. Several soldiers evacuated Nicolai; however, it was too late, and the brave lieutenant succumbed to his wounds.[52]

First Sgt. André Bizot attempted to carry out the lieutenant's last order. The communists were among the men of 1st Section; both sides had lost much of their unit cohesion. The battle had deteriorated into a hand-to-hand brawl.

Between 0530 and 0600 hours, word of 1st Section's precarious situation reached Capt. Léon Serre, 3rd Company's commander. Serre knew he had to retake the position. Despite the danger, he rushed to the embattled section and counterattacked with a makeshift force of soldiers he had rounded up along the way. This group, together with a machine-gun team from 4th Section, then took over 1st Section's battle position. By 0700 hours in the morning, the enemy fell back to lick their wounds. A silence descended over this segment of the perimeter.[53]

FEBRUARY 1, 0430–0700 HOURS: 1ST COMPANY, FRENCH BATTALION, 23RD INFANTRY REGIMENT, 2ND INFANTRY DIVISION, HILL 453

Third Company was not the only French unit under attack at 0500 hours that morning. Gérard Journet was serving in the machine-gun section assigned to 1st Company on Hill 453, where his machine-gun team anchored the southern flank of the company's battle position. Like many of the French and American soldiers, he was dog tired that morning. As he wrote in a postwar letter, "The company had progressed all day; when night fell, facing [the] Twin Tunnels, they [1st Company] installed themselves (isolated on Hill 453) in closed perimeter, in foxholes, which weren't very deep because of the frozen ground."

A few minutes before 0500 hours, Journet heard something in the darkness. "We heard voices and footsteps in the snow," he said. "The sergeant fired his carbine, weapons cracked simultaneously, Chinese bugles sounded with deep notes. The attack was broken up by [the] launching of grenades and 57mm recoilless rifle fire because most of the guns were frozen."

Around 0700 hours, Journet and the other men in his section discovered the grim results of their fusillade. Eleven bodies littered the ground in front of his machine gun. One body was only 5 meters from Journet's muzzle. Then the Frenchmen detected movement—one of the bodies was still moving within the carnage. The wounded man was the only survivor of the attack on Journet's machine gun. Journet and his comrades returned to their positions as a medic tended to the injured enemy soldier. They sensed the communists would strike again, and soon.[54]

FEBRUARY 1, 0400–0700 HOURS: 2ND AND HEADQUARTERS COMPANIES, FRENCH BATTALION, 23RD INFANTRY REGIMENT, 2ND INFANTRY DIVISION, SOUTHERN SLOPE OF HILL 279

While the soldiers of 1st Company repelled the first of many Chinese waves, the metropolitan infantry volunteers in 2nd Company, French Battalion, found themselves locked in mortal combat. Like many of the men in the 23rd Infantry, the soldiers of the 2nd were bushed. "The day's march had been difficult, with numerous peaks to climb, and there was fifty centimeters of snow on the ground," their commander, Captain Huschard, explained in a postwar speech. "The men were exhausted and didn't even have the energy to dig holes when they reached their positions at nightfall, the ground being so frozen. And that night it was extremely cold."

Huschard's company normally had three complete rifle sections (the French labeled their platoons "sections"). However, the command post required a reserve, so the battalion commander tasked 2nd Company with providing several groups for this mission, leaving Huschard with only three understrength rifle sections to defend his entire portion of the battalion perimeter. Even worse, Huschard had no direct communication with DeCastries's 1st Company to the south. If he wanted to send a message to Hill 453, he would have to send it through battalion first. For better command and control in his own company, Huschard established his command post in an abandoned village down the slope from his company's battle positions to the north. With him were his 57mm recoilless rifle and mortar sections.

Around 0400 hours, Huschard thought he heard small-arms fire coming from the direction of 3rd Company to the north. As Lt. Louis Leroux, his second-in-command, assured him, "Captain, it's not serious, you can stay lying down."

Huschard was not convinced. He later remarked, "I went up to the crest to see for myself. A half hour passes, and I don't know why, but I ask my assault section and section commander to get ready and come up onto the crest."

In response to the activity north of their location, Capt. André LeMaitre, the Headquarters Company commander, sent a section of 75mm recoilless rifles to reinforce the hard-pressed soldiers of 3rd Company at 0500 hours. Shortly after the rifle section left the village to link up, an entire battalion of 373rd Regiment rushed through the gap between 2nd Company and 1st Company. The only forces left to defend the valley were sections from LeMaitre's Headquarters Company. According to after-action reports, the attacking force of over a hundred Chinese emerged from the morning haze at 0620 hours, and the few remaining soldiers from the Headquarters Company were unable to stop them.

"It would seem an aberration to entrust the defense of his position to an escorting company [Headquarters]," read the after-action report. "We thought that the enemy [CPVF], following his usual habits, would not venture into the vast firing ranges. And then, we didn't have the choice. There was no one else to the do the job, except for a meager reserve (four combat groups and the engineer section)." Unfortunately for the soldiers defending the Muchon Valley, the Chinese had decided to change their tactics.

The same anonymous soldier from the headquarters company continued in the report: "A detachment that we see and estimate to be about a hundred men spills over the south buttress of the mountain pass by the breach opened wide between Hill 453 and the mountain pass of Muchon. Twenty men succeed in infiltrating by the valley, flowing over the buttress and attacking from the west."[55]

Huschard had sent his reserve to reinforce 3rd Company, so he had few options. "The Chinese having progressed between my company and the 1st Company fell in large numbers upon the Army Corps," he later said. ("Corps" was a French term for the battalion headquarters company.) "Major [André] LeMaitre who commanded [it], was killed point-blank. At several places, the combat turned to hand-to-hand." As evidence of the bitter contest, Lieutenant Leroux sustained an abdominal wound, but instead of seeking medical aid, he continued to fight for the next thirteen hours. His condition was not an exception; it was commonplace that morning among the soldiers serving in the French Battalion.[56]

Lt. Claude L. Jaupart was the section leader in charge of Headquarters Company's 75mm recoilless rifles. Prior to the Chinese attack upon the Muchon Valley, he had taken his section to reinforce 3rd Company. When word reached him that Captain LeMaitre was dead, he swung his section around and returned to the Muchon Valley, where, together with another section, he counterattacked to stabilize the lines. The fighting was fierce. Luckily, Jaupart's assault force was replete with heroes. PV2 Moise Borst was an ammo bearer for one of the 75mm recoilless rifle teams. When several Chinese attacked one of the French machine guns, Borst selflessly charged ahead and threw a grenade at the communist soldiers. His bravery cost him his life, but he saved the machine-gun team in the process.[57]

Another hero was 1st Sgt. Paul Amban of Headquarters Company, a decorated veteran who had served in Indochina, where he was cited for bravery three times. On the morning of February 1, he led thirteen other soldiers from his section as part of Jaupart's counterattack. According to the citation, "with ferocious energy, [he] retook the positions and forced the enemy to abandon two [of their] dead on our lines." The assault, however, left him seriously wounded.[58]

Despite the counterattack's success, Jaupart and Huschard sensed that it would be only a temporary reprieve. After sunrise, both had a better appreciation of what had befallen their battalion. It was far from ideal.

"We were a hair away from catastrophe," Huschard later remarked. "Three hundred Chinese had infiltrated between the 1st Company and mine during the night, and the first elements ended up several hundred meters from my command post, where there were no more reserves."

Huschard sensed the end was nigh. But something unexpected happened. "And then, we don't know why, towards 0700, we heard the Chinese bugles calling for a fall back. I saw the three hundred Chinese go [past] me and the 1st Company. Even pointing all my machine guns on them, I was only able to get a few of them, the others being too far away. 1st Company couldn't see them, being surrounded by fog. I requested . . . artillery fire, but could not obtain it, the situation being more serious on the American side."

In a postwar letter, Lieutenant Jaupert recalled the momentous and inexplicable Chinese withdrawal. "I still cannot understand why the Chinese, having taken the village and the small ridge over it, did not push on to the road, where there [were] no tanks, no riflemen, just our 81 mm mortars and the 75 RR [Recoilless Rifle] platoon of the 3rd Battalion."

It seemed that, for the moment, the French had dodged a bullet.[59]

FEBRUARY 1, 0400 HOURS: HEADQUARTERS COMMAND POST, FRENCH BATTALION, 23RD INFANTRY REGIMENT, MUCHON VALLEY

Despite the carnage along the perimeter, the mood inside Colonel Monclar's command post remained calm. The night before, the colonel had established his command post in a millhouse in the Muchon Valley, behind 2nd Company and the Headquarters Company. Cpl. Serge-Louis Bérerd, a soldier assigned to Monclar's command section, recalled first hearing incoming mortar rounds at approximately 0400 hours in the morning. "News soon arrived that we were encircled," he wrote in a postwar letter, "and that Colonel Freeman wanted those personnel, not already engaged in battle, to form a second line on the counter slope behind the first, American line. The order applied to us, and I found myself, with the others, in the position of gunner, lying down behind a small dam."

Like many soldiers, Bérerd did not relish the idea of fighting for his life beside perfect strangers. "My military education being sufficient enough to know that it's one thing to be on a line, in a dominating position, with friends from the section, who won't let you down, and with heavy arms well placed, in a company which can maneuver under a captain who can ask for support, and it's another thing entirely, to be on a line with people you don't know, who hardly know how to use their weapons, with no support and no command and on top of it, to be in a position which is dominated from all sides," he wrote.

For the young corporal, the chaos swirling around him eroded his confidence. Bérerd heard a voice from behind him say, "So, Bérerd, you're looking a little pale!" The corporal turned to face the man and saw Colonel Monclar. Bérerd remarked, "Taken aback, and not being in a very comfortable position, lying on the ground, I didn't know what to answer." Bérerd thought Monclar seemed composed and unruffled, oblivious to the swirling tempest around him. It was as if he were on an early morning stroll.

According to the corporal, the battalion intelligence officer, Captain Michelet, saved him by responding to Monclar, "Oh Bérerd is always pale. That's his natural state."

The corporal later admitted he was "a little tense." Monclar seemed larger than life, and deservedly so. In a postwar letter, Bérerd wrote, "First of all, not only did I never see the General afraid, but I've never met anyone else who has seen him frightened."

Monclar's imperturbability was crucial for the French defense. He refused to panic, and as result, the soldiers in the command post continued to perform despite the hailstorm of exploding mortar rounds. No one wanted to disappoint "the General," as his men affectionately called him. If the Chinese thought the French Battalion was an easy mark, Monclar proved them wrong. Accordingly, if the Chinese wanted a victory, they would have to find it on the American side of the perimeter.[60]

FEBRUARY 1, 0430–0830 HOURS:
HEADQUARTERS COMMAND POST, 23RD
INFANTRY REGIMENT, 2ND INFANTRY DIVISION,
INSIDE PERIMETER, TWIN TUNNELS

Like the men on the lines, the officers inside the regimental command post were not surprised when the Chinese struck the perimeter. Shortly after the attack began, Colonel Freeman remarked sardonically to

General Stewart, "I told you this was going to happen. What do you want me to do now?"

In a postwar interview, the general recalled the conversation he had with Freeman, saying, "the only choice we had was to stay put and kill as many Chinamen as we could. This we did."[61]

Freeman listened in on the fires nets as observers called for artillery and mortars against the advancing Chinese hordes. The colonel recalled the effectiveness of his indirect fire assets that morning. "Illuminating shells from mortars and illuminating grenades threw an erie [sic] light into the morning darkness as artillery and mortar forward observers called in defensive fires. Barrages came down with a crash and just where they were wanted. The impact stunned the attackers and made them change their bold assault tactics. There was a lull as the enemy pulled back to reorganize."[62]

Even though Freeman had predicted the enemy's attack, he wondered why the Chinese chose to assault so late in the morning. Prior to the Twin Tunnels, the CPVF usually conducted their offensives around midnight, fearing U.N. airpower, and the attacks typically lasted until 0500 hours in the morning or first light. This time, though, the Chinese initiated their assault at 0430 hours.[63]

Because of the change, the regimental commander conferred with his senior intelligence and operations officers. After discussing the issue for several minutes, Freeman concluded that his regiment's occupation of the Twin Tunnels had disrupted Chinese plans to such an extent that the communists felt they had to react rapidly with the forces at hand to eject the U.N. assets from the area. Because of the decisive nature of the terrain, the CPVF commanders were willing to risk battle during daylight hours. Freeman listened to reports, looking for more clues to either confirm or deny his hypothesis. After several hours of bitter combat, by around 0700 hours, the fighting died down along the perimeter. Despite the calm, he sensed he had a long day of fighting ahead.[64]

At 0800 hours, the Chinese resumed the offensive. Within minutes, 3rd Battalion reported that both Item and Love Companies were under attack. Even worse, the communists had opened a gap of nearly a thousand meters between the two companies. Ten minutes later, Item Company reported that it was "losing ground" and the gash between the beleaguered companies was widening. Freeman knew he needed help. At

0830, he ordered 1st Battalion to send reinforcements. The sun was up, but as Freeman wrote in his account, "An early morning haze had become a heavy black overcoat with low visibility." As a result, Freeman was unable to request close air support for the time being. This new development did not bode well for the 23rd Infantry Regiment.[65]

FEBRUARY 1, 0430–1600 HOURS:
2ND PLATOON, I COMPANY, 23RD INFANTRY
REGIMENT, 2ND INFANTRY DIVISION, HILL 333

Item Company and the soldiers of 2nd Platoon had been at 100-percent security since 0200 hours, when the echo of automatic weapons fire woke the men hunkered down inside their foxholes. PFC Cecil Eide was suffering from diarrhea when the Chinese assault kicked off later that morning, yet he refused to leave the safety of his foxhole. "I just dropped my drawers and let it fly," he said.[66]

Initially, most of the desultory shooting was in the French sector, which was several hundred meters to the rear of Item Company. Sometime after 0430 hours, the soldiers in 2nd Platoon heard a long bugle blast emanating from somewhere in front of the company command post. Seconds later, another bugle answered it, originating west of 2nd Platoon. North of their location, a firestorm erupted in front of Love Company's platoon battle positions.

SFC Dieter W. Rampendahl, the platoon sergeant, crept over to his 2nd Squad and told them to be prepared for an enemy attack that would likely emerge from the draw in front of their foxholes. Satisfied that the soldiers were prepared, Rampendahl proceeded to alert the other squads in the platoon. Within minutes, everyone was ready.

After Rampendahl and his platoon leader had arrived the previous night, they noticed that the small hill north of Hill 333 was defensible terrain. Therefore, they positioned squads to overwatch each cardinal direction. The 3rd Squad occupied a spot along the northwest side of the perimeter, and their leader oriented their one BAR gunner to face almost due west. Defending the position from the southwest was 1st Squad, with two BAR gunners whose weapons pointed west and south from their foxholes, respectively. The last rifle squad was 2nd Squad, which Rampendahl believed was positioned to overlook a possible enemy avenue of approach, a draw that provided defilade for an attacking force coming from the southeast. Because of this likely avenue of attack, 2nd Squad had three BAR gunners, two of which pointed south toward the draw. To provide early warning, the platoon leadership posted a two-man observation post in front of 2nd Squad. Finally, the Weapons Squad—commonly known as 4th Squad—had, at full strength, one .30-caliber light machine gun and one bazooka. Since the machine gun was capable of producing the most casualties, 2nd Platoon, Item Company, controlled the ground between the rest of Item Company and Love Company's flank to the north. The Item Company commander, Captain O'Neill, positioned the machine gun so that its principal direction of fire would enfilade the ground in front of Love Company's southern flank.[67]

Shortly after Rampendahl called on each squad around the platoon perimeter, CPVF soldiers crashed into 3rd Platoon, Love Company, north of 2nd Platoon, Item Company. For nearly ninety minutes, the men in 2nd Platoon were bystanders in the battle. Then, at 0600 hours, the GIs in 3rd and 4th Squads watched incredulously as a squad from Love Company ran past their foxholes and stampeded south toward King Company. Minutes later, both squads started to receive fire from the direction of 3rd Platoon, Love Company. The machine gunner in 4th Squad peered into the fog but could not see beyond the saddle that separated Item Company from Love Company.

M/Sgt. Junior Crayton was acting as an assistant machine gunner to a M1919 gun team, and was also the 4th (Weapons) Squad leader. He recalled hearing both Chinese and American voices emanating from the morning haze like whispers slipping out from behind a stage curtain. In between the fogbanks, the Tomahawks from 2nd Platoon spied spectral figures. As one of the soldiers described, "They were in a column of deuces hub to hub." It did not take long for the men in the two northernmost squads to realize the ghostly shapes were Chinese soldiers.

Sergeant Rampendahl hastily assessed that the two squads did not have the necessary combat power to repel such a massive wave of enemy troops. He needed to bolster their numbers immediately. Without a spare squad in reserve, he hurried over to 2nd Squad and grabbed one man from each of the squad's foxholes, leading them back to 3rd and 4th Squads' battle positions. Meanwhile, the soldiers hardly noticed the additional men—they were too busy plinking away at the enemy. Unable to see the communists, they could nevertheless make out shaking pine trees and shuddering bushes on the hill and along the saddle, and they could hear the cracking twigs and snapping branches in front of them. That was enough.

Sergeant Crayton and his gunner provided long-range direct fire, chugging away at the opposite hill with their machine gun. Unbeknownst to Crayton, several CPVF soldiers had crept up to the knoll, occupying a defilade below his machine-gun position. Amid the clinking and clanking of expended brass casings skipping away from his M1919, Crayton heard rustling from the underbrush several meters below his muzzle. The sergeant ordered the gunner to depress the M1919, but when he tried to fire, he heard the unwelcome *chunk* of the bolt slamming forward, hitting hard metal without shooting a single round. Crayton and the gunner instinctively opened the feed tray, noticing that the firing pin had sustained damage. The weapon was out of commission.

It did not take long for Sergeant Rampendahl to arrive, demanding answers as to why the only crew-served weapon in the platoon was silent. When he found out about the broken firing pin, Rampendahl assured the gunners that he would find another and disappeared into the haze. Armed only with a rifles and pistols, Crayton and the assistant gunner let loose at the charging enemy. Within moments, both men were wounded, but they continued to fight.

After ten minutes, the Weapons Squad leader determined that Rampendahl was not returning. Without an operating machine gun, they were dead men if they remained on the forward slope. Crayton yelled over to the remaining riflemen in other foxholes to fall back toward the reverse slope. There they could reorganize themselves and continue the battle. A deafening silence met Crayton's calls. Realizing the others were all dead or gone, the squad leader grabbed his gunner and the two began to scamper back toward 1st and 2nd Squads.

West of Weapons Squad, the soldiers in 3rd Squad were also battling for their lives. Shortly after 2nd Platoon came under fire, Cpl. Robert E. Logan, the squad leader, slumped over dead in his foxhole after receiving several hits from small-arms fire. Logan's death broke the men in the 3rd Squad. They scrambled out of their holes and ran pell-mell back to 2nd Squad.

The Chinese were hitting everyone in Item Company. Thomas C. Harris was an attached forward observer from M Company who had been calling in fire missions since 0400 hours that morning. At 0630 hours, his radio operator, James C. Strickland, collapsed after a bullet slammed into his upper left chest. Harris grabbed Strickland's radio and called for a medic. The lone observer then continued to request fire missions for the company. By 0700 hours, the medics had finally arrived, but the lead storm was so thick that they were unable to leave the position for another twenty minutes. Shortly after the medics lifted Strickland out of the hole, Harris himself was wounded in the foot. Despite the pain, he continued his mission.

Captain O'Neill arrived at Harris's position to inform the young soldier that he was the only forward observer left in Item Company. The communists had shot the other two observers, just as they had Strickland. Harris told the commander about his wound. O'Neill took one look at Harris's foot, and said, "It wasn't too serious." Harris was it in the Item Company commander's view—O'Neill needed a trained observer and could not afford to lose the young Kentuckian at this vital juncture in the battle. Luckily for O'Neill, Harris soldiered on and continued to call fire missions until a new crew relieved him at 0830 hours. Elsewhere, Item Company's position was deteriorating fast.[68]

Along the southwestern edge of 2nd Platoon, several Chinese had infiltrated past 3rd Squad and opened fire on 1st Squad's battle position. By this point, 1st and 2nd Squads were the only intact formations left in 2nd Platoon. Both had to defend the southern edge, including the draw, as well as the reverse slope, which faced north toward 3rd and 4th Squads' former positions. The attack on 1st Squad forced their leader to pull back some of his men from the reverse slope so that they could add their fire to that of the other squad members already in contact. The chances of survival seemed bleak for the remaining squads.

SFC James Jones, the leader of 2nd Squad, watched the Chinese swarming over the hill. "The enemy was so thick on that hill that the trees were actually shaking," he recalled. To cover the approach, Jones shifted some of his men to the knoll's reverse slope, replacing the soldiers from 1st Squad who had just left. Shortly after the men from 2nd Squad established a hasty battle position on the reverse slope, the survivors of

3rd Squad and the 2nd Squad replacements sent to bolster them staggered over the crest of the hill like punch-drunk boxers.

Rampendahl and Jones were fuming. Both of the sergeants brandished their rifles and ordered the men to secure the wounded recovering with the rest of the squads. One of the wounded was the 2nd Platoon leader, which left Rampendahl in charge of the platoon. He gathered the stragglers and, after several anxious moments, cobbled together the remnants of the Weapons and 3rd Squads into a fighting formation. It was not a moment too soon.

The Chinese attacked as the three remaining squads girded themselves for the inevitable assault. With rifles and BARs, the survivors of 2nd Platoon "sprayed" the knoll as the Chinese rushed toward them like a howling mob. Sprinting in front of the communists were two men: Sergeant Crayton and his gunner. The GIs held their fire.

One of them admonished Crayton as he dived into a foxhole, "They'll use the gun [the busted M1919] on us!"

Crayton assured him, "Oh no they won't. The firing pin's busted."[69]

At that moment, the platoon's fate seemed sealed. The Chinese were barreling down the hill in "droves." Without a working machine gun, the survivors of 2nd Platoon sensed the end was near. Suddenly, muzzle flashes flared up around the east side of the knoll. A soldier, thinking the flashes were coming from Chinese burp guns, opened fire.

Luckily, he missed. The flashes were from 1st Platoon, arriving to reinforce 2nd Platoon with two of their own squads. Leading the way was 2nd Lt. Thomas K. Craig, their platoon leader. Sergeant Jones grabbed the soldier's rifle barrel and shouted, "If you can't see, get the hell off the hill. You'll kill some of our own men."[70]

However, the CPVF grunts were close enough to lob grenades into the platoon's foxholes. Gravity aided the enemy—if the Chinese underthrew the potato mashers, the grenades would simply roll down the hill and into the holes. As a result, the GIs from 2nd and 3rd Squads jumped out of their holes, which had quickly become death traps thanks to the avalanche of grenades.

A single Chinese soldier tumbled down the hill and fell into one of the empty foxholes. Someone yelled, "Don't shoot him. It's a GI." But M/Sgt. Hubert Lee knew better. "GI, hell!" he remarked as he fired three rounds into the enemy's head. Lee was right. The communist soldier was wearing a GI pile cap but still sporting his quilted winter uniform.

The assault was ferocious, but the survivors of 2nd Platoon and the newcomers from 1st Platoon threw back the Chinese attackers, buying time for the company leadership to reorganize the defense north of Hill 333.

By 0900 hours, there was a break in the action. Sergeant Rumpendahl and Lieutenant Craig reconsolidated the perimeter. Craig had brought his platoon's lone machine gun, which he subsequently placed on the north side of the perimeter so that it could fire on the crest of the hill in front of 2nd Platoon.

On the opposite side of the crest were the Chinese, who were chucking grenades over the summit like children tossing water balloons over a neighborhood wall. One enemy soldier lobbed grenade after grenade, and after each throw, he taunted the Americans, shouting, "Okay, Joe!" The constant ridicule angered the men of Item Company. One of the Tomahawks "didn't want the Chinks to have the satisfaction of running us off the top."

But it was more than pride that forced the men of Item Company to counterattack. "It was suicide standing there with grenades [potato masher–type concussion grenade] coming down on us," Sergeant Jones said in a post-battle interview. Instead of fear, frenzy gripped the 2nd Platoon survivors. They wanted to "banzai"-rush the crest to chase off the Chinese, a deadly game of "King of the Mountain."

Initially, Lieutenant Craig ordered them to wait. He requested a fire mission from the 81mm mortar section. The first incoming shell was a white phosphorous round, which the forward observer normally used to mark targets before calling in for more. Alas, the round detonated on the company command post. Luckily, no one was injured. First Lt. Charles H. Roberts, leader of 3rd Platoon, saw what happened and ended the fire mission. He and the rest of the men lost faith in the observer who had replaced Private Harris only sixty minutes before. The original forward observers were either dead or wounded. The men would have to assault the Chinese without any softening up from artillery.

At 1015 hours, the survivors from 2nd Platoon and the additional reinforcements from 1st Platoon climbed out of their foxholes and steeled themselves for the assault on 2nd Platoon's former positions. Lieutenant Mewha, the Eighth Army historian, wrote:

The men in the three squads charged up the slope about ten feet, firing from the hip. The enemy grenades were "sailing" over their heads and landing to the rear near where they had been before. By laying down a terrific barrage of small arms and BAR fire, the enemy was forced to withdraw to the forward slope. When the men reached the crest, small arms and automatic weapons fire was received—from the hill to the front, and from the little finger which extended to the right off the knoll.[71]

PFC George R. Van Sciver III was a radio operator for 2nd Platoon. Braving enemy fire, he had carried wounded men down the knoll toward 1st and 2nd Squads after 3rd and 4th Squads had withdrawn from the forward slope. During the assault, he singlehandedly slayed several enemy soldiers with a fixed bayonet. For his bravery, the Army promoted him to corporal and awarded him the Silver Star.[72]

Though the counterattack had recaptured the hill summit, its effects were short-lived. Within minutes of the assault, the exhausted soldiers reported that they were running out of ammunition. It did not take long for the Chinese to realize the American fire had slackened. Like the GIs before them, the Chinese rushed up the hill. Frustrated and helpless, the men of Item Company yielded the crest and backpedaled down the reverse slope.

When they returned to their foxholes, Rampendahl and Lee ordered the men to stock up on ammo. The leaders of Item Company believed the knoll belonged to them, and they were determined to push the communists off their hill. At 1045 hours, Lieutenant Craig rejoined 2nd Platoon. With him was a squad from King Company under the command of SFC Carl Spencer from Lexington, Indiana. At approximately 1030 hours, 3rd Battalion commander Colonel Kane had instructed Captain Thompson of K Company to send elements of one platoon to reinforce Item Company. Thompson chose 2nd Squad, 1st Platoon, to carry out the colonel's order.

When Spencer arrived at the Item Company positions, he examined the hilltop, his squad's next objective. Between him and the opposing hill was a saddle. According to Spencer, it was "about forty feet deep and then the [ridge] finger ran out. The ground had many small pine trees and underbrush about waist high. The men [Item Company] were also firing into the saddle. The enemy (approximately a company) was on the finger and was trying to force his way across the saddle to the high ground. Heavy enemy small arms and automatic weapons fire was spraying the area."

After Spencer arrived, he reported to Lieutenant Craig, who asked him how many grenades each of the men had. Spencer informed the officer that each man had three. Resolved to recapture the hill, Craig wanted Spencer to distribute the grenades among the soldiers who were about to participate in the second assault of the morning. According to the 2nd Squad leader, "They were then to throw the grenades and charge the enemy in an attempt to force them off the ridge-finger."

In a postwar interview, Craig admitted he issued different instructions. According to him, he "then told all the men to fix bayonets; every *other* [emphasis added] man to throw a grenade; and to charge the crest. The other men were then to throw their grenades. However, most of the men threw their grenades the first time."[73]

Despite the face-value simplicity of the plan, it was not simple enough. Almost all of the soldiers hurled their grenades at the beginning of the assault instead of staggering the action. The Chinese defenders recovered their senses by the time the Tomahawks reached the top of the hill and opened fire on the Americans as they popped their heads over the crest.

Spencer later argued that "the enemy was not within range and the brush was too thick for them to be effective. The men expressed the opinion that the grenades should have been thrown later."[74]

The fighting atop the hill was brutal. "I wasn't scared right then and killed several gooks with my rifle; then I caught a slug in my leg and got scared as hell. Then I knew they were playing for keeps," Sergeant Jones remembered. It was 1110 hours. Sergeants Lee and Rampendahl knew that without more bullets and grenades, they could not hold the hill. They ordered the survivors to withdraw back toward their original assault positions on the reverse slope. The top of the hill became a no-man's-land for both sides.[75]

Spencer and the survivors from 2nd Squad, 1st Platoon, Company K, described what it was like fighting with Item Company. According to Spencer, "The men were forced to crawl on their knees to a point overlooking the saddle, where the men established a base of fire with their

BARs and M-1's. It was necessary to raise [*sic*] up to place fire on the enemy; and when the men did so, the enemy could be observed running from bush to bush on the slope."[76]

With GIs so close to the Chinese lines, the communists began to hurl hand grenades over the crest of the knoll. In quick succession, the exploding potato mashers wounded four men. Spencer saw a squad of communists trying to infiltrate around the eastern side of the forward slope. At that moment, a grenade detonated nearby, wounding Spencer, who refused to withdraw despite the burning shrapnel in his body. Instead, he continued to haul ammunition to the other soldiers. His squad was down to five men.

Luckily, help was on the way. Thirty minutes before noon, two more squads from King Company arrived to reinforce the remnants of Item Company. In addition to the soldiers was a single water-cooled machine gun from Mike Company. The gunner, SFC Richard W. Bass, was from K Company. The original gunner from M Company had died, and since Bass no longer had an operating weapon of his own (rifle fire had damaged it earlier that day during one of the many firefights), he took over the role of machine gunner.

Bass set up the water-cooled M1917 gun on a "small pimple" that jutted out from the ridgeline. From there, he could see the area to the southwest of the "ridge finger." With him were several riflemen who were now ammo bearers for the voracious crew-served weapon. Bass had four boxes of machine-gun ammunition. He loaded the first belt and cocked the bolt to rear.

Bass's and the machine gun's arrival were fortuitous. Shortly after, he spied twenty-five to thirty CPVF soldiers infiltrating around the hilltop; he opened fire and scattered the Chinese. In response, the communists began shooting from a spur northwest of Bass's location. The incoming fire pinned many of the Americans on their side of slope. Bass had to suppress the Chinese automatic fire, so he swung the machine gun toward the northwest. Within seconds, he had neutralized the offending enemy soldiers.

With this new group and crew-served weapon system, the grunts charged up the slope for a third time at 1300 hours. They drove the communists off, but this time, the CPVF left a sniper who wounded five to six Americans within minutes of the summit's capture. After several tense moments, the GIs found him hiding in a draw northwest of their position. One of the BAR gunners emptied his magazine and silenced the pesky sharpshooter. Despite killing the sniper and freeing a hilltop of communists, Item Company's hold on the hill was tenuous. Ammunition shortages bedeviled the Americans. Instead of waiting for the inevitable Chinese counterattack, Rampendahl and Lee reluctantly ceded the crest once more.[77]

Item Company had other problems. Soon after the unsuccessful third assault, enemy riflemen peppered Bass's machine gun with seven holes, shattering the water jacket and thereby knocking it out of commission. The near miss stunned Bass, who had luckily squirmed his way back behind cover while the surviving riflemen suppressed the Chinese.

Twice more that afternoon, the GIs tried to retake the crest. Each time, the Chinese threw them off when the Americans ran low on ammunition. Despite their best efforts, Item Company and the reinforcements from King Company could not hold the knoll.

By 1600 hours, the distance between the lines was less than a few meters in some places. Men lobbed grenades as often as they shot their rifles. Casualties on both sides were mounting. It had become a test of wills. Unbeknownst to the soldiers in Item Company, their French counterparts to the west fared even worse.[78]

FEBRUARY 1, 0830–1200 HOURS: 1ST COMPANY, FRENCH BATTALION, 23RD INFANTRY REGIMENT, 2ND INFANTRY DIVISION, HILL 453

At 0830 hours, the communists resumed their attacks against the men of 1st Company. Gérard Journet, the machine gunner from 1st Section, believed the Chinese wanted to use the heavy fog to mask their movements. At first, the Chinese tried to infiltrate around the northern and southern escarpments, but according to later accounts, these attempts failed. However, their frontal assault from the west breached the French lines near 3rd Section, which was under the command of Robert Girardot, an adjutant (a French rank).

A Chinese sapper team detonated an explosive charge, which left Girardot blind. Despite the wound, he persevered and continued to lead his men, but in the end he had to order his section to fall back. Meanwhile, other soldiers tried desperately to staunch the flow of enemy troops. PV2 François Couric hurled grenade after grenade at the Chinese—his bravery delayed the gushing torrents of communist soldiers, but it did not stop them. Finally, an enemy soldier shot him dead.[79]

Captain DeCastries realized he had to plug the hole. He immediately counterattacked, using an attached 75mm recoilless rifle team and machine guns. Leading the way was 1st Sgt. Gustave Gatoux, who, "At the head of his group, led a violent counterattack, permitting the recapture of his positions." The ferocity of the French riposte paralyzed and then pushed back the Chinese forces. Sensing a rout, the communists retreated, leaving behind thirty-nine bodies, six machine guns, thirty rifles, and five submachine guns. By noon, DeCastries's men had weathered three attacks; despite Chinese efforts to the contrary, the French still controlled Hill 453.[80]

FEBRUARY 1, 0800–1600 HOURS: 3RD COMPANY, FRENCH BATTALION, 23RD INFANTRY REGIMENT, 2ND INFANTRY DIVISION, NORTH OF HILL 279

The CPVF had better luck at Hill 279. Twenty-six minutes after sunrise, the Chinese resumed their assault on 3rd Company, who had barely recovered from the previous attack. They had no time to catch their breath or recover from the early morning mayhem. At 0800 hours, the Reds raced down the slope of Hill 319 like an unstoppable rockslide. The French fought hard, but the overwhelming number of Chinese soldiers wore on 3rd Company. The wounded began to pile up inside foxholes, the automatic fire preventing the U.N. forces from evacuating them.

Sometime before 0930 hours, Captain Serre requested heavy mortar support, which had to come from the regimental heavy mortar company since the French Battalion lacked their own heavy mortars. S/Sgt. Harley E. Wilburn, a forward observer, arrived with his radio operator, PFC Paul Fry. Wilburn, from St. Louis, Missouri, was only twenty years old when he arrived in Korea. Unlike many of his comrades, he was in the service when the war broke out, but he had bigger plans. In his leisure time, he played for the 23rd Infantry Regiment's amateur baseball team, and he wanted to play major league baseball for the St. Louis Browns. In fact, he was preparing to attend tryouts when North Korea invaded South Korea. With his baseball dreams now a distant memory, Wilburn and Fry went to meet the French.

Wilburn vividly remembered the fighting on February 1. "As I got to the top of the ridgeline," he said in an interview, "I kept asking the French soldiers, who couldn't hardly speak any English . . . where their company commander was, and they kept telling me [to] go on up further." After several minutes of searching, the two Americans reached the French command post. "I finally found the company commander of the French Company," recalled Wilburn, "and I told him who I was and what I was up there to do—to give him support with our heavy mortars."[81]

Serre led the pair up the slope. As they climbed up the hill, the French captain explained how the Chinese mortars had been pounding his company's position over the previous night and into the morning. He wanted the American forward observers to find the enemy tubes so that the U.N. artillery and mortars could neutralize them.

"I couldn't pinpoint exactly where the fire was coming from due to the fog and the echo's [sic]," Wilburn recalled in a postwar letter. "The French officer crawled up to the top of the ridge exposing himself to point out the mortars position."

Serre said, in broken English, "You look down my finger and I'll show you." Then, much to Wilburn's shock, "He got hit right in the head as he tried to point to the Gook mortars." It stunned Wilburn for a moment. "I grabbed him by his feet and screamed for help but it was to [sic] late, he died speaking French. I don't know if he was praying or what."[82]

Several minutes after Captain Serre fell, the Chinese attack from Hill 319 intensified. The enemy observer responsible for the heavy fire called for more Chinese artillery on the slopes of Hill 279. Lieutenant Baxerre, Serre's executive officer, assumed command of 3rd Company. Maj. Maurice Barthelemy assumed command over the entire northwest section of the battalion's perimeter, including the attached ROK Company on the southern flank of 3rd Company. Barthelemy was a spare major, and therefore assumed the de facto role of a battalion problem-solver. In fact, Barthelemy described himself in a postwar interview as "the eyes of the commander." Like many of the soldiers on the northern slopes of Hill 279, he was wounded, yet continued to fight and lead the two embattled companies.

Sometime around 1030 hours, Barthelemy received an urgent plea for assistance from Captain Huschard and 2nd Company. He quickly realized that if the Chinese penetrated Huschard's perimeter, they could then flank 3rd Company's battle position. The major grabbed two groups from 3rd Company and headed south to buttress Huschard's flagging unit. Unfortunately, this only weakened 3rd Company even further. The next CPVF assault slammed into 1st Sgt. André Bizot's section. According to later accounts, "The section Bizot, crushed by fire, maintained in place by the myth that they must hold the road, pulls behind 2nd section."

For several more hours, 3rd Company continued to clash with the Chinese. Finally, at 1400 hours, Lieutenant Baxerre requested permission to withdraw to Hill 279. Major Barthelemy reluctantly approved the request, and the 3rd Company survivors began to pull out at 1500 hours.

Meanwhile, the attached forward observer, Harley Wilburn, heard the French yelling, but he did not know what they were saying to him. After several minutes of silence, "I looked around," he said, "and they were all gone." The American sergeant looked at his radio operator, Private Fry, and said, "Let's get the hell out of here because they're going to overrun us." Their only chance of escape was calling for fire on their own position. Hearing the *thump-thump* of their own mortars, the two soldiers sprinted back toward the new French lines. "We ran," said Wilburn. "And my radio operator got hit with a piece of our own shrapnel in his rear end."[83]

By 1600 hours, 3rd Company was at the end of its tether. Everyone was low on ammunition. Without resupply, the men felt they could not withstand another major communist assault. Despite the shortages, Maj. Olivier LeMire ordered 3rd Company to hold their ground "no matter what." Alas, words were not bullets.[84]

FEBRUARY 1, 1000–1600 HOURS: HEADQUARTERS COMMAND POST, 23RD INFANTRY REGIMENT, 2ND INFANTRY DIVISION, INSIDE PERIMETER, TWIN TUNNELS

Even though they were behind the lines, the regimental command post was far from safe. Outside, enemy artillery and mortar rained down from the sky, while deadly machine-gun fire constantly interrupted activity inside the tents and buildings. Ricochets and errant bullets hit staff clerks passing messages, as if they were infantry dashing between foxholes.

As the fighting raged along the perimeter, Colonel Freeman and General Stewart controlled the battle by using their radios to call for resupply and artillery support. Freeman understood that his most glaring weakness was ammunition—he was running out of all types. Despite his pleas for more bullets, his supply columns could not bring up the crates of Class V (Ammunition) from the supply depots far to the rear in Che-chon fast enough. Wave after wave of Chinese soldiers forced the men in the foxholes to expend a prodigious amount of ammunition to keep the enemy at bay. So far, it had worked. Though the Chinese had breached the defenses in several places, they were unable to exploit the penetrations. In large part, this was because Colonels Monclar and Kane were able to divert forces within their respective battalions to plug the holes before the communists could rush reinforcements into gaps.

"Throughout the day's battle it appeared that the enemy had full confidence in his ability to exterminate us with his overwhelming mass and small arms fire and automatic weapons, a division against two under-strength battalions," Freeman later wrote in his account of the Battle of the Twin Tunnels. "With our inability to employ air, and our rapidly diminishing ammunition as a result of the tremendous fire required to stop his human sea attacks, he almost succeeded. We prayed for a break in the weather and we screamed to Rear CP to expedite ammo resupply."[85]

Freeman knew his chances would improve if his division commander, Maj. Gen. Clark Ruffner, would release his 2nd Battalion and place it under Freeman's direct control. In this regard, General Stewart's presence aided Freeman. According to Stewart, Ruffner wanted updates every thirty minutes from the assistant division commander. By mid-morning, Stewart informed his boss that the situation was beginning to deteriorate. Stewart said an interview, "I told him [Ruffner] of our increasing difficulties, and when he indicated a slight skepticism, I informed him that at the moment I was standing in a pool of blood from the wounded radio operator who had just been shot. I also held the microphone out the door so he could hear the firing."[86]

Ruffner relented, releasing 2nd Battalion and the rest of 1st Battalion to Freeman. It became a question of time: Would the newly released troops arrive in time to save Freeman's beleaguered combat team? According to radio reports, all of the distant and scattered elements of 1st

Battalion moved out around 1400 hours. However, since Maj. George Russell's battalion lacked motor transport, most of the riflemen had to walk to the Twin Tunnels.

It was the same story for 2nd Battalion. The only element Lt. Col. James Edwards could motorize was Easy Company, which he did. The other two rifle companies from 2nd Battalion would not reach the Twin Tunnels until after dark. Freeman glanced at his watch. Nightfall was a long way off. He knew how Custer felt at the Little Bighorn.

It seemed Stewart was thinking the same thing. "My party dug a circle of foxholes and gathered all the hand grenades they could find," he said in an interview. "We prepared to make a 'Custer's Last Stand.'"

The Air Force liaison officer standing next to General Stewart confided to the assistant division commander, "General, I don't like this." He asked, "What is going to happen?"

Stewart's answer was stark. "I replied that in about twenty minutes we would all be dead," the general remarked in a postwar interview. "He liked my answer even less than he did the situation."

At 1500 hours, Freeman sensed the battle was nearing a climax. It was bad news everywhere. "Ammunition was running low and our casualties were piling up," he later wrote. "It looked like we were going to cave in the center of both battalions. We had already designated an inner perimeter over the east tunnel to which we would fall back and defend if necessary, although it would have been a last stand—nothing more."[87]

General Stewart then asked the liaison officer about air support; according to Stewart, the officer replied that "several flights were stacked above us, but due to cloud cover, they could not see the ground."[88] Freeman recalled that shortly after Stewart asked the question, "Then, just like a Hollywood battle, the sun broke through!"[89] The liaison officer grabbed his radio and asked the lowest flight leader "if he could see the ground [through] the break in the clouds."

A voice answered over the static, "Yes."

A wave of excitement swept through the command post.

"We are directly below the break, and we need your help," the liaison officer radioed.

"Here we come," the voice announced. The cavalry had arrived.

FEBRUARY 1, 1630 HOURS:
2ND PLATOON, I COMPANY, 23RD INFANTRY
REGIMENT, 2ND INFANTRY DIVISION, HILL 333

It was 1630 hours, and despite the dwindling number of potential attackers, the survivors from 2nd Platoon, Item Company, and 1st Platoon, King Company, climbed out of their foxholes to assault the knoll once more. Sgt. Hubert Lee led the way, just as he had the previous five times. The enemy had wounded Lee twice, but the sergeant was determined to take the hill, despite the grenade fragments burrowed deep in his injured leg from an earlier explosion.

With a wave of his hand, Lee and the survivors charged the objective. As Lee rushed ahead, a grenade detonated in front of him. The resultant concussion knocked him to the ground. When his soldiers approached him to carry him away to safety, Lee waved them off and crawled up the hill, still barking orders and exhorting his men to continue the attack.

Lee continued to fire at the enemy from his knees. During the assault, Chinese soldiers managed to hit Lee with small-arms fire, wounding him a third time, but he continued to crawl up the hill. Amazingly, he survived. The Army credited his platoon with the destruction of eighty-three enemy soldiers.

George Collingsworth was a stretcher-bearer for much of the fighting at the Twin Tunnels and recalled seeing Lee hobbling down the hill. "He was hit all over," said Collingsworth, "and he was walking with a piece of a tree limb, and me and this other guy with a stretcher . . . wanted to carry him off."

Lee refused the service, saying, "There are people who need that stretcher worse than I do." In honor of his uncommon bravery and dogged determination, President Truman awarded Lee the Medal of Honor.[90]

Lee's attacks did not come without cost, however; 2nd Platoon had lost twenty-eight out of thirty-eight men. "Ammunition was so low that the men were searching the ground for loose rounds; some fixed bayonets," said Mewha, the Eighth Army historian. The Chinese were far from finished. "Enemy soldiers were seen jumping from tree to tree with straplings [*sic*] tied to their backs and as waists as camouflage," he wrote.

Then the exhausted and bedraggled soldiers of Item Company received the news: the tactical air observer, flying above the Twin Tunnels in his T-6 Mosquito, had decided the best place to deliver his close air support was near Item Company's battle positions along Hill 333. Colonel Freeman agreed. The news of incoming rockets and bombs was music to Lee's and the rest of 2nd Platoon's ears. "Air support's coming, and it's going to be close," someone from 2nd Platoon yelled above the cracking and popping of small-arms fire.

The previous night, the soldiers in 2nd Platoon had placed a brightly colored air panel on the ground to indicate the forward line of Allied troops. The panel was still in an ideal location between 2nd Platoon and the Chinese when Lieutenant Craig was informed about the approaching air support. By this point in the war, the Chinese knew what the panels meant. Like the GIs opposite them, they had seen the T-6 buzz overhead. They knew hell was coming if they failed to move the panel and disrupt the airstrike. Grenades started to fly out of the Chinese foxholes, and the survivors from I and K Companies could see CPVF infantry scampering out of the bushes in a desperate effort to move the panel. In response, the GIs banged away at them with their rifles, pinning them to the ground. Fortunately for the Americans, the Chinese failed to reach the panel in time.

The tactical air observer fired a yellow flare at the panel, which served as an aiming marker for the incoming fighter-bomber pilots. The soldiers watched as the flare landed harmlessly on the ground 25 meters from the platoon's forward foxholes. The fighter jockeys had a target.

The first flight was made up of four Air Force jets that came screaming in low shortly after the T-6 left the air space. On the first pass, they strafed the ridge north of Hill 333, circled around, and did it again. On their third pass, they plastered the Noll Valley to the northeast and showered the same ridge north of Hill 333 with rockets. When the Air Force pilots were done, four Marine Corsairs relieved them. Carnage continued to rain down from the air. Soldiers of Item Company said the air support "strafed 'every inch of ground to the front,' flying approximately fifty feet off the ground."[91]

Freeman vividly remembered the devastation from the air strikes:

They didn't waste one round! First, 500 pound bombs, daisy cutters, right into the middle of the closely packed Chinese who went up in pieces; next, back to work with rockets—"gook-goosers," our Infantry facetiously called them, then with the .50 calibers against the now disintegrating enemy. What beautiful air support! The next flight coming in before the Marines had barely started was laid on the Chinese in front of the center of the French position. This mass of Commies on the bare ridge went down like prairie grass in a windstorm. The pressure was immediately relaxed on the defenders as the enemy tried to rally or to dig in. Flight after flight came in up to a total of twenty-four and what was left of the enemy began to "bug out."[92]

For the Joes fighting and dying along the perimeter, the arrival of air support was a miracle. "I was not ashamed to admit tears were in my eyes when I saw those planes," remarked Sergeant Bass.[93]

The airstrikes broke the back of the Chinese. With the exception of a few stay-behind snipers, the fighting was over. The men of Item Company counted forty-seven bodies; they also discovered numerous blood trails crisscrossing the saddle north of the knoll. Shortly after sunset, elements from 1st and 2nd Battalion began to arrive and took over much of the perimeter from the French and 3rd Battalions.

FEBRUARY 1, AFTERNOON TO EVENING: 1ST COMPANY, FRENCH BATTALION, 23RD INFANTRY REGIMENT, 2ND INFANTRY DIVISION, HILL 453

While the men reconsolidated their lines and carted away the wounded and dead, Corporal Bérerd was on his own personal mission. The French Battalion's intelligence officer, Captain Michelet, had learned of an enemy survivor who was under guard atop Hill 453, where Captain DeCastries's 1st Company was located. Michelet wanted Bérerd to interrogate him and bring him back to the battalion headquarters. When Bérerd arrived at the top of Hill 453, he reported to the commander, who led him to the prisoner of war.

"Was he in bad shape!" Bérerd wrote in a postwar letter. "He was lying unconscious on a litter and probably had pneumonia on top of his wounds. I shook him all I could, and only got out of him a few grunts which were insufficient for my Koreans to decide whether he was North-Korean or Chinese. [Bérerd had two Korean translators accompanying him.] So I proceeded with searching the dead around the position, and on one young man who had a better uniform than the rest, I found an overlay showing the route to 453."

Bérerd then asked the two Koreans to carry the wounded POW on a litter down part of the hill. Bérerd was to meet them at the halfway point to relieve the older of the two men and carry the litter the rest of the way. After several minutes, the French corporal linked up with the two Koreans at the designated point and discovered that the Koreans had left behind the wounded enemy soldier. According to Bérerd, the Koreans told him "they were not as strong as I was, and that the litter and the man were too heavy for them so they come [sic] empty-handed."

The French corporal decided that the POW was near death and the grueling trip down the hill would likely result in his death. Bérerd chose to return to the command post without the prisoner. The overlay was the most important part of his mission, and if he returned that item to Captain Michelet, the officer would be satisfied. When he arrived at the command post without the wounded POW, Bérerd said Michelet "blew his stack."

The captain informed Bérerd that the POW had been the only survivor of the Chinese assault. Incensed, Michelet left the command post in a huff and brought the wounded POW back himself. After Michelet returned to the command post, a medic revived the wounded soldier, who turned out to be Chinese. Accompanying Michelet was regimental commander Colonel Freeman, who, because of his time in China, could speak fluent Chinese. He interrogated the prisoner himself. The prisoner admitted he was from the 373rd Regiment.

Twenty-four hours later, X Corps interrogators gleaned even more information from him. They discovered that the 373rd was part of the 125th Division, 42nd Army. More importantly, the 373rd Regiment had been undergoing refit operations in the mountains north of the Twin Tunnels when the division committed it to attack the 23rd Infantry Regiment at the Twin Tunnels. According to the POW, it only had a strength of 700 to 800 men prior to the attack. The analyst who typed the interrogation report added, "If strength figures are correct, it is an indication that the 125th CC Division did not receive sufficient replacements prior to commitment to battle." This confirmed Freeman's earlier assessment that the Twin Tunnels–Chipyong-ni area was so vital to the Chinese operational plan that they would commit forces prematurely and in broad daylight to control the crucial piece of terrain. What Freeman and the U.N. command could not know was that the Chinese would do it again two weeks later, on a much larger scale.[94]

The battle was not quite over. The Chinese role had changed—they were now the hunted. Freeman later remarked, "[The Chinese] didn't have a chance of getting away, though." He ordered his tanks and flak wagons to push north to interdict the fleeing Chinese. Freeman affectionately called the quad .50-caliber machine guns on the M16 half-tracks "meat choppers" in his postwar account. Out in the open, the communists were sitting ducks, and the tankers and their crews gunned them down as they tried to scurry north into the mountains.[95]

Later that night, Colonel Kane received the casualty reports from his companies. In total, his battalion suffered seventy-six casualties: nineteen killed in action, one missing in action, and fifty-six wounded in action. Item Company accounted for forty of those, while Love Company sustained an additional twenty-four casualties.

Across the valley, Colonel Monclar also counted his wounded, dead, and missing in action. His battalion suffered grievously: 27 killed in action, 2 missing in action, and 103 wounded in action, for a total of 132 casualties. Third Company sustained the most, with fifty of the total casualties; 1st Company sustained an additional twenty-eight, and 2nd Company added twenty-six more.[96]

It was not a fair trade for the Chinese. The X Corps G2 estimated the CPVF 125th Division hemorrhaged over 3,000 casualties for an objective it failed to capture. Of those, the G2 calculated over 1,000 were killed in action. Even with their overwhelming numbers, the Chinese could not afford to run up casualty tabs like those incurred at the Twin Tunnels. Eventually, the war of attrition would catch up with them. That was Ridgway's overall plan: use U.N. firepower to offset Chinese manpower. Even though it was close, it had worked. But despite the butcher's bill at the Twin Tunnels, the Chinese would try their luck again two weeks later at Chipyong-ni.[97]

CHAPTER 5

Eye of the Storm

"They [the Chinese] did not value life or seem to mind dying. In fact, a lot of them appeared to want to die."

—2nd Lt. Paul J. McGee, G Company

FEBRUARY 1–2, 1951:
HEADQUARTERS, X CORPS, CH'UNGJU

Freeman's success at the Twin Tunnels had only whetted General Almond's appetite. The corps commander wanted to keep pressing the enemy, and therefore ordered his entire command to push north. While the Tomahawks battled for their lives above the Twin Tunnels, Almond had already decided to go on the offensive.

On February 1, the X Corps commander held a conference at this headquarters in Ch'ungju with all of his major subordinate commanders and the ROK III Corps commanders, including Maj. Gen. Yu Jai Hung, the overall commanding officer. In the spirit of General Ridgway's mission to take the fight to the enemy, Almond devised an operation he called Operation Roundup. He scheduled the offensive to kick off on February 5. His plan was to envelop the bulk of communist forces located near Hongcheon. Leading the way would be two of his ROK divisions: the 5th and 8th ROK Divisions. (Eventually, the 3rd ROK Division would join them.) To secure his eastern flank, Almond wanted the ROK III Corps to advance abreast of X Corps and fix the communist forces in their sector. Shortly after the meeting with his commanders, Almond secured approval from General Ridgway.[1]

The new operation required Freeman to move his regiment to Chipyong-ni. In a postwar account, the 23rd's commander wrote that the Tomahawks' mission required them to "dominate the road center of Chipyong [*sic*] and occupy the high ground in the vicinity so as to protect the right flank of IX Corps and establish the western anchor of a X Corps line of departure for the offensive."[2]

Unbeknownst to General Almond and the rest of the U.N. forces, the Chinese were planning a much larger offensive. They sought to destroy U.N. forces north of Hoengseong. If they succeeded, the loss of two ROK divisions in the immediate area would leave a gaping hole in the U.N. lines—a hole the Chinese would exploit. Follow-on forces would advance and seize the road hub of Wonju, acting as a springboard for further offensive operations.

Marshal Peng Dehuai had not forgotten the Tomahawks at Chipyong-ni. The CPVF commander assigned the 39th Army to deal with the 2nd Infantry Division. The 115th and 116th Divisions had the task "to cut off other enemy forces stationed at Chipyong-ni . . . in order to prevent the enemy from escaping and to intercept enemy reinforcements." What Freeman could not know was that his tired and tested regiment was on a collision course with two Chinese divisions.[3]

FEBRUARY 2–3:
AREA OF OPERATION, 23RD INFANTRY REGIMENT, 2ND INFANTRY DIVISION, CHIPYONG-NI

While the rest of the X Corps readied itself for Operation Roundup, the Tomahawk regiment edged forward into the great unknown. For much of February 2, the regiment's artillery prepped the objective areas, hitting targets on Hill 319, while the tankers engaged targets withdrawing from an unnamed hamlet sandwiched between Hills 319 and 407 just northeast of the regiment's location and the village of Sindae to the northwest.

On February 3, the regiment secured Chipyong-ni. "The entire stretch of road and the hills along it were littered with bodies of Chinese testifying to the efficacy of our artillery and mortar and the air strikes of two days before," Freeman later wrote. In total, the regimental staff estimated that its soldiers collected over 1,300 enemy bodies from the 125th CPVF Division; nearly 600 of them were in front of 3rd Battalion alone.[4]

Freeman liked what he saw in the ground around Chipyong-ni. "The terrain around Chipyong [*sic*] was admirable for defense by a force of our size," he later wrote. "Here we could dig in our main position on low hills, which would facilitate defensive fires, resupply and construction of obstacles. Enemy seizing the higher ground around our position would not be able to direct effective small fires against us but would be vulnerable to our supporting fires."[5]

The most significant drawback of Chipyong-ni was the hills surrounding it. Most of the high ground around the town was higher than the hills that would form the 23rd Infantry's perimeter. Freeman had to make a choice. Even though he wanted to secure the six hills around Chipyong-ni, the distance between the various hilltops was too great. Instead, he chose to maintain a tighter perimeter. He would learn over the next two weeks whether he had made the right choice.[6]

To ensure that the regiment had the necessary combat power to accomplish its mission, General Ruffner allocated several more units to the 23rd Infantry from the division's task organization. In addition to its full complement of three infantry battalions, a tank company, an attached French Battalion, and an artillery battalion, the 23rd also gained a combat engineer company (B/2nd Engineers), a battery of 155mm towed howitzers (B/503rd Field Artillery, which would arrive on February 9), and a Ranger company (1st Ranger). Freeman also kept the self-propelled antiaircraft battery (B Battery) from the 82nd Antiaircraft Artillery Battalion. Even by Korean War standards, it was a well-equipped force. Most regiments had only nine infantry companies; thanks to the additions of the Ranger company and the French Battalion, Freeman had thirteen. He would use them all in the upcoming battle.[7]

As each unit arrived, Freeman sent them out to their designated spot along the new perimeter. Unlike at the Twin Tunnels, where the 23rd's southern flank was wide open, Freeman wanted a tight defense for Chipyong-ni. He had learned not to leave any holes for the Chinese. More importantly, he had two companies in reserve: B Company and, if needed, 1st Ranger Company.

Freeman placed 1st Battalion to the north, with C Company on the western side and A Company on the eastern side. B Company was the last unit to arrive and was therefore assigned as a regimental reserve. To the east was 3rd Battalion, with all of its companies on the line. Colonel

Kane placed his L Company in the north, I Company in the center, and K Company in the south. Along the southern flank was Colonel Edwards's relatively fresh 2nd Battalion, with E Company placed to defend his eastern flank, F Company in the center, and G Company anchoring his western flank. Finally, protecting the regiment's western sector was Colonel Monclar's French Battalion, with 1st Company serving as his link between 2nd Battalion and his own. From south to north, respectively, in the center were the ROK and 2nd Companies; securing the northern portion of Monclar's line was 3rd Company.[8]

While the men dug foxholes and cleared fields of fire, Freeman kept pressure on the enemy by ordering his battalions to send out patrols to maintain contact with Chinese forward lines. He wanted to know where the enemy was at all times. Freeman described how they patrolled. "At dawn each day, elements of our forces occupied the high ground about a thousand yards in front of the position on the north, west, and south. At dusk, and when they could not be observed, they withdrew, leaving the forward positions heavily mined and booby trapped [*sic*] and with trip flares set. Far-ranging combat patrols screened these positions and the enemy was never aware of our true dispositions." Freeman later scribbled a note in the margins, "These tactics were later to pay off in a big way."[9]

FEBRUARY 3–8:
HEADQUARTERS, 2ND BATTALION, 23RD
INFANTRY REGIMENT, CHIPYONG-NI

Lt. Col. James Edwards set up his command post shortly after he had arrived in Chipyong-ni. Capt. John H. Ramsburg, an officer in the headquarters, described the unassuming structure as a "long building . . . one end of wood and one of mud with [a] tin roof." The command post was located along the town's main east–west road, closer to Easy and Fox Companies because Edwards felt the enemy's likely avenue of approach was through those companies.[10]

Like Freeman, Edwards had proven himself to the men under his command. And like many of his fellow officers and soldiers, he hailed from Texas. His first test came on August 22, 1950, when the 23rd Infantry was defending the Pusan Perimeter. Edwards's 2nd Battalion came under attack from what the subsequent award citation claimed was an entire North Korean division. Despite the odds, Edwards kept his composure and ordered his battalion "to hold its position at all costs." To keep the NKPA units from overrunning his battalion, he ordered spoiling attacks and counterattacks. The Texan commander constantly exposed himself to enemy fire while acting as a forward observer for the artillery. Miraculously, his battalion survived the night, and instead of hunkering down the next morning, Edwards sensed the enemy was about to break and ordered another counterattack. The sudden assault stunned the NKPA units, and they eventually withdrew. For his gallantry, the Army awarded him his first Silver Star.[11]

Edwards was far from finished with his heroic acts. On November 26, 1950, he led his battalion against the unexpected onslaught of Chinese communists attacking the town of Kujang, North Korea. After an unsuccessful attempt to capture a hill near the town, Edwards conducted a dangerous retrograde operation, leading to the hasty evacuation of his command post. The battalion commander organized a counterattack and retook his post at 2300 hours that night. Throughout the engagement, Edwards exposed himself to machine-gun and mortar fire. According to his citation, "His heroic and inspiring leadership on this occasion was directly responsible for preventing any further enemy penetration." He earned his second Silver Star.[12]

Edwards had the respect of his subordinates. Capt. Bickford Sawyer, who had assumed command of Easy Company the previous month, recalled "Colonel Edwards was well liked and respected by the officers and men of the battalion. He was not, however, revered as was Colonel Freeman." What Sawyer appreciated most about Edwards was his hands-off leadership style. "The commander [Edwards] and his staff practiced the minimum of supervision. I was normally given a mission and I was never told or advised how to accomplish it, nor did the commander or his staff ever watch over me as my company moved to do its job. This worked fine with me, but I can't speak for other commanders. On the other hand, if I ever needed support, artillery, air or armor, Colonel Edwards moved heaven and hell to get it for me."[13]

Many of the soldiers shared the same basic opinion of Edwards as their officers did. "Edwards seemed more of the driving kind. Nevertheless, [he] looked after the troops well," said Ben Judd, a soldier in Fox Company.[14] Second Lt. Paul J. McGee, a recently arrived platoon leader in George Company, said in a postwar interview, "I felt about the same way toward Colonel Freeman as I did Colonel Edwards, that we had the best. They were the type of officers that instilled in their command the idea that we were the best." However, not everyone had a rosy view of Edwards. The radio operator for Easy Company, Douglas Graney, shared his mixed views in a postwar letter, writing, "Edwards—A tough battalion commander. I liked him although I thought he could have been better. He never visited the line troops."[15] Regardless of the men's opinions, Edwards was in charge, and he sensed that the fighting around Chipyong-ni was only beginning.[16]

While examining the map, Edwards replayed the last few days in his mind. Shortly after 2nd Battalion assumed their spot along the regiment's perimeter, Edwards dispatched patrols to ensure that he knew the location of the CPVF's screen line. On February 4, G Company sent a platoon southwest to Hill 129, and F Company sent one south to Hill 397. Neither found the enemy. However, platoon patrols from 3rd Battalion ran into Chinese units near Hill 506, east of Chipyong-ni; the communist units easily repulsed the American patrol.[17]

On February 5, both G and F Companies returned to Hills 129 and 397, and just as they had the previous day, found nothing. Meanwhile, 1st Battalion sent B Company to clear Hill 363, east of the regiment's position and midway between Hill 506 to the north and Hill 401 to the south. After several brief skirmishes with Chinese troops, 1st Battalion captured Hill 363. Since their mission did not call for 363's occupation, the U.N. soldiers trudged back to Chipyong-ni at nightfall.[18]

Freeman needed to push his screen line farther east to where most of the enemy activity was. However, he had learned his lesson from the ambush of the C Company patrol on January 29. If the enemy was near Sanggosong in force, then Freeman needed more than just two platoons of infantry to keep them occupied. Therefore, on February 6, he ordered Colonel Edwards to send out an entire reinforced company. To beef up the company's combat power, Freeman allocated three Sherman tanks from the regiment's tank company. Edwards chose Captain Sawyer's Easy Company to conduct the mission.

The next morning, Easy Company left the perimeter and headed east toward Hill 363. Several hours after they left, Sawyer received a message from a liaison plane flying ahead of his patrol. The plane did not have direct communications with the infantry, so the pilot dropped a message in a canister; Sawyer opened it and read the note: "Long column of enemy troops headed up the hill in your direction."

"The pilot didn't tell me how far the enemy force was from the top of the hill," Sawyer later wrote, "but I knew it was now a race." He hastened his men to the top. As they neared the summit, the enemy opened fire and "pandemonium took over."

Sawyer reported enemy contact at 1120 hours. As he wrote in a postwar letter, "The enemy had won the race and he was now firing down on us."

For much of the afternoon, Sawyer tried to maneuver his three platoons to gain an advantage against the Chinese on Hill 363. By 1518 hours, Sawyer realized he did not have the necessary combat power to seize the hill, even with his tanks. He was taking fire from Hill 401 to the southeast and from another enemy position to the northeast. To prevent further casualties, Colonel Edwards ordered him to withdraw.

Over the next twenty-four hours, the X Corps' G2 section tried to make sense of the Chinese Army's disposition east of Chipyong-ni. The analysts believed the Chinese were in the area and in force. However, Operation Roundup had kicked off, and with the westward push of 8th ROK Division, Col. James Polk, the new X Corps G2, concluded that the forces east of Chipyong-ni were enemy forces retreating from the advancing 8th ROK Division. It was a classic case of wishful thinking. Unbeknownst to Edwards and Freeman, the Chinese were not retreating: they were building up their force for a major offensive. Once again, the intelligence analysts got it wrong.[19]

As a result of the rebuff at Sanggosong, Freeman upped the ante, ordering Edwards to take most of his battalion and clear the town. On the morning of February 7, Edwards left Chipyong-ni with two infantry companies (G and F), the weapons company (H), and a platoon of four tanks. Since the force represented most of the battalion, Edwards led the operation in person, taking with him much of his headquarters. All that remained behind was 3rd Platoon, George Company, and Easy Company.

When F Company reached Hill 363, the soldiers discovered that the enemy had abandoned the hill and blocked the Sanggosong–Chipyong-ni road by cratering it with explosive charges. As a result, the tanks had to wait until the engineers arrived to fill in the massive holes. Edwards sent the infantry ahead without the tanks and requested that the regiment dispatch a platoon of combat engineers to open the road at 1055 hours. G Company reported that Hill 506 was also free of enemy forces. Regiment ordered Edwards to use his Pioneer and Ammunition Platoon to open the road instead of the regiment's engineers, which would have meant a longer delay.

Early that afternoon, Fox Company arrived at Sanggosong, and the F Company commander, Captain Tyrrell, reported it cleared at 1340 hours. Within fifteen minutes though, Chinese mortars, located northeast of Sanggosong, began to fire on F Company. In response, Edwards ordered Tyrrell to push northeast toward Hill 218 while G Company, under 1st Lt. Thomas Heath, moved east from Hill 506 to clear the town of Hagosong, due north of Sanggosong.

For several hours, the men inched forward under heavy mortar and machine-gun fire. Neither company was making any appreciable progress. The hilly terrain was as much an enemy to G Company as the Chinese were. Toward nightfall, Edwards pulled back because it was not a part of his mission to remain outside of the perimeter overnight. He had found the enemy. He estimated that one Chinese regiment was north of Sanggosong and knew that his battalion task force, with only two maneuver companies, did not have sufficient combat power to tackle a Chinese regiment of unknown strength, so he withdrew. By 1955 hours, his command had returned to Chipyong-ni.

Later that night, Colonel Edwards kept looking at the big operations map in his battalion headquarters, as if the answer would suddenly appear on the paper. His eyes were fixed on the hills to the east of his battalion. For the past several days, his units had run into dug-in Chinese infantry there, with most of the contact occurring in the valleys and low-lying ridges between the higher summits of Hill 506 to the north and Hill 401 to the south. The Chinese refused to cede the ridges to the U.N. forces. Edwards wanted to know why.

Meanwhile, the X Corps intelligence analysts pored over the various reports from their divisions. In their daily summary, they spent time discussing enemy activity west of Chipyong-ni, despite the fact that Edwards believed an unidentified Chinese regiment was in Sanggosong, east of the 23rd Infantry. Mounting evidence from Edwards's battalion went unanswered as Colonel Polk maintained that the Chinese were only capable of delaying actions and counter-reconnaissance. Remarkably, none of his predictive assessments mentioned another major offensive on the horizon.[20]

FEBRUARY 7–8:
E COMPANY, 23RD INFANTRY REGIMENT, NANCE AND SAWYER HILLS

T/Sgt. Martin Lee was nineteen years old, but despite his youth, he was a platoon sergeant for 2nd Platoon, Easy Company. He had joined the Army at fourteen years of age in April 1945, using someone else's birth certificate, and remained in the service until 1949, when he received his discharge papers. Like many of the soldiers in the 23rd Infantry, the Army recalled Lee to active service on July 1, 1950.

The young Hoosier had traveled to Fort Lewis, Washington, where he underwent refresher training for several weeks. Afterward, he left on a ship bound for Korea and disembarked at Pusan on October 21, 1950. Pending disciplinary actions meant the Army had demoted Lee to private first class. However, Capt. Perry Sager, the commander of E Company in November 1950, needed NCOs. When he saw that Lee had prior service, he promoted him to technical sergeant and ordered him to assume the role of platoon sergeant for 2nd Platoon.

Somehow, Lee survived the battles of Kunu-ri and the retreat south. His platoon occupied a position that overlooked a draw, and Lee emplaced his platoon's light machine gun in the center so that its arc of fire would cover the entire platoon front. To protect this key weapon system, the platoon sergeant flanked it with riflemen. Thanks to the replacement system, his platoon was now at full strength. Sharing his foxhole was the forward observer from the regimental heavy mortar company, Sgt. Richard J. Bradley, from Wheeling, West Virginia.

In front of his platoon were strands of barbed wire. "We hung C-rations on it so that it would make noise when they [Chinese] would hit it," said Lee, explaining his platoon's early warning system. "We'd take grenades and put them in the C-ration cans and pull the pin and then run the string across paths and when they'd hit [the] string and pull the grenade out and it would blow up and get'em."[21]

In addition to the makeshift trip-wire grenades, the men of F Company set up trip flares along the likely infiltration routes to provide additional early warning. Placing the trip flares was dangerous for the men given the task. PFC Grant Mead, a soldier in 3rd Platoon, positioned to the west of 2nd Platoon, recalled an incident when his foxhole comrade, who was new to the platoon, inadvertently triggered one of the flares. "He came up to join us," explained Mead. "And he was assigned to go out one day to set up booby traps and flares. And he accidentally set one off and he had happened to be leaning over the flare [when it] went off and took the top of his head off so that pretty well took care of him."

Not all acts of ingenuity were dangerous. Near the railroad tracks was a farm where the farmer and his wife had perished and left several oxen. The cooks assigned to F Company slaughtered the beasts and fed the meat to the soldiers with some coffee and donuts. Over sixty years later, Mead remembered the meal and said with relish, "We had some of the best cooks in the Army."[22]

FEBRUARY 2–8:
3RD PLATOON, G COMPANY, 23RD INFANTRY REGIMENT, SOUTH OF CHIPYONG-NI

Second Lt. Paul J. McGee was the new platoon leader for 3rd Platoon. When he arrived at George Company, he went straight to his new unit because of the dire need for infantry officers. In fact, the need was so acute that he did not even meet Colonel Edwards, his battalion commander. He replaced the previous platoon leader, who, according to McGee, had been "wounded or killed."

McGee's first impression of his platoon was not an auspicious one. "There wasn't really a Third Platoon when I got there; oh, there were a few men. But after I was there a few days we'd restrengthened [*sic*] into a full platoon. Most of the men were new like me. There were a few who'd had experience; Sergeant [Billy C.] Kluttz, my platoon sergeant, had some experience."[23]

Luckily for 3rd Platoon, McGee was not a green lieutenant. During World War II, he had attained the rank of staff sergeant and fought with the 66th Infantry Division in northwest Europe, where he had earned the Combat Infantryman Badge. McGee noted that the Germans and the Chinese did not fight in the same way. "The Germans fought to live

just like us," he said in a postwar interview. "They did not take unneces-
sary chances, they tried to kill the enemy, and they tried to stay alive.
They wouldn't charge you unnecessarily; didn't pull any frontal assaults
or come at you like mad people or animals."

His current enemy "was altogether different. They had no value of
life. They would charge right up to your hole. They'd even come up to
you sometime without weapons—just come running at you. Once you
got them cornered in a hole or a cave, they would not come out or surrender. They were a different sort of people. They did not value life or
seem to mind dying. In fact, a lot of them appeared to want to die."

According to McGee, the Chinese and North Koreans also used different tactics than the Germans. "A lot of the time the Chinese would
put their positions on the reverse slope of the hill," he observed. "The
Germans and we did not fight that way—we'd normally put our positions on the forward slope. They could live on practically nothing.
They'd take a sack full of rice, and sometimes five or six rounds of
ammunition with four or five people behind one rifle. They were just a
different sort of people—fanatics. You'd almost feel like—what's the use?
There was almost no end to them."[24]

Unlike other men the Armed Forces called back or drafted into
active service, McGee was already in the Army when the war broke out
in June 1950. He had grown up in Belmont, North Carolina, which he
described as a "little mill village." Like many young men a decade before,
he had rushed to the colors after the Japanese bombed Pearl Harbor in
December 1941, wanting to join the Marines to be with his older
brother. Alas, he was colorblind and ended up in the Army because the
Marines only wanted perfect physical specimens. After World War II, Paul
reenlisted in the Army. Ironically, his brother left the Marine Corps and
enlisted in the Army to be with his younger brother. The elder McGee
remained an enlisted soldier, but Paul eventually ended up at Officer
Candidate School and earned his commission as an infantry officer.

When the Korean War began, Paul's brother was serving with the
7th Infantry Division in Japan while Paul was in Airborne School. When
he finished, he immediately sought a combat assignment in Korea so that
he could join his older brother. His sibling was fighting with the 17th
Infantry Regiment, which eventually landed behind the Marines at
Inchon and subsequently found themselves trapped with them near the
Chosin Reservoir.

Paul reached Korea on January 1, 1950. Soon after his troopship docked at Pusan, he marched off the gangplank and asked for an assignment in the 17th Infantry Regiment. Unfortunately, no slot was available. Instead, most of the new arrivals headed north to join the 2nd Infantry Division. Paul figured it was the next best thing to his goal, so within a few weeks, he joined up with his new platoon in George Company. (He was able to link up with his brother later when George Company, 23rd Infantry, was located near the 17th Infantry in early January.)

Paul McGee was a new platoon leader in a platoon with many new faces, but the platoon sergeant was not one of them. "Sergeant Kluttz was a soldier," McGee said. "He should have been an officer. He was a lot like me. He had no schooling to amount to anything, and he didn't want to be an officer. I don't guess, but I wouldn't want a platoon sergeant any different from him. He was never afraid—or at least he never showed it. He wasn't nervous; he was always calm. He wasn't too much for military courtesy, but he was a real soldier." Like McGee, Kluttz was from North Carolina.

When the new platoon leader assumed command, his first task was integrating the new soldiers into the unit. He and Kluttz spent much of the latter half of January training the replacements in bayonet drills and hand-to-hand combat. Their first combat mission was on February 2 when they relieved the French Battalion's 1st Company on Hill 453. McGee remembered what he saw as they approached the hill:

> As we started to walk up that road to go to the hill to take our positions, I saw about six French soldiers lying in the back of a 2x6 truck. They were frozen stiff. As we kept going up the hill we saw more dead soldiers. They were all frozen, and they had a rope tied under their arm. One man in front and a man in the rear had ropes tied around their feet. They were just sliding them down off that hill; they were too heavy to carry. The French were just laughing and talking and carrying on while they did this, which I could not understand. It was amazing to me that they'd want to joke while dragging those bodies along with them.

McGee also recalled, "I saw quite a few dead Chinese up there on that hill where the French had been."

It was sobering experience for the new platoon leader. "When I first saw all those dead French soldiers up on top of that hill, I realized then that it was going to be tough," he later remarked.

On February 3, George Company and the rest of 2nd Battalion moved up to Chipyong-ni to assume defensive positions along the southern side of the regimental perimeter. "It was just a regular Korean village, mud huts with thatched roofs," McGee recalled. "We were told that it was a railroad junction, but I never saw a train. All I saw were the railroad tracks. I never really had an opportunity to observe the town; we went right on through the village and went on to preparing our positions."[25]

Leading George Company was 1st Lt. Thomas Heath, the acting commander at the time of the campaign. The actual commander, Capt. Aulbry C. Hitchings, was on R&R. Like McGee, Heath was also a WWII veteran who had served with the 82nd Airborne Division. At thirty-three years old, the officer from Coldwater, Oklahoma, was ancient compared to most lieutenants.[26]

Initially, Colonel Edwards positioned Heath's G Company along a shallow rise, which later became known as Heath's Hill. West of G Company was the French Battalion, and to the east was F Company, at the center of which was Edwards's line. Since F Company had the smallest sector, it only needed two platoons on the main line of resistance. Heath tried to do the same with his own company so that McGee's 3rd Platoon was originally in reserve, but soon realized that he needed all of his platoons rotating on the line, especially once Colonel Edwards required him to send out daily patrols. Fortunately, the first few days passed uneventfully.[27]

FEBRUARY 2–8:
L COMPANY, 23RD INFANTRY REGIMENT,
NORTH OF CHIPYONG-NI

Like G Company, L Company also received replacements. Chipyong-ni was a baptism by fire for many soldiers. PVT James Henkel was a new rifleman in 3rd Platoon and had arrived at Chipyong-ni on a truck loaded with supplies. When he hopped off, the soldiers from the adjutant office sent him to Captain Jackson's L Company, located on the northeast side of the perimeter.

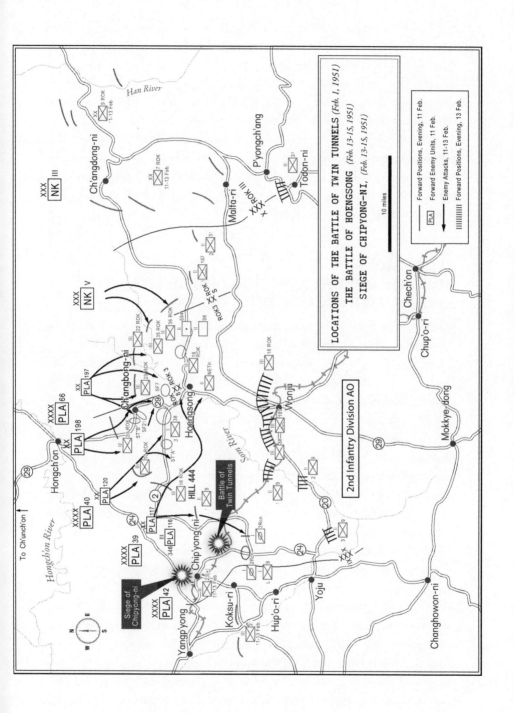

LOCATIONS OF THE BATTLE OF TWIN TUNNELS (Feb. 1, 1951)
THE BATTLE OF HOENGSONG (Feb. 13-15, 1951)
SIEGE OF CHIPYONG-NI (Feb. 13-15, 1951)

Forward Positions, Evening, 11 Feb.
Forward Enemy Units, 11 Feb.
Enemy Attacks, 11-13 Feb.
Forward Positions, Evening, 13 Feb.

10 miles

2nd Infantry Division AO

Battle of Twin Tunnels

Siege of Chipyong-ni

Han River

Ch'angdong-ni

P'yongch'ang

Todon-ni

Malt'a-ri

Hongch'on

Ch'angbong-ni

Hoengsong

HILL 444

Chip'yong-ni

Yangp'yong

Koksu-ri

Hup'o-ri

Yoju

Wonju

Chech'on

Chup'o-ri

Mokkye-dong

Changhowon-ni

To Ch'unch'on

Hongch'on River

Som River

Henkel's squad was still recovering from the shellacking it had sustained at the Twin Tunnels and numbered only five men at the time. Almost immediately, the soldiers went to work. "We dug . . . one great big fighting hole that would hold around four people, shoulder-to-shoulder, and in back of it, we dug a sleeping hole," Henkel said. "We worked on that, off and on, for three or four days."

Henkel described their field of fire, noting, "We looked down this one trail that was coming up. My platoon was hooked in to A Company, and my squad was the last squad that was hooked into A Company." He wondered if the Chinese would use that trail to attack his squad. But elsewhere, operations continued.[28]

FEBRUARY 8–10:
AREA OF OPERATIONS, 23RD INFANTRY
REGIMENT, EAST OF CHIPYONG-NI

February 8 was a day of reorganization for Edwards's 2nd Battalion. In the west, the French Battalion continued to probe out toward Hill 583. Every day, the Chinese greeted them with harassing fire, keeping the French at bay. However, the fire informed Freeman as to where the communist front-line trace was located.[29]

The situation to the east was more pressing for the Tomahawk commander. To prevent overtaxing his men, Freeman rotated the major reconnaissance patrols. On February 8, it was 3rd Battalion's turn to head east. Unlike the X Corps G2, Major General Ruffner, Freeman's boss, was concerned about the enemy buildup between his two regiments within his division's area of operations. In response, he ordered both the 23rd and 9th Infantries to conduct a clearance operation. In the process, the units would link up somewhere in the vicinity of Hill 444 to the east of Sanggosong. Representing the 9th Infantry Regiment was its 1st Battalion. Division ordered it to advance as far as the village of Sogu.

The two battalions left early on the morning of February 8, and within a few hours, both were locked in battle with unidentified Chinese forces. At 1012 hours, 3rd Battalion reported over the 23rd Infantry's command net that its lead elements were under fire from communist forces located atop Hill 444. Three hours later, at 1310, Colonel Freeman authorized Colonel Kane, 3rd Battalion's commander, to fight it out all night if the unit could not successfully link up with the

9th Infantry Regiment. Both Freeman and Ruffner wanted the zone cleared, and they were willing to commit forces overnight to do it.

Throughout the day, staff officers listened to the command net, tracking 3rd Battalion's snaillike progress. Most of the fighting was over a long distance, but the Chinese held the advantage by occupying the high ground. As the day inexorably drifted into night, Kane requested permission for his battalion to pull back into the old perimeter. The time was 1815 hours. A few minutes later, Freeman denied the request, ordering Kane to establish his own perimeter near Sanggosong. Freeman felt that if he could do it at the Twin Tunnels, Kane could, too.

At 2235 hours, General Ruffner issued an order for the 9th and 23rd Infantry Regiments. It read, "In addition to patrol activities continue present mission to objective assigned to block escape route north, to clear enemy from zone, and to link up with the 9th Infantry. When the missions are accomplished by the 9th and the 23rd the units will be returned to perimeters by Division order."

Above, aerial observers discovered large bodies of Chinese troops. According to the pilots, they were moving from west to east. Most were north of Chipyong-ni and thus beyond the range of the 105mm howitzers located within the town. The enemy knew Freeman's long-range fire capabilities and had mitigated the risk by marching outside of the howitzers' range fan. Edwards later wrote, "Aerial observers estimated that from two to three infantry divisions moved past CHIPYONG-NI during each twenty-four period."[30]

"The reason for the determined Chinese stand at SANGGOSONG and North of KOSAN was now apparent," the battalion commander concluded. "The Chinese had thrown at least one division into a defensive line to screen the movement of a group of their Armies from an assembly area east of SEOUL. . . . They were moving Eastward towards HOENGSONG [*sic*]."[31]

The next morning, February 9, 3rd Battalion resumed its clearance operation at 0815 hours. Most of the day's activity was on Hill 539, southeast of Sanggosong, and Hill 444 to its east. By 1430 hours, 3rd Battalion was in direct radio contact with 1st Battalion, 9th Infantry. Despite their close proximity, a large Chinese force remained between the two battalions. Moreover, the Chinese were fighting hard for both hills.

As a result, General Ruffner issued a new order over the regimental command net, instructing that "if increased resistance develops in vicinity of Hill 444 and objective area [Hill 539], CP-9th Infantry may be single over all commander of units engaged. This will be done by division order only." All of the commanders listening in on the net knew what that meant. If Kane and his counterpart could not link up before sundown, then Col. Edwin J. Messinger, the commander of the 9th Infantry Regiment, would assume control of 3rd Battalion until the clearance operation was complete.

By 1930, Ruffner informed Colonel Kane that he was temporarily under the control of the 9th Infantry Regiment. Kane passed the news along to Colonel Freeman. For Edwards and the other commanders in the 23rd, this meant their battalions would have to hold down a larger portion of the perimeter until 3rd Battalion returned. No one liked the circumstances, but they did not have much of a choice in the matter. They had to wait until Kane and his men returned.[32]

February 10 was more of the same for 3rd Battalion and the 9th Infantry Regiment. All day long, the U.N. soldiers battled the Chinese on Hill 444. Even after repeated artillery and airstrikes, the summit remained under enemy control. By 2035 hours, General Ruffner authorized the return of 3rd Battalion to the 23rd Infantry Regiment at the conclusion of the operation. The ever-growing number of Chinese forces moving from west to east, toward Hoengseong, had caused concern among the division staff. Ruffner did not want to leave Freeman's regiment undermanned and alone in enemy territory.[33]

FRIDAY, FEBRUARY 9: 3RD PLATOON, G COMPANY, 23RD INFANTRY REGIMENT, SOUTH OF CHIPYONG-NI

While the 3rd Battalion and the 9th Infantry Regiment tried and failed to rendezvous, the Tomahawks continued to improve their fighting positions as reinforcements arrived. On February 9, Baker Battery from the 503rd Field Artillery pulled in behind G Company. Because of the tight perimeter, Colonel Freeman determined that the southwest corner of the regimental area was the only spot for the big guns. As a result, Lieutenant Heath had to push out G Company's line to accommodate the battery of six towed 155mm howitzers with all of their accompanying trucks and other vehicles.[34]

Realizing he would have to adjust his section of the perimeter, Colonel Edwards, Heath's commander, examined the ground and decided the best place for Heath's company was along another low ridge, roughly three hundred meters south of the original one. In front of the new hill was open terrain that provided several hundred meters of grazing fire for most of the company. However, the new location also forced Heath to deploy all of his platoons along the perimeter to assure no gaps between his command, the French Battalion to his right, and Fox Company to his left. He was no longer able to hold assets back.

That was not the only problem with the new battle position. According to Colonel Edwards:

> 2nd Battalion was only issued enough wire to put up a double-apron fence in front of about one-half of the Battalion's MLR. Since Company G was digging its new foxholes, because of the extension of the perimeter in its area, and since . . . [I] considered the Company F sector and the West two platoon areas of Company E as the most vulnerable areas, the wire was issued to Company E and Company F. More wire was ordered but never arrived thus leaving Company G's sector without any wire except for a small section of about one hundred feet on SCHMITT HILL adjacent to the road. [35]

In a postwar interview, McGee recalled the new platoon position and the hill that later bore his name. "It was not a very big hill," he said. "It was kind of sloping. The left of the hill was rather steep, going toward the foot of hill 397; it wasn't a good position to defend. In fact, the whole thing was not a good position because of that 397. We had orders to dig in and prepare a two-man foxhole, which we did."

By this time, 3rd Platoon had received most of its replacements and was at full strength with forty men. McGee estimated that his platoon frontage was somewhere between 150–200 meters. He had an adequate number of soldiers with which to defend his sector. With Lieutenant Heath's permission, the platoon leader ordered his men to dig their fox-holes along the military crest of the hill.

Even though his battalion commander, Colonel Edwards, had ordered that the foxholes have overhead cover, McGee soon realized he had a problem. "We did not have anything to build cover with," he later said, "and we didn't have the time to go out and get it. The only cover I had on my hole was four little round sticks that we drove into the ground and attached a stick across each corner from corner to corner over the top of the hole and covered it with straw and limbs and our panchos [sic]. All that was for was to keep the snow out, but it wouldn't stop any type of fire."

Despite the decent frontage, the platoon leader wanted no gaps in the line. Therefore, he placed all three of his rifle squads on the main line of resistance. "I just spaced them out to try to cover all the ground we had to cover," McGee explained. "Some of them were six–eight yards between holes; some were ten–fifteen yards between holes, depending on the ground." By placing all his units on the line, he had no reserve.

McGee set his one crew-served machine gun up on the east side of his platoon battle position so that it would interlock with 2nd Platoon's machine gun farther east down the main line. As a result, the lieutenant did not like its field of fire in front of his own platoon. "There was a crop between hill 397 and the machine gun position, which the Chinese could use to crawl in and get closer to the gun," he explained. "There was also a cave right in front of the gun which they [Chinese] used."

The most troublesome spot in front of 3rd Platoon was the creek bed. From the west side of George Company, the stream hugged the road that led from Masan to Chipyong-ni. As it neared 1st Platoon's position, it dog-legged east until it reached McGee's 3rd Platoon. At that point, it turned north again and snuck toward the center of 3rd Platoon's position. When he first saw the stream, McGee knew it would provide defilade for the Chinese, and thus it was a likely infiltration route. "They [Chinese] could crawl out from there and on up into our position," he later remarked. He was right, but without more wire, he could not block it.

To cover the dead space, McGee wanted preplanned artillery concentrations on that spot. His attached forward observer was Harley Wilburn, who had survived his prior ordeal with the French at the Twin Tunnels. Wilburn recalled planning the mortar concentrations in front of G Company's positions. "A couple of my concentrations were in ravines that were coming down out of the biggest hill on the left hand side of the 3rd Platoon area," he later remarked, "and I laid a concentration in that ravine as it come [sic] down into the flat area of the hill and approached our positions."[36]

McGee had sound-powered telephones between the platoon command post and each of the squads, and a regular telephone linked his platoon command post with the company command post. According to the Carolina native, the signalmen had laid the communication wire on the surface. The open wire would come back to haunt McGee and his platoon later when the Chinese attacked the night of the fourteenth.

For command and control, McGee dug his own foxhole in the center of his line, while Sergeant Kluttz hollowed out a dirt house just to the west of his platoon leader. Several hundred meters behind 1st Platoon was Heath's command post in an abandoned house. To the east of Heath's headquarters were George Company's three 60mm mortars; to the west were the six guns of Baker Battery, 503rd Field Artillery. Like all defenders, McGee wished he had more wire, trip flares, and mines. Alas, he would not receive any more from supply.[37]

FEBRUARY 10–11:
G2 SECTIONS THROUGHOUT CENTRAL KOREA

Luckily for McGee's 3rd Platoon and the rest of George Company, February 9 and 10 passed without incident. However, events were spiraling out of control elsewhere. On February 10, the division sent a report to the 23rd Infantry's S2 section at 1030 hours. The news was not good. An aerial observer had spotted a "large number of CCF [Communist Chinese Forces] vicinity of Haengso-Ri." The analysts of the 23rd Infantry's S2 shop looked at a map and placed a pin on it to mark the location. By air, it was approximately eleven kilometers northeast of Chipyong-ni. Division had more news. According to the same observer, he saw 1,200 horses pulling numerous mortar tubes. The Chinese mission was "to envelop Chipyong-ni," he said.

As the day progressed, it got worse. At 2115 hours, Division reported that U.S. forces had repatriated forty-two U.N. prisoners whom the Chinese had released as part of a propaganda operation to sow dissent among the U.N. ranks. These same freed men reported seeing a battalion of Chinese forces the night of February 9–10. In addition, they said the CPVF units were using pack animals to help move the heavy equipment. When pressed, the soldiers claimed that the Chinese numbered around 5,000 to 8,000 men. Even more disturbing, they reported seeing the column marching "along a trail north of Sinchon." The analysts did not like the news because Sinchon was southeast of the 23rd Infantry's location. In short, the Chinese were now behind them.[38]

At 2100 hours that evening, the intelligence analysts at X Corps began to appreciate the danger they were facing. Gone was the bravado. The Chinese were not retreating—they were doing the opposite. "East of Chipyong-ni, an estimated enemy battalion not only made full use of the rugged terrain but added a minefield as well in a desperate effort to restrain the advance of elements of the 2nd US Division," the G2, Colonel Polk, wrote in the nightly summary. "This determined stand by an estimated enemy battalion appears to have the purpose of covering the concentration of several thousand troops who have been assembling for several days in the Piryong-ni area northeast of Chipyong-ni."

Even more worrisome was the information from a X Corps spy. Much of his reporting corroborated what the aerial observers had seen over the last forty-eight hours. The spy claimed that, as of February 7, the CPVF had massed over 2,000 men at Piryong-ni and more than 12,000 at Haengoso-ri. Both were less than a day's march from Chipyong-ni. At that point, U.N. forces had captured only one Chinese soldier, so it was difficult to determine which CPVF units were in the area. Regardless, analysts estimated that the communists had several armies within striking distances, and that the CPVF armies were roughly the same size as U.S. corps.

For Polk, the numerous sightings spelled trouble. "Recent agent reports and air sightings during the period have shown a large enemy build-up, presumed to be CCF, in the area northeast of Chipyong-ni, where elements of the 42nd CCF Corps have been previously identified," he concluded at the end of the nightly report. "The increasing build-up is believed to be an additional CCF Corps, possibly the 39th or 40th, arriving in the area to assist the 42nd CCF Corps in offensive action against X Corps." Polk labeled the Chinese units "corps," even though the communists themselves called them "armies."

The G2 finally realized that the Chinese forces now had the potential "to drive southeast past Chipyong-ni through the gap between the 23rd Infantry Regiment and elements of the 8th ROK Division. The enemy then has the capability of either turning southwest and enveloping the Chipyong-ni salient, or of continuing to the southeast to strike at Wonju."[39]

The next day, February 11, the news only worsened. An aerial observer reported seeing 300 to 400 enemy soldiers marching in column, nearly twenty kilometers northeast of Chipyong-ni. According to the pilot, they were heading east. Near the enemy column, the pilot also spotted an enemy mortar system. This troop sighting was the farthest east of all the other observations.[40] To an untrained eye, it would seem that Chipyong-ni was safe, but the enemy was planning a much wider envelopment. The two ROK divisions north of Wonju, several kilometers east of the 23rd Infantry, were the target. After the Twin Tunnels defeat, Commissar Peng Dehuai assessed that the 8th, 3rd, and 5th ROK Divisions were easy pickings compared to the 23rd Infantry. He was right.

That night, at 2200 hours, 1st Ranger Company raided a Chinese camp west of Chipyong-ni, near the town of Hwajeon-ri and Hill 583. Freeman authorized the raid because he knew it was tailor-made for the elite soldiers. They were eager to do it and wanted to show off their skills. Moreover, Freeman and the rest of X Corps needed Chinese prisoners. Other than one CPVF prisoner from the 66th Army, the G2 Section had no Chinese soldiers under interrogation. It was imperative for the raid to bring back live communists.

Unfortunately, the raid was a failure. Almost immediately, the Chinese discovered the infiltrating Rangers and opened fire. Worse, the Rangers quickly realized they had attacked an entire battalion. As a result, they withdrew without capturing a single Chinese soldier. Fortunately, they sustained only six casualties. Ironically, one of those killed was a French reporter who wanted to see some action but wanted to do so during a "safe" mission.

According to Colonel Edwards, the minor disaster chipped away at the Rangers' reputation among the regular infantry. "After this episode, particularly the abandonment of the wounded, the stock of the Rangers sank lower than ever among the combat infantrymen of the 23rd Infantry," he later wrote.[41]

As the Rangers hurried back to Chipyong-ni, safely tucked away behind friendly lines was Colonel Polk. That night, he looked over the daily intelligence summary for X Corps. The first few heady days of Operation Roundup were a distant memory. The Chinese were poised for a massive counterstroke. Polk predicted that the Chinese would likely "attack to the southeast through the Chipyong-ni–Hoengsong [sic] area with elements of the 42nd CCF Corps reinforced by one additional CCF Corps, in order to seize the Wonju road center, while at the same time employing elements of the 66th CCF Corps in a holding attack south and east of Hongchon [*sic*]." Polk had listed three other possible courses of action for the Chinese; however, he believed the most likely was the operation to seize Wonju and isolate Chipyong-ni.[42] This time, he was right. He was also too late.

FEBRUARY 11–12: AREA OF OPERATIONS, X CORPS, NORTH OF HOENGSEONG

Three ROK divisions faced the Chinese offensive north of Hoengong. From west to east, they were the 8th ROK, the 3rd ROK, and the 5th ROK Infantry Divisions. The 8th ROK Division was the most vulnerable, occupying a slight salient with all of three of its regiments on the main line of resistance. In the west was the 16th ROK Infantry, while the center was held by the 10th ROK Infantry. Positioned along the eastern sector was the 21st ROK Infantry. In the next twenty-four hours, the CPVF would destroy all three.

At 2030 hours, the predicted Chinese offensive commenced. Almost immediately, things began to unravel for the U.N. defenders. The CPVF 198th Division, part of the 66th Army, hit the 21st ROK Infantry Regiment with two regiments, while its third regiment bypassed the beleaguered ROK unit to the east. Meanwhile, the CPVF 120th Division, 42nd Army, bypassed the 10th ROK Infantry Regiment from the west and subsequently established blocking positions behind the 10th and 21st ROK Infantry Regiments. This denied the ROK units the ability to withdraw to the east. Regiments from the CPVF 117th Division, 39th Army, infiltrated past the 16th ROK Infantry Regiment and occupied blocking positions north of Hoengseong, thereby slipping in behind the ROK 21st and 10th Infantry Regiments, trapping them both and preventing them from retreating southward.[43]

The impact was immediate. By midnight, the 21st and 16th ROK Infantry Regiments were gone. They had lasted less than three hours. The 8th ROK Division had ceased to be an effective fighting force. Meanwhile, the remaining U.S. forces in the area—specifically 3rd

Battalion, 38th Infantry—were fighting a losing battle against over-whelming Chinese forces near the village of Saemal.

By the morning of February 12, it was clear to all that Almond's Operation Roundup was a failure. In fact, Almond's insistence on push-ing north, regardless of his flanks, had resulted in the overextension of his own command. This led to huge gaps between his units, which the CPVF exploited by infiltrating entire battalions behind U.N. lines. Once again, the U.N. was retreating and the communists were reaping the benefits of Almond's recklessness.[44]

At 2000 hours on February 12, Almond issued Operations Instruc-tion 104. In accordance with the new order, the corps commander wanted all of his units to withdraw and consolidate along the Chipyong-ni–Wonju–Saemal–Ungol line. Fortunately, the 3rd and 5th ROK Infantry Divisions, though under pressure, continued to fight. However, the 8th ROK Division had disintegrated, and Almond ordered its rem-nants to fall back to Chupo-ri. Ostensibly, Almond had selected the divi-sion to become the corps reserve, but the 8th ROK was a division in name only.

The communists' next target was the 2nd Infantry Division. General Ruffner sensed his division was next and pulled back his two regimental combat teams and the 187th Airborne Regiment to occupy the Yoju–Wonju line. However, while the 9th Infantry withdrew toward Yoju and the 38th Infantry and 187th Airborne consolidated at Wonju, the Tomahawks remained at Chipyong-ni.[45]

MONDAY, FEBRUARY 12, 0200–1610 HOURS: HEADQUARTERS, 23RD INFANTRY REGIMENT, CHIPYONG-NI

The soldiers operating the radios inside the tactical operations center learned about the Chinese offensive six hours after it began. At 0200 hours, division radio operators ordered the 23rd Infantry to postpone its battalion-sized reconnaissance to Hill 583. For the soldiers on radio watch, this was the first indicator that something was amiss.

Fifteen minutes later, the 37th Field Artillery headquarters chimed in over the division net and reported that the two ROK units directly to the east of the 2nd Infantry Division were under attack and withdrawing. For several minutes, the men probably wondered what that meant. At 0310 hours, division confirmed their fears.

The scratchy voice over the radio squawked, "Inspire, this is Ivanhoe [the division call sign; Inspire was the call sign for the 23rd Infantry]. Roadblock vicinity Zero—Five—Five—Three by estimated two hundred enemy." In response, several staff clerks hastily began to jot down the information while other soldiers plotted the incident on the operations map. The voice continued, "10th ROK command post has been under attack tonight . . . one thousand yards west of the enemy roadblock. Present status not known. Falling back One—Five—Zero—Zero yards."

The entire operations center was up and alert. At 0330 hours, division called in again, the voice over the radio listing the disasters as if calling a baseball game. "Divarty reports another roadblock by estimated enemy company located [at] Dog—Sugar—Zero—Two—Two—Five—Three—Four. The road has been blown as has been the road at the previously reported roadblock. No communication with the 10th and the 16th ROKs. 16th ROK command post believed to have been overrun. ROKs captured Chinese PWs. Early during the day they captured a PW from the 358th Regiment, 104th Division, 40th Army."

At 0545 hours, division reviewed the events of the last ten hours. None of it was good. "3rd Battalion, 38th Infantry being attacked from north and west," said the operator over the cracking static. He continued, "21st ROK coming down to the south hit a roadblock and are in a mess. Don't know the results. They have wounded. 21st ROK is falling back two thousand yards. 23rd ROK Regiment also falling back. . . . Higher headquarters putting out order to 9th Infantry to be prepare[d] on three hours' notice to assemble at Yoju. A similar order is given to the 38th Infantry to assemble at Wonju."[46]

The staff noticed that the division did not mention the 23rd Infantry Regiment, and many wondered why they did not receive a withdrawal order like the other regimental combat teams in the division. "Everybody expected to go up on the probe and pull back," Lt. Col. Frank Meszar, the regiment's executive officer, said later. "I started them digging in immediately when we got there."

Meszar thought it was a simple case of security. "If nothing happens," he later remarked, "so what? Let's be ready for anything." Now, with the looming possibility that the Chinese would soon surround and besiege their regiment, he was glad he had insisted on the defensive preparations.[47]

At 1010 hours, the 2nd Infantry Division's G2 section called down to the 23rd Infantry's S2 section and informed them that they had interrogated a prisoner, a deserter from an engineer battalion attached to the 116th Division. The interrogators learned that the division was part of the 39th Army and that it was now located only a few kilometers north of Chipyong-ni.

According to the prisoner, the division was near full strength, with over 12,000 soldiers. It also had an artillery regiment and a signal company in its task organization. The division's infantry battalions had ten mortars, three heavy machine guns, twenty-seven light machine guns, and nearly six hundred rounds of ammunition for each gun. Officers had told the deserter that the 116th Division was preparing for upcoming offensive operations. The interrogator believed the prisoner was exaggerating, but even so, the intelligence section could not completely discount the report. For the past week, aerial observers had called in numerous sightings of Chinese troops, moving in large formations, which corroborated the deserter's assertions. For the analysts at Chipyong-ni, it was another indicator that the CPVF were coming and wanted to annihilate the Tomahawk Regiment.[48]

Meanwhile, Captain Tyrrell's Fox Company reconnoitered the area hills west of Chipyong-ni. They rolled out on trucks at 1045 hours and debussed near the village of Okku, 5 kilometers southwest of Chipyong-ni. Like before, the three platoons headed toward the nearby hills and stayed off the roads. Within a few hours, soldiers from 2nd Platoon captured three civilians who claimed they saw numerous Chinese soldiers in the nearby villages of Uon and Chilsong. As if on cue, the platoon leader saw between thirty and fifty CPVF soldiers scurry from the west side of Uon, while another thirty to fifty Chinese scampered out of Chilsong. In response, the soldiers of F Company opened fire, scattering the enemy troops.

Later, at 1545 hours, F Company cleared the hamlet of Hwajon-ni, 2 kilometers north of Uon. There, the soldiers detained a group of military-aged males in civilian clothes. Edwards ordered Tyrrell to burn the village to deny the enemy from using it. Fox Company completed its clearance operation and returned to base. Under interrogation, the captured men later claimed the Chinese had a battalion to the northwest of Hill 583. The intelligence analysts knew the Chinese were closing in on Chipyong-ni from all directions.[49]

Unbeknownst to Freeman and the other officers in the 23rd Infantry, Generals Ruffner and Almond wanted to withdraw the regiment so that it could join the 9th Infantry near Yoju. Sometime on February 12, the corps commander sought permission from Eighth Army to pull back the Tomahawks. General Ridgway, however, had other ideas. After the Twin Tunnels victory, he had realized the 23rd Infantry was a unit that would stay and fight. He refused Almond's request and issued a direct order to the 23rd Infantry.[50]

At 1610 hours on February 12, the radio operators logged an important message from division. "Inspire 6, this is Ivanhoe 3," the voice began, "Our forces are executing a withdrawal except for [you]. [You] are to remain by order of Scotch [General Ridgway]."[51]

"Despite the ferocity of the fighting and the apparent determination of the enemy, I never had the slightest doubt over the outcome of this battle," Ridgway later wrote in his book, *The Korean War*. "Whether I was on the ground with the forward elements or flying over them for a more comprehensive picture, I felt confident they would hold."[52]

Colonel Edwards recalled a sergeant from George Company, who, after learning that the 23rd Infantry was staying put while the Chinese surrounded them, exclaimed, "Those stupid slant-eyed, yellow bastards! They don't realize it but they have just started to dig their own graves!"[53]

The Chinese soldiers marching toward Chipyong-ni from all directions probably did not care what the sergeant thought. Their mission was simple: destroy the Tomahawks—all of them. According to the X Corps G2, Colonel Polk, "The Chipyong-ni salient is a thorn in the side of the enemy, and it is expected that he will soon attempt to remove this irritation with the forces available to him in that immediate area."

Facing the one U.N. regiment at Chipyong-ni were elements from three Chinese armies. If the odds of a U.N. victory seemed long at the Twin Tunnels where Freeman had faced only one division, then at Chipyong-ni they were outside the ballpark.[54]

CHAPTER 6

Chipyong-ni: The First Night

"We had no place to go that you could not walk to in a few minutes.
The Regimental perimeter was not much bigger than the Pentagon."

—Capt. Albert Caswell Metts, M Company Commander

TUESDAY, FEBRUARY 13, 1951, 0900–2200 HOURS: AREA OF OPERATIONS, 23RD INFANTRY REGIMENT, CHIPYONG-NI

Ridgway's order to remain at Chipyong-ni galvanized many of the soldiers and officers, who knew that the Chinese attack was only hours away and began readying the perimeter for the impending battle. Colonel Freeman instructed his staff to arrange airdrops and air support for February 14. Fortunately, he already had planned for this possibility, and his soldiers had cleared an area for a makeshift airfield along the southwest side of the regimental perimeter. In addition, the colonel ordered Capt. William N. Payne, the Regimental Headquarters company commander, to establish an inner perimeter. Freeman had learned his lesson from the near-disaster at the Twin Tunnels and realized his regiment would need alternate battle positions in case the Chinese rendered the primary positions untenable.[1]

Meanwhile, the men continued to improve their foxholes while clearing fields of fire. To provide early warning, Freeman ordered the battalions to set up trip flares along the potential infiltration routes. "I remember getting the word that we were surrounded and to dig in deeper," recalled Peter F. Schutz, a soldier in A Company. "We also got some trip flares and were told to place them in front of our position. They were the first and only trip flares I remember setting out in Korea.

Sergeant [Tracy] Young had us place them about fifty feet or so in front of our position and install[ed] trip mines back to the foxhole so we could set them off as needed. I think we set out about six or seven at our position."[2]

The defenders had another ingenious weapon hidden among the rocks: buried in the ground were 50-gallon drums of gasoline (the military term for these obstacles was "fougasse"). According to Freeman, they "were emplaced in the earth as mortars, and pointed toward the natural avenues of approach. Several grenades were placed in the bottom and the drum was filled about one-third of the way with oil and gasoline."

Freeman explained how the soldiers used the devilish weapons: "As the leading waves of Chinese stormed down the hill the defenders pulled the wires and exploded the grenades and [sprayed] the enemy with a bath of fire. This was beautiful—but only a one-time weapon." Since the Chinese had encircled the regiment, Freeman's vehicles no longer needed their surplus fuel. As a result, the commander had an ample supply of ammunition for his fougasses.

"One thing we had plenty of and did not need was gasoline!" commented Captain Metts, commander of M Company, in a postwar letter. "We had no place to go that you could not walk to in a few minutes. The Regimental perimeter was not much bigger than the Pentagon. Further, cans of gas were air dropped every day along with ammunition, food and other supplies."[3]

While the men readied themselves, the division and the regiment continued to send out ground and air patrols to find the Chinese. They were not far from the Tomahawks. At 0900 hours, an air observer spotted 1,000 enemy soldiers 15 kilometers to the southeast of Chipyong-ni. According to the pilot, they were moving south. Two hours later, F4U Corsairs plastered the enemy column with napalm. Several minutes after the strike, the air observer reported that the close air support had halted the column.[4]

At 1200 hours, the 23rd Infantry's S2 section received a report from a civilian who told a roving reconnaissance patrol that the Chinese had established a blocking position 10 kilometers south of the 23rd Infantry, near the villages of Sangsok and Sŏhwohyŏn. After the analyst logged the report, he looked at the map to find the location and noticed how perilous the situation was for his regiment. The enemy forces had hidden

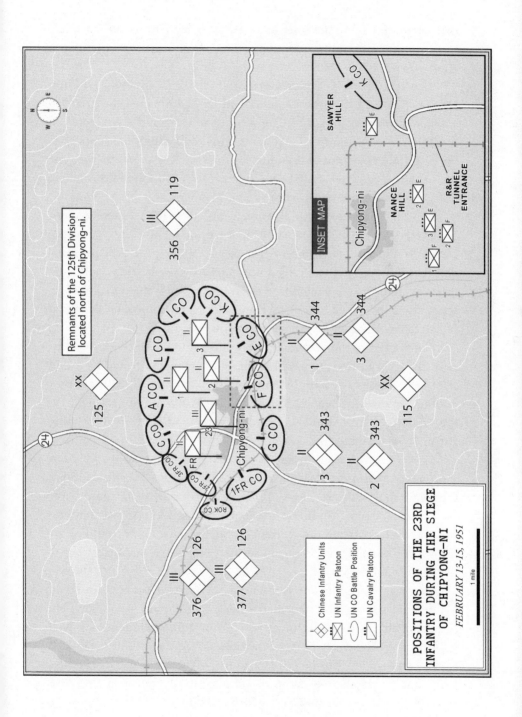

Remnants of the 125th Division located north of Chipyong-ni.

INSET MAP

SAWYER HILL   K CO

R&R TUNNEL ENTRANCE

NANCE HILL

Chipyong-ni

POSITIONS OF THE 23RD INFANTRY DURING THE SIEGE OF CHIPYONG-NI
FEBRUARY 13-15, 1951

1 mile

Chinese Infantry Units
UN Infantry Platoon
UN CO Battle Position
UN Cavalry Platoon

I CO   L CO   A CO   C CO
K CO   E CO   F CO   G CO
3FR CO   2FR CO   1FR CO   ROK CO
FR   23

Chipyong-ni

119   356   III
125   xx
126   376   III
126   377   III
115   XX
344   1   II
344   3   II
343   3   II
343   2   II

their ambushes along the sides of a narrow valley, cutting off the single east–west road between Chipyong-ni and Wonju. It was a textbook chokepoint.[5]

The reconnaissance patrol was from the 2nd Infantry Division Reconnaissance Company. General Ruffner had directed the patrol to advance north from Iho-ri to Chipyong-ni and screen the area between the 23rd and 9th Infantry Regiments. Providing additional support to the patrol was L Company from the 9th Infantry Regiment. By the time the analysts logged the civilian's report, the patrol had found the Chinese near the purported location, confirming the story.

At 1255 hours, the patrol fired their mortars at the Chinese soldiers. Within seconds, several shells landed in the troop formations, causing the enemy to disperse. The soldiers in the patrol watched the Chinese abandon their covered and concealed positions. As a result, they could estimate the number of enemy infantry. Ten minutes after the initial barrage, they radioed back to division and the 23rd Infantry, informing them that 300 to 400 communists were southeast of Chipyong-ni.[6]

For the rest of the afternoon, the scouts battled it out with the Chinese. By 1630 hours, the patrol requested permission to fall back and rejoin the division before the communist battalions wiped them out. Ruffner granted the request. It was clear to Ruffner and Freeman that the Chinese were behind the 23rd Infantry and ready to block any attempt to relieve the Tomahawks.[7]

Closer to Chipyong-ni, each of the infantry battalions sent out short-range patrols to clear the surrounding hilltops. Freeman limited the forays to 5,000 yards beyond the perimeter so that he could cover the advancing men with his own indirect fire assets in case they ran into trouble. By late afternoon, an Item Company patrol reported to regiment that someone was blaring bugles near Hill 506, 2 kilometers east of the town.[8]

Late that afternoon, one patrol from 1st Battalion brought back two Chinese prisoners, and Freeman interrogated them personally. He recalled that the two detainees were "not too intelligent nor well informed." However, after several minutes, the captured soldiers revealed to the commander that the CPVF had five divisions in the area around Chipyong-ni. If all five divisions simultaneously attacked the 23rd Infantry, the Chinese would have a 15:1 advantage.[9]

At 1806 hours, the sun disappeared behind Hill 248. Eighty minutes later, division headquarters informed the Tomahawk radio operators that a Firefly, a modified C-47 Skytrain, would drop flares throughout the night to provide illumination for the close air support missions over the next few hours. As the plane lumbered over the target, the crew would release the flares, which would float down to the earth, marking a potential aiming point for follow-on aircraft. The Air Force, Marine, or Navy fighter-bombers could see the flares, swoop down, and destroy the target. It was an effective technique, and some C-47s carried up to 400 flares in a single mission.[10]

However, some of the flares were in the east. This was a problem because the Firefly was loitering over the western side of the perimeter. At 2110 hours, 3rd Battalion reported seeing two flares appear to the southeast in front of Easy Company. Five minutes later, 2nd Battalion confirmed the nocturnal activity, informing regiment that its observers spotted flares emanating from Hill 319 to the southeast of Chipyong-ni. At 2150 hours, G Company soldiers claimed they saw flares rocketing into the sky with a launch point west of them and in front of the French Battalion.

Ten minutes passed. The next report came from 3rd Battalion. Soldiers from Item and Love Companies both claimed they saw flares to the northeast. For the officers and staff in the regimental command post, the sudden flare activity was an indicator of an impending attack. They were right.[11]

FEBRUARY 13, EARLY EVENING: MACHINE-GUN TEAM, H COMPANY, 23RD INFANTRY REGIMENT (ATTACHED TO E COMPANY), ALONG NANCE HILL

"I'm in a machine gun bunker and it is cold," wrote Seymour "Hoppy" Harris. "Brutally cold. It must be at least -10, but seems colder. There is not a cloud in the sky, and if you walk around the snow creaks under your feet. This is good, for if it creaks under our feet, it creaks under theirs [the Chinese]."

Harris was a replacement, and this was his first night with his new unit. He had arrived earlier on February 13 on the last convoy into

Chipyong-ni. In fact, when he hopped off the back of the truck, other soldiers inquired how he had made it through the Chinese cordon.

"If we're not supposed to be able to get out of here, how come you people got up here?" someone asked him. Harris did not have an answer.

Since he was new, squad leader Cpl. Stewart W. O'Shell teamed him up with the company reject. "And the guy in my bunker with me, yeah, he can speak English," Harris wrote in a letter, describing his comrade. "Loud and clear. I actually begin to believe he invented bitching." The young replacement wondered how he was going to last the night. From the moment he slipped into the hole, his companion started yapping. "I am already fucked up like a Chinese Fire Drill and listening to this guy's constant bitching nearly drives me nuts. He doesn't want to be here. . . . He's cold. He's sick of eating C-rations. The Chinks are coming in here to murder us all. Truman is a bastard, and his administration is worse than that."

That first night, Harris was on guard duty. Since he was new, he was not on a machine gun, but rather just a rifleman, providing security for the crew-served weapons. As such, he was armed with only a carbine. His machine-gun team was attached to 3rd Platoon, Easy Company's battle position, overlooking a draw that originated on Hill 397. "The mouth of the draw is about fifty yards away and has a barbed wire entanglement covering its mouth," wrote Harris. "It is so moonlit that I can see for over one thousand yards to the foot of a high hill known as Hill 397. If the Chinese come, this is supposed to be the most likely avenue of approach. I cannot but help wondering how anyone could be that stupid. To come down a draw, with no cover, not over fifty yards wide, and have to chogie [sic] over one thousand yards to get to us. To me it seems the most insane thing I'd ever heard of."

When he told his squad leader what he thought, the corporal replied, "These are not ordinary people we are dealing with." Satisfied with the answer, Harris sank back into his hole and scanned his sector for the enemy. He did not have long to wait.[12]

FEBRUARY 13, 2207–2210 HOURS: COMMAND POST, D COMPANY, 23RD INFANTRY REGIMENT, CHIPYONG-NI

Capt. Ansil L. Walker stepped out of the hut that served as his command post. He felt good. His men had collected over 1,000 rounds for the

This photo of Gen. Paul L. Freeman, Jr., was taken when he was the commander of the 2nd Infantry Division, several years after Chipyong-ni. Note the 2nd Infantry Division insignia on both shoulders. A unit patch on his right shoulder signifies that he served with the 2nd Infantry Division on a combat deployment. U.S. ARMY HERITAGE AND EDUCATION CENTER, PAUL L. FREEMAN, JR. COLLECTION

Lt. Gen. Matthew B. Ridgway (right), commander of the U.S. Eighth Army, with Lt. Col. Ralph Monclar (left), commander of the French Battalion, on March 1, 1951. Ridgway was there to present a battle streamer to Monclar's French Battalion after it distinguished itself at the battles of Chipyong-ni and the Twin Tunnels. REAL WAR PHOTOS

Another photo of Lieutenant Colonel Monclar (wearing the beret) and Lieutenant General Ridgway at the presentation of the battle streamer. REAL WAR PHOTOS

Col. Marcel G. Crombez, commander of the 5th Cavalry Regiment. His unit relieved the 23rd Infantry Regiment on February 15, 1951, after running a gauntlet of several Chinese Army units. This photo was taken on March 26, 1951. U.S. ARMY SIGNAL CORPS

Lt. Col. James W. Edwards (second from right, wearing a sweater). His 2nd Battalion was hit hard on the night of February 14–15, 1951. U.S. ARMY HERITAGE AND EDUCATION CENTER, PAUL L. FREEMAN, JR. COLLECTION

Pvt. Harley Wilburn, a forward observer. After the Battle of the Twin Tunnels, Wilburn found himself attached to 3rd Platoon, G Company. On the night of February 14–15, 1951, his platoon was the focal point of the main Chinese attack at Chipyong-ni. HARLEY WILBURN FAMILY

Private Wilburn stands next to an M2 4.2-inch mortar. His call-for-fire missions were instrumental in the Battle of the Twin Tunnels, where he called for fire on his own position. He was working with the 3rd Company of the attached French Battalion at the time. HARLEY WILBURN FAMILY

Sgt. Martin Lee, 2nd Platoon, Easy Company. His platoon fought the Chinese Army to a standstill outside a railway tunnel southeast of Chipyong-ni. This photo was taken when Lee was a sergeant in the 4th Infantry Division, several years after the war. MARTIN LEE FAMILY

First Lt. Kingston Montgomery Winget, a platoon leader in C Company, 23rd Infantry Regiment. His uniform is typical of what the soldiers wore at Chipyong-ni. He is also wearing a 1943 pile cap; the army eventually replaced this style with the M1951 pile cap, which was better suited for Korea's climate. LT. COL. KINGSTON WINGET

First Lieutenant Winget sharing some hot coffee with another soldier. LT. COL. KINGSTON WINGET

An M16 half-track from B Battery, 82nd Antiaircraft Artillery Automatic Weapons Battalion, mounting four .50-caliber machine guns on a rotating turret. B Battery used these weapons at Chipyong-ni with deadly effect against the Chinese infantry. REAL WAR PHOTOS

Soldiers from the 2nd Infantry Division's reconnaissance company ride in an M39 armored utility vehicle, which came into service at the end of World War II and used the same chassis as the M18 Hellcat tank destroyer. This photo was taken on February 10, 1951. REAL WAR PHOTOS

French officers and soldiers manning a .50-caliber machine gun at Chipyong-ni, February 5, 1951. REAL WAR PHOTOS

Colonel Freeman (second from left, wearing a sweater) questions a wounded Chinese soldier on February 13, 1951. Unlike many officers, Freeman was fluent in Mandarin Chinese, thanks to his assignments to China in the 1930s and 1940s. U.S. ARMY HERITAGE AND EDUCATION CENTER, JAMES W. EDWARDS COLLECTION

Another shot of 1st Lieutenant Winget, C Company, 23rd Infantry Regiment. LT. COL. KINGSTON WINGET

This photo of Chipyong-ni was taken around the time of the battle. The photographer was probably north of the town, near the battle position of 3rd Platoon, C Company, and likely facing south toward the town. LT. COL. KINGSTON WINGET

The mountains northwest of Chipyong-ni. The photographer was standing near the battle position of 3rd Platoon, C Company. Colonel Freeman positioned his forces on the hills around Chipyong-ni, but he did not have enough combat power to occupy the higher mountains that surrounded the town on all sides. Thus, the Chinese had excellent observation on the U.N. positions. LT. COL. KINGSTON WINGET

Another view of the mountains, shot from the same position. LT. COL. KINGSTON WINGET

C Company's battle position, as seen from the vantage point of the Chinese. Many of the U.N. positions were located on hills, which made an assault even more difficult for the Chinese attackers. LT. COL. KINGSTON WINGET

First Lieutenant Winget, 3rd Platoon, C Company, carries a Thompson sub-machine gun. According to Winget, the soldiers were not fond of the Thompson because it had a large muzzle flash when fired, thereby exposing the soldier's position at night. LT. COL. KINGSTON WINGET

G Company's rear area. North is to the right. In the foreground, denoted by the 1, is the location of G Company's command post. The 3 represents the location of B Battery, 503rd Field Artillery, and the 4 denotes the location of the B Battery squad tent. This photo was taken several months after the battle. U.S. ARMY SIGNAL CORPS

The battle position of 2nd Platoon, G Company, at Chipyong-ni. The 5 denotes the foxholes of the main line of resistance, and the 6 represents F Company's battle position in the distance. The directional arrow is pointing east. This photo was taken several months after the battle. U.S. ARMY SIGNAL CORPS

This photo was taken from Cpl. Eugene L. Ottesen's machine-gun position, looking southwest. Ottesen was instrumental in the defense of 3rd Platoon, G Company, on the night of February 14–15. The 9 denotes the direction of the Chinese attack on his foxhole. U.S. ARMY SIGNAL CORPS

The road to Koksu-ri, looking south. To the left would have been the location of 1st Platoon, G Company, and Schmitt Hill. The 18 denotes a machine-gun position, and the 19 marks the location of the minefield that disrupted Colonel Edwards's tank platoon on the afternoon of February 15. The 20 denotes a strand of barbed wire in the distance. U.S. ARMY SIGNAL CORPS

The battle position of 1st Platoon, G Company (Schmitt Hill), looking north from the perspective of the Chinese. The 16 denotes the location of hasty foxholes the Chinese dug after they captured the hill. The 17 represents the location of 1st Platoon's main line of resistance. To defend the captured hill, the Chinese soldiers used a reverse-slope defense, which bedeviled Colonel Edwards's counterattacks for several hours. U.S. ARMY SIGNAL CORPS

The village of Masan, looking east at the saddle that connected Hill 397 to G Company's battle position. The 7 denotes the battle position of 3rd Platoon, G Company, while the 8 represents the direction of the Chinese attacks. U.S. ARMY SIGNAL CORPS

Another photo of the road to Koksu-ri, looking south. The 10 denotes the direction of the Chinese withdrawal on the late afternoon of February 15, 1951. The 11 marks a culvert, and the 12 shows the route Task Force Crombez used to relieve the 23rd Infantry. The 13 denotes the creek bed, which, since it was dead space, the Chinese used to infiltrate toward the G Company lines. U.S. ARMY SIGNAL CORPS

A clump of trees overlooking the dry creek bed that caused so many problems for 3rd Platoon, G Company. The 14 in the center marks a makeshift shelter the Chinese dug to protect themselves from mortar fire. The 15 denotes dead space inside the creek bed. U.S. ARMY SIGNAL CORPS

A C-119 Flying Boxcar over Chipyong-ni. With the Chinese surrounding it, the only way the 23rd Infantry could receive supplies was through air drops. The standard C-119 could carry over 20,000 pounds of supplies. LT. COL. KINGSTON WINGET

Airdropped supplies after they landed inside the U.N. perimeter. Many of the soldiers complained that the shock of the landing damaged much of the ammunition inside the crates, which later caused weapons like 2nd Lt. Paul McGee's BAR to jam. REAL WAR PHOTOS

The road north into Koksu-ri, from the perspective of the soldiers of Task Force Crombez as they braved the gauntlet to reach the 23rd Infantry at Chipyong-ni. U.S. ARMY SIGNAL CORPS

Chinese dead in front of C Company's battle position after the Battle of Chipyong-ni. LT. COL. KINGSTON WINGET

Chinese dead in front of C Company's battle position after the Battle of Chipyong-ni. LT. COL. KINGSTON WINGET

More Chinese dead. This photo was taken on February 17, 1951, two days after the battle. The Chinese suffered thousands of casualties but failed to destroy the 23rd Infantry. REAL WAR PHOTOS

These photographs taken by Pvt. Harley Wilburn show Chinese dead in front of G Company's battle position. Many of the bodies are scorched from the napalm dropped from fighter-bombers by the U.N. forces. HARLEY WILBURN FAMILY

According to Private Wilburn, the Chinese mined the roads as they withdrew. This vehicle from the regimental mortar company hit one of the mines. One soldier lies dead nearby, covered by a poncho. HARLEY WILBURN FAMILY

Another wrecked truck that hit a mine laid by the withdrawing Chinese. HARLEY WILBURN FAMILY

The USS *General M. C. Meigs*, a fast troop transport that made several trips back and forth from Korea during the war. Private Wilburn was a passenger on the *Meigs*. HARLEY WILBURN FAMILY

Long after the Korean War, the officers of the 23rd Infantry would gather at reunions to remember their fallen comrades. This photo was taken on June 12, 1970, at the Infantry Ball. In the center is Gen. Paul Freeman. To his right is Col. Perry Sager, 2nd Battalion's S3 at the time of the Battle of Chipyong-ni. On the far right is Ansil L. Walker, commander of D Company at Chipyong-ni. U.S. ARMY HERITAGE AND EDUCATION CENTER, PAUL L. FREEMAN, JR. COLLECTION

Standing on Schmitt Hill in 2014, looking south toward Koksu-ri. The road is the same one Task Force Crombez used to reach Chipyong-ni. AUTHOR'S COLLECTION

Standing on Schmitt Hill in 2014, looking down the slope that became the killing ground for G Company's machine-gun teams. After the battle, hundreds of Chinese corpses littered the battlefield. AUTHOR'S COLLECTION

Another shot taken while standing on Schmitt Hill in 2014, looking south toward Koksu-ri. The road is the same one Task Force Crombez used to reach Chipyong-ni. AUTHOR'S COLLECTION

A foxhole near the old G Company positions, seen in 2014. Unfortunately, groups have conducted reenactments of the battle and dug their own foxholes on location. As a result, it is hard to distinguish what is an actual foxhole from the Korean War and what is a facsimile. AUTHOR'S COLLECTION

Hill 397, which overlooks all of Chipyong-ni, photographed in 2014 from near the G Company positions. The Chinese occupied Hill 397 before the battle, and it is easy to see how they had excellent observation of 3rd Platoon and the rest of G Company. AUTHOR'S COLLECTION

The highway to Koksu-ri. The notch in the distance is the location where the Chinese defenders ambushed the lead tanks that were part of Task Force Crombez, using captured American 3.5-inch bazookas. In one instance, they knocked out an American M46 heavy tank. AUTHOR'S COLLECTION

The village of Masan in 2014, from the perspective of the Chinese attackers. To the left is Schmitt Hill. To the right is McGee Hill, the location of 3rd Platoon, G Company, under the command of 2nd Lt. Paul J. McGee. AUTHOR'S COLLECTION

Another photo of McGee Hill, seen on the left. To the right is the saddle that connects McGee Hill to Hill 397 (behind and to the right of the photographer). AUTHOR'S COLLECTION

mortars, and his gunners had stockpiled 50,000 rounds of linked ammunition for the machine guns. Since his company was the weapons company for 1st Battalion, Major Russell, its commander, had divvied up Walker's heavy machines between A and C Companies, which were manning the northern sector of the regimental perimeter.

The Dog Company commander then described what happened next:

> Dim outlines of three bony cows appeared in front of Captain Glenn MacGuyer's A Company. As they tripped over a couple of flares and detonated an anti-personnel mine, an order was given to destroy them. No reason was given; none was needed, because the Chinese tactic of herding a few cows and running them into front-line areas was well-known. By so doing, the Chinese hoped that defenders would become trigger-happy, and disclose front-line positions. In this instance, a single gun obeyed the order.[13]

Realizing the ruse had failed, the Chinese forces opened up with everything they had at the American lines. At 2207 hours, 1st Platoon, Charlie Company, was the first to report contact. At 2210, the French Battalion, 1st, and then 2nd Battalion radioed that they also were under attack. In the sky, red and green flares arced high into the air like a fireworks show while bugles blared, adding to the percussion of chugging machine-gun fire and thumping mortars.

Walker looked north. As he later wrote, "A number of flares were tripped in front of A and C Companies as running Chinese stumbled over the installed wires, lighting the rice paddies and sloping hills." Within seconds, his machine gunners opened fire and bodies started to fall. Walker then watched the "shadowy figures as they tried to escape the illumination." It was carnage everywhere.[14]

Walker knew he had to return to his command post to control his company. "Suddenly the wild whistle of a single 120mm mortar shell sounded directly overhead," he wrote. "[SFC Joseph F.] Loy and I dived for the command post's trench, and it landed with a mighty ker-whomp on an unoccupied hut about thirty feet away. Rocks, frozen clods of dirt and shell fragments rained down as the hut collapsed."[15]

"Outta here!" a voice shouted from inside the D Company command post. Seconds later, First Sergeant Bockerich dived into a nearby hole; 1st Lt. Wilbert F. Klein soon followed him, carrying the company switchboard, its wires trailing behind him. It looked like he was dragging an open box of Christmas tree lights.

SFC Joseph F. Loy was with Captain Walker. When he saw Klein dive into the slit trench, Loy joined him and went to work reattaching the wires to the company switchboard. Walker needed to talk to the battalion and his unit, and he needed a working communication system to do that. As the NCO struggled to untangle the wires in the darkness, "another incoming, high-pitched whistle sounded directly overhead, suddenly ending in a booming explosion on the straw roof of the recently-vacated hut just a few feet away," Walker recounted. "The walls disappeared, the blazing roof collapsed, and the earth bounced and shook."

In response, Sergeant Bockerich sardonically remarked, "Captain, our field desk, company records, three hundred dollars in cash, bed rolls, and your letters from home are floating somewhere over Chipyong [sic] right now." Walker shook his head in frustration.[16] The Dog Company commander was lucky. On the front lines, the situation was worsening.

FEBRUARY 13, 2200–2300 HOURS: ALONG THE FRONT LINES, A COMPANY, 23RD INFANTRY REGIMENT, NORTH CHIPYONG-NI

Private Schutz waited in his foxhole. Though he was tense, he was ready. His squad leader, Sgt. Tracy Young, a smart veteran who had predicted the course of the Chinese assault, had primed him for battle. "Sergeant Young also told us to expect mortar rounds followed by an attack of a small squad type unit," Schutz later wrote. "He told us not to fire the machine gun to give away its position unless we were attacked by at least a unit of two squads or a platoon."

The Chinese attack began with an intense mortar barrage. "After the mortars stopped," wrote Schutz, "we could see movement up a small ridge line on our left. This ridge was blocked by a huge outcropping of rock. The machine gunner was Willie Bean from Alabama and he opened up on this group coming up the left [west] ridge." Bean's machine gun was lethal and cut down the Chinese in droves.

Meanwhile, another large group of communists attacked the center and eastern sections of Able Company's main line of resistance. Thanks to illumination rounds from the company mortars, Bean and the others saw them coming. The machine gunner swung his gun to the center and blazed away. Unbeknownst to the Americans, the Chinese had resumed their attack on the western side of the perimeter, using the outcropping for defilade.

Schutz saw them. "I used my carbine to hold them off until Willie could swing the gun around to the left again," he explained. According to the private, the Chinese onslaught continued unabated for an hour, but despite the numbers, Able Company held. Elsewhere, the red flood continued.[17]

FEBRUARY 13, 2230–2359 HOURS: ALONG THE FRONT LINES, C COMPANY, 23RD INFANTRY REGIMENT, NORTHWEST CHIPYONG-NI

PVT Donald Byers was an ammunition bearer for one of the D Company machine-gun teams located with C Company. He remembered the first attack and wrote about it in a postwar letter. "Around 10:30 pm on 13 February . . . rifle fire opened up on the French positions to my left [west], and then a burst of machine gun fire opened up in A Company area to my right [east]. Someone yelled, 'Here they come,' and I could see them: 200, 500, 1000 Chinese soldiers walking across the rice paddies directly towards our positions. All of a sudden, our entire line opened up with everything we had."[18]

The furious fusillade did not stem the Chinese tide. As it rolled forward, the communists blasted their bugles while their officers blew their whistles. The cacophony sounded like a drunken marching band to the defenders. At 2245, 1st Battalion staff telephoned the regiment and told them that A Company's western flank was under pressure and C Company was undergoing an intense mortar bombardment. The regimental S2 analysts reported to their division counterparts five minutes later, saying, "Main threat seems to be A and C companies." They were wrong. The main threat was everywhere.[19]

FEBRUARY 13–14, 2200–0830 HOURS:
ALONG THE FRONT LINES, 1ST COMPANY,
FRENCH BATTALION, 23RD INFANTRY REGIMENT,
WEST CHIPYONG-NI

Between 2200 hours and midnight, the Chinese probed the U.N. perimeter, searching for weak spots in the lines. While much of the action was in front of 1st Battalion, the communists also struck the French sector. In particular, the Chinese hit 1st Company, which was facing Hill 248.

At 2315 hours, forward observers hiding in a train station along the western edge of town radioed back to the main command post, located inside a village brewery near the town center. "Enemy on the crest in one hundred or two hundred [meters] of the forward post of the train station," they reported. Seconds later, they called again: "Request mortar fire on that crest to the left [south] of the railroad track."

Twelve minutes later, the French mortar tubes thumped. Within seconds, shells bracketed the crest in front of 1st and 2nd Companies. However, the first fire mission was a failure. Less than a minute later, the forward outpost chimed in, "Shot not observed. Request to fire three hundred [meters] from the forward post at the train station on the same hill where the enemy is located."

Hearing the news, the mortar crews adjusted their tubes, and for the next eight minutes the French indirect fire assets pounded the crest that paralleled 1st and 2nd Companies' positions. This barrage was also unsuccessful; on the contrary, the hellish bombardment only further incited the communists, who continued to fire their own mortars at the French defenders along the western edge of Chipyong-ni.

At 2350 hours, Maj. Maurice Barthelemy, who was at the forward outpost, alerted the French command, "Enemy is engaged about fifteen meters [from] the engineer section in Seven . . . Nine . . . Zero . . . Four . . . Seven . . . Seven. Request mortar fire on this point."

Despite the steel rain, the Chinese continued their assault. By midnight, the French command issued a net call for all their units. "All stations," announced the radio operator, "be careful about using up your ammunition."[20]

Feeling the pressure, Colonel Monclar buttressed the engineers and the forward observers at the train station. He sensed 1st Company was in danger and ordered 3rd Company to send a section to each location.

The old colonel knew his men could stop the Chinese if they had the ammunition. The question at hand was whether the U.N. forces would run out of bullets before the Chinese ran out of bodies.

Throughout the evening and into the next morning, the French mortars did most of the work. After sunrise on February 14, the soldiers from 1st and 2nd Company patrolled no-man's-land and found several wounded Chinese, whom they brought back to treat and interrogate. In total, they captured fourteen enemy soldiers, including an officer.[21]

FEBRUARY 13, 2335–2359 HOURS: COMMAND POST, 23RD INFANTRY REGIMENT, CHIPYONG-NI

For the defenders of Chipyong-ni, there was no safe place inside the perimeter. Early in the attack, Chinese artillery hit an M16 half-track, causing the ammunition to cook off. The damaged half-track then caught fire and burned most of the night, providing the enemy gunners with a target. Toward 2335 hours, the communists intensified their bombardment.

Freeman recounted the effects of the enemy artillery in his postwar memoir:

> Heavy mortars, 120mm, Russian jobs, which the Chinese had emplaced behind Hills 345 and 248 began to lob their shells inaccurately into the center of our position. . . . More shells began to fall with increasing accuracy and frequently near our vulnerable installations—Command post, artillery and mortar positions, supply dumps and aid stations. Officers and men whose duties required their continued functioning in these activities, and who thus could not seek cover, suffered heavily.[22]

At 2335 hours, the clerks inside the regimental command post logged the following report: "CP getting seven to eight rounds [of] arty fire. Inspire 3 gave SITREP to Inspire 6." Inspire 6 was Colonel Freeman, while Inspire 3 was Major Dumaine, the S3.

Five minutes later, a huge explosion from a near-miss rocked the command post. Around midnight, another six shells detonated nearby.[23] Freeman later commented on the intensity of Chinese indirect fire, "We hadn't received such a concentration of heavy weapons fire since the Naktong!"[24]

FEBRUARY 13–14, 2220–0515 HOURS: ALONG THE LINE, E COMPANY, 23RD INFANTRY REGIMENT, NANCE AND SAWYER HILLS

Along the eastern side of the perimeter, the action also was heating up. When the Chinese onslaught kicked off, Captain Sawyer's Easy Company was waiting for them, defending the base of two hills that Colonel Edwards had labeled (from west to east) Nance and Sawyer Hills after his officers (1st Lt. Marvin L. Nance of Easy Company and Sawyer, the company commander). In front of the position were a stream, a tunnel, and a railroad bridge.[25]

Sawyer positioned all three of his platoons along the main line of resistance, with 1st Platoon guarding the eastern flank of the company sector, 2nd Platoon in the center under the command of 2nd Lt. Charles H. Davidson, and 3rd Platoon protecting the western flank. A railroad running perpendicular to the company served as the unit boundary between the 1st and 2nd Platoons. For indirect fire support, Sawyer placed his 60mm mortars behind Nance Hill, which was to the rear of 3rd Platoon, and established his command post on the hill's forward slope. For extra support, Colonel Edwards had allocated one section of heavy machine guns, one team of forward observers, and one team of 75mm recoilless rifles to Easy. Lastly, Colonel Freeman provided Sawyer with several tanks from the regimental tank company and M16 half-tracks and M19 AA tanks from B Battery, 82nd Antiaircraft Artillery (Automatic Weapons) Battalion (Self-Propelled). With these attachments, Sawyer's Easy Company packed a powerful punch.[26]

Easy Company had more tricks up its sleeve. Sawyer dug a fougasse near the railroad tracks so that it faced the tunnel, and according to Douglas Graney, "Barbed wire, grenade traps and mines were set at all approaches. The inside of the tunnel was littered with traps."[27] The Chinese had no clue what was waiting for them.

The first communist wave crashed into 2nd Platoon around 2220 hours. Ten minutes later, another group slammed into 1st Platoon. According to Colonel Edwards, a company of Chinese soldiers emerged from the railroad tunnel shortly after the mortar and artillery barrage ended and charged 2nd Platoon. It was a bloodbath.[28]

When Sawyer observed the enemy company appear in front of 2nd and 1st Platoons, he ordered his men to detonate the fougasse. The gasoline drum exploded, showering the enemy soldiers with liquid fire. Sergeant Lee saw the blast from 2nd Platoon's battle position. "I remember when he [Sawyer] ignited that [the fougasse], it lit up the whole area," he recalled. "It was just like a shooting gallery for us. Hell, we could see them as if it was the light of day. . . . We were just picking them off one-by-one until the fire went down."[29]

The enemy officers ordered their soldiers to establish a support-by-fire position at the mouth of the tunnel. Within minutes, Chinese machine gunners opened fire on 2nd Platoon, clearly the signal for the Chines to resume their attack. The enemy soldiers shouted "Manzai!" and surged forward.

The Americans slaughtered them. "The Chinese first wave assaulted right through the antipersonnel mines, trip flares and booby traps, taking heavy casualties," Edwards later wrote. "This wave was mowed down by the U.S. small arms and machine gun fire. The tank and the M-16 (Quad 50) laid down a curtain of .50 caliber slugs in front of the 2nd Platoon. The Chinese continued to come on in waves until they were all killed or wounded."[30]

Lee agreed with his battalion commander's assessment. "We had a field day," he said. "All you had to do is fire and you'd hit somebody."[31] Darting through the swirling hurricane of bright tracers and fiery explosions was Lieutenant Davidson, the 2nd Platoon leader. Davidson's most important task was keeping his unit supplied with ammunition; throughout the battle, he ran back and forth, dropping off hand grenades to each of his squads. At one point, an enemy grenade detonated near him, injuring him, but he refused medical aid and continued to resupply his men. For his bravery, the Army later awarded Davidson the Silver Star.

In his postwar account, Colonel Edwards explained why his men preferred hand grenades: "The infantrymen always used a large amount of hand grenades in these night battles, as they preferred not to fire their rifles except in extreme emergencies, as the flash immediately pinpointed their position."[32]

Sergeant Lee agreed with the colonel's assessment. "We could roll a grenade right out of our hole and get them," he said. Like Davidson, Lee also ran back and forth, distributing ammunition. "That night, the lieutenant was dropping off ammo, and I was trying to get mortar rounds to the guys," he later remarked. In addition to the mortar rounds, Lee also divvied up BAR magazines to the men of Easy Company. "I suppose I delivered fifty to sixty bandoleers that night," he recalled.[33]

At 2320 hours, the Chinese attacked 2nd Platoon again. Ten minutes later, another group rushed out of the tunnel and assaulted 1st Platoon to prevent it from reinforcing 2nd Platoon. Ten minutes into the attack, a bazooka team from 2nd Platoon crept forward and drew a bead on one of the Chinese machine-gun crews located near the tunnel opening. The loader inserted a rocket into the tube and tapped the gunner's shoulder, letting him know the bazooka was ready to fire. Feeling the tap, the gunner pulled the trigger and the rocket screamed out of the launcher and slammed into the Chinese gun position, "destroying the gun and sending its crew into eternity." Thanks to the bazooka team, the Chinese lost their support-by-fire position. Without it, the Chinese attack collapsed and the survivors withdrew, returning to the tunnel.[34]

After distributing the ammunition, Sergeant Lee returned to his foxhole. "They [the Chinese] were really coming at us," he said. "I almost burned up my rifle when I finally did get to my hole. . . . I was picking them off just as fast I as could."

His foxhole comrade, Sgt. Richard Bradley, pulled him back down into his fighting position, yelling, "Those bullets are going right over your head. You know that?" Lee heeded his friend's advice and crunched down in the hole for several minutes until the firing subsided.[35]

Chinese sappers were approaching 2nd Platoon's foxholes, using satchel charges attached to long poles to drop the explosives into the foxholes when they were close enough. The men of 2nd Platoon saw the enemy coming. According to Lee, the Chinese tried to destroy two holes in his platoon, but thanks to timely illumination flares, the U.N. defenders detected them and killed them with hand grenades.[36]

James Bolen was a machine gunner in Easy Company. When the Chinese attacked, he opened fire with his M1919 light machine gun and kept firing. At several points during the battle, he lost control of his weapon. As a result, it would continue firing, even though Bolen was not pulling the trigger—he called it a runaway gun. The upper receiver and barrel had overheated from the high rates of cyclic fire. Because of this, Bolen burned out two of his barrels. Fortunately, he had replacements.[37]

Enemy activity in Easy Company's sector continued after midnight when a medical jeep and an M19-tracked AA gun roared down the road that passed through 1st Platoon, Easy Company's position. The half-track provided security for the medics from 3rd Battalion as the small convoy headed toward K Company. As they drove through 1st Platoon, the Easy Company soldiers tried to halt the two vehicles because they were heading toward a small village; unbeknownst to the commander of the column, a Lt. William Haire from B Battery, 82nd Antiaircraft Artillery Battalion, the Chinese had seized the hamlet earlier that evening.

Lieutenant Haire did not see the Easy Company soldiers, and his column continued into enemy territory. Within seconds of leaving friendly lines, the communists opened fire. "The jeep was smothered with Chinese small-arms fire and burst into flames," Colonel Edwards later wrote.[38]

Chinese soldiers emerged from the darkness and grabbed the wounded jeep driver, while an Easy Company soldier pulled the wounded medic back toward American lines. A nearby tank rolled forward to provide covering fire for the M19 as its crew tried to turn the tracked vehicle around while under fire. A Chinese soldier hit the tank with a shape charge, wounding the driver. At 0040 hours, B Battery radioed the regiment and informed them that the half-track and its crew were cut off. The battery commander wanted to send another M16 out to recover the M19.

After several minutes of debating over the telephones and radios, the commanders decided to leave the stranded half-track at its location. Its crew still had plenty of ammunition, and Colonel Edwards believed the crew could defend themselves until morning. Moreover, it added its pair of cannons to Easy Company's battle position. Thus, it remained with Easy for the rest of the night.

Inside the vehicle, Sgt. Nick M. Schelbrack operated the guns. While providing suppressive fire with his twin 40mm cannons, he also requested indirect fire missions on Hill 397. From his vantage point, he had excellent observation of its slopes.[39]

Elsewhere, the battle continued. Despite their losses, the communists charged Sawyer's company three more times, and each time the

Americans threw them back with more casualties. The last attack began at 0515 hours and ended with the Chinese back inside the tunnel. Shortly after sunrise, the E Company soldiers saw the results of their handiwork. "The slaughter was evident with bodies draped over and under the wire and many were crying wounded," Douglas Graney described in a postwar letter. "Dead and wounded Chinese were everywhere in front of our lines." According to Graney, though the siege continued for another thirty-six hours, the Chinese never again attacked from the tunnel.[40]

His commander, Captain Sawyer, added, "The most memorable sight was about a half dozen enemy bodies laid out in a perfect line with a long Bangalore torpedo in front of them pushed under our barbed wire fence. They were obviously killed by our grazing machine gun fire."[41]

FEBRUARY 13–14, 2220–0650 HOURS: ALONG THE LINE, G COMPANY, 23RD INFANTRY REGIMENT, MCGEE HILL

Several hours earlier, Capt. John H. Ramsburg, Colonel Edward's S2, assessed that the most vulnerable spot along the 23rd Infantry's perimeter was the southern sector. Because of this, he told Lt. Paul McGee, 3rd Platoon's leader, that the main Chinese attack would strike G Company. McGee recalled Ramsburg's words as he watched two flares shoot up into the sky from the hamlet of Masan, which was in front of his unit and at the base of McGee Hill. He wondered if this was the main assault he'd been warned about. It was 2220 hours.

Seconds later, McGee heard the telltale thuds and crumps of mortar rounds whooshing out of their tubes. Instinctively, everyone in 3rd Platoon hunkered down inside their two-man foxholes and waited. In an instant, explosions rocked the two hills that made up 3rd Platoon's battle position: McGee Hill in the west and Curtis Hill in the east. By 2230 hours, the first wave struck Curtis Hill.[42]

Cpl. Herbert G. Ziebell was a rifleman in 1st Squad, 3rd Platoon. When the attack began, he woke up the other GI in his foxhole, PFC Roy F. Benoit, and said to him, "There is some firing going on over by the rest of the platoon. Get up and get ready."

Ziebell stared out into the darkness. "I didn't start firing right away . . . because I didn't see anybody to fire at," he later said in an interview. "To fire at the darkness would draw fire." Hence, he waited.

Several meters to the northeast of Ziebell's hole was 2nd Squad, 2nd Platoon. Like the other platoons, the soldiers of 2nd Platoon had dug in on a mound labeled Finn Hill, named after 2nd Lt. Kenneth G. Finn, their platoon leader. PFC Donald E. Nelson, a bazooka gunner for 2nd Squad, was awake when the attack began. In fact, he had been arguing with his foxhole buddy, Pvt. Jack Ward, when they heard someone digging several hundred meters south of their position. Then they heard the shrill scream of a whistle.[43]

The first enemy group crept forward and approached G Company along a spur that jutted out from Curtis Hill. When they were within 70 meters of the American lines, they tossed three hand grenades at the closest squad. Cpl. Eugene L. Ottesen was waiting for them and opened fire with his .30-caliber light machine gun.

When McGee heard Ottesen's machine gun open fire, he alerted his other squads and his commander, Lieutenant Heath, over the field phone. Paul McGee sensed it was going to be a long fight and told his platoon, "Watch for the enemy [and] do not fire unless you see them." He understood that his soldiers did not have an infinite amount of bullets or grenades. Since the Chinese had surrounded them, resupply would have to come from the air.[44] Meanwhile, another squad attempted to sneak around the western flank of 3rd Platoon by infiltrating through a creek bed. When they were close, they attacked the BAR gunner in Sgt. Franklin H. Querry's squad.

To the west, in 1st Platoon's sector, Cpl. Roland J. Jarvey scrambled out of his foxhole to find a better firing position. He crawled to a new spot and opened fire on the attackers. As a result, the Chinese shifted their fire toward Jarvey's location. The corporal refused to withdraw and kept plugging away at the enemy with his rifle. Eventually, after sustaining several hits from hand grenades, mortar rounds, and bullets, Jarvey slumped over and died. However, he had stymied the Chinese for several critical minutes, and the Army posthumously awarded him the Silver Star for his bravery.[45]

Farther to the east, Privates Ward and Nelson saw the group that had attacked Ottesen's machine gun. In retaliation, they grabbed their bazooka and crawled out of their foxhole. When they were close, Nelson loaded the bazooka and told Ward to open fire. The gunner aimed his weapon at the flashes 800 yards away from their position and fired three times. Meanwhile, the machine gunner for 2nd Platoon, Pvt. Andrew C. Warf, also detected the infiltrators in front of Ottesen's position and opened up with his light machine gun. The crossfire was too much for the Chinese. Most them of died in front G Company, and the few survivors withdrew.[46]

At 2256 hours, the communists returned. The Chinese initiated the attack with a large-caliber, direct-fire weapon. Soon after the bombardment of George Company began, 2nd Battalion radio operators first reported, "G Company getting tank fire from Hill 129. Enemy blowing horns."[47]

Four minutes later, McGee saw two more flares pop up from the village of Masan. Responding to the signal flares, a Chinese company emerged from the hamlet and began to climb up Schmitt, McGee, and Curtis Hills. (Schmitt Hill was 1st Platoon's location, named after SFC Donald R. Schmitt.) This time, the communist horde reached several of the American foxholes and the fighting devolved into hand-to-hand combat.

In one instance, PFC Anthony J. Castiglia, who was fetching ammunition for one of G Company's machine guns, spotted a group of Chinese infiltrators sneaking up on his gun team, who were unaware of the impending assault. Without hesitation, Castiglia charged the enemy soldiers, tossing several hand grenades at the attackers while firing at them with his rifle. Instantly, he gunned down two of the communists and wounded several more, but during the melee he was shot and killed. His devotion to his comrades, however, had saved their lives.

Despite their often-unprotected maneuvering, not all the ammunition bearers died. PFC William G. Mason survived the gauntlet of enemy machine-gun fire, bringing much-needed ammunition to his machine-gun team. For his bravery, the Army awarded him the Silver Star.[48]

McGee was still in the thick of the action. At the height of the attack, Cpl. James C. Mougeat, one of McGee's squad leaders, decided to report to his lieutenant personally, letting him know that a squad of CPVF had reached his battle position. As the corporal climbed out of his foxhole, two Chinese soldiers emerged from the darkness and hurled grenades at him. The resulting explosion blew the stock off his rifle. Fortunately, his fellow U.N. soldiers saw the two Chinese interlopers and sprayed them with rifle fire, killing them both. Mougeat was in intense pain and dropped his Garand as if he were tossing a baseball bat after hitting a fastball in freezing weather. "Lieutenant McGee, I'm hit," he called out. The corporal looked down and saw that a piece of shrapnel had punctured his calf. Despite the pain, he hobbled over to the platoon command post.

When Mougeat arrived, McGee asked him how bad the wound was and what the situation was in front of his squad. The corporal responded, "The Chinks are hitting us on the left." He informed his platoon leader that the Chinese had maneuvered a squad in front of his position. After several minutes of discussion with McGee, the corporal recovered his wits, told his lieutenant, "I am not hit bad," and left the command post to return to his squad.

Within minutes of Mougeat's departure, the Chinese surged again. Amid the screaming whistles and blasting bugles, McGee detected a large group of enemy infantry less than 25 meters from his foxhole. His hole was higher up the hill, so the lieutenant began to roll hand grenades down the slope. Corporal Ottesen swung his machine gun around and opened fire on the same group, while the company's 60mm mortars showered the area with high-explosive rounds. McGee even killed one of the enemy soldiers with a BAR. It was total destruction, and once again, the Chinese slinked back toward their line of departure. The second wave had failed.[49] "Again the Chinese 'human sea' tactics had hit a stone wall," Colonel Edwards later commented.

G Company had sustained twelve casualties: ten wounded and two killed. In some places, especially in 1st Platoon's sector on Schmitt Hill, fewer men occupied the main line of resistance. In response, Lieutenant Heath requested support from B Battery, 503rd Artillery. The battery commander answered the call and provided a section of soldiers and a .50-caliber machine gun. Heath positioned the reinforcements and the crew-served weapon in the middle of 1st Platoon's battle position.

The Chinese were not finished with G Company, though, and they attacked again at 0100 and 0218 hours. The soldiers of George Company easily defeated the two assaults. According to Colonel Edwards, these were minor affairs. The attack at 0100 hours was only a probing operation—the communists were searching for weak spots in the American lines.[50]

In between the Chinese waves, McGee circulated among his men. "I would try to check every position, every man," he said in a postwar interview. "I'd see how many wounded we had, our ammunition supply, and encourage them to stay in their holes, be alert that it wasn't over. But at a couple of different times, we thought it was over, that they'd withdrawn. Of course, we treated our wounded, got the ones off the hill that needed treatment. We'd discuss what we'd do if they hit us again."[51]

McGee's foresight paid off. Around 0330 hours, the lieutenant watched a pair of flares pop above the village of Masan, signaling yet another attack. The communists supported this one with a long mortar bombardment that continued throughout the assault. The focal point of the attack was the seam between 1st Platoon and 3rd Platoon, a saddle between Schmitt and McGee Hills. At 0343 hours, 2nd Battalion requested tank support for G Company.[52]

The shelling did not help the Chinese. According to McGee, the mortars were "Not very accurate at that time, because they didn't hit any of us. They were falling all around us, mostly in front of us."

The platoon leader then described the Chinese bounding techniques. "At times they would crawl four or five yards," he said in an interview, "then they'd raise up and fire. Then when they got in close to us, they'd use a lot of grenades. They continued firing until we stopped them by shooting them. The first night, they didn't get close enough to us to use their satchel charges and their Bangalore torpedoes. We took care of them all before they could get that close to us."[53]

Despite the mortar support, the latest CPVF attack shared the same outcome as its predecessors, failing to penetrate the American lines. The Chinese lost three irreplaceable mortars to American counter-battery fire after a G Company forward observer spotted the mortars in Masan and requested an artillery concentration on top of the village.[54]

At 0430 hours, 2nd Battalion radio operators informed the regimental staff, "G Company okay now. Enemy brought mortars twenty-five meters in[to] the front lines, but stopped."[55]

Two hours later, at 0650, Lieutenant Heath reported that his men heard bugles in front of their foxholes, an indication, he knew, that the Chinese were withdrawing back toward Hill 397. The first night of combat was over for G Company. Heath's command had sustained twenty-three casualties, the highest loss within 2nd Battalion. Five of the casualties were dead. Luckily for McGee, none of the departed were from his platoon.[56]

Even though their attacks had fallen short, the Chinese commanders had discovered a potential infiltration route: they had found the creek in front of McGee's platoon and 1st Platoon. The soldiers who survived that first night told their officers how the creek bed offered defilade for a potential attack. Because of this information, the next attack would have a much greater chance of success. Moreover, the Chinese could reinforce the southern sector throughout the day with two battalions from the 343rd Regiment, 115th Division. Overnight on February 14–15, the Chinese would outnumber G Company more than six to one.[57]

WEDNESDAY, FEBRUARY 14, 0220–0835 HOURS: ALONG THE LINE, K COMPANY, 23RD INFANTRY REGIMENT, CHIPYONG-NI

The real fighting began early on the morning of February 14 for K Company, but its soldiers were prepared. According to Tom Ryan, a soldier in King Company, the men had scrounged and scavenged the battlefields in the months leading up to Chipyong-ni. As a result, "every other man carried a BAR, [while] those not carrying a BAR, carried BAR ammo," commented Ryan. The unit also had more than triple the allotment of SCR-300 radios, which meant every platoon had a radio to augment its wire communication with the company. Thus, the company had redundant communications and plenty of firepower on the eve of the siege.

Several minutes prior to the main assault on King Company, the Chinese prodded several oxen to lumber through no-man's-land with the purpose of detonating American mines along the road and drawing fire from the American positions. One of Ryan's comrades saw the beasts of burden and wondered what they were. He later remarked to Ryan that they "looked like the devil with horns."

Capt. Charles Thompson, K Company's commander, heard the bugles and braced for the inevitable. His command post was in a ravine about a hundred meters behind 2nd and 3rd Platoons. He had positioned all of his platoons on the main line of resistance, with 2nd Platoon covering the northern flank while 1st Platoon held the southern flank. In the center was 3rd Platoon. There was no sizeable reserve if the Chinese penetrated his lines.

Within seconds of the bugle blasts, the enemy opened fire on Thompson's company. Ryan recalled how the Chinese assault began with a hurricane of mortars and grenades, later describing how "the hill felt like it was shaking." The initial barrage leveled one of the mortar pits, killing two soldiers almost instantly.[58]

At 0220 hours, 3rd Battalion radio operators called regiment and informed them, "K Company [is] getting hit hard—all platoons engaged."

Colonel Kane offered to shift one platoon from Item Company to reinforce King Company. Before regiment could reply, another Chinese wave hit K Company. At 0242 hours, wounded soldiers from 3rd Battalion inundated the regimental aid station, reporting that the Chinese had penetrated K Company's lines. In response, Major Dumaine left the regimental command post to see the commander of 3rd Battalion. Within minutes of speaking with Colonel Kane, the regimental S3 informed the main command post that King Company was still in the fight.[59]

One of the reasons for K Company's survival was a single soldier, PFC Lawrence Numkena from Bernalillo, New Mexico, a BAR gunner in K Company. During the assault, he saw a group of communist soldiers climbing up a draw in front of his squad. He waited until they were almost on top of him, then opened fire. The initial bursts were devastating—he singlehandedly killed sixteen outright. Terrified and leaderless, the survivors scrambled back down the hill.

Numkena was not finished. A few minutes after 0400 hours, the Chinese wave came crashing down on K Company again. The BAR gunner saw another group of communist soldiers negotiating the draw in front of his squad. The enemy was in defilade, so he crawled out of his foxhole to find a better firing position. As he moved, the Chinese saturated K Company's main line of resistance with mortar rounds and sprayed the ridge with machine-gun fire. Undaunted, Numkena kept crawling. Finally, he found a spot, stood up, and tossed several grenades at the onrushing Chinese platoon. After chucking his grenades, he opened fire with his BAR, shooting from the hip like a cowboy in the Wild

West. His fusillade caught the Chinese out in the open, and, within seconds he had killed twenty-seven more enemy soldiers. With most of their platoon lying dead along the hillside, the survivors withdrew, yielding the ridgeline to K Company and Private Numkena. The young New Mexican later received the Silver Star for his actions.[60]

Numkena was not the only soldier in K Company to receive the prestigious award for his actions that morning. SFC George H. Glassman was a platoon sergeant from Maryland. During the battle, Glassman resupplied his men with ammunition while dashing from foxhole to foxhole under fire. At one point, he discovered that the enemy had penetrated his platoon's northern flank. He personally plugged the hole when he charged a group of enemy soldiers by himself, killing the first three with grenades and then chasing off the rest. After securing the position, Glassman remained there until the end of the attack.[61]

Not far from Glassman's location was Sgt. Leo Blevins from Virginia. On the morning of February 14, Blevins was a squad leader whose squad had the task of protecting the flank of his platoon's light machine gun. During the main assault on K Company, Blevins detected a platoon of Chinese soldiers trying to infiltrate past the machine-gun position. He yelled at the gunner to shift fire, and the gunner swung the M1919 over and cut loose with several bursts. However, the enemy was in defilade. Undeterred, the squad leader climbed out of his foxhole and skirted the ridge to find a better spot to engage the communist platoon. After several minutes, Blevins found it and opened fire with his rifle. Singlehandedly, the Virginian took out seventeen enemy soldiers, breaking the back of the enemy assault. Like Numkena and Glassman, Blevins was awarded the Silver Star. Thanks to these heroic actions, K Company weathered the Chinese wave.[62]

Much like G Company's experience, the communists hit Thompson's command several times that morning. At 0630 hours, the enemy tried one more time to penetrate K Company's MLR. Forty-five minutes later, Colonel Kane reported that Thompson's men were "having [a] hard time" and ordered elements of L Company to reinforce K Company. Thompson would not need them. Unbeknownst to Kane, the Chinese attack had culminated, and by 0800 hours, the fighting in front of King Company had petered out.

By 0835 hours, Colonel Kane's soldiers were counting the corpses in front of their foxholes. The numbers were staggering. K Company estimated 200 to 300 bodies in front of their positions, while I Company calculated the Chinese had left behind between 30 to 40 dead in front of their battle position.

In front of 1st and 2nd Battalions and the French Battalion, the tally of enemy dead was also high. According to Colonel Edwards, soldiers from E Company found 137 bodies, while soldiers from G Company found another 283. Major Russell reported his soldiers found 81 bodies scattered throughout C and A Companies' sectors. In total, nearly 1,000 frozen dead bodies lay outside the Tomahawks' perimeter.

As Colonel Edwards later observed, his men found most of the bodies in the company kill zones; therefore, the Chinese could not have dragged them out without risking the lives of the living. Leaving the bodies behind was not the normal practice: the communists did not want the U.N. forces to know their casualties, and they tended to evacuate even the dead to deny U.S. military intelligence the ability to estimate enemy unit effectiveness. Under these circumstances, 2nd Battalion's commander believed Chinese losses were much higher than just the bodies in front of his companies. Edwards estimated his battalion alone was probably responsible for 1,680 enemy casualties, nearly four times the number of enemy corpses. Regardless, it had been a bad night for the Chinese, and despite the human waves, they had not even dented the U.N. position at Chipyong-ni.[63]

FEBRUARY 14, MORNING:
COMMAND POST, X CORPS, CHUNGJU

Ridgway's plan was working. He wanted the Chinese to bludgeon themselves against the American defenses. At Chipyong-ni and Wonju, he had his wall against which they could beat their heads. To ensure that everyone understood his intent, Ridgway traveled to Almond's headquarters at Chungju to outline his plan personally. There, he met with General Almond; Col. John S. Guthrie, the X Corps chief of staff; Col. James H. Polk, the G2; and Lt. Col. John H. Chiles, the G3.

Ridgway's first concern was the relief of the 23rd Infantry at Chipyong-ni. Almond told him that the British 27th Commonwealth Brigade was fighting its way northward from Yoju to accomplish that mission. Ridgway knew that one brigade combat team was not sufficient, and he later ordered IX Corps, which shared a boundary with X Corps near Chipyong-ni, to send another regimental combat team to relieve the Tomahawks from the west.

Ridgway dictated a list of instructions to Almond and his key staff. "The Chinese attack," said the Eighth Army commander, "appears to be on about a twenty-mile front. I want to be sure the shoulders are held." He continued, "Major units should be maintained intact. [Eighth] Army is assuming responsibility for the III ROK Corps." He looked at the other officers with a stern gaze and said, "No equipment is to be abandoned."

Ridgway then pointed at a city on the operations map and declared, "Wonju must be held, and the attack checked in that area." He moved his finger to Chipyong-ni and added, "The highest priority is the opening of the MSR with the 23rd Infantry Regiment."

The officers in the room nodded in agreement. The paratrooper general said, "All echelons must be impressed with the importance of every hour. Many times one small group, by determined action, can influence the entire situation."

Ridgway spoke for several more minutes and concluded his instructions by saying, "We will do everything we can to assist you in stemming this attack."[64]

With that, he left Almond's command post. For the X Corps staff, Ridgway's confidence buoyed them. Moreover, as he spoke to them, artillery and close air support had ripped apart an attacking Chinese division northwest of Wonju. West of Wonju, the battle for Chipyong-ni was far from finished. In fact, the most dangerous phase was yet to come.[65]

FEBRUARY 14, MORNING: ALONG THE FRONT LINES, C COMPANY, 23RD INFANTRY REGIMENT, NORTHWEST CHIPYONG-NI

All Donald Byers could see in front of his position was carnage. It was eerie. "In the morning, it was all quiet," he said. "We got up [and] walked out of our foxholes and saw the dead Chinese . . . close to our positions in the snow."

He did not need to walk far. The bodies were only a few feet from his foxhole and well within hand-grenade range. The corpses dispelled the notion of the Chinese superman. To his surprise, many of the dead were unarmed. Byers later remarked, "They looked kind of pathetic. . . . They're frozen and their arms sticking up in the air, stiff."

"We stopped them cold. They did not penetrate," he recalled in a postwar interview. His unit suffered only one casualty—a machine gunner who had been shot and killed. Despite the human waves, the Chinese attack had failed miserably.[66]

FEBRUARY 14, 0725–LATE AFTERNOON: COMMAND POST, 23RD INFANTRY REGIMENT, CHIPYONG-NI

By midmorning, Colonel Freeman felt somewhat relieved. The Chinese had concentrated their attacks along two seams: the boundary between the French Battalion and 2nd Battalion, and the boundary between 2nd and 3rd Battalions. Both operations had ended in failure.

At 0725 hours, division updated the 23rd Infantry on the progress of the battle near Wonju. According to the division radio operator, Wonju was under attack from two sides, while between Wonju and Chipyong-ni the division Reconnaissance Company and elements of the 9th Infantry were fighting for their lives. More important to the Tomahawks, the radio operator informed them that the British 27th Commonwealth Brigade was on the way to relieve them.

A little after 0800 hours, the division's G3 Air Operations officer contacted the 23rd Infantry with bad news: weather forecasts predicted nine hours of lousy weather, and Mother Nature had grounded all aircraft flying out of Japan and from the carriers offshore. This meant close air support would be spotty at best, since it would come from the makeshift airbases on the Korean Peninsula. The G3 assured the staff of the 23rd Infantry that the Tomahawks would be a priority for any air support that could fly.[67]

At 0847 hours, the French Battalion transferred fifteen enemy prisoners, including one wounded officer. Freeman questioned them and, according to the communist officer, learned the 23rd Infantry was facing units from five different Chinese divisions, approximately 30,000 enemy soldiers. The officer later revealed that he was a second lieutenant in the 376th Regiment, 126th Division. According to the Chinese officer, the entire 126th Division was in the area; the division alone numbered over 10,000 men, and the 42nd Army had equipped it with captured Japanese howitzers from the Second World War. The 42nd Army had tasked the 126th Division with the mission of seizing Chipyong-ni.

The officer pointed to a location on a map and informed his captors that the division mortars were located in the village of Sinchon, behind Hill 129. He added that if the attack failed, his division had orders to reassemble near the division's mortar sections. This was vital data, and Freeman's intelligence team quickly relayed this information to the division G2.[68]

At 0907 hours, Freeman felt comfortable enough to give General Ruffner a situation report. He radioed division: "Ivanhoe this is Inspire Six. Our situation . . . Chinese dug in on MSR. We have about two hundred wounded who must be evacuated right away. Must have ammo, arty, mortar and the works . . . Over."

A voice squawked over the intercom: "Inspire 6 this is Ivanhoe. The General [Ruffner] is anxious that the position be held. Will do all possible to help. Captain Noel will fly over in L-5 with message [at] about 1000. Out."[69]

After this report, Freeman returned to his tent. There, he chatted with his S2, Maj. Harold W. Shoemaker, and his executive officer, Lieutenant Colonel Meszar, about the previous night. Suddenly, a 120mm mortar shell screamed in and exploded. It was a direct hit. The blast killed Shoemaker instantly, and the resultant concussion knocked everyone else over.

"We'd been fighting all day and all night," recalled Colonel Freeman in a postwar interview. "And I had a little torn-up tent which I shared with Colonel Meszar and it was about daylight and the fighting, the shooting was still going on. I was sitting . . . on the ground in that tent, with the telephone in my hand. We had one bottle of whiskey left—Old Grandad . . . I had offered that to any patrol that could bring in a Chinaman who was still alive. My S2, Shoemaker, was standing there to the entrance of that tent . . . telling me what was going on from his viewpoint."

"A fragment of it [the mortar shell]," he continued, "I guess, about two or three inches, hit the bottle of Old Grandad; glass and whiskey flew all over the place, and then it went into my leg—the fragment—and it made a very nasty looking hole." Luckily, the shrapnel did not shatter the bone in Freeman's calf. According to the colonel, "It didn't bother me too much. The medic bandaged it up and I could hobble around."[70]

Capt. Robert M. Hall was the first doctor to examine Freeman's wound. According to Hall, the wound would have warranted evacuation under normal circumstances, but as the medic noted, "This was not a normal situation," so he did not request a helicopter to airlift the colonel to safety. "There was no medical reason for his [Freeman's] evacuation but that there was every tactical reason for his remaining," Hall said.

To replace Shoemaker, Colonel Freeman appointed Capt. John H. King as the new S2 for the regiment, effective at 0951 hours.

For the next few hours, Freeman watched the skies, hoping for the anticipated aerial resupply. When it finally arrived, it was underwhelming. "Twenty-four flying boxcars [Fairchild C-119 transport aircraft] came over," he wrote, "and dropped us ammo and other supplies. This was truly a Godsend, but unfortunately no heavy mortar ammunition or illuminating shells were included and the rifle cartridges were not placed in clips, serious handicaps for night fighting."[71]

Unforeseen problems kept coming. When General Almond learned of Freeman's injury later that day, he ordered Lt. Col. John H. Chiles, Almond's operations officer at X Corps, to replace him. According to General Stewart, 2nd Infantry Division's assistant division commander, Almond did not even consult with General Ruffner before he pulled the trigger on Freeman.

The order to relinquish his command shocked Freeman, and he refused to leave. After he heard the news of his relief, the Tomahawk commander supposedly said, "I brought them [the 23rd Infantry] in and I'll take them out."

In spite of Freeman's intransigence, Almond insisted that Chiles take over the 23rd. Eventually, General Ruffner asked General Stewart to call Freeman over the radio to work out the change of command details. According to Stewart, the Tomahawk commander argued that "he was being relieved from command while his regiment was in combat, and that was the worst disgrace an officer could suffer; he said he was not going to come out."

The assistant division commander assured him. "No one questioned his performance," wrote Stewart. He told Freeman "that he would undoubtedly be decorated and promoted." Freeman finally acquiesced.

Colonel Chiles arrived by plane that afternoon, and Freeman was supposed to fly out on the same bird. To Chiles's chagrin, the plane could not take off. According to Freeman, the plane had blown a tire. Therefore, Chiles had to wait another twenty-four hours before Freeman would relinquish his command. Fortunately for everyone involved, the new commander took it in stride.[72]

In a postwar interview, Colonel Meszar claimed that Almond did not like Freeman and had been waiting for the right opportunity to relieve him. According to Meszar, Almond was "waiting for Freeman to do something wrong." Moreover, like many generals, Almond wanted his handpicked team under his command. Chiles was on Almond's team—Freeman was not.[73]

The officers of the 23rd Infantry viewed Freeman's dismissal as a grave injustice. "I felt then that the replacement of the commander of the 23rd RCT at that critical time and ostensibly for a medical reason when no medical reason existed was reprehensible," Captain Hall later wrote. "I think so even more now in light of what I have learned since then. It is an illustration of why I think that Almond was unfit to command." Regardless of Hall's feelings, Freeman was on the way out and would be gone in the next twenty-four hours. Elsewhere, the battle continued.[74]

At 1430 hours, Col. Marcel G. Crombez, the commander of 5th Cavalry Regiment, received a warning order from 1st Cavalry Division. It had a new mission: clear the Koksu-ri–Chipyong-ni highway and relieve the 23rd Infantry Regiment.[75] Later that night, 2nd Infantry Division radioed the staff of the 23rd Infantry to tell them about the relief operation. At 1753 hours, a voice on the radio called the Tomahawks: "Inspire this is Ivanhoe. Firefly request granted. Starts at 2000 hours. Continues all night. Relief about 0200. 5th Cavalry on way up west road. Possibly arrives tonight late or early morning. Nottingham [27th Commonwealth Brigade] has no change. Are engaged lightly."

News of another relief column bolstered the spirits of the men inside the regimental command post. Thirty minutes later, they received an update from division confirming the change in operation. The voice over the radio said, "5th Cavalry may reach this perimeter tonight. Presently lightly engaged at 35 grid."

The operations staff telephoned the French Battalion to let them know that a friendly armored column might drive up the road from Koksu-ri that night. Unbeknownst to the staff, it would be almost another twenty-four more hours before the cavalry would arrive. Furthermore, the Chinese had plans to end the siege before then. However, the Navy and the Air Force would punish the Chinese for remaining at Chipyong-ni.[76]

FEBRUARY 14, 1545–1810 HOURS:
SKIES ABOVE CHIPYONG-NI

John Collins was a T-6 Mosquito pilot flying the forward air controller missions above Chipyong-ni on February 14, 1951. The last twenty-four hours had been busy for him and his co-pilot, Capt. George Wolf. Late on February 13, while flying a reconnaissance mission, they had spotted Chinese troop concentrations massing between the 23rd Infantry Regiment and the 24th Infantry Division.

"It soon became apparent that the 2nd Division was headed for trouble," Collins wrote later. "All quadrants around their positions were teeming with enemy and the problem seemed to be the 2nd was not fully aware of their predicament. . . . *Mosquito Spirit* (George and I) continued reconnoitering and the more we looked, the more enemy activity we found. Our numerous reports caused the 24th Division headquarters to become alarmed and they asked if we could land at their forward airstrip and give a detailed briefing, one on one."

On Valentine's Day, Wolf and Collins took off and left the 24th's forward command post. They flew to Chipyong-ni on what, according to Collins's notes, was Mission Number #49, arriving over at the contested village at 1545 hours.

"14 February, 1951, was a day I'll never forget," penned Collins in a postwar article. "We departed our riverbed airstrip, just missing a tank at the far end, and reported on station to Major Smith [air liaison officer]. Apparently, Air Force and Navy ground crews had been working all night and fully loaded fighters and bombers checked in. We had F-4U Corsairs, F-51s, Douglas A.D. Skyraiders (our favorite), F-80s, F-9s, A-26s and of course our own T-6. . . . I squeezed the mile button to call the fighters in and I talked for hours it seemed. When I wasn't talking a flight on target, George was. We had never then and never since had so many aircraft to control in one day."

The sky was a traffic jam. "At times mid-air collisions were almost a problem," Collins later wrote. "Normally the attacking aircraft flight path was a recommendation of Mosquito and a decision of a fighter. At Chipyong with so many aircraft it was necessary for us to specify and require the fighters to follow our lead or orders."

Despite the danger, the close air support was deadly. "We hit so many targets that day I can only remember a few. One time I spotted an unusual sight, a group of about two hundred Chinese infantry in sleeping bags hidden (so they thought) in a gully. We put four F-51s [Flight Wild West Able] with napalm, completely filling the draw with no sign of visible survivors."

The Chinese faced an exploding volcano of strafing and bombing. "As the afternoon wore on, we had the Chipyong area looking like a scene from Hell, fires, explosions, napalm going on all over the place," Collins continued.

After flying for nearly three hours, *Mosquito Spirit* safely landed at the airfield outside of Inchon at 1810 hours.[77]

FEBRUARY 14, 0721–LATE AFTERNOON: ALONG THE LINE, G COMPANY, 23RD INFANTRY REGIMENT, MCGEE AND CURTIS HILLS

Lieutenant McGee felt relieved and confident: relieved because his platoon had not lost a single soldier, and confident because his platoon had defeated several Chinese attacks in one night. However, he knew the fighting was far from finished.

Shortly after sunrise, his platoon sergeant, Bill Kluttz, shouted that he saw five figures, hiding in the nearby creek bed. The sergeant shot several tracers at them to mark their location for McGee, who saw the enemy soldiers and realized they were in defilade. He ordered Kluttz to find a bazooka and blast them out of the creek bed.

Kluttz left and returned a few minutes later with a bazooka team. After several minutes of searching, the two-man team could not find the target. Kluttz grabbed the bazooka and fired it himself. The rocket swished out of the tube and slammed into a tree that overhung the creek. The subsequent blast showered the area with bits of shrapnel and shards of wood. Realizing they were no longer safe, the communists burst out of the creek and dashed over the rice paddy. McGee counted forty as they scampered and scurried through the field while his 2nd Squad and 1st Platoon opened fire on them, killing several.[78]

The lieutenant knew the presence of forty enemy soldiers so close to his lines meant he had to clear his platoon's kill zone. "There was a kind of calm in the morning mist," said McGee in a postwar interview. "I could see there were quite a few dead bodies around, and some wounded that couldn't walk. I took six men with me and we went out to the front to check for weapons, check to make sure that the dead were actually were dead, because they were tricky."

As the lieutenant walked past a body, he would poke and prod to see if it moved. One body looked dead—a leg was mostly gone—so he did not bother with it. While checking another lifeless stiff 15 feet away from the first by lifting the body with the barrel of his carbine, he detected movement out of the corner of his eye. The legless corpse was not a corpse. Hidden underneath him was a burp gun, and the enemy soldier began to shift his torso so that he could fire on McGee. It was a race. The officer tugged at his carbine, but it was stuck under the first corpse. Luckily, Cpl. Boleslow N. Sander, who was close by, saw the wounded enemy soldier and rushed over to bayonet him before the Chinese soldier could spray the lieutenant with his submachine gun.

Now, they were alert. Sergeant Kluttz spotted another communist crawling out of a haystack. When the enemy soldier realized that Kluttz had seen him, he raised his rifle to open fire on McGee, but Kluttz was quicker on the draw. He dropped the enemy rifleman with a single shot from his M1. Fortunately, the remaining wounded had lost the will to fight and surrendered.

Later in the morning, McGee and his patrol discovered a cave. He listened and heard voices coming from inside it. "We knew there was more than one," the lieutenant later said. "We didn't even know how big the cave was; we weren't about to go in it. In fact, I cautioned the men that were with me not to go in it. We yelled for them to come out, but of course we couldn't speak Chinese. None of them came out, so we threw a couple of WP (white phosphorous) grenades and a couple of fragmentation grenades in there."

The resultant explosion showered the inside of the cave with hot metal and burning sparks. No one likely survived. For McGee, the choice was obvious. "I felt sort of numb, realizing that I had killed some human beings," he said, "but I also tried to keep in mind that they were trying to do the same thing to me. It's a feeling that I don't have words for. I just can't explain it. Of course, I was glad it was them and not me."

McGee's patrol netted twelve prisoners. Seven of the twelve were wounded, one of whom was a bugler. The lieutenant counted eighteen corpses in front of his platoon. He noticed that the enemy soldiers carried a hodgepodge of weapons—some had rifles while others had submachine guns. Some had no individual firearm and carried only satchel charges or Bangalore torpedoes. According to McGee, they all had grenades strapped to a belt on their waist.

Later that afternoon, the lieutenant learned that the Chinese had surrounded them. Help was on the way, but it was still 8 miles south of their location. His commander told him that the Chinese would attack again that night, so McGee returned to his platoon and told them to lock and load. As his men readied themselves, the veteran officer wondered if he had enough ammunition to make it through the night.[79]

McGee's group was not the only patrol from G Company; two squads from 2nd Platoon departed at 1400 to clear the hamlet of Masan. As the men scoured the ground, they found leaflets that the Chinese had left for the Americans to find. They read:

GIVE UP ARMS!
YOUR SAFETY INSURED!
   Now you are entirely besieged and all routes of retreat have been cut out. If you but lay down your arms we would undertake to insure your safety, no mental insult and oppression, as well as no confiscation of personal property. It is not worthwhile to lay down your lives for Wall Street monopolists. Stubborn resistance means death while giving up arms means living. Call your fellowmen to lay down arms and cease resistance immediately. Come over to our side.
   THE CHINESE PEOPLE'S VOLUNTEER FORCES.

According to Colonel Edwards, the leaflets failed to entice any soldier to desert. In fact, most of them laughed when they read them. If the Chinese wanted victory, they would have to earn it the hard way.[80]

FEBRUARY 14, LATE AFTERNOON–EARLY EVENING: 115TH DIVISION, 39TH ARMY, CPVF, SOUTH OF CHIPYONG-NI

Beyond earshot of Allied ears and behind the hills that surrounded the U.N. perimeter like an amphitheater, the Chinese were waiting for nightfall as they licked their wounds. The previous night, they had thrown wave after wave at George Company. Despite overwhelming numbers, the attack had ended in failure. In the east, in Easy and King Companies' sector, the communists had hurled hundreds of soldiers at the American lines, many of whom perished in the railroad tunnel or were burned to death when Captain Sawyer detonated his fougasse.

Despite the butcher's bill, the surviving regiments and divisions would resume the attack at nightfall. In the French sector, the 376th and 377th Regiments of the 126th Division would attempt to fix Monclar's battalion. Farther east, in 2nd Battalion's sector, the survivors of the 356th Regiment, 119th Division, would try to breach the American lines in G Company's area.

In addition to these forces, the commander of the 39th Army brought up a fresh division from the Twin Tunnels area to continue the attack if the 356th, 376th, and 377th Regiments failed. This was the 115th Division, which had three intact regiments: the 343rd, the 344th, and the 345th. Unlike the previous night, the communist officers had a better grasp of the terrain. This time, instead of probing for weak spots, the 115th Division commander planned to conduct an all–out assault. From west to east, the 3rd Battalion of the 343rd Regiment would occupy Hill 129, and from there it would attack Monclar's 1st Company with the task of fixing it so that it would be unable to reinforce G Company. In the center, 2nd Battalion, 343rd Regiment, and 3rd Battalion, 344th Regiment, would be the decisive operation with the task of breaching G Company's main line of resistance. In the east, 1st Battalion, 344th Regiment, would attack to fix F and E Companies. At the decisive point, the enemy would have approximately a six-to-one advantage. The division commander allocated the entire 345th Regiment as a reserve and an exploitation force. It was a formidable enemy.[81]

As the Americans readied themselves for another night of combat, another storm was gathering only a few kilometers south of Lieutenant McGee's location. That evening, it would make landfall on 3rd Platoon.

CHAPTER 7

Chipyong-ni: The Second Night

"This time the Chinese had a plan."

—Col. Paul Freeman, commander, 23rd Infantry Regiment

FEBRUARY 14–15, 1951, 1732–0045 HOURS: ALONG THE LINE, G COMPANY, 23RD INFANTRY REGIMENT, MCGEE AND CURTIS HILLS

As the sun slipped behind the western ridgeline, the bushes and trees on Hill 397 began to stir as if they were alive. From his vantage point, Lieutenant McGee saw tiny dots appear along the slopes of Hill 397. The platoon leader thought they looked like worker ants scampering down an anthill. He knew what was coming. His commander, Lieutenant Heath, also saw the coming invasion.

Harley Wilburn recalled what he witnessed that night. "We saw the Chinese coming from probably two miles south of George Company," said Wilburn. "And they were carrying torches of all things. I couldn't believe it, but there were so many of them, they weren't afraid of nothing. They came right across that flat ground carrying torches towards our position. . . . You see thousands of lights coming at you like that at night and you're just a young nineteen [or] twenty year old man, it really shakes you up."[1]

At 1732 hours, the G Company commander requested that the battalion register their 81mm mortars in front his position. Like McGee, Heath wanted to be ready. Several minutes later, the radio operators from 2nd Battalion reported to regiment "many gooks on [Hill] 397, firing on them now."[2]

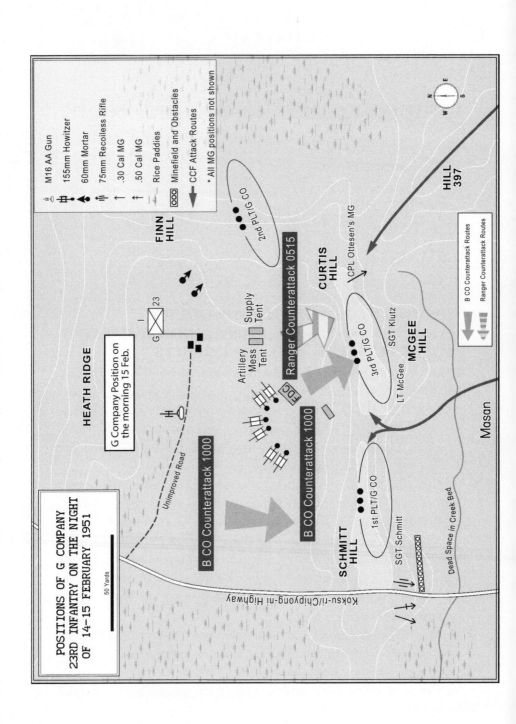

POSITIONS OF G COMPANY
23RD INFANTRY ON THE NIGHT
OF 14–15 FEBRUARY 1951

50 Yards

HEATH RIDGE

FINN HILL

G Company Position on
the morning 15 Feb.

Unimproved Road

G | 23

Artillery

Mess Tent

Supply Tent

FDC

Ranger Counterattack 0515

CURTIS HILL

CPL Ottesen's MG

B CO Counterattack 1000

B CO Counterattack 1000

2nd PLT/G CO

3rd PLT/G CO

SGT Klutz

MCGEE HILL

LT McGee

HILL 397

SCHMITT HILL

1st PLT/G CO

SGT Schmitt

Dead Space in Creek Bed

Masan

Koksu-ri/Chipyong-ni Highway

M16 AA Gun
155mm Howitzer
60mm Mortar
75mm Recoilless Rifle
.30 Cal MG
.50 Cal MG
Rice Paddies
Minefield and Obstacles
CCF Attack Routes

* All MG positions not shown

B CO Counterattack Routes
Ranger Counterattack Routes

N
W   E
S

The forward observer for the 37th Field Artillery Battalion was Lt. William H. Gibson. He requested a fire mission, its target the saddle that connected Hill 397 with McGee Hill. Within minutes, twenty rounds of 105mm HE exploded on the spot. Corporal McCormack, the forward observer for the G Company 60mm mortars, directed his own fire mission on the same target. Despite the barrage, the Chinese kept streaming down the hill.[3]

Around 1800 hours, the anticipated attack began. "There were more bugles and whistles," McGee later said. "And we thought we even heard something similar to drums. Some of the men heard digging, and we thought we could hear some of their machine guns that they pulled on carts. So we could tell that they were coming in force."[4]

This attack was different for Colonel Freeman. He later wrote:

This time, the Chinese had a plan. First, there was a heavy concentration of mortar and artillery fire which rained down on our position just at dark. This preparation lasted an hour and at seven o'clock the weird bugle calls rang out to the south. The enemy went to work again on the two roads leading into our position on each flank of the Second Battalion. Here the enemy concentrated his force. In column of companies he came down Hill 397 against G Company.[5]

Unlike the previous night, when 2nd Battalion faced large probing attacks along the length of its perimeter, the swarming Chinese targeted a particular spot along G Company's main line of resistance. Almost immediately, McGee knew he and his platoon were in for a long evening. "They hit us just about the full length of my whole platoon's position, plus the left flank of the First Platoon," he said. "They were coming in pretty steady, more of them, and they were firing more . . . they were standing—some of them even came at us running—and firing."[6]

Heath heard the firing in 3rd Platoon's sector and alerted Colonel Edwards that G Company was under attack. In response, the battalion commander requested a section of tanks from the regimental tank company to buttress the G Company lines.[7]

Meanwhile, the enemy claimed its first casualty of the night. Within minutes of the opening fusillade, the light machine gunner attached to

Cpl. Eugene L. Ottesen's squad slumped over in his foxhole, wounded. McGee had positioned the machine gun to cover the eastern flank of his platoon on Curtis Hill. Without hesitation, Ottesen jumped behind the gun and opened fire while the platoon medic treated the wounded soldier.

The corporal from Minnesota operated the M1919 gun as if it were his primary weapon. Despite the stream of incoming direct fire from an enemy squad on Hill 397, Ottesen chugged away at the onrushing Chinese, who piled up in front of his machine-gun pit as their bodies crumpled onto the frozen ground. Wave after wave crashed against Ottesen's lead wall. For several hours, the men of 3rd Platoon battled the Chinese to a standstill, but they could not hold out forever. The enemy was far too numerous.[8]

Lieutenant Heath had no reserves to plug the holes. Instead, he went to Baker Battery of the 503rd Field Artillery and asked for reinforcements. Since the enemy was too close for howitzers, the 155's of the 503rd were useless. Therefore, the gun crews pulling security on the gun line had little else to do. The battery commander agreed to lend Heath some of his artillerymen, but each time the G Company commander left with a group, they magically disappeared by the time Heath reached the main line. After the third attempt, Heath gave up. It was obvious to him that the gunners did not want to be infantrymen, even though their lives depended on it.

One man kept trying to recruit more men. Between 2100 and 2200 hours, Capt. John A. Elledge, the liaison officer between the 37th Field Artillery and B Battery, 503rd Field Artillery, found a squad of eleven soldiers from the 503rd who were willing to fight. Moreover, they had a .50-caliber machine gun. Elledge led them to 1st Platoon's section of the G Company line, where five of the men and their squad leader set up their machine gun while the other five occupied foxholes around the crew-served weapon and acted as security for it.[9]

While enemy infantry fixed the soldiers of 3rd Platoon, an enemy demolition unit crawled up the hill, using the dead space between 1st and 3rd Platoons, and closed within a few meters of 1st Platoon's eastern flank. There, the demolition team detonated several pole charges, which killed three U.S. soldiers and a Korean volunteer. Worse, it meant the Chinese had taken out two foxholes and were now on the main line of resistance.

In a postwar interview, McGee described how the Chinese used the pole charges. "They had satchel charges attached to the ends of sticks or poles, and they'd push that pole right up to the edge of our holes. We stopped a lot of them, but once they got a satchel charge into a hole, it was too late. They were using grenades and small arms to try to keep the occupants of the foxholes down to where they could get close enough to deposit their satchel charges." The old platoon leader added, "When you put a satchel charge in on top of two men, you know there's really . . . nothing left."[10]

After the ear-splitting explosions, the communists did not waste any time. They immediately brought up a machine-gun team and occupied one of the captured foxholes. Within seconds, the enemy gunners opened fire on McGee's 3rd Platoon, cutting a swath across its flank. The first victim was one of McGee's BAR gunners, who stumbled into McGee's foxhole, where the medic bandaged his wounds. The lieutenant dropped his carbine and grabbed the automatic rifle from the wounded soldier.[11]

Realizing that the machine-gun fire was emanating from 1st Platoon's area, McGee grabbed the field phone and rang up Lieutenant Heath, his commander. "Heath," he shouted into the receiver as tracers skipped past his foxhole, "is the 1st Platoon still up in position?"

After several seconds, the George Company commander replied, "Yes."

In fact, Heath had no inkling what was going on atop Schmitt Hill. When McGee had asked about 1st Platoon, the company commander called the 1st Platoon leader, M/Sgt. Emery S. Toth, who told him that his men were still in position. The problem was the platoon leader was not on the hill with his unit; his command post was behind the hill. SFC Donald R. Schmitt, the platoon sergeant, was running the platoon atop the ridge; however, he was in a hole on the western side of the line. From his position, he could not have known that his eastern flank was gone. Lulled into a false sense of security, Schmitt told Sergeant Toth that his platoon was still in position. Toth then informed Heath that everything was under control. Unfortunately for G Company, 2nd Battalion, and the 23rd Infantry Regiment, he was wrong. It was now almost 2200 hours. The Chinese had breached the main line of resistance, and the only U.N. officer who knew about it was Lieutenant McGee.[12]

Sergeant Kluttz, McGee's platoon sergeant, also wanted to know what had happened to 1st Platoon. From his foxhole, he yelled, "Anyone from 1st Platoon?" McGee shouted out the same question.

No one answered. McGee rang up Heath and asked him again if 1st Platoon was still in position. Heath's answer was the same. Before the platoon leader from 3rd Platoon could find out what the situation was with Toth's platoon, he watched several CPVF soldiers duck into a hole on his western flank near his 2nd Squad. They were now behind Sgt. Franklin Querry's hole. McGee tried to phone the threatened squad leader, but enemy mortars had cut most of the communication wire to his squads.

Determined to alert his sergeant, he shouted to Querry, "There are four of them at the rear of your hole. Toss a grenade up and over."

Querry heard his lieutenant, but when he tried to lob his grenades, the enemy machine-gun team occupying the foxhole in 1st Platoon's area swung the barrel over and opened enfilade fire on Querry, pinning the sergeant in his hole.

Clearly, McGee's platoon was in danger. The Chinese were in a position to flank his entire platoon and roll up the rest of G Company. With few options, the platoon leader then tapped his runner, Pvt. Cletis D. Inmon, and ordered him to open fire on the four infiltrators. Meanwhile, McGee emptied the magazine from his own recently acquired BAR. The deadly burst from the two guns killed the four CPVF soldiers instantly. The battle, though, was only beginning. It was now 2210 hours.

Meanwhile, Ottesen continued to fire away at the dark shapes charging up McGee Hill. According to McGee, the corporal's attention was fixated on the slope in front of his position. Therefore, he did not see the fifteen to twenty Chinese scrambling up the hill toward the saddle between Schmitt and McGee Hills. Luckily, the lieutenant saw them. "About fifteen or twenty of them are coming up to your right front," warned McGee.

By the light of the half-moon, McGee saw Querry's hole, but he did not see Querry firing from it. He saw a bobbing head and realized his squad leader did not intend to expose himself to shoot at the approaching soldiers when an enemy machine gun was firing at him from his western flank. Once again, McGee and his runner, Private Inmon, raised their weapons and began to chip away at the oncoming Chinese mob.

Despite the furious fire from the lieutenant's BAR, the Chinese closed in on Querry's hole. Finally, they were within hand–grenade range, and several enemy infantry chucked some potato mashers at the sergeant's position. McGee yelled at the 2nd Squad leader, ordering him to toss his own grenades back at the Chinese.

Instead, the enemy grenades detonated, wounding the foxhole's occupants. Querry and another soldier climbed out of the hole and scrambled toward McGee and Inmon, screaming, "Lieutenant McGee, I'm hit! Lieutenant McGee, I'm hit!" They left a single private behind to face the Chinese alone. Within seconds, a satchel charge landed inside Querry's former home and exploded, obliterating the soldier.

The two survivors braved the enemy tracers and stampeded into McGee's hole, collapsing on top of the lieutenant and the runner. Querry had some shrapnel wounds from a grenade, but otherwise was unharmed. The other soldier, though, had a more severe injury. McGee was furious—with two bodies on top of him, he could not fire. "Get the hell out of here and get back with your squad!" he roared at his squad leader.

The officer's words spurred Querry to climb out of the foxhole and return to his unit. He had not gotten far when a bullet slammed into his shoulder, spinning him around. McGee shouted for a litter team. Within minutes, they arrived and evacuated Querry and the other injured soldier from 2nd Squad.[13]

McGee and Inmon remained and continued to blaze away at the never-ending swarms of Chinese. However, soon McGee's BAR began to misfire. McGee later explained, "The ammunition we had been supplied with was mostly from the airdrop. The planes had to come in so low over those frozen rice paddies, that when they dropped the ammo, the concussion of it hitting the ground had crimped some of the cartridges, and it was these cartridges that were jamming our weapons. About every fifteen rounds or so, the BAR would jam." But he had a solution: "I had a little pen knife," he said, "which I'd use to eject the shell from my BAR when it jammed."[14]

By 2300 hours, 3rd Platoon no longer had wire communications with the company. Facing annihilation, McGee ordered PFC John N. Martin to race back to the company command post and ask Lieutenant Heath for more men, ammunition, and litter-bearers. The intrepid private dashed back toward the company headquarters, dodging random tracer rounds and mortar shells. When Martin arrived, he informed the commander about the situation on McGee Hill, and Heath secured fifteen men from the 503rd Field Artillery to send to 3rd Platoon as reinforcements. Around 2350 hours, Martin set out.

McGee saw Martin's group as they approached his position from the command post. When the men from the 503rd reached the crest of McGee Hill, Chinese soldiers opened fire, scattering them and leaving only three with Martin. They did not last long either. A mortar round exploded, killing one and injuring another. McGee never knew what happened to the third man. Undeterred, Martin returned to his foxhole.[15]

The beleaguered platoon leader could only swear at his misfortune, but not for too long. The enemy did not give him the respite to recover his wits. Waiting for Martin to return, his BAR had become a liability after he dropped his penknife during the fighting; as a result, he had no way to eject the spent cartridges from the chamber. Fortunately, his carbine still worked, and with it he plinked away at the onrushing communist hordes.

At one point, McGee spotted a charging CPVF soldier who was only 10 feet from his foxhole. The lieutenant raised his carbine and squeezed the trigger. *THUNK!* The bolt refused to close. The bitterly cold weather had frozen the oil inside the carbine, causing it to gum up the receiver. McGee had only moments before the enemy plunged a bayonet into his head. The officer shoved his palm against the charging handle. The brute force worked, and the bolt hit home. He fired four rounds at the enemy soldier, killing him.[16]

Before McGee and Inmon could enjoy their good fortune, the enemy machine-gun team in 1st Platoon's sector discharged several bursts toward their foxhole. One round hit Inmon in the eye. He reeled back into the hole with his hands over his face. Inmon cried out: "I am hit in the face. I am hit in the face. I don't want my mother to see me this way. Get me back off the hill."

McGee could see that Inmon's wound was serious. He watched blood spurt out from between his runner's fingers, as if the injured private were plugging a hole in a dike with only his hands. The lieutenant spoke to him, "Lay down, I can't take you out now." He called over to his platoon sergeant for help. "Hey Sergeant Kluttz," McGee shouted, "Send the medic over. Inmon's been hit."

Shortly afterward, a medic appeared and bandaged Inmon's face. The lieutenant asked his runner if he could still fire his M1 Garand. Inmon replied that he could not. The platoon leader needed to keep Inmon in the fight to prevent him from panicking.

"Can you load the magazines for my carbine?" asked McGee.

Inmon nodded and said he would try. For twenty minutes, Inmon and the medic hunkered down in the foxhole while McGee blazed away at the enemy. When the lieutenant felt the enemy fire slacken, he ordered the medic to take the injured private back to the casualty collection point at the company command post.[17]

Ten minutes after the medic evacuated Inmon, McGee noticed that Ottesen's machine gun was silent on Curtis Hill. "What happened to the machine gun? It stopped firing," he asked Sergeant Kluttz, who was still in the next hole.

Like McGee, Kluttz had no idea what had happened to Ottesen, but he did know that the Chinese were now between them and Cpl. Raymond Bennett's 1st Squad, which occupied the eastern flank of the platoon. They realized that Ottesen's squad had ceased to exist. The platoon leader called Bennett on the phone (fortunately, the enemy mortars had not cut the line between him and Bennett's 1st Squad). When Bennett answered, McGee ordered him to send a couple of soldiers to plug the hole between his squad and the platoon leader's foxhole.

Signalmen had reestablished the communication between Heath and McGee. With enfilade fire now coming from both of his flanks, the platoon leader was convinced that the enemy occupied a portion of 1st Platoon's main line of resistance. He called his commander again and asked, "Heath, is the 1st Platoon still there?"

The acting G Company commander assured him that Schmitt was in control and 1st Platoon was still on the hill. After several minutes of arguing and another visit from Private Martin, McGee finally persuaded his commanding officer that the Chinese had breached the main line of resistance. In response, Heath called over to Fox Company and asked for reinforcements. Captain Tyrrell, the Fox Company commander, selected 2nd Squad, 3rd Platoon, under the command of Sgt. Kenneth G. Kelly, to head out. The time was now 0045 hours: it was already too late.[18]

FEBRUARY 14, 2210 HOURS:
MACHINE-GUN TEAM, H COMPANY,
23RD INFANTRY REGIMENT (ATTACHED TO
E COMPANY), ALONG NANCE HILL

To keep other units from reinforcing the beleaguered G Company, the Chinese hit other sectors in 2nd Battalion's area of operations. At 2200 hours, CPVF units mounted a major assault up the draw that served as the boundary between F and E Companies. Waiting for them were four machine-gun teams from H Company, Seymour "Hoppy" Harris's team among them.

At first, Harris wondered if the Chinese would even come that night. Initially, all the action seemed to be to his left, but not to his front. "The only sounds are firefights taking place in the distance," he wrote in a letter. "Off to my left, I can hear the sound of automatic weapons and rifle fire. Green and red tracers arch through the sky like a 4th of July fireworks display at home. It would be beautiful, I think, if it weren't for the fact men were dying over there."

Earlier that evening, Corporal O'Shell had issued clear instructions to Harris, telling the replacement not to open fire until the first man had reached the barbed wire in front of his hole. Harris did not agree with his NCO's plan. He asked himself sardonically, "Why don't we just let them come into the bunkers with us?"

Shortly after 2200 hours, Harris thought he saw something in the wire. "I see the gooks coming, but at first it doesn't register on me. I look away," wrote Harris. "I thought, God, they look like ghosts. I must be going nuts! Then I slowly turn my head and look back up the draw. What I see makes my stomach do a backflip. Chinese! My God, the draw is full of them. They are about 100 yards from the wire. They come silently. Like little clowns. There is no chatter. The night is still as death. On and on they come. I wonder if anyone else sees them. My God, am I the only one who sees them?"

He kicked his companion and whispered, as if shouting under his breath, "Wake up! They're here!"

Groggy, but awake, his comrade asked, "Who's here?"

"The gooks! Who the hell do you think? Get the hell up, the balls going to open!" replied Harris.

Alarmed, the other soldier peered over the edge of the fox-hole. When he saw the oncoming Chinese horde, he started to mutter uncontrollably, "Oh, no! Holy Jesus, we've had it! Oh Jesus! Oh Jesus!" Instead of preparing for battle, the terror-stricken soldier burrowed into his sleeping bag, cocooning himself.

Disgusted, Harris raised his carbine and looked down the barrel of his weapon. "The gooks are nearly to the wire," he said. "I have been told to keep my carbine on semi-automatic, but I have my sights on three gooks who are rather close together, and without hardly thinking, I slip the selector lever forward, putting the weapon on full automatic."

It did not take long for a Chinese soldier to reach the first strands of barbed wire. On cue, Corporal O'Shell opened fire with his Garand, and Harris heard it *thump*. He inhaled one more time and squeezed his trigger.

Bedlam ensued. Harris described the scene:

It is like every weapon is wired together. They all go off at once. Tracers like laser beams streak out and I see them go clean through the gooks. I hear them scream, and go down like stalks of corn before a corn cutter. It is only seconds and the mortars start to rain in. And right behind them come the 105's, time fuse and point detonated. They turn the draw into an orange-gray hell. The noise is deafening beyond description. I am frozen, spellbound by the sight and sound of it. For a time I just kneel and stare at the horrible sight before me. Finally, I come to my senses and start to fire, although I cannot see a thing to fire at because of the smoke and flying debris. But the feel of the weapon jumping in my hands makes me feel better. By God, I'm doing something at least. It is 2210 hours.

After several minutes, the firing died down. The only sounds anyone could hear were the whimpers and murmurs from the wounded and dying Chinese soldiers. One of them sounded like a broken record. "Banzai, Banzai, Banzai!" he cried.

"Does anybody see that bastard?" asked a perturbed soldier.

According to Harris, the caterwauling ended several minutes later. Unfortunately, the communists were far from finished. Before he could catch his breath and relax, someone shouted, "Look sharp! Here comes them stupid shits again!"

"I look out the bunker and sure enough, here they come again," wrote Harris. "The draw is crawling with them. My God, I can't believe it. No one could be that stupid. Again, they are to the wire before O'Shell opens the ball. And it is a repeat performance."

But this time was different. Seconds after the gunfight resumed, a huge explosion rocked the earth; when the smoke cleared, a hole had appeared in the barbed wire. The enemy had detonated some type of Bangalore torpedo to clear a path through it. As if they had rehearsed it, the Chinese flooded into the gap. However, they failed to suppress the H Company machine guns before they attacked.

"Our machine guns pour their fire into this opening and soon it is clogged with dead gooks," explained Harris. Before he could celebrate the carnage, a nearby sapper opened fire. "I see a blue flash that seems to come out of the ground," he wrote. "It is a burp gun. The slugs rip up the dirt right in front of my face. I feel as if someone has stuck a lighted cigarette against my upper lip. I drop my carbine and in panic fall to the back of the bunker, pawing at my mouth. I cannot imagine what has happened. I can feel my lip swelling, but as far as I can see, there is only a little blood. My fingers keep catching onto something. Each time this happens it feels like a bee sting."

Fortunately, the wound was superficial, and Harris continued to fight. In his mind, he did not have a choice. The Chinese seemed unstoppable.[19]

FEBRUARY 14–15, 2100–0142 HOURS: COMMAND POST, 23RD INFANTRY REGIMENT, CHIPYONG-NI

The staff of 23rd Infantry Regiment knew they were not going to sleep that night. They continued to operate the radios and phones, sending out information to the subordinate units while receiving reports from division. At 2100 hours, the regimental radio operator alerted the battalions. "British lead elements reached East/West Three-Six grid line," he began, "[British] are staying there overnight. Will not come up tonight but will come first light in the morning."

The operator added good news about the American relief column: "5th Cavalry passed thru them . . . cut towards the northwest. [5th Cavalry] will stay there overnight. Will not come tonight but will come up first light in the morning."

Maj. John H. Newell was the regiment's S4, or senior supply staff officer for the 23rd Infantry. At 2130 hours, he informed the regiment that, despite the airdrops, the Tomahawks were short of 60mm and 81mm mortar ammunition. Even worse, the men did not have enough grenades—an essential weapon for night fighting. The messages confirmed that whatever they had on hand would have to last through the night.

At 2315 hours, both 2nd and 3rd Battalions reported receiving several rounds from a possible self-propelled gun. Five minutes later, the deluge intensified. The Tomahawk command post informed division that it was receiving "heavy" self-propelled, mortar, and small-arms fire. In addition, 2nd Battalion was under attack from Hill 397. By 2330 hours, the news coming in from Easy and Fox Companies indicated that the Chinese had concentrated their main attack against Colonel Edwards's battalion.

For another ninety minutes, the fighting seesawed back and forth along the southern side of the perimeter. By midnight, the Chinese 356th Regiment was a spent force. It had attempted to breach 2nd Battalion lines on two occasions, and with the exception of the penetration in G Company's western flank, it had failed. Unfortunately, the CPVF had more infantry. Following the 356th were the men of 1st Battalion, 115th Regiment. Shortly after midnight, they attacked.

The regiment had no clue that G Company was under tremendous strain. At 0050 hours, a Firefly dropped flares over Hill 397 to provide better targets for the machine gunners and mortar men, but it was not until 0142 hours that regiment received its first report that G Company was in trouble. At that moment, Colonel Freeman only knew that Heath's company was under heavy attack; he did not know that the Chinese already had penetrated his lines.[20]

THURSDAY, FEBRUARY 15, 0110–0130 HOURS: ALONG THE LINE, E COMPANY, 23RD INFANTRY REGIMENT, NANCE AND SAWYER HILLS

Elsewhere, the Chinese continued to probe along the length of 2nd Battalion's main line of resistance. At 0110 hours, a probing attack hit 2nd and 3rd Platoons. Shortly after, Captain Sawyer lost landline contact with 1st Platoon, and in response, he ordered his radioman, Douglas Graney, to fix the connection. Graney could not send his other linemen because they already were repairing the wire for 2nd and 3rd Platoon. With no one else available, he set out to complete the task himself.

"I grabbed a spool of wire and started down the hill toward the 1st Platoon," he wrote. "Heavy machine gun and rifle bullets slapped the frozen ground along our entire front. Chinese still trying to cut through our barbed wire were killed only to be replaced by more cutters. Boxcars flew overhead as I ran across the rice paddies. The flyboys launched flares by parachute that gave light to help us spot the enemy. I froze where I stood, as trained, when the light of a flare caught me in the open."

Tony Rego, a machine gunner in Easy Company, spotted Graney and shouted, "What the hell are you doing?"

"I'm pretending to be a tree," replied Graney.

"Trees don't grow in rice paddies. Get your ass out of there," yelled Rego.

Graney ducked into Rego's foxhole and waited for the flare to burn out. When it did, he climbed out of the hole and scampered over to the railroad embankment. There, he found Lt. Charles Davidson, the 2nd Platoon leader. The lieutenant and several other soldiers, including a machine-gun team and a bazooka gunner, were firing into the railroad tunnel.

Graney asked the lieutenant, "I thought we boobie [sic] trapped the tunnel?"

Davidson nodded and replied, "We did. The gooks kept pushing their men to blow up all the traps we set. The Chinese must have a hundred dead soldiers in there. And still they come. But as long as we have ammo, we'll hold. Are you going up to the 1st Platoon with that wire?"

"Yeah," answered Graney.

"Watch yourself," warned Davidson. "The gooks are all over the place."

"Thanks. See you later," said Graney. He ran up Sawyer Hill to link up with 1st Platoon. After several minutes of bumbling in the dark, he found the 1st Platoon leader's foxhole and climbed in to check the wire. After reconnecting the field phone to the wire on the spool, he began to unwind it, trailing the new wire behind him as he walked back to his foxhole at the company command post.

Suddenly, the Chinese attacked again. "I reached the top of the hill near my foxhole as tracers and blasts from grenades erupted," wrote Graney. "The enemy launched another attack. It didn't last long. Our front quieted as Chinese, who were able to run, dashed back up the hills to our front. The moans of the wounded and dying Chinese lying in the blood soaked snow could be heard across our entire front."

Though the attack had ended in front of Easy Company, Graney could hear the sounds of battle elsewhere. He wrote, "Machine gun and rifle fire from George Company's position continued. The Chinese had opened a hole through George's defenses."

At the time, he did not know how precarious the situation was west of his location. If George Company fell, then the rest of 2nd Battalion, including Easy Company, would be in grave danger.[21]

FEBRUARY 15, 0045–0300 HOURS: ALONG THE LINE, G COMPANY, 23RD INFANTRY REGIMENT, MCGEE AND CURTIS HILLS

Cpl. Raymond Bennett stumbled into the darkness with a couple of his men. Thanks to McGee's warning, he knew the Chinese were somewhere out in front of him. Fortunately, his 1st Squad had beaten all comers, but now he needed to roll back the Chinese on his western flank or risk being overrun. Within minutes of leaving his hole, he found the enemy and even shot and killed one of the enemy buglers as he was sounding his second note.

The communists fought back. One of them hurled a grenade at Bennett's squad, and the subsequent explosion sent shrapnel everywhere. One piece blew a chunk off Bennett's hand. Before the squad leader could recover from the shock, another enemy soldier shot him in the shoulder, sending him staggering backward. Another grenade detonated, and this time a fragment hit him in the leg. Bennett, now seriously wounded, could not remain on the line. He hobbled down the hill toward the command post with another wounded soldier from 1st Squad, PFC Roy F. Benoit.[22]

Meanwhile, Sergeant Kelly's squad from F Company arrived at 0100 hours and linked up with Sergeant Kluttz, who had recovered Ottesen's machine gun, which was still operable. The platoon sergeant led them past McGee's hole. Heath had ordered McGee to counterattack with

Kluttz and the new squad to recapture the area on 1st Platoon's eastern flank. When the platoon sergeant was in position, he charged forward. Waiting for him were two Chinese soldiers with submachine guns. Kluttz killed them both, but not before they had wounded everyone in Kelly's squad. The platoon sergeant returned to his foxhole with the recaptured light machine gun.

When Kluttz walked past McGee's position, he told them that everyone in Kelly's squad was wounded. Despite the casualties, the platoon sergeant knew they had to stay on the hill for long as possible: "McGee, we have to stop them."[23]

Cpl. Herbert Ziebell was one of the few men still alive on McGee Hill from 3rd Platoon. Like many of the soldiers, he was a replacement who had arrived in late January. Originally, he had been military police, but the 2nd Infantry Division did not need police—it needed infantry. The men at the replacement depot took away his carbine and gave him an M1 Garand, which he never had a chance to zero. "I couldn't hit nothing with that M-1 and I was hunting all my life," Ziebell later said.

Now, he was stuck in a foxhole with the Chinese swarming all around him. He quickly realized that engaging targets to his front would only mark his position for the enemy, so he held his fire. When the Chinese broke through on his west side, he banged away at them with his Garand.

"And when I shot I was pointing to the side of me," he said, "so they [the Chinese] saw that flash over on my right of my rifle. And the bullets were hitting over there first. And boy did I get down in the hole, my partner and me both. Well I didn't shoot for quite awhile, and they left me alone because they thought they got me."[24]

At 0200 hours, G Company's main line of resistance disintegrated. Without receiving orders, 2nd Platoon, which held the eastern flank of G Company's line, pulled out. This unplanned movement unhinged Heath's entire battle position and meant disaster for McGee's platoon. McGee said the Chinese would "get in those holes and start assaulting. It got to the point where my positions were being hit from the front, right, flank, and the rear. They were hitting with grenades, small arms fire, and machine gun fire, and that's how I started losing my positions."[25]

The platoon leader called over to Kluttz and asked him about the remnants of Bennett's 1st Squad. "I think that three or four are still left," his platoon sergeant replied.

Kluttz's machine gun was jamming. McGee heard it sputtering and shouted, "It looks like they have got us Kluttz."

The sergeant declared, "Let's kill as many of the sons-of-bitches as we can before they get us."

At 0215 hours, a round jammed in the chamber of Kluttz's M1919 machine gun, and he could not eject it. The platoon sergeant told his lieutenant, and McGee decided it was time to leave. "Let's try to get out," McGee said. "Let's throw what grenades we have left, fire what we can and try to get back over the hill toward Bennett's squad."

The Chinese were now all over McGee and Curtis Hills, and the two survivors had to fight their way down the slope. After several minutes of searching, Kluttz and McGee found only two men left from their entire platoon: the runner, Private Martin, and Corporal Ziebell from 1st Squad. Sergeant Schmitt had withdrawn the remnants of 1st Platoon from its position. By 0300 hours, no one alive remained along G Company's section of the main line of resistance.[26]

Lieutenant McGee wondered how he had survived the night when most of the soldiers in his platoon had not. In a postwar interview, he confessed, "All of my men stayed in their holes until they were killed or wounded."[27]

Individual acts of heroism went unseen, but when the survivors returned the next day, they found many of their comrades still in their foxholes. Pvts. Burl J. Mace, Paul C. Baker, and Bruce M. Broyles were among those heroes. When the soldiers of George Company pulled out, they remained in their holes and fought to the death. The survivors found them the next morning, surrounded by piles of enemy bodies. Each received posthumous Silver Stars for their gallantry.[28]

Like Mace, Baker, and Broyles, Cpl. Hal McGovern chose to stay and fight, manning a machine gun in 1st Platoon. With the Chinese flooding past him, he ordered the men who were part of his team to withdraw to safety. Then he stood up in his hole and opened fire with his light machine gun, holding it like a rifle. His blistering fusillade delayed the Chinese so his comrades could escape, but he could not save himself. He died in his hole, where they found him the next day.[29]

Pvt. Paul Stamper was another hero who died trying to save his friends in G Company. For much of the fighting, Stamper ran around the battlefield, repairing signal wire so that the platoons could communicate with each other and the company. At one point, he ran across an open field, dodging incoming mortar rounds, to repair a break in the line. Once fixed, he came under fire from a nearby enemy machine gun. Without a second thought, he crawled toward the enemy soldiers. When he was close enough, he tossed a grenade at the machine-gun team, destroying it and the gunners. Unfortunately, another enemy soldier killed him shortly thereafter. G Company survivors found his body the next morning. [30]

When Pvt. Albert H. Enger saw an abandoned machine gun, he jumped into the foxhole and opened fire at the charging Chinese. For several minutes, he mowed down wave after wave. Eventually, like the others, he was overwhelmed, and like his compatriots, was found dead in his hole behind his machine gun.[31]

Pvt. Richard L. Svitck refused to leave his wounded comrades behind on the battlefield, several times carrying injured soldiers from Curtis Hill back to the aid station. He continued to return to the ridge even after the Chinese had captured some of the positions. Eventually his luck ran out, and the survivors found his body the next morning on the hill.

For their selfless service, the Army also awarded McGovern, Stamper, Enger, and Svitck posthumous Silver Stars.[32]

Not all of the heroes were riflemen. Pvt. Delmar Patton of Ohio was a mortar man serving as an ammo bearer for G Company's 60mm mortar section. When he saw the wounded men from the line platoons staggering down from the ridgeline, he grabbed his rifle and headed up the hill. Patton remained there and fought off the Chinese until he died; he was found in a hole the next day, and like Svitck, awarded a posthumous Silver Star.[33]

However, not all of the Silver Stars were posthumous. PFC Harry L. Nace survived. When he reached the command post after the rest of G Company had withdrawn from its primary battle position, he discovered they had left two working .30-caliber machine guns on the hill and volunteered to retrieve them. Braving a deadly grazing fire, he crossed 400 meters of open ground four times to bring back the two guns and all of their ammunition. During one of the trips, he was wounded when a rifle round hit him, but the wound did not prevent him from completing his mission. He saved the two weapons and prevented the Chinese from using them against their owners.[34]

PFC William D. Gilleland was a platoon runner for G Company. At one point in the fighting, shrapnel from enemy mortar rounds cut one of the wires from the command post to his platoon. The young soldier from Iowa dashed out into the open and traced the wire to the break. When he found it, he immediately repaired it, even though mortar rounds were exploding everywhere around him. He then returned to his platoon. Shortly thereafter, he treated a wounded comrade and evacuated him off the front line, crossing the deadly open area between it and the aid station. Later, he carried .30-caliber ammunition across the same open space so that his platoon machine gun could keep firing.[35]

PFC Pete Lucas, Jr., was the gunner for one of G Company's 60mm mortars. When the line collapsed, he remained at his post and kept hanging rounds as the remnants of G Company streamed past him. When he felt a sting in his arm, he knew an unseen enemy soldier had shot him, but the fresh wound only slowed him down; it did not stop him. He continued to shoot his mortar until everyone had withdrawn from Curtis and McGee Hills.[36]

Cpl. Joe E. Halbrook was the section leader for one of G Company's 57mm recoilless rifle teams. He led his unit of Filipino-Americans and one Korean on a mission to neutralize some of the enemy mortars firing from the cemetery near the village of Masan. Braving the incoming rounds, he took one of the recoilless rifles and moved to a better firing position on Finn Hill in 2nd Platoon's sector. As he crept across the battlefield, he was under constant enemy fire. Despite the zipping tracers, he survived and loaded his weapon, firing it at one of the enemy mortar teams. His recoilless rifle shell shot through the air at a speed of 365 meters per second and detonated on contact, silencing it. "You'd see a fire from a mortar, and I'd fire at it," said Halbrook in a postwar interview. "I fired a lot of rounds. I don't know how many."

When the G Company line buckled, Halbrook refused to leave. He ordered his men to withdraw, but remained at his position to provide cover for them. With only hand grenades, his recoilless rifle, and his carbine, he held off the enemy until his men escaped. A few moments after the men withdrew, one of the attacking Chinese soldiers shot him, and the corporal realized it was time to go. He destroyed the recoilless rifle with a thermite grenade and left. Against the odds, Halbrook survived and later returned to duty.[37]

Not all of the heroes were in G Company. PFC Leslie E. Alston was a jeep driver and part of the forward observer team for B Battery, 503rd Field Artillery Battalion. When the Chinese broke through the main line, Alston dashed through enemy fire to help replace inoperable machine guns while resupplying other soldiers with ammunition. He rescued several wounded comrades while under fire and carried them back to the battalion aid station.[38]

Nace, Gilleland, Lucas, Halbrook, and Alston all received the Silver Star for their gallantry that night.

Sadly, the survivors never found Corporal Ottesen's remains. The Army initially listed him as missing in action, but later the adjutant changed his status to died-while-missing. His bravery, though, was not in doubt. The Army awarded him a Silver Star in absentia shortly after the battle. Kluttz and McGee also earned the Silver Star for their daring and courageous leadership of 3rd Platoon. Alas, McGee's fighting was far from finished.[39]

FEBRUARY 15, 0020–0225 HOURS: ALONG THE LINE, I COMPANY, 23RD INFANTRY REGIMENT, CHIPYONG-NI

Unbeknownst to Lieutenant McGee and the rest of G Company, the Chinese were attacking the U.N. perimeter at multiple locations simultaneously so that no one could reinforce the beleaguered soldiers of G Company. At 0020 hours, the communists struck K and I Companies.

Earl Becker was a recoilless rifleman in Item Company. "They'd come in big bunches," Becker said in a postwar interview, remembering the Chinese attacks at Chipyong-ni. "The first bunch had weapons, and if you killed them, then the second bunch would pick up their weapons. It was something else."[40]

Item Company, like everyone else, was short on rifle bullets, mortar rounds, and hand grenades. George Collingsworth, a jeep driver, had spent much of the night carrying crates of small-arms ammunition from his trailer to the front line. "We had very little ammunition left," he said. "And if they ever knew that we didn't have the ammunition that [they thought] we had, [then] they would've just come in and slaughtered us because we would have never fought our way out after that."[41] By 0225 hours, the Chinese had captured several foxholes in the Item Company sector, and 3rd Battalion reported to the regiment that it was shifting two squads from King Company to plug the hole.[42]

Attached to I Company were several heavy machine guns from M Company. These machine-gun teams were high-value targets for the Chinese sappers, and thus were the focus of several assaults. SFC William S. Sitman was the team leader for the one of the machine-gun sections. Born in 1923 and hailing from Altoona, Pennsylvania, like many NCOs he was a veteran of World War II. He had served in northwest Europe, where he had earned a Bronze Star for extinguishing a fire on an ammunition trailer.[43] That morning, his machine-gun team overlooked a draw that was a likely avenue of approach for any would-be attacker. As a result, his gun crew was busy, slaughtering wave after wave of Chinese soldiers.

As the Chinese closed in, they began to lob hand grenades at Sitman's gun team. At one point, one knocked out his machine gun. With Sitman's gun out of action, the Chinese had an infiltration route into the northeast section of the 23rd Infantry's perimeter. In response, the I Company commander ordered Cpl. John G. Larkin to replace Sitman's weapon with his own light machine gun.

After Larkin arrived, he set up his M1919 and resumed firing at the communist attackers. According to the corporal "the sergeant [Sitman] and his crew remained in the emplacement to give us security as there were several defilade approaches leading in."

With Larkin's machine gun chugging away, the Chinese threw themselves again at the position. Suddenly, Sitman shouted, "There's a grenade in our hole!" Without a second thought, the sergeant threw himself on top of the grenade and absorbed the subsequent blast. It killed him instantly, but the five other men in the foxhole lived. "Sergeant Sitman's heroic action, I feel sure, saved the lives of the other comrades in the emplacement and enabled us to deliver machine gun fire from our position throughout the attack," Larkin said later.

Herb Drees was one of the soldiers who survived thanks to Sitman's actions. He recalled the incident, decades after the war. "When that grenade came in, there was a hell of an explosion. Sitman caught the blast, the whole darn thing in his groin area." Drees lifted Sitman out and called for help. When the medic arrived, he took one look at Sitman and said, "He's gone."

For his selfless act, the Army awarded Sitman the Medal of Honor. Thanks to him, the Chinese were unable to breach the I Company lines. Unfortunately, the communists had better luck along the southern edge of the perimeter.[44]

FEBRUARY 15, 0315–0550 HOURS: COMMAND POST, G COMPANY, 23RD INFANTRY REGIMENT, RAMSBURG BOWL

The news of G Company's collapse was a thunderclap for the commander and staff of 2nd Battalion. At first, Colonel Edwards thought the soldiers of G Company had "panicked." In response, he alerted the regiment at 0315 hours and requested reinforcements. Meanwhile, his staff scrounged together elements from F Company's support platoon to seal the breach. Within two minutes of Edwards's request, Colonel Freeman authorized the commitment of one Ranger platoon to augment Edwards's reserves. With the additional combat power, Edwards ordered 2nd Lt. Robert W. Curtis, an Assistant S3 officer, to assume command of the composite force and recapture the old G Company positions.

Though he was a staff officer, Curtis was no slouch. He had earned a battlefield commission earlier in the war, and Edwards had wanted him to take a break from the line to receive additional training to help him become a better lieutenant. Now, with a new task and purpose from the battalion commander, the new lieutenant left for the G Company command post to meet up with the Ranger platoon.

Curtis remembered that night, writing, "As I walked down the road, I could hear enemy and friendly fire from all sides of the RCT perimeter and could see tracers crisscrossing the night sky. Frequently the whole area was eerily illuminated by enemy or friendly flares. I could hear the platoon of rangers coming up the road long before I could see them and I could tell that they were extremely perturbed about something."

He was correct. The Ranger officers and men complained they were not the right force for the job because they did not have best mix of weapons and men to hold a position after seizing it. First Lt. Alfred Herman, the Ranger company commander who had accompanied his platoon, thought defense was a job for regular infantry soldiers. According to Curtis, Herman was not complaining about the assault mission, but instead arguing against using his Rangers as part of a follow-on defensive operation.

The debate between Curtis and Herman continued until they reached the G Company command post. "On arriving at the CP," wrote Curtis, "I found the situation was desperate. There had been extremely high casualties. . . . Many of the key leaders were wounded and there was much confusion in the area. Lieutenant Heath was trying to complete a company reorganization and preparation for a counterattack."[45]

According to Curtis, the last five hours of combat had reduced Heath's company to the size of a platoon. In addition to the remnants of George Company, 2nd Lt. Charles F. Heady had brought his 3rd Platoon from Fox Company to Heath's command post. However, his platoon was already down a squad since it had given up its 2nd Squad earlier that morning to reinforce McGee's 3rd Platoon. Only the Ranger platoon was intact. In total, the composite force was three units from three different companies. After several minutes of discussion, the group decided that Curtis would assume command of the counterattack force since it was an ad hoc unit.

In addition to the platoons, Curtis had three George Company 60mm mortars, two tanks, and three of Heath's light machine guns at his disposal. (G Company's 2nd Platoon had pulled back but was still manning a sector on the main line.) Then, the Ranger platoon leader, 2nd Lt. Mayo Heath (no relation to the G Company commander) discovered that he had a date of rank that made him senior to Curtis. The Ranger company commander found that the rank issue made it impossible for him or his platoon leader to take orders from a junior officer. Lieutenant Herman declared that he would not move until he received a direct order from Colonel Freeman, because his company was the regimental reserve and not 2nd Battalion's reserve.

Realizing that no one had the authority to force Lieutenant Herman to move, Curtis called Colonel Edwards and informed him of the problem. The staff officer recalled the conversation in his postwar account: "I informed him [Herman] that since he was the senior commander on the ground he was welcome to take charge of all the forces in the area and lead the attack and that George Company and the platoon from Fox Company would follow his commands. I told him that I could put him in touch with Colonel Freeman but all it would get him was an ass chewing for delaying attack."

When Edwards learned of the delay, he was furious. He ordered his battalion S2, Capt. John H. Ramsburg, to "straighten out" the Ranger platoon leader, telling the captain, "Well, John, I guess you better go up and take command of that company and get that hill back."

Ramsburg left for G Company. Outside of the G Company command post, he ran into Lieutenant Curtis, whom he had known since August. The exasperated lieutenant said to him, "Christ, John, am I ever glad to see you. I can't do a damn thing with the Ranger company commander." It was now 0330 hours.[46]

For the next ninety minutes, Ramsburg collected the disparate groups and organized them for a counterattack. According to Ramsburg, when he walked over to the shallow hill where the soldiers had gathered he "found all the men mixed up, [and] decided they had to be sorted out and put into their own units."

First, Ramsburg sent Lieutenant McGee to find the G Company 60mm mortar teams. Then he sent Lieutenant Curtis to coordinate with M/Sgt. Andrew Reyna, who commanded the nearby section of tanks, and the three light machine-gun teams. He also told Curtis to scrounge up three radios so that the platoons could talk to each other and to him.[47]

After several minutes, McGee returned with the mortar section. Captain Ramsburg directed the mortar crews to drop one round on the ridgeline so that he could adjust fire on the objective. In response, the crew plopped a mortar round in one of their tubes and then watched it detonate on the crest.

"That where you want them?" the section leader asked Ramsburg.

Ramsburg nodded. "That's exactly right," he said. "Now go ahead and sweep the crest of the hill in both directions. I want a five minute concentration on that hill."

The section leader informed the captain that they were short on 60mm ammunition. Ramsburg responded, "Then fire all you have."

After several minutes, Curtis returned with three SCR-536 radios. Ramsburg allocated one to the Rangers, one to the F Company platoon, and one to himself. To coordinate with his battalion and regiment, Ramsburg then grabbed Harley Wilburn and his radio operator, Paul Fry, who was humping a SCR-300 radio. With command and control established, the S2 went over his plan one more time.

Ramsburg's scheme of maneuver was straightforward: the mortars would suppress the enemy on the hills, and as the teams expended their last rounds, the two platoons would advance. Heady's platoon, with twenty-eight men, would seize Curtis Hill in the east, while Heath's Ranger platoon, which had thirty-six men, would clear McGee Hill in the west. As the soldiers approached the objectives, the three light machine-gun teams would continue to suppress the enemy by firing over the heads of the two platoons. For additional combat power, Ramsburg had Lieutenant McGee and the last three soldiers from G Company's 3rd Platoon to augment Heady's platoon. According to Ramsburg, he wanted the tank crews to hold their fire because of the potential for fratricide (he did not have direct communication with the tanks, nor were they collocated with him).[48]

At 0515 hours, the counterattack began. As planned, the mortars started thumping, and after several minutes Ramsburg ordered the three machine-gun teams to open fire on the ridge. This precipitated a response from the Chinese, who retaliated with their own mortars. Roughly a dozen shells exploded around the soldiers gathering in the assault position. Among the wounded were Lieutenant Heady, the F Company platoon leader, and five other men.

The Chinese barrage resulted in a brief period of bedlam. Lieutenant Herman thought the incoming projectiles were short rounds from G Company's 60mm mortars, and he began to yell at the mortar teams. Ramsburg knew they were from the Chinese and ordered Herman to secure the wounded and return with them to the battalion aid station. Disgusted with the operation, the Ranger commander left the area. With Herman finally gone, Ramsburg restarted the counterattack.

Several minutes after the argument, the mortar section informed the battalion S2 that they had three rounds left. It was the signal. Ramsburg shouted, "Okay, let's go, let's go!" He repeated the phrase on his radio.

Ramsburg described what happened next in an interview conducted several months after the battle. "On the order to move out, the men stood up and walked forward, firing toward the hill during [that] time. The snow through the gulley was knee deep in places, only six or eight inches deep on the side of the hill. The snow had a crust on it. The Rangers were doing a lot of yelling on the way up." Ramsburg marched up the ridge behind the two platoons.

Meanwhile, 3rd Platoon from F Company was climbing up Curtis Hill. According to Lieutenant Curtis, the Rangers were moving faster than the soldiers from F Company. He estimated that the Rangers would reach the top several minutes before the others. Ominously, the Chinese defenders had held their fire. Curtis walked over to speak with Ramsburg about the situation. When he reached him, "all hell broke loose along the entire attack line."

Leading the soldiers from F Company was Sgt. Cuillaula B. Martinez from Texas. When the machine guns and mortars blasted away at the advancing soldiers, the men from F Company sought cover wherever they could find it. As a result, the enemy pinned them down in the open. Martinez realized it would only be a matter of time before the incoming mortars would cause casualties. He stood up and charged ahead. Almost immediately, a shell fragment nicked him in the face. Undaunted, he kept running toward the crest of Curtis Hill. His courageous example inspired the men around him, who jumped up and joined him in the charge. Within minutes, they were almost to the top of Curtis Hill. But as he neared the top, Martinez suffered another wound and fell to the ground.[49]

McGee was also scrambling up the ridge with Heady's platoon from Fox Company when the Chinese opened fire. Almost immediately, men started falling. On the eastern flank, it was even worse. The initial fusillade killed Lieutenant Heath, the Ranger platoon leader.

McGee later explained why the Chinese fire was so devastating:

> One of the problems with the support fire that we did have was that the Chinese were on the reverse slope mostly. And our fire did not affect them because it was going over the ridge and beyond them; if the Chinese had been on the forward slope, there would have been more hits, more damage. As the rangers approached the crest of the hill, the Chinese would come up out of their holes and use their small arms fire.[50]

"I could hear the Rangers shouting that they had taken their objective and needed litter bearers, medics and more ammunition," Curtis later recalled. "Shortly after the Rangers hollered that they needed help or they couldn't hold any longer."

Then, disaster struck. From the east, a single light machine gun left off a long burst of green tracers. Afterward, the gun ripped off several more short and steady bursts. Ramsburg thought the fire originated in the French sector, but according to Curtis, the source of the fire was forward of the French lines. Either way, the enfilade fire caused several more Ranger casualties.

When the tankers saw the tracers, they, too, thought it was a French machine gun, and blasted away with their own machine guns at the same target, which, unfortunately, were the Rangers on McGee Hill. Simultaneously, a Chinese machine-gun team that had occupied the former G Company positions on Finn Hill let loose on 3rd Platoon, F Company. The interlocking fire from all of the belt-fed weapons resulted in horrendous casualties for the Rangers and F Company. Among the fallen were the Ranger company's first sergeant and several other Ranger NCOs.

Ramsburg was livid. As Curtis recalled, "Captain Ramsburg hollered at me to go back and stop the damn tanks from firing into the Rangers. I ran back to the tanks as fast as I could, ordered them to cease firing and told them that we had taken the hill back and not to fire again unless given an order to fire."

Meanwhile, the Chinese continued to fight back. An unknown enemy soldier lobbed a grenade at Ramsburg. It exploded, spraying shrapnel and hitting him in the foot. The S2 never saw the grenade, and the blast stunned him. Initially, he thought he had shot himself in the foot with his submachine gun. Despite the agonizing pain, all he could think about was how he was going to explain his embarrassing injury to Colonel Edwards, the battalion commander.

As the S2 massaged his foot, Lieutenant Heath emerged from the darkness. "What happened to you?" he asked Ramsburg.

The ashamed captain explained his wound, but assured Heath that his condition was not serious. He told Heath that the Rangers needed reinforcements. Hearing this news, the G Company commander grabbed Ramsburg's SCR-536 radio, strapped it over his shoulder, and headed up the hill to assume control of the forces atop the ridge.

Unfortunately, Heath's attempt to regain control of the situation was short-lived. When he reached the crest of the ridge, Chinese soldiers saw him and opened fire. The G Company commander tried to reach for his carbine, but to his horror he had slung the radio over his weapon and could not disentangle his gun in time to shoot back at the enemy. Within seconds, the CPVF soldiers drew a bead on Heath and shot him in the chest. Before anyone could shoot back at them, they vanished in the swirling snow and darkness.

Moments later, a wounded U.S. soldier found Heath lying on the ground. The unidentified soldier had only one working arm, his other hanging lifeless with only strips of flesh keeping it from falling off. He grabbed Heath's leg with his good arm and began to drag him down the hill. Midway, he met Captain Ramsburg limping up the slope.

"Where you going?" asked the S2 sternly. He then saw the soldier's arm and realized the GI was not deserting the battlefield. Next, he saw the wounded man on the ground and inquired, "Who's that you're dragging behind?"

The soldier answered that it was Lieutenant Heath. Ramsburg told him to head the down the hill to the battalion aid station. Meanwhile, the S2 continued to stagger up the ridge. Moments later, he intercepted a small group of three or four Rangers. At first, he thought they were Chinese, hitting the deck and yelling, "Who are you?"

They replied they were the last Rangers on the hill. Even worse, they were withdrawing. They told the S2 that the Chinese were swarming everywhere along the ridge.

"What about F Company?" asked Ramsburg. They informed him they had not seen anyone from Fox Company on the ridge. Crestfallen, the S2 knew the counterattack had failed, and he returned with the Rangers to the G Company command post. On the way down, he met Lieutenant Curtis heading in the opposite direction and told him, "Get as many men as you can possibly gather up and get them on this hump to hold off the Chinese if they come over the hill."

Wilburn was still with Ramsburg and recalled a radio conversation between the S2 and Colonel Freeman. "He changed the channel on it to the headquarters [channel] to Colonel Freeman," said Wilburn. "And I heard him tell Colonel Freeman that we were in danger of not being able to get that hill back . . . and Colonel Freeman said 'don't fall back any further because if they get into this perimeter we're all going to be in trouble.'"[51]

Meanwhile, Lieutenant Curtis kept climbing. "I continued on up the hill," he wrote. "And [I] encountered only wounded men coming down, assisting more seriously wounded soldiers. As I continued to the top I suddenly realized that the shouting in the Ranger area no longer came from on top of the hill but from the bottom of the hill near where I could just make out the silhouettes of the 155 howitzers. Also little firing was occurring along the entire hill mass and I could hear only Chinese commands and I realized that I might be the only American left in the objective area."[52]

Shortly after Ramsburg and Wilburn spoke with Curtis, Wilburn left the stricken S2 and continued up the slope to occupy his former foxhole on McGee Hill. He later recalled, "I jumped in on my foxhole, and when I jumped in, my feet went down like I had jumped on a mattress or something."

The forward observer asked himself, "What the hell is this here?" He felt around the base of his hole and discovered a field jacket. "I pulled on that cloth," he said. "And it was an arm of a redheaded kid that was with the Rangers [who] had been killed there. And the Chinese just threw dirt on him and stood on top of him and kept shooting."[53]

After several minutes of waiting, Wilburn realized he was alone. No one else was coming to occupy the former G Company positions with him. Despite the bravery of the Rangers, the composite force had failed to recapture the hill. After hearing the word to pull back, Wilburn climbed out of his hole and returned to the G Company command post.

On the eastern side of McGee Hill, the survivors from F Company were falling back as well. PFC Clell E. Van Dorin volunteered to remain behind to provide covering fire so that his comrades could escape. With only his Garand, he held off the Chinese until his friends were safe and then returned to the G Company command post, wounded but alive.[54]

After the platoon from Fox Company withdrew from the ridge, SFC Clifford Logan found himself in a defilade position. From it, he saw a wounded soldier still on McGee Hill. Without a second thought, Logan raced back up the crest to evacuate him. Zigzagging through enemy tracers, Logan reached the injured soldier and pulled him off the hill. The sergeant from North Carolina made this hazardous trip several times until all of the wounded were off the ridge. For their bravery, the Army awarded both Van Dorin and Logan the Silver Star.[55]

During the counterattack, the seemingly invulnerable Sergeant Kluttz had suffered a gunshot wound to the stomach, but fortunately survived. As a result, Paul McGee was the only leader from 3rd Platoon still in the fight; all the others were either dead or wounded. McGee later remarked matter-of-factly, "We were in a really bad situation."[56]

West of McGee's position was Sergeant Reyna's tank section. There, the situation also was bleak. Colonel Freeman had originally positioned the tanks to block the road that served as the boundary between G Company and the French Battalion. SFC Kenneth Paul Pitlick was a tank commander in the other M4. He recalled what happened that night after the Chinese captured the two hills, explaining how he was standing inside his turret when an unidentified sergeant ran past him and said, "They are breaking through on us! You've got to do—"

Pitlick interrupted the soldier, "I know it."

The tank commander climbed out of his tank and walked across the road. He found some soldiers huddled in the ditch that lined the road and saw another U.S. soldier standing near them. At the time, he did not know that the unidentified soldier was a captain. Pitlick yelled at the officer, "You better get these men turned around. We are going to get wiped out."

"Yes, sir," the soldier said, adding, "I got [a] concussion."

Pitlick barked, "I don't care. Get them turned around and start—"

Before the tank commander could finish his sentence, he noticed an M16 half-track in the dark that had rolled on its side. "Look at that quad fifty laying there," said Pitlick. "It's turned over. Somebody has got to get that thing to work. You can hold off a battalion with that thing."

The captain and Pitlick bolted in two different directions to find a crew to help them rescue the stranded vehicle. When the sergeant returned to his tank, he told his crew, "There's nowhere to go. We're surrounded completely." He recalled, "I told them to pull back and I kept on firing until they got organized, you know, and then we pulled up and started opening up again."

Soon after the failed counterattack, Reyna's platoon leader, 1st Lt. Arthur J. Junot, arrived in his tank. Pitlick told his officer about the battle. It was still dark; however, there was enough light for Junot to scan the ridgeline in front of him. After doing so, he realized that nothing was between them and the enemy on the crest. Unbeknownst to the Chinese, the southern sector was wide open. The time was now 0550 hours.[57]

FEBRUARY 15, 0605 HOURS:
COMMAND POST, 2ND BATTALION,
23RD INFANTRY REGIMENT, CHIPYONG-NI

The failed counterattack stunned Colonel Edwards. Reports from the survivors indicated that a Chinese regiment occupied the old G Company positions. With this new information in hand, Edwards realized he needed more combat power if he wanted to throw the communists off the southern ridge. He informed Colonel Freeman of the situation, but the regimental commander had other problems beyond G Company. According to Freeman, 1st Battalion also was under attack, and more important, his unit was running low on 81mm and 4.2-inch mortar ammunition. He could only allocate the rest of the Ranger company to 2nd Battalion.

Edwards acknowledged the order and began to gather his remaining forces for the next operation. At 0605 hours, he contacted Captain Ramsburg, who was still at the George Company command post, telling him to prepare for the arrival of the rest of the Rangers. After he put down the phone, the battalion commander briefed his command post that he intended to organize and lead the next counterattack. Meanwhile, Lieutenant Curtis and the remnants from the composite force readied themselves for the next assault.[58]

FEBRUARY 15, 0600–0645 HOURS:
G COMPANY COMMAND POST,
23RD INFANTRY REGIMENT, RAMSBURG BOWL

Lieutenant Curtis wondered where everyone had gone. "As I reached the CP area all firing had stopped and the whole area fell silent except for Chinese digging on the reverse slope of the hill, evidently improving the old George Company positions," he later wrote.[59]

Inside the command post, the injured Captain Ramsburg argued with Lieutenant Herman, the Ranger company commander. According to Curtis, Herman felt the ground was not suitable for a defense. After much wrangling, an exasperated Ramsburg told the Ranger commander to leave and take his men with him.

When Ramsburg saw Curtis, he ordered him to find whomever he could and establish a new defensive line along the slight rise that ran in front of the G Company command post. Curtis left and searched the immediate area, finding a squad from F Company and several survivors from G Company. He also rounded up clerks and other support soldiers to add to the defense. All told, he counted twenty-five men on the line, including those who were slightly injured.

He realized that twenty-five men were not enough to stop a determined Chinese assault and asked Ramsburg for permission to grab a radio and head back up the hill to see if any survivors were still there. The S2 approved his request. Curtis left for the former G Company positions. As he approached the hill, Curtis ran into several artillerymen from the 503rd Field Artillery, whose howitzers were still in position. Amazed to see American soldiers in the area, Curtis asked if they intended to remain in position. The artillery officers assured him they were not going to abandon the howitzers.

Pleased that he had found more combat power, Curtis continued his search. He combed the base of the hill and found no survivors from G Company, nor from the earlier counterattack. After several minutes, he returned to the George Company command post. When he arrived, he heard a Chinese bugler. Seconds later, several enemy soldiers appeared on the crest of the hill. In response, the Americans opened fire, and the enemy disappeared.

After seeing the Chinese, Curtis and Ramsburg realized the wounded soldiers huddled around the G Company command post were sitting ducks. Curtis told Ramsburg to herd them back toward the battalion aid station. The S2 agreed and shouted, "Come on everyone, we are going back to establish a new defensive position."

Unfortunately, the radio operators and staff clerks thought Ramsburg's words were meant for them. They left with the wounded. Curtis tried to stop them, but they vanished in the darkness before he could reach them. The premature exodus meant Curtis now only had fifteen men in front of the G Company command post. Despite the miscommunication, he still had the one abandoned M16 half-track and the artillerymen from the 503rd. He reported his situation to Colonel Edwards and asked for reinforcements. The battalion commander replied that help was on the way.

"I found the squad leader from Fox Company," Curtis wrote, "and asked him to move all of the infantrymen left in the area into the far side of the road ditch and to extend the men south down the road towards the tanks as far as they could go and that the artillerymen would tie in with them and they would extend towards the Chinese. . . . He [the squad leader] asked me that if we were not going to make it that he would like to go back to Fox Company and go down with them. I promised him that he could go back to Fox Company as soon as we got help."[60]

Curtis walked over to the gun line to coordinate with the cannon cockers of the 503rd Field Artillery. There, he met the battery commander and asked him, "Why don't you turn the 155's around and put some fire on that hill?" Curtis later revealed that his suggestion was in jest—he didn't think they could do it.

To Curtis's surprise, the battery commander replied, "Sure, we can do that."

Within several minutes, a crew had turned around one of the howitzers. A soldier pulled the lanyard, and the big gun boomed. They fired it six times, shooting white phosphorous rounds at the Chinese defenders. Curtis later wrote, "From where I was standing I knew that the rounds scared the hell out of the Chinese as they burst very close to their positions."

Not be outdone, one of Lieutenant Junot's tanks let loose with its main gun. "The rounds hit the frozen, icy road and reverberated down the valley," wrote Curtis. "The echo off the surrounding hills made a terrifying sound. I thought the Chinese would think that we had brought up a new type [of] weapon. After this demonstration of firepower the night grew silent."[61]

FEBRUARY 15, 0645–0800 HOURS: BETWEEN FRENCH 1ST COMPANY AND G COMPANY, 23RD INFANTRY REGIMENT, RAMSBURG BOWL

After Lieutenant Junot heard the howitzers from the 503rd Field Artillery thunder across the valley, a group of ten French soldiers approached his platoon of tanks and asked the tankers for grenades. The French allies had seen the failed counterattack, and this tiny group had decided to retake the hill themselves. It was also a matter of survival for the French: if they allowed the Chinese to occupy Schmitt Hill, the enemy would have enfilade fire on the entire French line. Wanting to help, Junot gave them some grenades. Captain Elledge, the artillery liaison officer, joined the group, armed with a BAR.

The small group climbed up Schmitt Hill. When they were within 20 meters of the crest, the Chinese retaliated. According to Junot, it was a "grenade fight." He ordered his tank driver to move his vehicle closer to the road so that they could engage targets on the back side of the hill. Repositioned, Junot engaged the enemy with all of his machine guns. Unfortunately, the Chinese were too far up the ridge, and Junot could not elevate his main 76mm cannon high enough to engage or hit them.

The Chinese emplaced a machine-gun team inside a culvert, opening fire on the attacking French. The culvert provided defilade for the gun team; therefore, Junot could not suppress it with his own guns. As a result, Elledge and the French had to withdraw back down the hill. The tank platoon leader later estimated they had killed about fourteen or fifteen enemy in total. It was now 0800 hours.[62]

Sometime that morning, one of Junot's tanks had towed the M16 half-track out of the ditch. When Captain Elledge saw it, he decided to shoot the quad .50-caliber machine guns at the hill. The half-track was inoperable, but the onboard weapons system worked. According to Curtis, Elledge asked Ramsburg before he left whether he could expend all the ammunition on the half-track. Ramsburg approved Elledge's request, so Elledge climbed on board the damaged vehicle and opened fire with all four guns. The artillery officer wanted to use up all the ammunition and melt the barrels so the enemy could not capture it and use it against the U.N. forces.

At the time, Curtis did not know Elledge's plan; in fact, the M16 half-track was an essential part of Curtis's own overall defensive scheme. When he saw Elledge open fire, he was furious. "My first thought was to shoot the son of bitch off the weapon," Curtis later wrote. "I jumped on the closest tank and laid the machine gun on the quad 50 intending to scare the gunner off the weapon."

However, he realized it was too late. "I saw that by firing the quad 50 [on] full automatic the barrels were red hot and were being burned out. They were glowing red in the darkness and seemed to be bending down."

Together with another soldier, Curtis ran over to the M16 after Elledge abandoned it. He discovered that the barrels on the quad .50-caliber machine guns had indeed melted. "When I found out the condition of the weapon I was mad as hell, as I had just lost the most important weapon we had to use against a massed Chinese attack," he later wrote. Fortunately, for Curtis and the other survivors, help was finally on the way.[63]

FEBRUARY 15, 0803–0945 HOURS: TEMPORARY 2ND BATTALION COMMAND POST, 23RD INFANTRY REGIMENT, HEATH RIDGE

At 0803 hours, the Ranger company command post reported to regiment that it did not have the necessary combat power to execute a successful counterattack. Nine minutes later, Colonel Freeman committed Baker Company to retake the G Company positions and also designated his engineer company as an ad hoc reserve. At 0817 hours, the forward air controllers alerted 2nd Battalion that the next air strike would hit the G Company positions on McGee and Curtis Hills.[64]

Colonel Edwards learned about the change in plan moments before leaving his permanent headquarters to assume command at a temporary command post atop Heath Ridge. Once he arrived at the new post, he consulted with 1st Lt. Carl F. Haberman, the mortar platoon leader, who assumed control of G Company after Lieutenant Heath's injury. Haberman listed what was left of his command. McGee had survived. Moreover, 2nd Platoon, which had assumed a new defensive position, was intact. However, other than the mortars, 2nd Platoon, and a handful of survivors, nothing else was left of G Company.[65]

According to Colonel Edwards, the B Company commander, Capt. Sherman W. Pratt, arrived at the makeshift forward command post to receive his instructions around 0945 hours. Edwards informed Pratt that he had attached several units to his company, including the remaining Ranger platoons, the tank platoon, and the recently arrived section of two M16 half-tracks. In addition, Pratt would have direct support from G Company's 60mm mortars, H Company's 81mm mortars, the remnants of G Company (including 2nd Platoon), and the forward observers for the artillery and mortars. He would have a ten-minute bombardment prior to the assault.

Edwards described the old G Company positions. "George Company's positions are just up there to the left and right of those points," the colonel said, pointing to McGee and Schmitt Hills. Seconds later, a mortar round exploded nearby, and an unseen man shrieked. Unflappable, Edwards continued his brief.

"Are there any of your men still in position atop the hill?" Pratt asked.

"No, there are only enemy troops there," replied Edwards.

Not convinced, Pratt countered, "I saw some bodies moving, I thought, a few moments ago."

"If you did, it has to be Chinks," said the colonel.

"And if we reach the top, there are emplacements in existence that we can drop into?" inquired Pratt.

According to the B Company commander, Edwards told him, "Piece of cake, Pratt. We had great positions up there. All your men have to do is ease back up the slope, rush quickly over the crest, and drop into our well prepared and protected positions."

Satisfied with his instructions, the battalion commander said farewell to Pratt, who left to conduct his own troop-leading procedures with his company. Edwards later wrote that he had "erred in issuing his order to the Commanding Officer of Company B. He [Edwards] should have issued definite detailed orders to the Company B Commander and should not have assumed that he was as expert as the 2nd Battalion rifle company commanders."[66]

Like many Korean War officers, Pratt was a veteran of World War II. He had served in Europe and earned a Silver Star while fighting on the Rhine River in early 1945. Now he was a company commander whose job was to retake a hill.[67]

According to Pratt, he had seen the G Company positions several days earlier. Since he was the reserve, Freeman had wanted him to check out all of the company battle positions in the regiment's perimeter so that he would know the ground in case he had to fight on it. He recalled that the G Company foxholes were not very deep because G Company did not have same the amount of preparation; it had to move because of the 155mm howitzer battery's arriving several days after everyone else had showed up at Chipyong-ni.

"I studied Edwards for a moment or so, and glanced at my officers. We were reading each other's mind," Pratt later wrote. "We had been in these positions only a couple of days earlier before the big attack, and had found the positions wanting in many respects, as we had pointed out to the regimental S-3. I looked at Edwards again and tried to imagine what he was thinking."

The Baker Company commander reflected, "I realized that the 2nd Battalion's positions might have been improved since we last saw them, but I had the feeling that Edwards was being far from candid. I was tempted to ask him if the mission was such a piece of cake then why in hell didn't his own battalion reoccupy their own positions."

However, orders were orders. With his new task and purpose, Pratt conducted his troop-leading procedures. With him were his two platoon leaders, 2nd Lt. Maurice Fenderson of 1st Platoon, and Lt. Richard S. Kotite of 3rd Platoon. Pratt did not have an officer in charge of 2nd Platoon because of the loss of its leader several days prior to Chipyong-ni, but he had picked up two replacement officers from headquarters: 2nd Lt. Herschel "Hawk" Chapman, a West Pointer, and 2nd Lt. Raymond Dupree.

"If the retaking of his positions was such a snap, Captain, why had the earlier counterattack under his command not succeeded?" Chapman asked Pratt. "Or why did he not make another effort?"

Pratt looked back at the new lieutenant and replied, "Hawk, my boy, you couldn't have said my thoughts more clearly."

Suddenly, machine-gun fire ripped through the area. One bullet slammed into the stock of Pratt's carbine, shattering it. Instinctively, the men hunkered down. Seconds later, the B Company commander heard Chapman groan.

"Are you hit, Chapman?" asked Pratt.

Chapman grimaced and said, "I think so, Captain."

"Where?" inquired the B Company commander.

The new lieutenant shrugged his shoulder and said, "My arm stings."

Pratt then noticed the rivulet of blood dripping down from Chapman's hand. "Are you dizzy, lad? Are you about to pass out?" he asked him.

"Not really," said Chapman.

The company commander leaned over and said, "Here, let me take a look at you." Even though he was not a medic, Pratt quickly surmised that the wound was superficial. Still, Chapman was injured.

"Make your way back and out of here when you can, Hawk," ordered Pratt. "Looks like you have the million-dollar wound—not serious but good enough to get you off the front lines."

Hawk shook his head. "No way Captain," he declared. "I'm staying. If I withdraw with this slight wound I will be the laughing stock of my graduation class at the Academy. I would never live it down. Just give me an assignment and let's get on with it."

Impressed with the lieutenant's toughness, Pratt relented. "Okay fellow," the captain began. "If you feel that way, are you up to taking over the [2nd] platoon at this time? As you know, we have the platoon sergeant in charge and I'm sure he could use some help. I was going to wait a few days for you to get your feet better planted, but we have a bit of an urgency now, I think."

"Damned right Captain. Thought you would never ask," replied Chapman.

Pratt smiled. "Then up and away. The platoon is just behind us. Find the platoon sergeant and let him know you're now in charge. I think he will welcome your arrival. Get ready to be committed. I'm sure we are going to have to commit the reserve platoon but [I] don't yet know just where. I'm going to send Ray Dupree along to help you or take over in case you get hit."

Pratt knew the situation was far from ideal. In a postwar interview with Thomas M. Ryan, another Eighth Army historian, Pratt said, "I didn't trust Edwards as far as I could throw one of our medium General Sherman tanks. I had seen his positions earlier and formed my own conclusions as to their unsuitability, which had now been confirmed, in my judgment, by his forced withdrawal from them."[68]

Unfortunately, it was too late to do anything about it. B Company had a rendezvous with the Chinese, who were waiting for them.

FEBRUARY 15, 0945–1130 HOURS: B COMPANY, 23RD INFANTRY REGIMENT, RAMSBURG BOWL

Pratt's company was already assembling on Heath Ridge when he returned from his meeting with Colonel Edwards. Pratt wanted his most experienced officers leading the attack, so he grabbed Lieutenants Kotite and Fenderson. The three climbed over the spur that served as the boundary between the Ranger and B Company assembly areas.

From there, Pratt explained his plan. First, mortars and artillery would pound Schmitt and McGee Hills while Junot's tanks provided suppressive fire on Schmitt Hill from the road. Pratt's own 60mm mortars would also provide indirect fire support for both platoons. Fenderson's mission was to clear and seize Schmitt Hill, while Kotite's objective was to do the same with McGee Hill. The two assaults were supposed to be mutually supporting.

Pratt concluded his orders by saying, "Fendy, you and Kotite charge out. The time has come to bite the bullet." Both platoon leaders returned to their platoons and quickly briefed their soldiers on the upcoming operation.[69]

Shortly after 1000 hours, the artillery and mortars initiated their bombardment. During the barrage, both platoons moved to their assault positions. Fenderson followed Junot's tanks down the road. When he neared his objective, his platoon left the highway and pushed up Schmitt Hill.

Junot ordered his tanks to drive up the hill. Initially, the tankers had some success, but eventually, the tank platoon leader found the ridge was too slippery because of the snow. His tank lost traction, sliding down the slope like an out-of-control sled. Sergeant Pitlick's tank also experienced problems negotiating its way up the hill and remained at the base of a nearby draw. In response to the American armor presence, the Chinese shot at Junot's tanks with recoilless rifles.

It was a slog for the infantry. Despite the preparatory bombardment, the enemy soldiers were firing back at the two platoons. Even before Kotite's platoon could reach the base of McGee Hill, it came under heavy flanking fire from Schmitt Hill. Consequently, his men had to move forward in short rushes, slowing their advance. Instead of two platoons hitting their objectives simultaneously, Fenderson's unit reached its hill first at 1015 hours, while Kotite's platoon took more than forty minutes to reach the base of its objective. The attack appeared disjointed and piecemeal.

Around 1115 hours, Kotite's platoon began its ascent of McGee Hill. In a letter written several months after the battle, Kotite described the final phase of the assault:

When we were about two-thirds of the way up, mortar[s] started
coming in. We hit the ground and then I gave the signal to
assault so we continued up to about five yards from the top and
threw grenades then charged over the crest. The Chinese were
on the reverse slope in holes. They had three machine guns that
I saw myself as well as other riflemen, and they opened up. We
pulled back about five yards below the crest and laid in the
snow.

Kotite's platoon sergeant reported that Fenderson's men had pulled
out, which meant 3rd Platoon now had an unsecured flank. Kotite's only
option was to withdraw and reorganize for another attack. He ordered
his men to fall back. When he reached the bottom of the hill, he went to
look for Captain Pratt for further orders. The latest attempt to retake the
G Company positions had failed—again.[70]

FEBRUARY 15, 1105 HOURS:
HELICOPTER LANDING ZONE,
WEST SIDE OF CHIPYONG-NI

As Pratt's men labored up the snowy slopes of Schmitt and Curtis Hills,
Colonel Edwards had left his command post to say good-bye to the
injured Colonel Freeman, who was leaving on a helicopter that had
touched down at the makeshift landing area behind the French lines. By
his own admission, Edwards was not at his command post for thirty crucial minutes.

At 1105, the helicopter blades were spinning for takeoff. Freeman
asked Edwards about the status of Pratt's counterattack. Edwards later
admitted that he lied to Freeman, telling him "the Chinese penetration
had been eliminated."

As justification for the lie, Edwards later wrote: "If the Regimental
Commander had known that the situation was still very critical, he never
would have left and would probably have been court-martialed by the
Corps Commander."

As ordered, but against his better judgment, Col. Paul Freeman
boarded the chopper and left behind his beloved regiment. Several weeks
later, he wrote a letter to the soldiers of 23rd Infantry. In it, he explained

why he departed: "It is with deep disappointment and sincere regret that during your recent crisis at CHIPYONG-NI I was ordered evacuated. While my wound was slight, the Corps Commander wished me evacuated for other reasons. Although I protested, I was finally ordered out." He continued: "I want to say to you that there is no grander fighting regiment in all-the-world than the 23rd RCT. Your determination, courage and ability was demonstrated magnificently during the recent action at CHIPYONG. I hated leaving without seeing the fight through to its successful conclusion. . . . I salute each of you and wish that I could shake every hand of the men who have so valiantly served."

His soldiers felt the same way about him.[71]

FEBRUARY 15, NOONTIME:
B COMPANY, 23RD INFANTRY REGIMENT,
HEATH RIDGE

As Colonel Freeman's helicopter lifted off and flew away, the survivors of Pratt's failed attack streamed back toward their original assault positions, with the Chinese mortaring the assembly areas. Dewey R. Andersen, a mortar man in B Company, was a raw recruit, having arrived only a few days before the battle. Now he was in the thick of combat. According to Andersen, within an hour of the initial assault the Chinese had neutralized his B Company 60mm mortar with their own heavy mortars. Andersen was huddled in a foxhole while the incoming shells intermittently exploded around him.

Andersen's platoon sergeant ordered him to climb out of his foxhole and join him on the top of Heath Ridge, 20 feet above the private's foxhole. "Initially, I was reluctant to leave my foxhole," Andersen later explained in a postwar later, "but he [the platoon sergeant] was insistent and I finally decided that I had better follow his orders. Within a couple of minutes, a mortar shell landed on the corner of the foxhole that I had left. Unfortunately, a BAR man and his Korean assistant had jumped in my hole when I left."[72]

Nearby, Sgt. Joe R. Marez continued to hang rounds over his 60mm mortar tube. The Chinese counterbattery fire had already severely injured his ammunition bearer and assistant gunner, leaving him alone. He ordered both men to evacuate, but continued to operate the weapon even though he, too, was wounded. For several minutes, Marez fired his mortar, despite the incoming fire. He survived, and for his bravery the Army later awarded him the Silver Star.[73]

Meanwhile, Lieutenant Kotite had linked up with Captain Pratt at the bottom of McGee Hill. There, Kotite learned that the first attack had shredded Fenderson's platoon. Pratt decided to combine the survivors of 1st Platoon with Kotite's 3rd Platoon for another try. The platoon leader returned to his men and readied for another assault. After several minutes of constant bazooka fire from the Chinese, he rethought the action, withdrawing his platoon back toward Heath Ridge. He wanted to discuss a new plan with the B Company commander.

By this point, Pratt had realized that Schmitt Hill was the decisive terrain. "Just as I was about to rise and go to the waiting reserve platoon, another shower of mortar rounds landed all around us," he wrote later. "Several men were knocked down, and I felt shell fragments tearing through my right pant leg and my waist area. I swore in annoyance. When I felt liquid running down my leg, I concluded I had been hit. Finally my luck had ended."

Clearly, Pratt thought he was wounded. "But the liquid running down my leg was cold," he wrote. "I remember wondering why my blood would be so cold. . . . I glanced anxiously down at my leg. To my chagrin and relief, I saw that the fragment had only torn the bottom out of my canteen and its cover. The water inside had doused my leg and clothing. But two of the men in the company headquarters were not so lucky. They lay bleeding to death from those rounds."[74]

Pratt ordered his reserve platoon (the 2nd), under the command of 2nd Lt. "Hawk" Chapman, to assault the hill, using the same route Fenderson had used earlier. When Kotite arrived at the commander's location with his 3rd Platoon, Pratt added its combat power to Chapman's ongoing attack. He instructed his 3rd Platoon leader to approach the objective using the same route as Chapman's platoon, but told Kotite he would have to wait until after a planned airstrike on Schmitt Hill. Elsewhere, the battle raged.[75]

FEBRUARY 15, 1200–1228 HOURS:
TEMPORARY 2ND BATTALION COMMAND POST,
23RD INFANTRY REGIMENT, HEATH RIDGE

Colonel Edwards returned from the helicopter landing area and, upon his arrival at his temporary command post on Heath Ridge, learned of Pratt's failure. He was livid. The battalion commander sat down with his staff and discussed what had happened. The Chinese were on the reverse slopes of Schmitt and McGee Hills, therefore making it nearly impossible to suppress the Chinese defenders with any direct fire.

Edwards looked out from his location, his eyes drawn to the Chipyong-ni–Kanhyon highway that bisected the perimeter and served as the boundary between the French Battalion and his command. He wondered if he could send a platoon of tanks down the road and past Schmitt Hill. If the tanks made it, the M4s would be on the back side of Schmitt, McGee, and Curtis Hills. From there, they would have enfilade fire on all the Chinese defensive positions. The biggest obstacles to his plan were the mines his men had laid on the road several days before to prevent the Chinese forces from using it. Now, these mines blocked his soldiers and tanks.

Resolved to try, he ordered Capt. Perry Sager, his S3, to cobble together a task force of tanks and soldiers from the Pioneer and Ammunition (P&A) Squad to execute his plan. It was simple: the tanks would provide cover for the soldiers of the P&A Squad, who would disarm and remove the mines from the road. Edwards labeled this command Task Force S. Shortly after 1200 hours, Sager's force moved out, and by 1228 hours they reported that they were conducting the route clearance operation.[76]

FEBRUARY 15, 1207–1238 HOURS:
HEADQUARTERS, 23RD INFANTRY REGIMENT,
CHIPYONG-NI

Lt. Col. John H. Chiles was finally in command. However, other than monitoring the radio and coordinating air support, he had little to do. The fate of the regiment was out of his hands because his predecessor, Colonel Freeman, had committed all of the reserves. As of 1236 hours, the only designated reserve remaining was the regimental staff. Fortunately, help was on the way.

At 1207 hours, division reported that 5th Cavalry was 9,000 yards south of the perimeter. Seventeen minutes later, the aerial observer confirmed that the relief column was approaching the lines, but moving slowly. Could the regiment hold out until they arrived?

The regimental radio operator called them at 1238 hours and pleaded, "Reach us as soon as possible. In any event reach us."

Airdrops were delivering much-needed supplies while close air support pounded the surrounding hills. However, Chinese mortars disrupted the supply recovery operations by plastering the landing area. The mortars targeted the regimental command post as well, resulting in several casualties. Even if the cavalry made it, the battle was far from finished.[77]

FEBRUARY 15, 1200–1300 HOURS: B COMPANY, 23RD INFANTRY REGIMENT, SCHMITT HILL

Captain Pratt climbed up Schmitt Hill, following behind his reserve platoon. When he arrived near the crest, he learned of the horrendous casualties his company had sustained, including one of his platoon sergeants, Eugene L. Nabozny. Kotite's wounded platoon sergeant had led his men up the slope, and when he was near the top he launched an attack on the enemy's eastern flank. However, doing so exposed him and cost him his life. The advance bogged down near the top.[78]

WO Ralph E. Dusseau, the administrative officer for B Company, linked up with Pratt in a ravine on the side of the hill. "Captain," he began, "it looks like we got a real stalemate on our hands!"

Pratt replied, "It sure seems so, Dussy. What news from the platoons?"

"Our men are just short of the crest of the hill, and the enemy forces are just a few feet away, over the crest and near the top of the slope on the other side, or south side," said Dusseau.

"What are they doing?" asked Pratt.

"It's hairy, Captain. They mostly can't see each other, but they know each other are there. They're within a hand grenade's throwing distance and have been doing just that for over an hour," explained Dusseau.

Pratt later wrote about the tactical dilemma he faced. "The picture could hardly have been more grim. The platoons reported that each time they rose up to charge over the crest, enemy gunfire could cut them down in their tracks. The platoon leaders insisted that further efforts were simply suicidal, and wanted to know what to do."

Pratt's first idea was artillery. He asked his platoon leaders what they thought about an artillery barrage to suppress the Chinese defenders. They refused.

"You don't want artillery?" asked Pratt over the radio. He could not believe it.

His 1st Platoon leader, 2nd Lt. Maurice Fenderson, squawked back, "We don't think so. The enemy is so close to us that I fear any rounds aimed at them are sure to fall on us also."

Pratt wondered if tanks would work. Unbeknownst to him, Colonel Edwards already had ordered the tanks to push forward down the Chipyong-ni–Kanhyon highway. Several minutes later, the B Company commander watched the tanks rolling down the road past his position.[79]

FEBRUARY 15, 1257–1512 HOURS: TANK COMPANY, 23RD INFANTRY REGIMENT, ALONG THE KOKSU-RI–CHIPYONG-NI HIGHWAY

First Lt. Charles W. Hurlburt's 4th Platoon provided the bulk of the armor support for the route clearance operation. When the Chinese defenders saw the tanks rumbling down the highway, they opened fire with bazookas on the lead pair of tanks. Luckily, the first few rockets were ineffective. Still, the hidden antitank ambushes were enough to cause the two tanks to reverse gears and pull back toward their start positions. Without the tanks, the P&A Squad also had to withdraw. At 1257 hours, 2nd Battalion reported to the regiment that the clearance operation had a hit a snag. "It looked like it was going to be a stalemate," Edwards later wrote in a letter to Colonel Freeman.

After Edward's S3, Captain Sager, reported the issue, the battalion commander marched down to the assembly area to see him and solve the problem. Everyone was exhausted and few had slept. Tempers were high. The long night of battle had taken its toll on the officers and men. When Edwards arrived at the tanks, he spoke with Sager and Capt. George E. Vontom, the executive officer for the tank company.

The Fort Benning schoolhouse answer for antitank ambush teams was infantry; after several minutes of discussing the situation, Edwards quickly realized it was their best option. The problem was the lack of infantry: the only available soldiers were the few Rangers left on Heath Ridge. Edwards spoke with Lieutenant Herman and told him he needed his Rangers to clear out the enemy ambush teams. Once again, the Ranger officer protested, insisting his men were not suited for that mission since they were "hit and run specialist[s]."

"I told him by God that now he was an infantryman and would do what I told him to or report to the rear under arrest," Edwards later wrote. With his back against the wall, the Ranger officer acquiesced and led his men toward Schmitt Hill.[80]

Captain Vontom returned to his tanks, and Task Force S rolled out. Once again, the Chinese opened fire. Vontom, manning a .50-caliber machine gun on one of the tanks, blasted away at the CPVF defenders on Schmitt Hill while incoming tracers zipped by him. One round hit him in the heel, but he refused evacuation.

The P&A Squad went to work. Initially, the maelstrom of fire was too much for the clearance teams, but several men finally crept forward and began removing the mines. Cpls. Ernest C. Lawson, Jr., and George P. Munhall, Jr., and PFC Keith C. Karschney were the first to clear a path through the minefields for the tanks. By 1512 hours, the M4s had inched past Schmitt Hill. For their contributions clearing the road, Vontom, Lawson, Munhall, and Karschney all received the Silver Star.[81]

East of the highway, Pratt's two platoons made progress up Schmitt Hill from the north side. It was slow going. Close air support had saturated the hilltop at 1445 hours with napalm and it was danger-close. "At one point, some of the burning napalm bounced over the crest and was blazing throughout a Baker squad position," Pratt later wrote. "Some small amounts landed on the clothing of a couple of my men. Because of the heavy winter clothing, they were not burned on the skin, and the flames were doused. But they had a frightening experience from it and for some weeks afterward would not surrender their burnt clothing as they proudly showed off their 'battle scars.'"[82]

By 1512 hours, the B Company soldiers had made some progress. Still, it was a knife fight. As Kotite described the combat, "We played catch with grenades . . . for awhile and got an interpreter to tell them to surrender."[83]

Despite the success of Baker Company and the tanks, the Chinese kept battling. Many of the U.N. soldiers wondered if the Chinese would ever quit. What the soldiers of the 23rd Infantry did not know yet was that the Chinese were close to the breaking point.

CHAPTER 8

Rescue

"We walked right into an ambush."

—Pvt. Dick Barham, L Company, 5th Cavalry Regiment

THURSDAY, FEBRUARY 15, 1951, 0700–1700 HOURS: 5TH CAVALRY REGIMENT, KOKSU-RI–CHIPYONG-NI HIGHWAY

Salvation for the 23rd Infantry Regiment was only 10 kilometers to the south. Preparing for their final push through the gauntlet were the soldiers of the 5th Cavalry, known as the "Black Knights," part of the 1st Cavalry Division.

Like the 23rd Infantry, the 5th Cavalry had a long and illustrious lineage. Established in 1855, the regiment first saw action fighting the Comanche in west Texas. When the Civil War broke out, many of its former officers became famous Confederate generals, including Robert E. Lee, Albert Sidney Johnston, and John Bell Hood. However, the regiment remained in the Union Army and participated in several battles, including the Battle of Gaines' Mill. After the Civil War, the regiment headed to the frontier and fought in Indian campaigns for several decades.

For much of the early twentieth century, the Black Knights patrolled the West. When World War II broke out, the troopers exchanged their horses for jeeps and left for the Pacific. In 1944 and 1945, the 5th Cavalry was instrumental in the campaign to recapture the Philippines. Between the wars, the regiment performed occupation duties in Japan. In late July 1950, the regiment shipped out to Korea and fought the

NKPA along the Pusan Perimeter. Like the rest of the division, it participated in the Pusan breakout in September and October 1950 and the
retreat from the Yalu in the winter of 1950–51.[1]

Leading the regiment was Col. Marcel G. Crombez. The fifty-year-
old Belgian-born colonel was a controversial figure. A naturalized U.S.
citizen, he spoke with a heavy accent. He graduated from West Point in
1925, and during the Second World War served in a variety of stateside
assignments, eventually reaching the rank of colonel. However, he did
not see combat until the end of the war. When the conflict ended, he
returned to the rank of lieutenant colonel. Like Freeman, his career
seemed destined to end without a major combat command. In 1949, the
Army promoted him back to the rank of colonel. When the Korean War
began, he assumed command of the 5th Cavalry. Now he had the chance
to achieve the glory that had eluded him during World War II.[2]

Unlike Freeman, Crombez engendered feelings of hostility in the
rank-and-file soldiers. "I lost many good men because of bad orders
issued by Crombez," wrote 1st Sgt. Arnold E. Mitchell, the senior
enlisted man for Item Company, 5th Cavalry. "I lost 92 in one battle of
which there was no cause other than bitterness on the part of Crombez.
I loved my men and they never wanted for nothing as long as I was there
[sic] First Sergeant."

Mitchell had an opinion about Crombez's military bearing, too. "He
was always sloppy dressed," wrote the first sergeant. "He would stand and
chew an enlisted man out for not having his pockets buttoned or cap
not on straight when you could look at him and every pocket was un-
buttoned, no helmut [sic], pistol belt not fastened and just poorly dressed.
This is what I mean when I say I had no respect for him. Enli[s]ted men
couldn't talk back and he knew they couldn't."[3]

His staff had a more nuanced view of Crombez. Capt. Keith M.
Stewart was the assistant S3 for the regiment in February 1951. "Certainly, he [Crombez] was no great tactician," wrote Stewart. "But he knew
with a certainty that in Korea, at least, one would do well to stay to the
high ground—a number of commanders never learned that lesson."

Stewart recalled Crombez "was an arbitrary, stubborn, opinionated
individual but he was devotedly loyal to his command. He listened to
those he had confidence in and let his battalion commanders do their
jobs once a mission had been assigned." Stewart wrote that Crombez

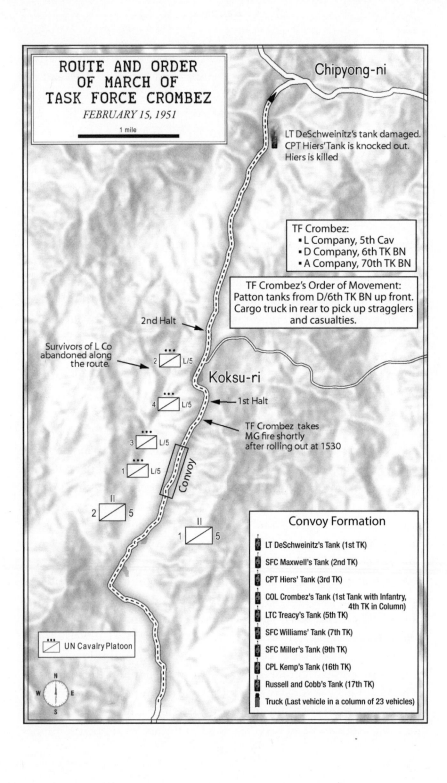

ROUTE AND ORDER OF MARCH OF TASK FORCE CROMBEZ

FEBRUARY 15, 1951

1 mile

Chipyong-ni

LT DeSchweinitz's tank damaged.
CPT Hiers' Tank is knocked out.
Hiers is killed

TF Crombez:
- L Company, 5th Cav
- D Company, 6th TK BN
- A Company, 70th TK BN

TF Crombez's Order of Movement:
Patton tanks from D/6th TK BN up front.
Cargo truck in rear to pick up stragglers
and casualties.

2nd Halt

Survivors of L Co
abandoned along
the route.

2 / L/5

Koksu-ri

4 / L/5

1st Halt

TF Crombez takes
MG fire shortly
after rolling out at 1530

3 / L/5

1 / L/5

Convoy

2 || 5

1 || 5

Convoy Formation

LT DeSchweinitz's Tank (1st TK)

SFC Maxwell's Tank (2nd TK)

CPT Hiers' Tank (3rd TK)

COL Crombez's Tank (1st Tank with Infantry,
4th TK in Column)

LTC Treacy's Tank (5th TK)

SFC Williams' Tank (7th TK)

SFC Miller's Tank (9th TK)

CPL Kemp's Tank (16th TK)

Russell and Cobb's Tank (17th TK)

Truck (Last vehicle in a column of 23 vehicles)

UN Cavalry Platoon

N
W E
S

"wanted to be a general more than anything else in this world. Unfortunately by his own actions, he was often, to his detractors, the object of derision."

Stewart concluded: "Colonel Crombez was considered by some to be somewhat of an amusing, slightly incompetent character who somehow or another got through this whole thing without being relieved. In my judgement [*sic*], those who had this opinion of him were wrong—true he was no tactical genius nor was he an outstanding leader—but in his own way he did get the job done."[4]

Crombez had been under tremendous pressure since February 14. His command had received orders from IX Corps to relieve the 23rd Infantry at Chipyong-ni the previous day at 1500 hours. Its commander, Maj. Gen. Bryant E. Moore, called Crombez personally over the phone to tell him to reach Chipyong-ni as soon as possible. At 1655 hours, Maj. Gen. Charles D. Palmer, Jr., commander of the 1st Cavalry Division, arrived at Crombez's location to personally convey the importance of 5th Cavalry's upcoming mission. At 1700 hours, Moore called Crombez again to say, "You'll have to move out tonight, and I know you'll do it."[5]

On the night of February 14, the 5th Cavalry crossed the Han River near the town of Hupo-ri. Though the Army labeled the 5th as a cavalry regiment, it was one in name only, with the same task organization as an infantry regiment. For the Chipyong-ni operation, Crombez's command included its three infantry battalions, a medical company, and A Company from the 8th Engineers. For tank support, it had several platoons from A Company of the 70th Heavy Tank Battalion, and all of D Company from the 6th Tank Battalion. For artillery support, it had the 61st Field Artillery Battalion and the 92nd Armored Artillery Battalion.

At 0700 hours on February 15, the regiment pushed north from Hupo-ri. The main axis of advance was the Koksu-ri–Chipyong-ni highway. Leading the way was 1st Battalion, which made contact with enemy forces 2 kilometers south of Koksu-ri, near the villages of Oktae and P'yongch'on, sometime between 0900 and 1000 hours. In response, the battalion commander deployed B and C Companies along the east side of the road and A Company on the west side. A little after 1000 hours, with enemy activity increasing, the regimental S3, Maj. Charles J. Parziale, recommended the commitment of Crombez's 2nd Battalion. The colonel agreed and ordered the battalion to deploy along the western side of the road, ahead of A Company.[6]

By 1100 hours, Colonel Crombez realized the Chinese defenders did not intend to yield to the two infantry battalions without a fight. According to the regimental S2, Maj. Robert A. Humphrey, spotter planes and the forward elements of both battalions had reported large enemy troop formations. Analyzing the reports, Humphrey estimated that the Chinese numbered around 2,000 soldiers. Even worse, they were dug in and ready for Crombez's regiment.[7]

Hearing the bad news, Crombez and Major Parziale, his operations officer, decided that a fast-moving, armored fist was better than a deliberate but plodding infantry steamroller. Crombez decided to use both platoons from A Company, 70th Heavy Tank Battalion, and all of the tanks from D Company, 6th Tank Battalion. In total, the column would have twenty-three to twenty-four tanks. To accompany the tanks, Crombez chose L Company to provide infantry support. He wanted the infantry "to remain on the tanks at all times unless forced off by fire to protect the tanks from fanatic enemy troops who might attempt to knock out the tanks at very close range." In addition to the infantry, Crombez added four engineers from the engineer company to clear any potential minefields along the route.[8]

Since the enemy would attack the vanguard first, Crombez ordered that no infantry ride on the tanks of the lead platoon. He wanted the M46 tanks from the 6th Tank Battalion to lead the column. The M46 Patton tank was a beast compared to the lighter and smaller M4 Shermans of the 70th Heavy Tank Battalion. A "heavy tank battalion" meant it had four platoons in each of the line companies instead of the standard configuration of three platoons; the designation had nothing to do with the type of tank. But the Patton *was* heavy, weighing nearly 50 tons and sporting a 90mm cannon as its primary weapon. It could withstand a lot more punishment than the Sherman and could dish out more death than its predecessor. Moreover, it had the ability to turn completely around on its axis like a wheel; this unique ability made it ideal in Korea where many of the roads were narrow, windy, and unimproved.

The rest of the column was comprised of M4 Sherman tanks, with the engineers riding on the second tank in the convoy. (It should be noted that a discrepancy exists in the primary sources as to the actual number of total tanks in the column.) To intimidate the Chinese, whom the U.N. soldiers considered superstitious and backward, Crombez ordered the tank crews to paint snarling tiger faces on the front of each tank so that each machine looked like a metal monster.

After the column cleared the road and arrived at Chipyong-ni, Lt. Col. Edgar J. Treacy, Jr., the 3rd Battalion commander, was to lead the ambulances and supply trucks to link up with them. Treacy would have to wait for Crombez's call before he could move out.[9]

According to those who served in 3rd Battalion, Crombez resented Treacy's success. Like Crombez, Treacy was a graduate of West Point, Class of 1935, but his World War II career was more successful. He served in the G2 section of the XIV Corps and participated in several Pacific campaigns. The Army promoted him to colonel before he was thirty, evidence of his ability. Even though he was ten years behind Crombez, he had attained the same rank by the end of the Second World War. When hostilities ceased, Treacy's rank reverted back to lieutenant colonel, his rank when he assumed command of 3rd Battalion, 5th Cavalry.[10]

Capt. Norman F. J. Allen was the commander of I Company at the time of Task Force Crombez. "We in 3rd Battalion that knew what was going on hated him [Crombez]. He never had any use for 3rd Battalion, and disliked Lieutenant Colonel Treacy immensely," he wrote in a postwar letter to a friend.[11]

Allen underscored the hostility Crombez felt for Treacy and his battalion. In September 1950, the 3rd Battalion was fighting to gain control of a piece of high ground known as Hill 174 on military maps. The 3rd Battalion had seized the hill nine times, but after each success the North Koreans recaptured it. According to Allen, Crombez ordered Treacy to send I Company to take the hill one more time. Treacy questioned his commander's judgment and supposedly told Crombez, "The enemy knows that we'll be coming and no matter how Allen tries to attack it, it went that way at least once before and the gooks will be ready for them. I Company is the only company of good strength in the regiment, and probably all of the 8th Army . . . and if they get chewed up, that will be the last strong company, gone to hell."

Crombez did not budge. On the contrary, he accused Treacy of cowardice. To clear his name, Treacy led the company assault up Hill 174. Allen later found out that Treacy was with the lead squad. When he asked Treacy why he was up front, Treacy replied, "Norm, I had never participated in a company attack before, Crombez had accused me of

being a coward in not ordering I Company to attack Hill 174, and
would relieve me if I Company didn't attack. I intended to refuse any
further orders to take Hill 174 if you were unable to hold it through the
night which no company had been able to do . . . and in order to refute
any implication of cowardice, I had to go with the attacking elements."[12]

Crombez's enmity extended to Treacy's entire battalion. No one
from 3rd Battalion was earning awards higher than Silver Stars, according to Allen, because Crombez reputedly said, "3rd Battalion wasn't
pulling its weight and he wasn't recommending approving any recommendation for higher than the silver star [sic]."[13]

When Treacy heard that Crombez wanted the men from L Com-
pany to ride atop the tanks, he did not like the plan, as it placed his soldiers in a vulnerable position. Capt. John C. Barrett, the L Company
commander, also disliked the concept. Barrett later commented in an
after-action report, "the infantrymen riding tanks are in effect 'sitting
ducks silhouetted against the sky, ideal targets for enemy fire.'"[14]

Orders were orders, though, so the soldiers and officers readied
themselves for the impending operation. After the mission, others
defended Crombez's controversial decision to mount the infantry on the
back of the tanks. For example, although Lt. Col. George B. Pickett, an
armored officer from IX Corps, was not part of Task Force Crombez, he
spoke with several armor officers who were involved in the action on
February 16—the day after the operation. According to Pickett,
Crombez had created the right task organization for the mission. In
1951, the 1st Cavalry Division was an infantry division and therefore did
not have armored personnel carriers like the M3 half-track. The only
way infantrymen could accompany a moving tank was by riding on top
of it. Crombez thought speed was essential, so he was willing to risk
exposing the infantry riding on top of his tanks in order to reach the
23rd Infantry Regiment in the shortest amount of time. Pickett finished
his interview with the remark, "the people who formed Task Force
Crombez knew what they needed, but what they needed was not
available."[15]

Regardless of his own reservations, Captain Barrett began conducting his troop-leading procedures. The time was 1215 hours. Essential to
the plan was the close coordination between the tanks and the infantry.
Barrett spoke with Capt. Johnnie M. Hiers, the commander of D Company, 6th Tank Battalion. Together, they formulated a basic scheme:

whenever the tanks halted, the infantry would dismount and establish hasty defensive positions along the road, 50 to 75 meters from the tanks. Whenever Crombez ordered the column to roll out, Hiers "would inform the tanks by radio, and the tankers in turn would inform the infantry by voice." Barrett made the erroneous assumption that the tank commanders would *not* be "buttoned up" inside their tanks during the operation. This costly misunderstanding would have fatal results for many of Barrett's infantry.

Trailing the tanks was a single 2½-ton cargo truck intended to serve as a makeshift ambulance. On board were several Korean soldiers Barrett had designated as litter-bearers. Unfortunately, the truck was soft-skinned and vulnerable to small-arms fire, unlike the tanks.

Barrett would ride on top of the seventh tank for command and control, along with ten enlisted men. Despite orders to the contrary, Colonel Treacy insisted on riding with his men, even though Crombez wanted him to remain behind with the supply convoy. It was a danger-ous mission, and Treacy wanted to share the risk. Bringing up the rear was First Lieutenant Johnson, Barrett's executive officer, who was to ride on the last tank. Both officers had SCR-300 radios, while the platoon leaders and Barrett had SCR-536s.[16]

In the meantime, Colonel Crombez had to meet with several visit-ing general officers. At 1250 hours, Major General Ruffner, the 2nd Infantry Division commander, arrived at Crombez's forward command post. He wanted to know when the 5th Cavalry would reach his besieged 23rd Infantry. Crombez assured Ruffner that his column would reach Chipyong-ni by sundown. To guarantee its success, Crombez told Ruffner that he would lead the column personally. Shortly after Ruffner left, General Palmer, Crombez's boss, returned to the 5th Cavalry com-mand post, inquiring about the progress of the relief column. He offered Crombez the use of his helicopter to conduct a reconnaissance of the route.

Around 1500 hours, Major Parziale received a call from Major Dumaine, the S3 of the 23rd Infantry. Dumaine explained to Parziale that the 23rd needed his column to reach them as soon as possible. Parziale told Colonel Crombez about the radio message, and Crombez realized that he could not wait for the rest of the supply trucks and ambulances to arrive from his division rear supply area. Time was running out. The Belgian-born commander finally made the decision to depart.[17]

Between 1530 and 1545 hours, Task Force Crombez rolled out. The colonel commanded the fifth tank in the column while his S3, Major Parziale, remained behind at the line of departure. Air support plastered the ridges. The Chinese responded with a hail of gunfire and 60mm mortars. Almost immediately, the tanks clanked to a halt and fired back at the Chinese positions. Fortunately, the pause was short, and within seconds the beasts groaned and heaved, resuming their trek. Clearly, the fearsome feline faces emblazoned on the tanks were not mystical totems after all. These were not superstitious Chinese.[18]

Pvt. Dick Barham was one of the L Company soldiers riding on the back of a tank. "We walked right into an ambush," he said in a newspaper interview. At the time of the operation, Barham was only nineteen. Minutes after the convoy started, he thought the engine on his tank had exploded. He then felt a sharp pain in his lower body as a bullet zipped through his buttocks and out his leg. "I'm hit!" he shouted to another man riding with him.

"Boogie!" the other soldier shouted to him. ("Boogie" was soldier parlance for "get out of harm's way.")

Barham rolled off the tank and staggered over to a nearby rice paddy, diving for cover as bullets zinged past him. A medic saw him, ran over to his location, and performed first aid. He cut open Barham's pants and then stuck him with a morphine syringe as he dressed the wound with a first aid bandage. When he was done, the medic scurried to the next casualty.

The young soldier from Chicago was now alone. He removed his grenades, laid them out in front of him, and waited for the enemy. Bullets pelted the puddles and snow around him. "You heard chheeewww and a splash. I hugged the ground and prayed for rescue," he said.[19]

Meanwhile, other soldiers were fighting for their lives as the armored leviathans rumbled northward. Two kilometers south of Koksu-ri, the road dog-legged to the west and then north into the village. There, the communists had established battle positions on two hills north and east of the bend, respectively. Their machine guns and rocket launchers had interlocking sectors of fire along the length of the road.

When the column approached, the enemy opened fire. The blistering fusillade from the enemy guns forced the line of tanks to lurch and stop at the bend. In response, the infantry on the tanks hopped off as planned, pushing off the road and establishing firing positions on either side while the tankers banged away at the hills with their machine guns. The sky was thick with lead as bullets crisscrossed through the cold air.

The infantry on the fifth tank were the first to dismount. PFC Homer Bassford and Cpl. George E. Reed were from 1st Platoon, L Company. As ordered, they jumped off, and from their position, they saw several of the Chinese infantry hiding in the nearby rice paddies. According to Bassford and Reed, the paddies lacked cover, becoming funeral plots for the enemy soldiers as machine gunners on the tanks ripped into them.

One of the gunners was Cpl. Paul Campbell. When everybody jumped off, his squad leader ordered him to stay on the tank and cover them with its .50-caliber machine gun. He gladly remained on the vehicle and opened fire with the M2. According to Campbell, the enemy was 50 to 200 meters from the road. He watched a M1919 machine-gun team struggle to set up their weapon after climbing off his M46. Suddenly, the corporal felt the tank shudder beneath his feet. The machine-gun team heard the tanks gunning their engines. They turned and saw the tanks clinking and clanking away. They tried to break down their crew-served weapon and race back to the departing convoy, but they were too late: the tanks had left them and several other soldiers behind.[20]

SFC Billy R. Williams was a tank commander in D Company, 6th Tank Battalion. "I was in the ninth tank in the column and could observe the Infantry dismounting under the machine gun fire," wrote Williams. "We moved through small arms, mortar and automatic weapons fire with the Infantry remaining in their exposed position. Each time we stopped we had to fire continuously to stop the enemy, even then, the Infantry killed many as they attempted to climb on the tanks."[21]

Riding on the eleventh tank was SFC George W. Miller, a platoon sergeant in L Company. When his tank rolled to a stop, he helped one of his wounded soldiers off the tank. Several minutes later, without warning, the tank drove off, leaving him and several soldiers lying in the rice paddies that lined the road. With bullets splashing the half-frozen puddles around him like lead raindrops, Miller realized they were dead men if they did not find cover. The sergeant saw a culvert on the west side of the road and led his group there.

Inside one of the tanks was M/Sgt. Jessie O. Giddens, a platoon leader in D Company, 6th Tank Battalion. Giddens later wrote:

> ... after moving about five hundred yards down the road, my platoon, which was the third in the column, began receiving intense small arms, machine gun, and anti-tank rifle fire, and the Infantry Platoon leader riding on my tank was wounded and one other soldier. The column was halted for about five minutes, due to a by-pass in the town of Koksu-ri. At this time, the enemy fire became so intense that all the Infantry riding my tank had to dismount to take cover. In doing so, the Infantry Platoon Leader was killed.

The master sergeant saw the carnage from his turret and sprang into action. "I had ordered my platoon to lay down as much fire as possible on the high ground and to cover the Infantry as much as possible," he explained later. He heard the call from his commanding officer over the radio. "As the infantry mounted we were ordered to move out and keep going due to the heavy fire coming in on my tanks," wrote Giddens. He knew he was abandoning the infantry, but he had little choice in the matter.[22]

Cpl. Hiram E. Cornelius was a tanker from A Company, 70th Tank Battalion, and recalled the ferocity of the Chinese defenders around Koksu-ri in a witness statement he wrote less than a week after the battle. "The column moved forward about a thousand yards and at that time, started receiving a tremendous amount of automatic weapons and very accurate mortar fire. The fire was deadly and accurate that most of the Infantry was forced to dismount from the tanks and take cover along the road. The tanks returned the fire and as the Infantrymen remounted, continued moving forward toward the objective."

Cornelius also described the fanatic bravery of the Chinese, who attacked the column as if they were berserkers. "Along the entire route," he wrote, "the task force was attacked by enemy personnel armed with pole charges and blocks of TNT, but due to the intense fire layed [sic] down by the tanks and Infantry, they were unable to get in close enough to disable the tanks."[23]

Farther back in the column, M/Sgt. Lloyd L. Jones, another platoon sergeant for 3rd Platoon, L Company, was traveling on top of one of the last tanks. Seconds after his tank halted, enemy gunfire sprayed his vehicle, wounding two of his soldiers. In response, Jones ordered his men off the tank. He knew the tank was the best cover in the area and told the wounded soldiers to get behind it. Suddenly, the turret swung abruptly to the right and knocked him off. Without warning, the tank engine sputtered, and then the beast heaved, its bogie wheels starting to turn. Before the stranded soldiers could climb back on the tank, it was gone. Jones and the others dashed over to the same culvert where Miller sought cover. After reaching it safely, Jones saw the trailing cargo truck drive up and stop as the litter-bearers got out to help the wounded. Braving the enemy fire, they lifted three injured soldiers from 1st Platoon into the back of the 2½-ton truck while rounds pinged off the sides like hailstones.

Jones made a snap decision, reasoning that the soft-skin truck was a potential hearse. He chose to wait. After the truck sped off, Jones found Private Bassford and the others, including several wounded soldiers, one of whom was the platoon leader, First Lieutenant Lahey. They were sitting ducks, so Jones ordered Bassford and another soldier to sneak back through enemy lines to the assembly area and tell one of the commanders that the column had left behind several groups of infantry south of Koksu-ri. Soon afterward, Lieutenant Johnson arrived at the culvert and consolidated the group into a hasty battle position.

Meanwhile, another group of abandoned soldiers from 2nd and 4th Platoons were fighting for their lives several hundred meters away in a ditch northwest of the culvert. Jones saw them, ran over to their location, and told them to join Johnson's group. For several minutes, the NCOs from 2nd and 4th Platoons organized the disparate group into a combat formation before setting out for the culvert. The pause probably saved their lives.

Back at the culvert, men were scraping the icy ground with their trench shovels, trying to dig hasty fighting positions. As tracers zipped over his head, Sergeant Miller crawled over to Lieutenant Johnson. He suggested that he take some of the unwounded men back to F Company and Capt. Joe W. Finley. Miller estimated the Fox Company positions were only 2,000 meters from their location. Johnson agreed, and Miller left to find help.

A few minutes later, machine-gun fire raked the area around the sewer pipe. Simultaneously, eight mortar rounds detonated on top of it, filling the air with shrapnel. The sudden attack was costly for the Americans, the barrage resulting in the death of Lieutenant Lahey and leaving Johnson wounded. Unbeknownst to Johnson, the Chinese had moved one of their machine guns to a new position from which they had enfilade fire on the culvert. Powerless, the men hunkered down and waited for the tanks.[24]

Fortunately, Bassford and Miller made it back to the assembly area and alerted everyone about the unfolding disaster along the highway. By 1645 hours, another column of tanks from the 5th Cavalry rolled down the road to rescue the abandoned soldiers. Private Barham's account said one tank rolled by his location and the crew rescued him.

However, the field hospital where they took him was hardly an improvement. The big Red Cross painted on the side of tent was a fat target for enemy mortars, and inside the field hospital the cries of the wounded filled the air. "They were calling for their mothers," said Barham. "Mom, mom, I need you," they whimpered, as if they were children.

The surgeons had to evacuate the wounded. The orderlies placed Barham and the others on stretchers and carried them to waiting ambulances. Barham looked up from his litter and noticed the windows on his ambulance were shattered. He soon discovered why. "Every time a mortar shell landed close, it would rock the ambulance. The fear is unbelievable because there is nothing you can do," he said.[25]

Not all of the stranded soldiers reached friendly lines. The enemy kept up a steady stream of fire as the column plowed through the village of Koksu-ri. Captain Barrett and Colonel Treacy's tank was the second tank to carry infantry in the column. Shortly after their tank exited the village, the column halted again. Barrett and Treacy jumped off.

Carroll Gifford Everist was one of the infantrymen with them. "We were riding our tanks when we came under fire from all sides," he wrote years later. "Staff Sergeant John Sollie was killed that day. He had been my buddy from the beginning to the end. The two of us shared a foxhole (a bunker would have been safer, but we were never in one), made jokes, and sang songs like 'Maresedotes.' John was killed and I was shot in the left knee."

Everist's account continued: "The tanks stopped and I got off to find cover (there was none) and to return fire, but I wasn't of much use. I had no mobility. Lieutenant Colonel Treacy, who had been shot in the mouth, carried me on his back to about fifteen feet off the road. He also gave me his first aid pouch."[26]

Everist and Treacy were not alone; with them were seven to nine other wounded soldiers. They all huddled together in a ditch by the road and waited for help. Several minutes after the tanks left, the enemy arrived.

"Once off the road, about fifteen Chinese swarmed in on us and we were all captured," wrote Everist. "Because I was shot in the knee and couldn't walk, Colonel Treacy carried me. We were taken to a wooden building (like a gazebo) with no walls and no furnishings. It was one big room in an open area close to the top of a hill. That was the area where all of us were before they took two men away. I don't know who the one man was taken from our group—I just remember that he was very tall. We never saw him again. He was probably shot. The other man taken away that night was Colonel Treacy."[27] At the time, Crombez had no idea that Treacy had hitched a ride on one of his tanks when the column moved out, let alone that he had been captured.

Unlike Treacy and Everist, Barrett managed to escape injury and capture. When the column rolled out again, the L Company commander missed his tank, but jumped on the eleventh one that passed by his location.

Atop the rumbling tanks, the carnage and chaos continued. Cpl. Wayne O. Kemp was a M1919 machine gunner riding on the eighteenth tank in the convoy. As ordered, he got off the tank at the first stop, handing the machine gun to the assistant machine gunner. When the tank started to roll, he raced back to it. As Kemp ran alongside the tracks, something stung him in the arm and he fell behind, wounded. Since he had given away the M1919, Kemp could only defend himself with his Colt .45 pistol. He joined his platoon sergeant, SFC George A. Krizan, and one of the squad leaders from his platoon, who were hiding in a ditch.

Several minutes later, Kemp and the others saw the cargo truck roll down the road. They waved it down, and the truck halted. As the three rushed over to it, enemy fire stitched the cab, wounding the driver. Sergeant Krizan pushed aside the wounded man and got behind the wheel as enemy fire continued to rip through the canvas. After everyone had climbed onto the truck bed, Krizan hit the accelerator and jammed the transmission into first gear. The shredded vehicle took off. After passing through Koksu-ri, it reached a pass where it came under intense enemy fire. As Krizan negotiated the narrow road, several rounds punctured the engine block of the truck, causing it to roll a stop only a few kilometers south of Chipyong-ni. Everyone inside was severely wounded; their only option was to wait for someone to rescue them before the Chinese found them first.[28]

PFC Donald F. Russell was a runner for 4th Platoon, L Company. He and Cpl. Hubert M. Cobb were on the nineteenth tank in the column. As their tank wove its way through Koksu-ri, bullets ricocheted off the steel behemoth and wounded several riders. Russell and Cobb remained unharmed, but they wondered how long their good fortune would last. When the column staggered and halted north of Koksu-ri, both men climbed off the tank and ran over to a roadside ditch. Huddled in the shallow trench, they debated whether to jump back on the tanks or stay where they were. Despite barely surviving the last hour on a veritable death ride, they concluded their chances of survival were slightly better if they remained with the column rather than alone in hostile territory.

As the tanks started to move again, both men got up and ran back to their vehicle. Cobb scampered up the side of the tank first, and Russell was still running alongside it, as if he were trying to hop into an accelerating freight car, when a mortar round suddenly exploded. A single fragment tore into his left hand, rendering it useless. Thinking fast, he handed Cobb his carbine so he could use his one good hand to lift himself up on the tank. However, when he tried to mount the monster, he stumbled and fell. Fortunately, the next tank did not crush him. Despite his injury, Russell was able to clamber onto one of the last tanks and held on until they reached Chipyong-ni.[29]

As the commander, Crombez was up front, inside the fifth tank. Despite his location in the vanguard, he knew that every time his column stopped and started he was leaving behind groups of soldiers along the road. It was a calculated choice for Crombez. He estimated that the Chinese had over 2,000 soldiers between them and Chipyong-ni.

Despite the firepower of his tanks, Crombez believed that a slugfest with a Chinese regiment would only end in disaster for his task force. First Lt. Martin Blumenson, who interviewed Crombez a month after Chipyong-ni, wrote, "Immediately after the column passed through KOKSU-RI, about one hundred additional riflemen were forced from the tanks, but Colonel Crombez, feeling that the success of the task force depended on the ability of the tanks to keep moving, directed the tanks to continue."[30]

Inside Crombez's tank was M/Sgt. Joe Kirkland, the vehicle commander. "We buttoned-up after the first five hundred yards," wrote Kirkland. "Colonel Crombez directed fire for our gunner and was in complete charge of the task force. If the column slowed down he would urge them to move on. When the lead tank was slowed and we had no communications with them, Colonel Crombez told the number two tank to close in on it. This kept the lead tank moving and the column continuing toward its objective."[31]

PFC Thomas Bayes, Jr., was the gunner in Crombez's tank and recalled how Crombez behaved under fire. "He [Crombez] gave me clear, short fire commands and spotted two or three rocket launcher teams," wrote Bayes. "He was very calm throughout the action and urged the tanks to keep moving through the heavy enemy fire."[32]

Crombez's tank driver, PFC George C. Lee, agreed with Bayes's assessment of the commander, writing, "He was very calm, made sound decisions and continuously controlled the maneuvering of the column and the fire of the tanks in which he was riding."[33]

Four kilometers north of Koksu-ri, the road threaded through a narrow pass in the hills. SFC James Maxwell was the tank commander for the second tank in the column. From his turret, he saw that the enemy had dug in along both sides of the road and sensed the approaching chokepoint would be a deadly kill zone.

"When were about two thousand yards from Chipyong-ni, I spotted a bazooka man moving over a hill of a pass in which we had to go," wrote Maxwell. "I called First Lieutenant Lawrence L DeSchweinitz, my platoon leader, who was the point tank but I was too late with my call and the lieutenant's tank was hit through the top of the turret, wounding First Lieutenant DeSchweinitz, Corporal Donal P. Harrell the gunner, and Private Joseph Garland, the loader."

Maxwell tried to raise DeSchweinitz over the radio but heard only static. His vehicle assumed the lead as it passed the lieutenant's stricken tank. Moments later, Maxwell heard a thud. "As I came through the pass my tank was hit in the two road wheels, one on each side of tank," explained Maxwell. Fortunately, the damage was not critical, and the tank continued north.[34]

Capt. Johnnie Hiers's tank was fourth in the column. As Cpl. John A. Calhoun navigated the M46 Patton through the pass, a Chinese soldier lined it up in his sights. Unbeknownst to Hiers and the Americans, the Chinese were using captured 3.5-inch bazookas. Designed to kill the newer, heavier Soviet tanks, the M20 bazooka packed a wallop compared to its predecessor, the M9, which had only a 2.36-inch diameter rocket. Against a Patton, the 3.5-inch rocket would have little trouble penetrating its thick armor. American and ROK units had abandoned scores of bazookas and other weapons during the bugouts of November, December, January, and early February, and the Chinese had picked them up, along with the ability to slay the Pattons and other tanks with ease.

Without warning, the Chinese soldier pulled the trigger. The rocket whooshed out of the tube, hurtling through the air at a speed of 340 feet per second, and slammed into the left side of Hiers's tank, detonating inside the ammunition ready rack. In less than a second, the rounds started to cook off inside the tank like popping popcorn, killing Hiers, the gunner, and his loader. Miraculously, Calhoun survived. Suffering from painful burns, he drove the tank off the road so that it would not become a roadblock. First Lt. William R. Bierwirth, 3rd Platoon Leader, D Company, was now the acting commander for all of D Company.

Soldiers later found the fins from the rocket that hit Hiers's tank, confirming that the Chinese were using captured M20 bazookas. They also found the gunner's emplacement near the defile. Looking at the scorch marks on the ground, they estimated the Chinese soldier had fired three to four rounds from that location.[35]

Meanwhile, Sergeant Maxwell had no idea that his commander was dead. He was too busy staying alive, acting as the eyes for the regimental commander and speaking directly with Colonel Crombez over the radio. Several hundred meters south of Chipyong-ni, he saw several tanks. From where he was, he did not know if they were friend or foe. He figured it was better to be safe than sorry.

"I started to fire on them," explained Maxwell. "But the lead tank turned its turret and I recognized it as one of our friendly forces. We came up to a halt and both just s[a]t for awhile. We had no radio contact with each other, so I dismounted from my tank and went forward on foot and made contact with the lead tank from the 23d Infantry Regiment and told him to pull back so we could get on through. When we entered Chip'yong-ni some of the men of the 23d Infantry and some of the French troops came out and kissed my tank."[36]

Shortly after Maxwell's vehicle rolled into the perimeter, Colonel Crombez's Patton tank slipped through the notch and reached Schmitt Hill. Behind him, the Chinese continued to fire at them as they raced through the narrow pass. "As the columns approached a point three-thousand yards from the town of Chip'yong-ni," Sergeant Giddens described, "we entered a pass with high ground on both sides and hundreds of small troop dug-outs. Here we came under the most intense fire."

When his tank started to thread the gauntlet, Giddens and his crew braced themselves. "As my platoon entered the pass, a bazooka hit the top of my turret, but failed to explode," wrote Giddens. Relieved they had survived, the master sergeant ordered his driver to enter the perimeter.[37]

One by one, the rest of the tanks rolled past Schmitt Hill. Between 1645 and 1710 hours, most of the vehicles of Task Force Crombez passed through the 23rd Infantry's front lines and into Chipyong-ni. The arrival of 5th Cavalry signaled disaster for the Chinese.[38]

Sgt. Martin Lee from Easy Company, 23rd Infantry, recalled the arrival of the 5th Cavalry. "All at once, we saw these damn cavalry patches on the sides of tanks coming around the corners," he said. "They came up through and around a hill and up through a draw there. They started opening up with those tanks and machine guns, and the gooks started running, and we just had a field day. We could pick them off because they were running up through the area."

The drubbing the Chinese had received for the last forty-eight hours finally bore fruit. The stoic peasant soldiers of the CPVF had had enough, and they broke down and ran. All discipline was lost as thousands of soldiers suddenly decided it was every man for himself.

Lee described the ensuing carnage. "I don't know how many we killed at that time but we had to have killed, between us and the cavalry . . . many thousands, I think, because we could see bodies all over the damn hillsides there."[39]

Grant Mead, another Easy Company soldier, also remembered the final, dramatic act of the siege. "When the Chinese broke," he recalled, "it was like ants on a hill when they skedaddled. They lost a lot of people. They lost a helluva lot more people than we did. We were trying to shoot as many of them as we could, and guys were opening up with their machine guns and everything."[40]

It was a total victory for the U.N. forces. "Thousands of Chinese on all the close and distant hills could now be seen running in long files away from the perimeter," Colonel Edwards wrote a decade later. "Every available rifleman and weapon on and inside the perimeter began firing and there were more targets than weapons. Two Chinese Armies were in complete panic! The Chinese ran like terror-stricken deer and stumbled over their own dead and wounded in their wild desire to get away from the perimeter."[41]

Afterwards, when Edwards saw Colonel Crombez, he walked up to the cavalry trooper and exclaimed, "You are a sight for sore eyes! God, but we're glad to see you!"

That evening, it was still tense inside friendly lines. The Tomahawks thought Task Force Crombez had brought up ammunition. More important, they had believed that they could evacuate their wounded that night. Neither would happen. Crombez informed them he had no ammunition for them, and since it was now dark, he did not want to risk calling for his supply column to drive through enemy territory to reach them. As a result, they would have to wait one more night.

"The situation was serious!" wrote Edwards. "If the Chinese attacked on that night, 15–16 February 1951, as savagely as they did the night before, most of the 23rd Infantry would die in savage, hand-to-hand fighting."

Fortunately, Task Force Crombez's final assault had broken the enemy's will. The evening passed without incident. The next day, Colonel Crombez brought the desperately needed trucks to resupply the soldiers and evacuate the wounded. However, the trucks were also there to remove the bodies of the fallen American and French soldiers.[42]

Decades after the war, Grant Mead recalled, "I remember as we were leaving all these trucks were loaded with dead bodies. . . . It made me think how very lucky I was."[43]

After the siege, forward observer Sergeant Wilburn returned to his foxhole on McGee Hill and surveyed the devastation. "I went back up on that hill to see the damage that was done up there," he said. "[There were] dead people laying around; they were all over the place. You could hardly take a step without stepping on a body part."[44]

After he returned from seeing his platoon medic, a wounded Seymour Harris also went back to his foxhole to see the results of the previous night's work. It was a sobering experience for him, even though he was staring at the bodies of the enemy. "My God, what a sight. Some had arms missing. Some had been decapitated, some had guts hanging out. Chinese soldiers lay in every way, shape, and form. On top of one another like corded wood."

He looked up and noticed an officer writing notes. "A tall captain with a clipboard is using his pen as a pointer, taking a head count of the dead gooks," explained Harris. "Slowly he walks up the draw. Counting away. I do a little counting myself, and get up to 50 before I stop. It was the tip of an iceberg."

Harris later wrote in a letter, "I really have no idea how many we killed that night. I heard it was five hundred and something, but I just can't say. All I know is that the draw was littered with dead nearly up to the base of the high hill."[45]

February 15 was not the end of the fighting for the abandoned soldiers of L Company. The Chinese had captured many of them. Despite the odds, Carroll Gifford Everist escaped from his communist captors and survived the war. "They [Chinese] were going to shoot me in the head," he later wrote. "I went in to hysteria. . . . G2 stated to me that Chinese believe if you are nuts you are worst [*sic*] off than dead."

The ruse worked. The Chinese abandoned him when they retreated into the mountains. Later, on February 18, a staggering and wounded Everist intercepted a U.S. patrol along the Koksu-ri–Chipyong-ni highway. His first meal was franks and beans. He said he still remembered how they tasted, even after half a century.[46]

Colonel Treacy was not as fortunate. He died in captivity on May 31, 1951. Several weeks after the battle, the survivors from L Company and others from 3rd Battalion lobbied the regimental command to submit Treacy for the Medal of Honor. Capt. Norman Allen, the Item Company commander, initiated the paperwork.

After several days, Allen inquired about the status of the award from the regimental executive officer, Lt. Col. Edward Mayer. The response was less than enthusiastic. "Christ, Norm, forget it!" Mayer said to Allen. "I hand carried your recommendation directly to Colonel Crombez as you asked me to, and he threw it on the floor, and ground it with his boot, saying, 'MOH, no Goddamn it no, if he ever returns to military control I will try him!'"[47]

Many of the men of L Company and 3rd Battalion never forgave Colonel Crombez for how he had treated them and their fallen commander. James Cardinal, a veteran from the 5th Cavalry, summed it up best, writing:

> Thus, it should come as no surprise that his [Crombez's] conduct in ordering the men of L Company to ride on top of the tanks, over the opposition of Lieutenant Colonel Treacy, the 3rd Battalion Commander, and Captain Barrett, commanding L Company, while he was safely ensconced inside the fifth tank was widely regarded within the 3rd Battalion as criminal and cowardly. His abandonment of Treacy, who was well liked and highly respected by the men of the 3rd Battalion, was seen as contemptible and despicable, since, rightly or wrongly, it was regarded as a treacherous act to get back at a man whom, many believed, he hated and who held him in contempt.[48]

On the other hand, Colonel Crombez received the Distinguished Service Cross for his actions on 15 February. His award was controversial, and Brig. Gen. Henry I. Hodes, the Eighth Army chief of staff, initially rejected its submission. Undeterred, Crombez lobbied General Ridgway, who ordered Hodes to approve the award. On January 29, 1952, Crombez received his Distinguished Service Cross.[49]

The award, though, did not silence his critics. In July 1951, the Department of the Army informed Crombez that he would be heading home. Capt. Keith M. Stewart, his assistant S3, later wrote, "There was no question about his courage—and, yes, he was promoted, after the war to Brigadier General—then put out to pasture."

Crombez knew his reassignment back to the United States would be the end of his career. According to Stewart, he fought it, but in the end it was a losing battle. He returned to the United States and retired shortly thereafter. For the men of 3rd Battalion, it was a small victory.[50]

L Company had suffered grievously. On the morning of February 15, 1951, it had a strength of 186 men. According to the unit administrative officer, 160 of these soldiers accompanied the task force. When it arrived at Chipyong-ni, only 23 infantry and 4 engineers were still riding on the tanks, and of those 13 were wounded. Crombez later claimed approximately 100 soldiers returned to friendly lines throughout the night.

Captain Barrett, the L Company commander, said his company had 20 killed in action, 20 missing in action, and roughly 40 wounded in action. In total, his company had around 80 casualties out of 160 men: 50 percent. The headlong charge up the Koksu-ri–Chipyong-ni highway had decimated his company.[51]

The 23rd Infantry also suffered serious casualties. According to the records, the Tomahawks sustained 404 battle and non-battle casualties. Of those, 52 were killed in action and 42 were missing in action. The majority of the losses were in G and B Companies. Colonel Edwards later wrote that G Company incurred 112 casualties in the forty-eight hours of fighting. Of those, 28 were killed in action and 29 were missing in action.[52]

For the 23rd Infantry, the three weeks between the end of January and the middle of February were some of the bloodiest for the entire regiment. "When we went over there [Korea], we had 210 men in our company," said Leo Dobbs, the Item Company, 23rd Infantry, mail clerk. "The day they [the Army] started to rotate us back, there was thirty-four of us left from the original bunch."[53]

EPILOGUE

"Win a quick victory if you can; if you can't, win a slow one."

Mao Zedong, leader of China

The battles of Chipyong-ni and the Twin Tunnels were not the end of the Korean War. In fact, the conflict continued until July 27, 1953. However, they were the turning point—the Midway and Stalingrad of the Korean War. It was the first time the United Nations had defeated a major Chinese offensive. Sure, there were small tactical U.N. victories prior to February 1951, but the first two weeks of February were operational-level triumphs. Peng Dehuai's vaunted Chinese Fourth Phase Offensive had failed to live up to its expectations.

As at Midway and Stalingrad, the aggressor did not realize the strategic initiative had passed to the defender, and like the Japanese and Germans, the Chinese tried one more time to wrest victory from the United Nations with the Fifth Phase Offensive. By then, however, Eighth Army's confidence was much greater, and in the end, the Fifth Phase Offensive was an even worse fiasco than the previous one.

After the Fourth Phase Offensive, Comrade Peng Dehuai left the Korean theater for Beijing. There, he met with Chairman Mao Zedong. The failure of the Fourth Phase Offensive had convinced Dehuai that the Chinese could not win the Korean War quickly, and he conveyed his misgivings to Mao. According to Peng, Mao said to him, "Win a quick victory if you can; if you can't, win a slow one." With new orders, Peng then returned to Korea to continue the conflict.

General Ridgway was also keen on continuing the conflict. Shortly after Chipyong-ni, he initiated Operations Killer and Ripper, respectively. In both operations, he did not seek territory or prisoners: his

241

intent was to kill as many Chinese as possible while preserving the lives of his own soldiers. He wanted to make the war in Korea so painful that the Chinese would come to the bargaining table, pleading for mercy.[1]

In April 1951, other events intervened. Ridgway was promoted after Gen. Douglas MacArthur overstepped his authority with President Truman and made public statements about expanding the war into China— statements he had not cleared with the president. As a result, he was fired, and Truman appointed Ridgway to replace him. Gen. James A. Van Fleet took over Eighth Army on April 11, 1951, and continued Ridgway's successful strategy of firepower over manpower. During that time, the Chinese launched their Fifth Phase Offensive, but did not get very far. Its small acquisition of real estate did not justify the horrendous losses the Chinese Army suffered for such meager gains.

By June 1951, the Russians had signaled a willingness to reach an agreement on Korea. Alas, it took two more years for both sides to reach an accord. However, the initiation of armistice talks did alter the character of the conflict. For the next twenty-four months, the Korean War resembled World War I more than World War II; it had transitioned from a fluid war of movement to a static war of position. Gone were the ambitious amphibious landings and major Chinese offensives. Trench lines and barbed wire replaced armored thrusts and airborne landings. Like in World War I, artillery now played a huge role.

Both sides wanted the war to end on their terms. By this time, the U.S. government was pursuing an objective: the resumption of the *status quo ante bellum*. It was up to the Eighth Army to get the Chinese and the North Koreans to accept the terms, and it took the United Nations two more years to do it. By July 1953, both sides finally realized that an armistice was the only achievable goal. In the end, they traded their prisoners of war and settled on their respective sides behind a new DMZ that, for the most part, follows the same path today across the peninsula.

For many of the men and women who fought in Korea, the war became the defining experience of their lives. Col. Paul Freeman's command of the 23rd Infantry Regiment at Kunu-ri, the Twin Tunnels, and Chipyong-ni catapulted his career. After his regimental command, he attended the National War College. The Army promoted him to brigadier general in July 1952, and he assumed command over U.S. Army Forces, Austria. Six months later, he transferred to the staff of Supreme Headquarters Allied Powers Europe, and for the next two years served as a staff general. In August 1955, he returned to Fort Lewis, Washington, to take command of his favorite unit: the 2nd Infantry Division. In October of that same year, the Army promoted him to major general, and he led the Indianhead Division for the next twelve months. Later, Freeman took over the 4th Infantry Division, which he ably led for another six months. He went to Washington, D.C., in the spring of 1957, where he worked for a year until the Army selected him to become the commandant of the U.S. Army Infantry School at Fort Benning, Georgia, where he served for nearly two years.

Impressed with his service, the Army promoted him to lieutenant general. His next job was as the deputy commander, U.S. Army Continental Command, in Virginia. He served in that capacity for two years. In May 1962, he earned the rank of general and became the commander-in-chief, U.S. Army Forces, Europe. In 1965, he returned to the United States and became the commander of the U.S. Army Continental Command. After serving his country for nearly forty years, Paul Freeman finally retired from the Army in 1967. He passed away on April 17, 1988. On his memorial citation, someone wrote, "His many friends will miss him, his warmth, and gentleness (albeit, behind a gruff exterior), his integrity, his honesty, and his loyalty. He was one of the last stalwarts of the old school . . . a credit to the Long Gray Line."[2]

Unlike Colonel Freeman, Col. Ralph Monclar's career ended after Korea. He returned to France, where his last posting was as the governor of Les Invalides. He passed away on June 3, 1964, and his body was laid to rest in the Vault of Governors, inside the Chapel of Saint Louis at Les Invalides. His neighbors include Napoleon Bonaparte and Ferdinand Foch.[3]

Chipyong-ni was the highpoint of 3rd Platoon leader Paul McGee's military career. After he made first lieutenant, McGee left Korea and the Army upon learning his father was on his deathbed. McGee took over the family business, the McCain & McGee Machine Shop in North Carolina. He remained in the Tarheel State for the rest of his life, marrying Ann Belk McGee. Together, they had four children: daughter Trill and sons Paul, David, and James. After a long, happy life, Paul died on May 11, 2009, in Charlotte, North Carolina.[4]

For others, the events of Chipyong-ni became a source of lasting acrimony. After the war, both Lt. Col. James Edwards and Capt. Sherman Pratt wrote accounts of what happened on the morning of February 15,

1951. Edwards penned his interpretation in 1964. In his version, Pratt was incompetent. To the 2nd Battalion Commander, the B Company attack was disjointed and piecemeal, and as a result the Chinese easily defeated it.

On the other hand, Pratt maintained that Edwards did not provide him with all the information he needed. According to Pratt, the G Company fighting positions were not deep enough. Moreover, though his attack appeared piecemeal, Pratt had intended to hit the Chinese positions with two platoons abreast, but enemy mortars and machine guns prevented his two platoons from reaching the objective simultaneously.

In the end, Pratt's initial counterattack was too late. According to Chinese accounts, the 344th Regiment had occupied the G Company positions with its 2nd and 3rd Battalions. The Chinese after-action report even mentioned the failed American counterattacks. If the Chinese did have two battalions on the three hilltops north of Masan (and by all accounts they did), then a company of GIs would have been far short of the required amount of combat power to attack a prepared defensive position. In short, both Pratt and Edwards were wrong in blaming each other.[5]

As noted, the G Company position fell at 0300 hours. It took Captain Ramsburg over two hours to prepare the first counterattack. By that point, it was already too late. The turning point was at 2200 hours, when the Chinese first secured a toehold inside the G Company positions. If Lieutenant Heath, the G Company commander, had a reserve, then he should have committed it when 1st Platoon lost its first foxholes to Chinese sappers; however, Heath refused to believe what Lieutenant McGee was telling him about the enemy machine gun on his flank. In Heath's defense, he believed Sergeant Toth's assessment over McGee's because Toth was an old-timer in the unit, while McGee was a new officer with only a few weeks of experience as a member of George Company.

When Ryan, the Eighth Army historian, asked McGee if a committed reserve would have made a difference earlier in the battle, the lieutenant replied, "I think so, because at first, there was only one hole taken over by the Chinese. That's when I informed the CP that the Chinese were in the hole. If at that time, the CO would have used the squad that they sent up to me later, I think we could have retaken that hole at that time."[6]

Regardless, the controversy at Chipyong-ni did not affect either Edwards's or Pratt's Army careers. After the war, Edwards retired as a full colonel, then became a prosecutor for the city of San Antonio, Texas. Meanwhile, Pratt stayed in the service and retired as a lieutenant colonel. Like Edwards, Pratt chose the law upon retirement. After attending law school at the University of Arkansas, he started a private practice in Arlington, Virginia. Later, he worked as a lawyer for the Federal Communications Commission, retiring in 1979. He died on September 23, 2013.[7]

Medal of Honor recipient M/Sgt. Hubert L. Lee believed Chipyong-ni was the high point of his military service. After the war, he left the Army and went to work repairing communications equipment in the town of Greenville, Mississippi. He never married and passed away on November 5, 1982, at the age of sixty-seven.[8]

Many of the other survivors of Chipyong-ni and the Twin Tunnels returned to the United States and became productive members of society. Sgt. Martin Lee from Easy Company eventually became Sergeant Major Lee, retiring from the Army in 1968. After the service, Lee became an insurance claims agent and retired in 1991. He was twice married and has four children. When asked by the author if he had served in Vietnam, Lee replied, "No, I was one lucky sucker. I didn't get called. I didn't want that extra star on my damn badge."[9]

Harley Wilburn was discharged from the Army and married his wife in 1952. He has four children: one daughter and three sons. He and his wife have been married for sixty-two years at the time of this publication. After the war, Harley worked as a specialized welder in St. Louis and retired in 1982 after undergoing heart surgery. He is still alive, a grandfather with eighteen grandchildren.[10]

As for the 23rd Infantry Regiment and L Company, 5th Cavalry Regiment, both received Presidential Unit Citations (23rd Infantry also received one for the Battle of the Twin Tunnels). This citation was the equivalent of an individual receiving the Distinguished Service Cross, and only the Commander-in-Chief could award it. In the citation for the 23rd Infantry Regiment, President Truman wrote:

The dogged determination, gallantry and indomitable espirit [*sic*] displayed by the 23rd Regimental Combat Team, when completely surrounded and cut off; the destruction of attacking Chinese hordes which enabled the United Nation Forces to maintain their front and resume the offensive; and the steadfast and stubborn refusal to allow a fanatical and numerically superior force to dislodge them, are in keeping with the finest traditions of the United States Army and reflect great credit on all members of the units who participated in this historical combat action.

General Ridgway added his own tribute, speaking to a joint session of Congress on May 22, 1952:

I wish I could pay proper tribute to the magnificent conduct of United Nations troops throughout these operations. It is difficult to single out any one unit or the forces of any one nation, but to illustrate, I shall speak briefly of the Twenty-Third United States Infantry Regiment, Colonel Paul L. Freeman, Commanding, with the French Battalion and the normal components of artillery, engineer and medical personnel from the United States Second Infantry Division. These troops in early February of 1951 sustaining [sic] two of the severest attacks experienced during the entire Korean campaign. Twice isolated far in advance of the general battle line, twice completely surrounded in near zero weather, they repelled repeated assaults by day and night by vastly superior numbers of Chinese infantry. They were finally relieved by an armored column from the United States First Cavalry Division in as daring and dramatic an operation as the war provided.

Ridgway finished his statement by saying to Congress, "I personally visited these magnificent men during both operations and personally directed the attack of the relieving armored column which finally broke through and contributed to the utter and final rout of the enemy forces. I want to record here my conviction that these American fighting men with their French comrade-in-arms measured up in every way to the battle conduct of the finest troops America or France has produced throughout their national existence."[11]

★ ★ ★

Though Korea remains divided, thanks to the efforts of the men of 23rd Infantry and its French Battalion, part of it is a free country. Sadly, with each passing day, another veteran from that war dies, and unlike the Second World War, most people do not know what their parents and grandparents sacrificed in Korea. At Chipyong-ni, they saved a nation. It was a heavy burden and a gallant act worth remembering.

NOTES

PREFACE

1. There is an interesting story concerning Anderson. According to Fockler, Anderson was in his squad and was killed when he went to retrieve his weapon, which he had left behind in one of the weapons carriers. Fockler then wrote that the Chinese soldier who killed Anderson died shortly after when one of the GIs shot him. It was not a different Anderson from the Silver Star citation, since it would be highly unlikely that both Andersons had the same first name. According to the citation, Anderson had tried to sneak out after the ambush and during his second attempt, the Chinese saw him and engaged him in hand-to-hand combat, which made sense since Anderson no longer had a weapon. We'll never really know what happened. Perhaps someone saw Anderson do something. Gerald G. Epley, "General Orders Number 192, 2nd Infantry Division," Korean War Project, June 18, 1951, accessed August 9, 2014, www.koreanwar.org/html/2011_2ID_korean_war_records _go.html, p. 5; Richard C. Fockler, "Letter 81: Letter of Richard Fockler to Korean War Project," Korean War Project, October 29, 2006, accessed August 9, 2014, www.koreanwar.org/html/letters_to_the_lost_from_korea.html?set=75.
2. Richard C. Fockler, "Afternoon at Twin Tunnels," Patriot Files, November 17, 2002, accessed February 8, 2014, www.patriotfiles.com/index.php?name=News&file= article&sid=344; Russell A. Gugeler, *Combat Actions in Korea* (Washington, D.C.: Center of Military History, 1987), 80–88; John H. Chiles, "23rd Infantry Regiment—Command Report," Korean War Project, January 1951, accessed September 2014, www.koreanwar.org, 4–7; Headquarters, 2nd Infantry Division 1951, "Command Report, 2nd Infantry Division, From 1 January to 31 January 1951," Korean War Project, January 1951, www.koreanwar.org, accessed September 2014, pp. 20–25; Paul L. Freeman, *Wonju Through Chip'yong: An Epic of Regimental Combat Team Action in Korea* (College Park, MD: Department of the Army, 1951), 1–9.

INTRODUCTION

1. Lynnita Jean Brown, "Korean War Casualty Information—China," Korean War Educator, 2014, accessed November 3, 2014, www.koreanwar-educator.org/topics /casualties/p_casualties_chinese.htm; Lynnita Jean Brown, "Korean War Casualty Information—Participating Nations," Korean War Educator, 2014, accessed November 3, 2014, www.koreanwar-educator.org/topics/casualties/p_casualties _participating_nations.htm.
2. United Nations Statistics Division, "National Accounts Main Aggregates Database," UNSTATS, 2014, accessed November 3, 2014, unstats.un.org/unsd/snaama /dnllist.asp.

CHAPTER 1

1. Joint Chiefs of Staff, United States, General Order No. 1, Center for Strategic and International Studies, August 17, 1945, accessed June 20, 2014, csis.org/files/media/csis/programs/taiwan/timeline/sums/timeline_docs/CSI_19450902b.htm.

2. Mark O'Neill, "Kim Il-Sung's Secret History," *South China Morning Post*, October 17, 2010.

3. Cold War Files, "Syngman Rhee," The Cold War Files: Interpreting History through Documents, 2014, accessed June 23, 2014, legacy.wilsoncenter.org/coldwarfiles/index-33794.html.

4. Allan R. Millett, *The War for Korea, 1950–1951: They Came from the North* (Lawrence: University of Kansas Press, 2010), 21–22.

5. Ibid., 11, 18.

6. National Security Council, "A Report to the President by the National Security Council on the Position of the United States with Respect to Korea," Truman Library, April 2, 1948, accessed June 24, 2013, www.trumanlibrary.org/whistlestop/study_collections/korea/large/documents/pdfs/kr-7-1.pdf, pp. 8, 12–13.

7. Ibid.

8. Allan R. Millett, *The War for Korea, 1950–1951*, 29–30.

9. Ibid., 32.

10. Central Intelligence Agency, "Daily Report," Baptism By Fire: CIA Analysis of the Korean War Overview, January 13, 1950, accessed June 25, 2014, www.foia.cia.gov/collection/baptism-fire-cia-analysis-korean-war-overview#Daily Reports 1950.

11. Robert K. Sawyer, *Military Advisors in Korea: KMAG in Peace and War* (Washington, D.C.: Center of Military History, 1988), 111–13; Millett, *The War for Korea*, 48–49.

12. John J. Muccio, interview by Jerry N. Hess, "Oral History Interview with John J. Muccio," February 10, 1971, www.trumanlibrary.org/oralhist/muccio1.htm; G-2, Army Department Teletype Conference, June 25, 1950, Naval Aide Files, Truman Papers, Truman Library, accessed June 27, 2014, www.trumanlibrary.org/whistlestop/study_collections/koreanwar/documents/index.php?documentdate=1950-06-25&documentid=ki-21-11&pagenumber=1, p. 2.

13. Matthew B. Ridgway, *The Korean War* (New York: De Capo Press, 1967), 8.

14. James L. Stokesbury, *A Short History of the Korean War* (New York: Quill, 1988), 19–32.

CHAPTER 2

1. Bob Beeby, letter to Col. Kenneth Hamburger, November 9, 1992 (Kenneth Hamburger Collection, Sierra Vista, AZ).

2. United Nations Security Council, "Resolution 82 (1950) of 25 June 1950," Refworld, UNHCR, The UN Refugee Agency, June 25, 1950, accessed June 27, 2014, www.refworld.org/cgi-bin/texis/vtx/rwmain?docid=3b00f15960.

3. J. Lawton Collins, "Army Department Teletype Conference ca June 1950," Truman Library, June 27, 1950, accessed June 27, 2014, www.trumanlibrary.org/whistlestop/study_collections/koreanwar/documents/index.php?documentdate=1950-06-00&documentid=ki-215&pagenumber=1, pp. 1–2.

4. Allan R. Millett. *The War for Korea, 1950–1951: They Came from the North* (Lawrence: University of Kansas Press, 2010), 94–5, 102–3, 107.

5. William J. Sebald, telegram, William Sebald to Dean Acheson, June 30, 1950, Harry S. Truman Administration File, Elsey Papers, Truman Library, accessed June 29, 2014, www.trumanlibrary.org/whistlestop/study_collections/koreanwar/documents/index.php?documentdate=1950-06-30&documentid=ki-4-1&pagenumber=1; General Order No. 1, Joint Chiefs of Staff, August 17, 1945, accessed June 20, 2014, http://csis.org/files/media/csis/programs/taiwan/timeline/sums/timeline_docs/CSI_19450902b.htm.

6. Marlene Elizabeth Heck, "The Blair House. Inside the Home: The Truman Study," 1989, accessed June 30, 2014, www.blairhouse.org/about/inside-the-home/truman-study.

7. Harry S. Truman, handwritten note, June 30, 1950, President's Secretary's Files, Truman Papers, Truman Library, accessed June 30, 2014, www.trumanlibrary.org/whistlestop/study_collections/koreanwar/documents/index.php?documentdate=1950-06-30&documentid=ma-2-2&pagenumber=1; White House, "Press Release, June 30, 1950," Harry S. Truman Administration File, Elsey Papers, Truman Library, June 30, 1950, accessed June 30, 2014, www.trumanlibrary.org/whistlestop/study_collections/koreanwar/documents/index.php?documentdate=1950-06-30&documentid=ki-4-23&pagenumber=1.

8. Historical Section, G-2, Headquarters, 2nd Infantry Division, "2nd Infantry Division and the Korean Campaign: Vol. 1, 8 July 1950–31 August 1950," Korean War Project, August 1950, accessed September 2014, www.koreanwar2.org/kwp2/usa/2id/003/USA_2ID_070013_0850.pdf, pp. 2–3.

9. Headquarters, 23rd Infantry Regiment, "War Diary, 23rd Infantry Regiment. July 1950," Korean War Project, July 1950, accessed July 19, 2014, www.koreanwar.org/html/2011_2ID_korean_war_records_unit.html?pid=3, p. 10.

10. There was a 23rd Infantry Regiment that fought in the War of 1812, but it was disbanded after the war. U.S. Army Center of Military History, 2013.

11. Frank Meszar, "Operational Annex to Command and Unit Historical Report Period 9 July–31 July 1950, 23rd Infantry Regiment," Korean War Project, July 1950, accessed September 2014, www.koreanwar2.org/kwp2/usa/2id/003/USA_2ID_070013_0750.pdf, p. 7.

12. Historical Section, G-2, Headquarters, 2nd Infantry Division, "2nd Infantry Division and the Korean Campaign," 10.

13. Donald W. Hoffman, letter to Col. Kenneth Hamburger, September 2, 1992, Stow, OH (Kenneth Hamburger Collection).

14. Morris V. Evans, letter to Col. Kenneth Hamburger, November 30, 1992, Marlboro, NJ (Kenneth Hamburger Collection).

15. Unknown, "Paul Lamar Freeman," April 1988, Arlington, VA (Kenneth Hamburger Collection).

16. Headquarters, 23rd Infantry Regiment, "War Diary, 23rd Infantry Regiment. July 1950," p. 13.

17. Meszar, "Operational Annex, 9 July–31 July 1950, 23rd Infantry Regiment," 7–8.

18. Headquarters, 23rd Infantry Regiment, "War Diary, 23rd Infantry Regiment. July 1950," pp. 13–14.

19. Frank C. Butler, letter to Thomas Ryan, October 13, 1987, New Harbor, ME (Kenneth Hamburger Collection), 1.

20. Frank C. Butler, letter to Col. Kenneth Hamburger, January 9, 1993, New Harbor, ME (Kenneth Hamburger Collection), 1.

21. Ibid., 1–2.
22. The 82nd Airborne Division was also a TO&E unit. At the time, the Army only had two deployable divisions: the 2nd Infantry and the 82nd Airborne. Butler, letter to Col. Kenneth Hamburger.
23. Butler, letter to Col. Kenneth Hamburger, 1–2.
24. James L. Stokesbury, *A Short History of the Korean War* (New York: Quill, 1988), 45–46.
25. Historical Section, G-2, Headquarters, 2nd Infantry Division, "2nd Infantry Division and the Korean Campaign," 10, 28–29, 41–42.
26. John H. Chiles, "Narrative Summary of Command and Unit Historical Report, Period 1 September–30 September 1950," Korean War Project, September 1950, accessed September 2014, www.koreanwar2.org/kwp2/usa/2id/003/USA_2ID_070013_0950.pdf, pp. 5–13.
27. Ibid., pp. 11–13.
28. James S. Lay, Jr., "A Report to the National Security Council by the Executive Secretary on the United States Courses of Action with Respect to Korea (NSC 81)," Truman Library, September 1, 1950, accessed July 17, 2014, www.trumanlibrary.org/whistlestop/study_collections/korea/large/documents/pdfs/ki-17-1.pdf#zoom=100, pp. 1–2.
29. Joint Chiefs of Staff, "Directive to the Commander of the United Nations Forces Korea," Harry Truman Library, September 27, 1950, accessed July 17, 2014, www.trumanlibrary.org/whistlestop/study_collections/korea/large/documents/pdfs/ki-18-3.pdf#zoom=100.
30. Headquarters, 23rd Infantry Regiment, "Narrative Summary, Period 1–31 October 1950," Korean War Project, October 1950, accessed July 17, 2014, www.koreanwar2.org/kwp2/usa/2id/003/USA_2ID_070014_1050.pdf, pp. 6–8.
31. Scott R. McMichael, *A Historical Perspective on Light Infantry* (Fort Leavenworth, KS: Combat Studies Institute, 1987), 66–69.
32. Douglas MacArthur, "MacArthur Telegram to JCS," Truman Library, November 4, 1950, accessed July 17, 2014, www.trumanlibrary.org/whistlestop/study_collections/korea/large/documents/pdfs/ki-22-13.pdf#zoom=100.
33. Douglas MacArthur, "Telegram from Douglas MacArthur to the Secretary of the Army," Truman Library, November 6, 1950, accessed July 18, 2014, www.trumanlibrary.org/whistlestop/study_collections/korea/large/documents/pdfs/ki-22-23.pdf#zoom=100; Joint Chiefs of Staff, "Telegram from JCS to CINCFECOM," Truman Library, November 6, 1950, accessed July 18, 2014, www.trumanlibrary.org/whistlestop/study_collections/korea/large/documents/pdfs/ki-22-14.pdf#zoom=100; Lay, "A Report to the National Security Council," 1–2.
34. Joint Chiefs of Staff, "Views of the Joint Chiefs of Staff," Truman Library, November 9, 1950, accessed July 17, 2014, www.trumanlibrary.org/whistlestop/study_collections/korea/large/documents/pdfs/ci-3-6.pdf#zoom=100; Lay, "A Report to the National Security Council," 1–2.
35. Philip C. Jessup, "Memorandum of Conversation about the Situation in Korea," Truman Library, November 21, 1950, accessed July 18, 2014, www.trumanlibrary.org/whistlestop/study_collections/korea/large/documents/pdfs/ki-15-11.pdf#zoom=100, pp. 1–5.
36. Millett, *The War for Korea, 1950–1951*, see chapter 9.
37. Martin Lee, interview by author, January 31, 2015.

38. Headquarters, 23rd Infantry Regiment, "Narrative Summary, Period 1–30 November 1950," Korean War Project, November 1950, accessed July 18, 2014, www.koreanwar.org/html/2011_2ID_korean_war_records_unit.html?pid=3, pp. 9–12; Headquarters, 2nd Infantry Division, "War Diary, Headquarters, 2nd Infantry Division 1–30 November 1950," Korean War Project, November 1950, accessed July 19, 2014, www.koreanwar.org/html/2011_2ID_korean_war_records_unit.html?pid=1, pp. 30–32.

39. Headquarters, 23rd Infantry Regiment, "Narrative Summary, Period 1–30 November 1950," pp. 12–13; Headquarters, 2nd Infantry Division, "War Diary, Headquarters, 2nd Infantry Division 1–30 November 1950," pp. 32–35.

40. Douglas Graney. *Cottonseed Easy Six* (Denver: Outskirts Press, Inc., 2010), 89–90.

41. Headquarters, 23rd Infantry Regiment, "Narrative Summary, Period 1–30 November 1950," pp. 13–15; Headquarters, 2nd Infantry Division, "War Diary, Headquarters, 2nd Infantry Division 1–30 November 1950," pp. 35–37; Paul L. Freeman, letter to T. R. Fehrenbach, August 31, 1966, San Antonio, TX (Kenneth Hamburger Collection).

42. Headquarters, 23rd Infantry Regiment, "Command Report, Period 1–31 December 1950," Korean War Project, December 1950, accessed July 20, 2014, www.koreanwar.org/html/2011_2ID_korean_war_records_unit.html?pid=3, pp. 5–6.

43. "Le Battalion Francais de l'ONU en Coreé, Decembre 1950–Novembre 1953," n.d., EMAT (Kenneth Hamburger Collection), 5–7.

44. "Rauol Monclar." Ordre de la liberation, February 21, 2006, accessed July 21, 2014, www.ordredelaliberation.fr/fr_compagnon/686.html.

45. Kenneth E. Hamburger, *Leadership in the Crucible: The Korean War Battles of Twin Tunnels and Chipyong-ni* (College Station: Texas A&M University Press, 2003), 78–79; William R. Guthrie, letter to Col. Kenneth Hamburger, October 16, 1992, Winter Haven, FL (Kenneth Hamburger Collection), 5.

46. Albert Caswell Metts, letter to Col. Kenneth Hamburger, 1992, San Antonio, TX (Kenneth Hamburger Collection), 4.

47. Douglas Graney, letter to Col. Kenneth Hamburger, n.d., Houston, TX (Kenneth Hamburger Collection), 7. Many of the U.S. officers liked Monclar, but they also thought he made some poor decisions. Robert W. Curtis, a second lieutenant at the time of Chipyong-ni, felt that the French were great attackers but made too much noise and built too many fires while in the defense. Robert W. Curtis, interview by Kenneth Hamburger, October 23, 1992, p. 3.

48. This is a great story. The soldiers of French Battalion held their commander in high esteem, and many truly felt that no one or nothing could frighten the general. History has shown that the men's opinion was well founded. François DeCastries, interview by Kenneth Hamburger, December 15, 1992.

49. Headquarters, 2nd Infantry Division 1950, "Command Report, From 1 December 1950 Through 31 December 1950," Korean War Project, December 1950, accessed July 22, 2014, www.koreanwar.org/html/2011_2ID_korean_war_records_unit.html?pid=1, p. 5; Roy E. Appleman, *Disaster in Korea* (College Station: Texas A&M University Military History Series, 1989), 292.

50. Arlington National Cemetery, "Matthew Bunker Ridgway," March 1993, accessed July 22, 2014, www.arlingtoncemetery.net/ridgway.htm; Matthew B. Ridgway, *The Korean War* (New York: De Capo Press, 1967), 79–80.

51. Ridgway, *The Korean War*, 81–83.

52. Guthrie, letter to Col. Kenneth Hamburger, 7.

53. Metts, letter to Col. Kenneth Hamburger, 5.

54. Graney, letter to Col. Kenneth Hamburger, 6–7.

55. Headquarters, 2nd Infantry Division 1950, "Command Report, From 1 December 1950 Through 31 December 1950," pp. 14–15.

56. Glenn C. MacGuyer, letter to Col. Kenneth Hamburger, December 29, 1992, Olympia, WA (Kenneth Hamburger Collection), 2.

57. Frank C. Butler, letter to Col. Kenneth Hamburger, November 6, 1992, New Harbor, ME (Kenneth Hamburger Collection). Not everyone hated Almond. William Guthrie thought his decision on soldiers changing their socks daily was a good one. Almond made it a standing order and wanted to know every night that the squad leaders and above had checked their soldiers. Guthrie, letter to Col. Kenneth Hamburger, 4.

58. Ralph H. Krueger, letter to Col. Kenneth Hamburger, November 18, 1992, Sierra Vista, AZ (Kenneth Hamburger Collection), 1.

59. Hoffman, letter to Col. Kenneth Hamburger, 17–19.

60. Graney, letter to Col. Kenneth Hamburger, 8.

61. Evans, letter to Col. Kenneth Hamburger, 6.

62. Bickford E. Sawyer, letter to Col. Kenneth Hamburger, October 6, 1992, Honolulu, HI (Kenneth Hamburger Collection), 9–10.

63. Headquarters, 2nd Infantry Division, "Command Report, 2nd Infantry Division, From 1 January to 31 January 1951," Korean War Project, January 1951, accessed September 2014, www.koreanwar2.org/kwp2/usa/2id/003/USA_2ID_070015_0151.pdf, pp. 1–23; John H. Chiles, "23rd Infantry Regiment—Command Report," Korean War Project, January 1951, accessed September 2014, www.koreanwar2.org/kwp2/usa/2id/003/USA_2ID_070015_0151.pdf, pp. 4–7; William W. Quinn, Periodic Intelligence Report No. 120, Period 232100I–242100I Jan 51, X Corps (Kenneth Hamburger Collection, College Park, MD: Department of the Army, 1951, Annex 1).

CHAPTER 3

1. Glenn A. Stackhouse, "They Stood and Fired: Brothers in 37 Survivors of 600-Man Red Trap." *Knickerbocker News,* January 30, 1952: 2A.

2. Ibid.

3. Russell A. Gugeler, *Combat Actions in Korea* (Washington, D.C.: Center of Military History, 1987), 86–87.

4. Ibid., 87.

5. Ibid., 87–88; Headquarters, U.S. Eighth Army, Korea: General Orders No. 114, "Harold P. Mueller, Distinguished Service Cross," Military Times Hall of Valor, March 4, 1951, accessed August 4, 2014, http://projects.militarytimes.com/citations-medals-awards/recipient.php?recipientid=6774.

6. As usual, there is a discrepancy in the time hacks. According to the 2nd Battalion journal, the report from Major Engen came in at 1245, whereas the same report did not reach regiment until 1330 hours. That does not correlate with the 2nd Battalion journal, which reported that F Company was alerted at 1320, ten minutes before regiment knew what was happening. This is impossible since regiment coordinated the F Company relief column. S2 Section, 23rd Infantry Regiment, S2 Journal,

290001 January 1951 to 292400 January 1951 (Kenneth Hamburger Collection, College Park, MD: Department of the Army, 1951); Headquarters, 2nd Battalion, 23rd Infantry Regiment, Daily Journal, 29 January 1951 (Kenneth Hamburger Collection, College Park, MD: Department of the Army, 1951), 3–5.

7. Paul L. Freeman, *Wonju Through Chip'yong: An Epic of Regimental Combat Team Action in Korea* (College Park, MD: Department of the Army, 1951), 9.

8. Headquarters, 2nd Battalion, 23rd Infantry Regiment, Daily Journal, 29 January 1951, p. 4.

9. Unknown, "Company 'F' 23rd Infantry Regiment, 'Rescue Patrol'—Part of the Twin Tunnels After Action Report" (College Park, MD: Department of the Army, 1951); World War II Army Enlistment Records, "Stanley C. Tyrell," 2014, accessed August 1, 2014, http://wwii-army.findthebest.com/l/2120201/Stanley-C-Tyrrell; Headquarters, U.S. Eighth Army, Korea: General Orders No. 278, "Stanley C. Tyrell, Distinguished Service Cross," Military Times Hall of Valor, May 31, 1952, accessed August 1, 2014, http://projects.militarytimes.com/citations-medals-awards/recipient .php?recipientid=6846. Not everyone shared the colonel's confidence. Sgt. Donald Hoffman was a squad leader in Fox Company and recalled the rescue operation: "Our company commander at the time . . . was Captain Tyrell [*sic*]. In my opinion, he was a rotten, no-good, yellow son of [a] bitch. To my knowledge, no one in the unit had any use for him. . . . He was a man who was about 5'8" tall, heavyset, and he gave the impression he didn't belong in the infantry. It was rare when any of us in the ranks ever saw the man." Donald W. Hoffman, letter to Col. Kenneth Hamburger, September 2, 1992, Stow, OH (Kenneth Hamburger Collection).

10. Headquarters, 2nd Battalion, 23rd Infantry Regiment, Daily Journal, 29 January 1951, pp. 4–5.

11. Russell A. Gugeler, *Combat Actions in Korea* (Washington, D.C.: Center of Military History, 1987), 88–89; Richard C. Fockler, "Afternoon at Twin Tunnels," Patriot .Files, November 17, 2002, accessed February 8, 2014, www.patriotfiles.com/index .php?name=News&file=article&sid=344.

12. Gugeler, *Combat Actions in Korea*, 89–90.

13. Gerald G. Epley, "General Orders Number 119, 2nd Infantry Division," Korean War Project, May 29, 1951, accessed August 6, 2014, www.koreanwar.org/html/ 2011_2ID_korean_war_records_go.html.

14. John H. Chiles, "23rd Infantry Regiment—Command Report," Korean War Project, January 1951, accessed September 2014, www.koreanwar.org, p. 98.

15. S2 Section, 23rd Infantry Regiment, S2 Journal, 290001 January 1951 to 292400 January 1951; John B. Dumaine, "After Action Report Covering Operations of the 23rd Regimental Combat Team during the Period 290630 January to 152400 February 51" (College Park, MD: Department of the Army, 13 March 1951), 1.

16. John Collins, "'Mosquito Spirit' Leads Operation Punch through 'Dark Days,'" Kenneth Hamburger Collection, *Atlantic Flyer*, March 1988: A5.

17. Stackhouse, "They Stood and Fired," 2A.

18. There is definitely some discrepancy as to when the air support and the liaison planes arrived. Gugeler said the air support arrived first, and then the liaison planes (L-5s) shortly thereafter. Some of the soldiers on the ground maintained that, for the most part, the liaison planes were usually there. Paul L. Freeman, "Periodic Operations Report 134 for Period 281800 to 291800 January 1951, 23rd Infantry

Regiment" (Kenneth Hamburger Collection, College Park, MD: Department of the Army, 1951), 1; Headquarters, 1st Battalion, 23rd Infantry, "Battle of the Tunnels," Draft After Action Report (Kenneth Hamburger Collection, College Park, MD: Department of the Army, 17 March 1951), 1–3.

19. Gugeler, *Combat Actions in Korea*, 91; Headquarters, 1st Battalion, 23rd Infantry, "Battle of the Tunnels," 3.
20. Gugeler, *Combat Actions in Korea*, 91–92.
21. Gerald G. Epley, "General Orders Number 88, 2nd Infantry Division," Korean War Project, April 29, 1951, accessed August 9, 2014), www.koreanwar.org/html/2011_2ID_korean_war_records_go.html, p. 2.
22. Stackhouse, "They Stood and Fired," 2A.
23. Gugeler, *Combat Actions in Korea*, 92.
24. Epley, "General Orders Number 88, 2nd Infantry Division," 2.
25. Richard C. Fockler, "Letter 81: Letter of Richard Fockler to Korean War Project," Korean War Project, October 29, 2006, accessed August 9, 2014, www.korean war.org/html/letters_to_the_lost_from_korea.html?set=75; Fockler, "Afternoon at Twin Tunnels"; American Battle Monuments Commission, "Clement Leonard Pietrasiewicz," January 25, 1954, accessed August 9, 2014, www.abmc.gov/search-abmc-burials-and-memorializations/detail/Korea_25223#.U-aZpGO8Phs.
26. Rupert D. Graves, "General Orders Number 299, 2nd Infantry Division," Korean War Project, July 16, 1951, accessed August 11, 2014, www.koreanwar.org/html/2011_2ID_korean_war_records_go.html, p. 2.
27. Gugeler, *Combat Actions in Korea*, 93–94; Graves, "General Orders Number 299, 2nd Infantry Division," 2.
28. Gugeler, *Combat Actions in Korea*, 94–95.
29. Ibid., 95–96.
30. Ibid., 96.
31. Gerald G. Epley, "General Orders Number 87, 2nd Infantry Division," Korean War Project, April 28, 1951, accessed August 6, 2014, www.koreanwar.org/html/2011_2ID_korean_war_records_go.html, p. 1.
32. Gugeler, *Combat Actions in Korea*, 96–97.
33. Epley, "General Orders Number 88, 2nd Infantry Division," 2; Gugeler, *Combat Actions in Korea*, 97.
34. Gugeler, *Combat Actions in Korea*, 95–97.
35. Perry A. Sager, "Periodic Operations Report 79, Headquarters, 2nd Battalion, 23rd Infantry Regiment" (Kenneth Hamburger Collection, College Park, MD: Department of the Army, 30 January 1951), 1; Dumaine, "After Action Report Covering Operations of the 23rd Regimental Combat Team during the Period 290630 January to 152400 February 51," p. 1.
36. Headquarters, 1st Battalion, 23rd Infantry, "Battle of the Tunnels," 3.
37. Freeman, *Wonju Through Chip'yong*, 9.

CHAPTER 4

1. S3 Section, 23rd Infantry Regiment, S3 Journal, 30 January (Kenneth Hamburger Collection, College Park, MD: Department of the Army, 1951), 2.
2. Ibid., 1; G3 Section, X Corps, Combat Notes Number 5—Part of The Twin Tunnels After Action Report Collection (College Park, MD: Department of the Army, 1951), 1–2.

3. John B. Dumaine, "After Action Report Covering Operations of the 23rd Regimental Combat Team during the Period 290630 January to 152400 February 51" (College Park, MD: Department of the Army, 13 March 1951), 2; Paul L. Freeman, *Wonju Through Chip'yong: An Epic of Regimental Combat Team Action in Korea* (College Park, MD: Department of the Army, 1951), 10–11.

4. Freeman, *Wonju Through Chip'yong*, 10.

5. Clark L. Ruffner, "2nd Infantry Division—February 1951 Command Report," Korean War Project, February 1951, accessed September 2014, www.koreanwar2.org/kwp2/usa/2id/003/USA_2ID_070015_0251.pdf, p. 1; Matthew B. Ridgway, *The Korean War* (New York: De Capo Press, 1967), 104–5.

6. Ruffner, "2nd Infantry Division—February 1951 Command Report," 1; Ridgway, *The Korean War*, 104–5.

7. Ruffner, "2nd Infantry Division—February 1951 Command Report," 1; Freeman, *Wonju Through Chip'yong*, 15; James H. Polk, Periodic Intelligence Report No. 129, Period 012100I–022100I Feb 51, X Corps (Kenneth Hamburger Collection, College Park, MD: Department of the Army, 1951), 1–2.

8. G2 Section, 2nd Infantry Division, Intelligence—Staff Section Report of the G-2, 2nd Infantry Division—Part of the Twin Tunnels After Action Report (College Park, MD: Department of the Army, February 1951), 1–2.

9. Ibid., 1–3.

10. Freeman, *Wonju Through Chip'yong*, 12; John B. Dumaine, "After Action Report Covering Operations of the 23rd Regimental Combat Team during the Period 290630 January to 152400 February 51" (College Park, MD: Department of the Army, 13 March 1951), 2; Unknown, "Battle of the Tunnels Area," After Action Report (Kenneth Hamburger Collection, College Park, MD: Department of the Army, 1951), 1.

11. Beverly T. Richardson, "After Action Report for Period 29 Jan to 16 Feb 51, 3rd Battalion, 23rd Infantry—Part of The Twin Tunnels After Action Report Collection" (College Park, MD: Department of the Army, May 2, 1951), 1.

12. Kane was originally awarded the Bronze Star, but it was upgraded to the Silver Star with General Order 333-51. Gerald G. Epley, "General Orders Number 1, 2nd Infantry Division," Korean War Project, January 1, 1951, accessed August 28, 2014, www.koreanwar.org/html/2011_2ID_korean_war_records_go.html, p. 8.

13. Albert Caswell Metts, letter to Col. Kenneth Hamburger, 1992, San Antonio, TX (Kenneth Hamburger Collection), p. 4.

14. John Kamperschroer, interview by author, January 20, 2015.

15. Charles M. Thompson, interview by John Mewha, "After Action, Twin Tunnels—Part of the Twin Tunnels After Action Report," May 17, 1951, p. 1; Charles H. Roberts, Anthony Durante, Robert C. Whitton, Charles M. Robinson, Arland A. Lottman, James E. Jones, Junior Crayton, Major R. Ramey, Anthony T. Hardon, Charles R. McCullough, Charles B. Ellis, Alfred G. Adler, and Cecil Eide, interview by John Mewha, "After Action Report for Item Company Twin Tunnels—Part of the After Action Report Twin Tunnels," May 17, 1951, p. 1; John Mewha, "Narrative—Twin Tunnels, 3rd Battalion, 23rd Infantry Regiment—Part of the Twin Tunnels After Action Report" (College Park, MD: Department of the Army, 1951), 1–2.

16. Freeman, *Wonju Through Chip'yong*, 12.

17. Ibid.
18. Roberts, et. al., interview by John Mewha, 1.
19. Leo Dobbs, interview by author, January 23, 2015; Earl Becker, interview by author, January 25, 2015; George Collingsworth, interview by author, January 25, 2015.
20. Dobbs, interview by author.
21. Roberts, et. al., interview by John Mewha, 1–3.
22. William P. Barenkamp, interview by John Mewha, "After Action Report—Part of the Twin Tunnels After Report," May 16, 1951, p. 1; Richard A., Palmer, interview by John Mewha, "After Action Interview with Richard A. Palmer—Part of Twin Tunnels After Action Report," May 16, 1951, p. 1.
23. James Henkel, interview by author, January 29, 2015.
24. Thompson, interview by John Mewha, 1; Freeman, *Wonju Through Chip'yong*, 12–13; "Rapport sur la Guerre en Corée," n.d., France, EMAT (Kenneth Hamburger Collection), 309–11.
25. François DeCastries, interview by Kenneth Hamburger, December 15, 1992.
26. Gérard Journet, letter to Col. Kenneth Hamburge, n.d., Horbourg-Wihr, France (Kenneth Hamburger Collection), 2; Unknown, "Battle of the Tunnels Area," 2.
27. Freeman, *Wonju Through Chip'yong*, 13; G3 Section, X Corps, Combat Notes Number 5, Accompanying Maps.
28. Thompson, interview by John Mewha, 1–2, Accompanying Map.
29. George C. Stewart, interview by Tymothy W. Caddell, "Service in WWII & Korea," June 7, 1985, pp. 7–8.
30. Richard C. Fockler, "Afternoon at Twin Tunnels," Patriot Files, November 17, 2002, accessed February 8, 2014, www.patriotfiles.com/index.php?name=News&file=article&sid=344.
31. Henry Bagley, Herman L. Seabolt, Leland L. Cargle, Joseph A. Talotta, Billy M. Lloyd, Richard D. Goldsberry, and George F. Bammert, interview by John Mewha, "After Action Interview with the Soldiers of L Company—Part of The Twin Tunnels After Action Report Collection," June 16, 1951, p. 3.
32. In Freeman's account, it was a bazooka that caused the damage to the flak wagon, not a grenade. Since many of the L Company soldiers said it a grenade, I decided they probably had a better idea what happened to the tanks and flak wagon attached to their company than their regimental commander. Freeman, *Wonju Through Chip'yong*, 14.
33. Willis P. Brooks, interview by John Mewha, "After Action, Twin Tunnels—Part of the Twin Tunnels After Action Report," May 17, 1951, pp. 1–2.
34. Thompson, interview by John Mewha, 1–3.
35. The trucks that Green saw were probably part of Chief Brooks's column. Edward L. Green, interview by John Mewha, "After Action Interview with Edward L. Green—Part of Twin Tunnels After Action Report," May 17, 1951, pp. 1–2.
36. Richard M. Bass, Carl A. Spencer, William A. Shelton, Marvin J. Mueller, and Richard J. Laba, interview by John Mewha, "After Action Interview with 1st Platoon, Company K, 23rd Infantry Regiment—Part of Twin Tunnels After Action Report," May 16, 1951, p. 2.
37. Thompson, interview by John Mewha, 2–3; George H. Glassman, John W. Dravecky, Dean A. Davidson, and Robert Gilbreath, interview by John Mewha, "After Action, Twin Tunnels—Part of the Twin Tunnels After Action Report," May 17, 1951, pp. 1–2.

38. William A. Sanford, interview by John Mewha, "After Action Report with William A. Sanford—Part of the Twin Tunnels After Action Report," May 17, 1951, pp. 1–2; S3 Section, 23rd Infantry Regiment, S3 Journal, 1 February (Kenneth Hamburger Collection, College Park, MD: Department of the Army, 1951).

39. William Tuttle, interview by author, January 30, 2015.

40. Bagley, et. al., interview by John Mewha, 3–4; Palmer, interview by John Mewha, 2.

41. John Kamperschroer, interview by author, January 20, 2015.

42. S3 Section, 23rd Infantry Regiment, S3 Journal, 1 February.

43. Palmer, interview by John Mewha, 2; Sanford, interview by John Mewha, 2; Bagley, et. al., interview by John Mewha, 4.

44. Larry Hauck, letter to Col. Kenneth Hamburger, July 2, 1986, San Antonio, TX (Kenneth Hamburger Collection), 2.

45. Unknown, "Battle of the Tunnels Area," Accompanying Map for 0800 Feb 1.

46. Since individual awards do not designate a soldier's platoon, it is difficult to determine which platoon was Kenolio's. I believe he was either in 3rd or 1st Platoon, since the citation could match either's actions that morning. Gerald G. Epley, "General Orders Number 128, 2nd Infantry Division," Korean War Project, June 1, 1951, accessed September 4, 2014, www.koreanwar.org/html/2011_2ID_korean_war_records_go.html, p. 2.

47. Bagley, et. al., interview by John Mewha, 3–6.

48. Sanford, interview by John Mewha, 2.

49. Lieutenant Aldrich later claimed he was not the one who gave the order to withdraw. He reported that the platoon forward observer had made the call. Since the forward observer died on the hill, no one could confirm or refute his assertion. Bagley, et. al., interview by John Mewha, 6.

50. Sanford, interview by John Mewha, 2–3; Gerald G. Epley, "General Orders Number 154, 2nd Infantry Division," Korean War Project, June 15, 1951, accessed September 5, 2014, www.koreanwar.org/html/2011_2ID_korean_war_records_go.html, p. 5.

51. Bagley, et. al., interview by John Mewha, 6–7.

52. Headquarters, 3e Company, *3e Company Journal de Marche, February 1, 1951. Battle of the Twin Tunnels* (EMAT, Box 288: French Army, 31 May 1952), 1.

53. Award Citation for André Bizot (Kenneth Hamburger Collection, French Army, July 1951); Headquarters, 3e Company, *3e Company Journal de Marche;* "Rapport sur la Guerre en Corée," 314–15.

54. Journet, letter to Col. Kenneth Hamburger, 1.

55. "Rapport sur la Guerre en Corée," 312.

56. Award Citation for Louis Leroux (Kenneth Hamburger Collection, French Army, July 1951).

57. Award Citation for Moise Borst (Kenneth Hamburger Collection, French Army, July 1951).

58. Award Citation for Paul Amban (Kenneth Hamburger Collection, French Army, July 1951).

59. Captain Huschard, speech, 1951, EMAT, (Kenneth Hamburger Collection,); Claude L. Jaupart, letter to Col. Kenneth Hamburger, December 31, 1992, Nice, France (Kenneth Hamburger Collection), 1–2.

60. Even though Monclar was a lieutenant colonel in the U.N. forces, the French soldiers always thought of him as a lieutenant general, which was his rank in the French Army. As such, they referred to him as general, befitting of his rank.

Serge-Louis Bérerd, letter to Col. Kenneth Hamburger, April 3, 1992, Poitiers, France, trans. by Kenneth Hamburger (Kenneth Hamburger Collection), 4–5.

61. Stewart, interview by Tymothy W. Caddell, 8–9.
62. Freeman, *Wonju Through Chip'yong*, 15.
63. William W. Quinn, "Enemy Tactics and Equipment, Combat Intelligence Bulletin Number 1, G2 Section, X Corps, Ridgway Papers Box 117" (Carlisle Barracks, PA: Department of the Army, 1951), 1–5.
64. Freeman, *Wonju Through Chip'yong*, 15.
65. Ibid., 16; S3 Journal, 1 February.
66. Roberts, et. al., interview by John Mewha, 3.
67. Ibid., Sketch 1.
68. Thomas C. Harris, "Experience in Action, Twin Tunnels, Wonju, Korea area," October 15, 1992, Gulfport, FL (Kenneth Hamburger Collection), 1.
69. Roberts, et. al., interview by John Mewha, 1–5, sketch 1–2; Gerald G. Epley, "General Orders Number 121, 2nd Infantry Division," Korean War Project, May 27, 1951, accessed September 15, 2014, www.koreanwar.org/html/2011_2ID_korean_war_records_go.html, p. 1.
70. Roberts, et. al., interview by John Mewha, 5–6, sketch 1–2; Gerald G. Epley, "General Orders Number 90, 2nd Infantry Division 1951," Korean War Project, April 3, 1951, accessed September 15, 2014, www.koreanwar.org/html/2011_2ID_korean_war_records_go.html, p. 1.
71. Roberts, et. al., interview by John Mewha, 6.
72. Gerald G. Epley, "General Orders Number 123, 2nd Infantry Division," Korean War Project, May 29, 1951, accessed September 18, 2014, www.koreanwar.org/html/2011_2ID_korean_war_records_go.html, pp. 2–3.
73. Roberts, et. al., interview by John Mewha, 7.
74. Thompson, interview by John Mewha, 3; Bass, et. al., interview by John Mewha, 2–4.
75. Roberts, et. al., interview by John Mewha, 7.
76. Bass, et. al., interview by John Mewha, 2–3.
77. Roberts, et. al., interview by John Mewha, 6–8.
78. Ibid.; John Mewha, "Narrative—Twin Tunnels, 3rd Battalion, 23rd Infantry Regiment—Part of the Twin Tunnels After Action Report" (College Park, MD: Department of the Army, 1951), 13–15; Bass, et. al., interview by John Mewha, 3–4.
79. Award Citation for François Couric (Kenneth Hamburger Collection, French Army, July 1951); Award Citation for Robert Girardot (Kenneth Hamburger Collection, French Army, July 1951).
80. Journet, letter to Col. Kenneth Hamburger, 2; "Rapport sur la Guerre en Corée," 309–11; Award Citation for Gustave Gatoux (Kenneth Hamburger Collection, French Army, July 1951).
81. Harley E. Wilburn, interview by author, January 18, 2015.
82. This is an interesting account. Wilburn does not mention the officer's name in his letter, but Wilburn is noted in 3rd Company's journal as arriving sometime around 0930, the time of Serre's death. Therefore, I made the deduction that the officer mentioned in Wilburn's letter was most likely Serre. Harley E. Wilburn, letter to Col. Kenneth Hamburger, February 20, 1993, Centralia, MO (Kenneth Hamburger Collection), 1–2; Wilburn, interview by author.
83. Wilburn, interview by author.

84. Maurice Barthelemy, interview by Kenneth Hamburger, December 15, 1992; Head-quarters, 3e Company, *3e Company Journal de Marche*, 1–2; Wilburn, letter to Col. Kenneth Hamburger, 2; "Rapport sur la Guerre en Corée," 314–15.

85. Freeman, *Wonju Through Chip'yong*, 17.

86. Stewart, interview by Tymothy W. Caddell, 9.

87. Freeman, *Wonju Through Chip'yong*, 20.

88. Stewart, interview by Tymothy W. Caddell, 9–10.

89. Freeman, *Wonju Through Chip'yong*, 20.

90. There is some question as to the number of assaults on the hilltop. Was it five or six times? Was the sixth time the final assault? I decided, using the data available, that were six total assaults, and it was on this assault that Lee earned his Medal of Honor. William E. Bergin, "General Order Number 21, Award of the Medal of Honor to Hubert L. Lee," Medal of Honor Citation (Washington, D.C.: Department of the Army, 25 February, 1952); Collingsworth, interview by author.

91. Roberts, et. al., interview by John Mewha, 9.

92. Freeman, *Wonju Through Chip'yong*, 20.

93. Roberts, et. al., interview by John Mewha, 9.

94. Serge-Louis Bérerd, "Misunderstandings in the Field," letter to Col. Kenneth Hamburger, Poitiers, January 27, 1993, p. 1; Polk, Periodic Intelligence Report No. 129, p. 2.

95. Freeman, *Wonju Through Chip'yong*, 21.

96. James E. Stacy, interview by John Mewha, "Interview with James E. Stacy, Executive Officer, 3rd Battalion, 23rd Infantry Regiment—Part of the After Action Report Twin Tunnels," May 17, 1951, p. 3; Roberts, et. al., interview by John Mewha, 9; Headquarters, French Battalion, "Le Battalion Francais de l'ONU en Coree, Decembre 1950–Novembre 153," Ministre de Defense, February 1, 1951, accessed September 30, 2014, www.memoiredeshommes.sga.defense.gouv.fr/fr/arkotheque /inventaires/ead_ir_consult.php?ref=SHDGR_GR_7_U_287_301_jmo&fam=9, pp. 19–21.

97. Polk, Periodic Intelligence Report No. 129, p. 2.

CHAPTER 5

1. Headquarters, X Corps, Command Report, X Corps, February (Kenneth Hamburger Collection, College Park, MD: Department of the Army, 1951), 4, 15.

2. Paul L. Freeman, *Wonju Through Chip'yong: An Epic of Regimental Combat Team Action in Korea* (College Park, MD: Department of the Army, 1951), 23.

3. Headquarters, XIX Army Group, CPVF, "Chinese Critique of Tactics Employed in the First Encount," U.S. Force Korea, March 29, 1951, accessed October 5, 2014, www.usfk.mil/usfk/Uploads/120/ChineseCritiqueofTacticsEmployedintheFirst Encount.pdf, p. 1.

4. Headquarters, 23rd Infantry Regiment, "23rd Infantry Regiment, February 1951," Korean War Project, February 1951, accessed October 5, 2014, www.koreanwar2. org/kwp2/usa/2id/003/USA_2ID_070015_0251.pdf, pp. 6–8; Freeman, *Wonju Through Chip'yong*, 24.

5. Freeman, *Wonju Through Chip'yong*, 24.

6. Headquarters, 23rd Infantry Regiment, "23rd Infantry Regiment, February 1951," p. 8.

7. G3 Section, X Corps, Combat Notes Number 11—Chipyong-ni (Kenneth Hamburger Collection, College Park, MD: Department of the Army, 1951), 1–2.

8. Freeman, *Wonju Through Chip'yong*, 40.

9. Ibid., 24; Headquarters, 23rd Infantry Regiment, "23rd Infantry Regiment, February 1951," p. 8.

10. John H. Ramsburg, interview by unknown, "Interview with Captain John H. Ramsburg," July 2, 1951 (Kenneth Hamburger Collection, Sierra Vista, AZ), 1; James W. Edwards, "The Siege of Chipyong-ni," in *Staff Ride Read Ahead Packet, Battle of Chipyong-ni, 13–15 February 1951*, by U.S. Eighth Army Staff (Seoul: 2nd Infantry Division, 1990), sketch 5.

11. Gerald G. Epley, "General Orders Number 61, 2nd Infantry Division," Korean War Project, October 9, 1950, accessed October 12, 2014, www.koreanwar.org/html/2011_2ID_korean_war_records_go.html, p. 2.

12. Gerald G. Epley, "General Orders Number 149, 2nd Infantry Division," Korean War Project, June 15, 1951, www.koreanwar.org/html/2011_2ID_korean_war_records_go.html, pp. 2–3.

13. Bickford E. Sawyer, letter to Col. Kenneth Hamburger, October 6, 1992, Honolulu, HI (Kenneth Hamburger Collection), 9.

14. Ben Judd, letter to Col. Kenneth Hamburger, April 1, 1993 (Kenneth Hamburger Collection, Sierra Vista, AZ), 11.

15. Douglas Graney, letter to Col. Kenneth Hamburger, n.d., Houston, TX (Kenneth Hamburger Collection), 9.

16. Paul J. McGee, interview by Thomas M. Ryan, "Interview with Paul J. McGee, Platoon Leader, 3rd Platoon, G Company," August 11–12, 1988 (Kenneth Hamburger Collection, Sierra Vista, AZ), 8.

17. Edwards, "The Siege of Chipyong-ni," 114; Freeman, *Wonju Through Chip'yong*, 23.

18. Edwards, "The Siege of Chipyong-ni," 116; Freeman, *Wonju Through Chip'yong*, 25; S3 Section, 23rd Infantry Regiment, S3 Journal, 5 February (Kenneth Hamburger Collection, College Park, MD: Department of the Army, 1951), J45.

19. Edwards, "The Siege of Chipyong-ni," 116–118, sketch 2; Freeman, *Wonju Through Chip'yong*, 25; Sawyer, letter to Col. Kenneth Hamburger, 3–4; S3 Journal, 23rd Infantry Regiment, 6 February (Kenneth Hamburger Collection, College Park, MD: Department of the Army, 1951), J57, 65, 73. This report is a classic example of mirror-imaging. The analysts believe the Chinese are withdrawing, which would indicate the increased activity east of Chipyong-ni. On its face, it makes sense. However, in the same report the analysts inform us that NKPA deserters are talking about an upcoming offensive set to begin on February 8. Colonel Polk, the G2, discounts it and assesses that the Chinese will conduct counter-reconnaissance and harassment attacks. James H. Polk, Periodic Intelligence Report No. 133, Period 052100I–062100I Feb 51, X Corps (Kenneth Hamburger Collection, College Park, MD: Department of the Army, 1951), 5.

20. Edwards, "The Siege of Chipyong-ni," 118–22, sketch 3; S3 Journal, 23rd Infantry Regiment, 7 February (Kenneth Hamburger Collection, College Park, MD: Department of the Army, 1951), J55, 57, 62, 65, 69, 72, 90, 93, 103, 111; Freeman, *Wonju Through Chip'yong*, 25. It is interesting to speculate why Polk was convinced the Chinese were withdrawing. Perhaps he did not have the report from Edwards. However, it is puzzling to wonder why the corps did not seem concerned with the

results of the battalion patrol. Maybe, since X Corps analysts had focused on the progress of Operation Roundup, they were not paying attention to other parts of their area of operation. James H. Polk, Periodic Intelligence Report No. 134, Period 062100I–072100I Feb 51, X Corps (Kenneth Hamburger Collection, College Park, MD: Department of the Army, 1951), 2–3.

21. Martin Lee, interview by author, January 31, 2015.

22. Grant Mead, interview by author, January 31, 2015.

23. McGee, interview by Thomas M. Ryan, 15.

24. Ibid., 4–5.

25. McGee did not say it was 453, but he mentioned it was before the Twin Tunnels and on the left (west) side of the main supply route, which leads me to believe it was 1st Company that they relieved. McGee, interview by Thomas M. Ryan, 1–19; Paul J. McGee, interview by Edward C. Williamson, "Interview First Lieutenant Paul J. McGee, 3rd Platoon Leader, G Company, 23rd Infantry—Part of the G Company After Action Report, Chipyong-ni," October 18, 1951, p. 1.

26. Korean War Project, "First Lieutenant Thomas Henry Heath," Korean War Project Remembrance, 2014, (accessed October 10, 2014, www.koreanwar.org/html/korean_war_project_remembrance.html; Scott Slate, "Chipyong-ni high-water mark of the Korean War," Indianhead, www.2id.korea.army.mil/news/Indianhead, August 1, 2005: 9.

27. Edwards, "The Siege of Chipyong-ni," 113, sketch 5; McGee, interview by Edward C. Williamson, 1.

28. James Henkel, interview by author, January 29, 2015.

29. Freeman, Wonju Through Chip'yong, 26–27.

30. Clark L. Ruffner, "2nd Infantry Division—February 1951 Command Report," Korean War Project, February 1951, accessed September 2014, www.koreanwar.org, p. 7; Edwards, "The Siege of Chipyong-ni," 123–4; S3 Journal, 23rd Infantry Regiment, 8 February (Kenneth Hamburger Collection, College Park, MD: Department of the Army, 1951), J22, 23, 31, 33, 36, 38, 40, 44, 48, 55, 56, 75, 86, 91, 107, 112; Edward J. Messinger, Command Report, February 1951, 9th Infantry Regiment (Kenneth Hamburger Collection, College Park, MD: Department of the Army, 8 March 1951), 3–4.

31. Edwards, "The Siege of Chipyong-ni," 123.

32. S3 Journal, 23rd Infantry Regiment, 9 February (Kenneth Hamburger Collection, College Park, MD: Department of the Army, 1951), J23, 41, 44, 56, 61, 62, 76, 77, 78, 89, 105; Edwards, "The Siege of Chipyong-ni," 126.

33. S3 Section, 23rd Infantry Regiment 1951, J67, 85, 88.

34. Edwards, "The Siege of Chipyong-ni," 124.

35. Schmitt Hill was on the west side of G Company's position. Edwards had named all the hills after officers in his battalion. G Company's new position was on top of three hills: Schmitt, McGee and Curtis. Edwards, "The Siege of Chipyong-ni," 124, sketch 7.

36. Harley E. Wilburn, interview by author, January 18, 2015.

37. Even though McGee did not like the position of his light machine gun, it made sense in regard to his battalion's overall defense plan. Usually in an area defense, battalion and company commanders sight the crew-served weapons for the entire battalion to ensure proper interlocking fields of fire. Hence, even though the platoon

leader owns the machine gun and is tasked to operate and defend it, he usually does not position it in a battalion or company defense. McGee, interview by Thomas M. Ryan, 19–22; Edwards, "The Siege of Chipyong-ni," 113.

38. S2 Section, 23rd Infantry Regiment, S2 Journal, 100001 February 1951 to 102400 February 1951 (Kenneth Hamburger Collection, College Park, MD: Department of the Army, 1951).

39. James H. Polk, Periodic Intelligence Report No. 137, Period 092100I–102100I Feb 51, X Corps (Kenneth Hamburger Collection, College Park, MD: Department of the Army, 1951), 1–5.

40. S2 Section, 23rd Infantry Regiment, S2 Journal, 110001 February 1951 to 112400 February 1951 (Kenneth Hamburger Collection, College Park, MD: Department of the Army, 1951).

41. In his account, Edwards was off by a day. He wrote that the raid occurred on the night of 10–11 February; in fact, it was the next night. Regardless, it was a failure. Edwards, "The Siege of Chipyong-ni," 127–28; Freeman, *Wonju Through Chip'yong*, 28; Polk, Periodic Intelligence Report No. 137, p. 2; S3 Section, 23rd Infantry Regiment, S3 Journal, 11 February (Kenneth Hamburger Collection, College Park, MD: Department of the Army, 1951).

42. James H. Polk, Periodic Intelligence Report No. 138, Period 102100I–112100I Feb 51, X Corps (Kenneth Hamburger Collection, College Park, MD: Department of the Army, 1951), 5.

43. J. D. Coleman, *Wonju: The Gettysburg of the Korean War* (Washington, D.C.: Brassey's Publishing, 2000), 109–13.

44. Ibid., 112–54; Headquarters, 38th Infantry Regiment, "Hoengsong—Section of the Command Report for 38th Infantry Regiment, February 1951" (Kenneth Hamburger Collection, College Park, MD: Department of the Army, 1951), 1–17.

45. Headquarters, X Corps, Command Report, 7.

46. S3 Section, 23rd Infantry Regiment, S3 Journal, 12 February (Kenneth Hamburger Collection. College Park, MD: Department of the Army, 1951), J7, 8, 11, 12, 15.

47. Frank Meszar, interview by Kenneth Hamburger, November 17, 1992 (Kenneth Hamburger Collection, Sierra Vista, AZ).

48. James H. Polk, Periodic Intelligence Report No. 139, Period 112100I–122100I Feb 51, X Corps (Kenneth Hamburger Collection, College Park, MD: Department of the Army, 1951), 2; S2 Journal, 120001 February 1951 to 132400 February 1951 (Kenneth Hamburger Collection, College Park, MD: Department of the Army, 1951).

49. There is little mention of the F Company patrol outside of Edwards's account; however, the S2 logs mentioned a patrol returning from 2nd Battalion at 1725 hours with nine civilian prisoners. Edwards, "The Siege of Chipyong-ni," 131–33; S2 Journal, 120001 February 1951 to 132400 February 1951.

50. Ruffner, "2nd Infantry Division—February 1951 Command Report," 12.

51. S3 Section, 23rd Infantry Regiment, S3 Journal, 12 February, J57.

52. Matthew B. Ridgway, *The Korean War* (New York: De Capo Press, 1967), 107.

53. Edwards, "The Siege of Chipyong-ni," 134–35.

54. James H. Polk, Periodic Intelligence Report No. 140, Period 122100I–132100I Feb 51, X Corps (Kenneth Hamburger Collection, College Park, MD: Department of the Army, 1951), 4.

CHAPTER 6

1. Headquarters, 23rd Infantry Regiment, "23rd Regimental Combat Team Perimeter Defense of Chipyong-ni," After Action Report (Kenneth Hamburger Collection, College Park, MD: Department of the Army, 1951), 6.
2. Peter F. Schutz, letter to Col. Kenneth Hamburger, n.d. (Kenneth Hamburger Collection, Sierra Vista, AZ), 1.
3. Paul L. Freeman, *Wonju Through Chip'yong: An Epic of Regimental Combat Team Action in Korea* (College Park, MD: Department of the Army, 1951), 32; Albert Caswell Metts, "Humorous and Human Interest Stories," n.d., San Antonio.
4. S3 Section, 23rd Infantry Regiment, S3 Journal, 13 February (Kenneth Hamburger Collection, College Park, MD: Department of the Army, 1951), J21, J35.
5. S2 Section, 23rd Infantry Regiment, S2 Journal, 130001 February 1951 to 142400 February 1951 (Kenneth Hamburger Collection, College Park, MD: Department of the Army, 1951).
6. S3 Section, 23rd Infantry Regiment, S3 Journal, 13 February, J40, J46–47.
7. Ibid., J64, J69; John B. Dumaine, "After Action Report Covering Operations of the 23rd Regimental Combat Team during the Period 290630 January to 152400 February 51" (College Park, MD: Department of the Army, 13 March 1951), 4; Headquarters, 23rd Infantry Regiment, "23rd Regimental Combat Team Perimeter Defense of Chipyong-ni," 5.
8. Headquarters, 23rd Infantry Regiment, "23rd Regimental Combat Team Perimeter Defense of Chipyong-ni," 5; S3 Journal, 13 February, J52.
9. Freeman, *Wonju Through Chip'yong*, 31.
10. S3 Section, 23rd Infantry Regiment, S3 Journal, 13 February, J84; Jimmy Tomlin, "Trinity veteran's Korean War memories remain vivid," *High Point Enterprise News*, August 4, 2013, accessed November 22, 2014, http://debug.paxton.zope.net/highpoint/life/features/x135060486/Trinity-veterans-Korean-War-memories-remain-vivid.
11. S3 Section, 23rd Infantry Regiment, S3 Journal, 13 February, J84, J98–102.
12. Seymour Harris, "Return to Heartbreak Ridge," Korean War Project, February 1951, accessed February 27, 2015, www.koreanwar.org/my_html/korea010.htm.
13. Ansil L. Walker, "A Battle of the Forgotten War," February 1990, Tacoma, WA (Kenneth Hamburger Collection), 11.
14. Ibid., 12.
15. Ansil L. Walker, "Ansil L. Walker Recalls the Battle of Chipyong-ni During the Korean War," Historynet, August 21, 2006, accessed November 22, 2014, www.historynet.com/ansil-lwalker-recalls-the-battle-of-chipyong-ni-during-the-korean-war.htm.
16. Walker, "A Battle of the Forgotten War," 12; Walker, "Ansil L. Walker Recalls the Battle of Chipyong-ni"; S3 Journal, 13 February, J104, J106.
17. Peter F. Schutz, letter to Col. Kenneth Hamburger, n.d. (Kenneth Hamburger Collection), 1–3.
18. Donald M. Byers, "Speech at Chipyong-ni," February 13, 1991 (Kenneth Hamburger Collection, Sierra Vista, AZ).
19. S3 Journal, 13 February, J115; S2 Journal, 130001 February 1951 to 142400 February 1951.
20. Headquarters, French Battalion, "Compte Rendu Minute Sur le deroulement des Operations de Defense de Chipyong Ni," February 1951, Chipyong-ni (Kenneth Hamburger Collection), 1.

21. Raoul Monclar, "Report of the Battle of Chipyong-ni," trans. by Kenneth Hamburger (Kenneth Hamburger Collection, Vol. 7, Box 404: French Army, 1951), 5; Freeman, *Wonju Through Chip'yong*, 33; Headquarters, French Battalion, "Compte Rendu Minute Sur le deroulement des Operations de Defense de Chipyong Ni," 2–3; S2 Journal, 130001 February 1951 to 142400 February 1951.

22. Freeman, *Wonju Through Chip'yong*, 31.

23. S3 Section, 23rd Infantry Regiment, S3 Journal, 13 February, J133, 135, 138; Frank Meszar, interview by Kenneth Hamburger, November 17, 1992 (Kenneth Hamburger Collection, Sierra Vista, AZ).

24. Freeman's comparison to the Naktong was in reference to August 1950 when the North Koreans still had many of their heavy weapons, courtesy of the Russians. Hence, unlike the later Chinese who used mainly pack howitzers and mortars, the NKPA at the beginning of the Korean War closely resembled the contemporary Russian Army with its long-range artillery and other heavy howitzers. The concentration of heavy mortars and pack howitzers must have been considerable at Chipyong-ni for him to make such a statement. Freeman, *Wonju Through Chip'yong*, 31.

25. Douglas Graney, letter to Col. Kenneth Hamburger, n.d., Houston, TX (Kenneth Hamburger Collection), 13.

26. Bickford E. Sawyer, letter to Col. Kenneth Hamburger, October 6, 1992, Honolulu, HI (Kenneth Hamburger Collection), 6–7; James W. Edwards, "The Siege of Chipyong-ni," in *Staff Ride Read Ahead Packet, Battle of Chipyong-ni, 13–15 February 1951*, by U.S. Eighth Army Staff (Seoul: 2nd Infantry Division, 1990), 20–22.

27. Graney, letter to Col. Kenneth Hamburger, 14.

28. Ibid.

29. Martin Lee, interview by author, January 31, 2015.

30. Edwards, "The Siege of Chipyong-ni," 22.

31. Lee, interview by author.

32. Rupert D. Graves, "General Orders Number 504, 2nd Infantry Division," Korean War Project, September 3, 1951, accessed November 25, 2014, www.koreanwar.org/html/2011_2ID_korean_war_records_go.html; Edwards, "The Siege of Chipyong-ni," 22–23.

33. Lee, interview by author.

34. Edwards, "The Siege of Chipyong-ni," 22.

35. Lee, interview by author.

36. Ibid.

37. James Bolen, interview by author, "James Bolen Questionnaire," January 29, 2015.

38. Edwards, "The Siege of Chipyong-ni," 24; S3 Journal, 14 February (Kenneth Hamburger Collection, College Park, MD: Department of the Army, 1951), J8; George M. Gilbert, interview by Kenneth Hamburger, "Interview with George M. Gilbert—Driver for Lieutenant Haire, B Battery, 82nd AAA Battalion," December 5, 1992.

39. Edwards, "The Siege of Chipyong-ni," 24; S3 Journal, 14 February, J8, 9, 13; John B. Dumaine, "After Action Report Covering Operations of the 23rd Regimental Combat Team during the Period 290630 January to 152400 February 51" (College Park, MD: Department of the Army, 13 March 1951), 6.

40. Graney, letter to Col. Kenneth Hamburger, 14.

41. Sawyer, letter to Col. Kenneth Hamburger, 7.

42. Paul J. McGee, interview by Edward C. Williamson, "Interview First Lieutenant Paul J. McGee, 3rd Platoon Leader, G Company, 23rd Infantry—Part of the G Company After Action Report, Chipyong-ni," October 18, 1951, p. 2; Edwards, "The Siege of Chipyong-ni," 23.

43. Kenneth C., Green, Roy F. Benoit, Donald E. Nelson, Bernard Jack, and Herbert G. Ziebell, interview by Edward C. Williamson, "G Company, 23rd Infantry—Part of the G Company After Action Report, Chipyong-ni," October 18, 1951, p. 1; W. H. Melhorn, "Combat Information: Small Units in Defense, Training Bulletin #3" (Kenneth Hamburger Collection, Fort Monroe, VA: Department of the Army, April 23, 1952), 6.

44. McGee, interview by Edward C. Williamson, 3.

45. Ibid., 2; Melhorn, "Combat Information," 6; Gerald G. Epley, "General Orders Number 192, 2nd Infantry Division," Korean War Project, June 18, 1951, accessed August 9, 2014, www.koreanwar.org/html/2011_2ID_korean_war_records_go .html, p. 3.

46. Melhorn, "Combat Information," 6–7; McGee, interview by Edward C. Williamson, 2; Green, et. al., interview by Edward C. Williamson, 1.

47. S3 Section, 23rd Infantry Regiment, S3 Journal, 13 February, J120. Edwards believed the gun was a self-propelled gun. He also said it could have been a 75mm pack howitzer. In other locations, the Chinese used captured American tanks and would fire the guns until they ran out of ammunition. Edwards, "The Siege of Chipyong-ni," 25.

48. Edwards, "The Siege of Chipyong-ni," 25. It is possible that Castiglia was the other soldier with Mason. Mason's citation mentions another soldier who went with him but was killed on the return trip from the ammunition bunker. Castiglia's citation mentions that he died on the return trip after securing ammunition for his machine-gun team. Gerald G. Epley, "General Orders Number 146, 2nd Infantry Division," Korean War Project, June 15, 1951, accessed November 28, 2014, www.koreanwar.org/html/2011_2ID_korean_war_records_go.html, pp. 2, 8.

49. McGee, interview by Edward C. Williamson, 2–3.

50. Edwards, "The Siege of Chipyong-ni," 25; S3 Journal, 14 February, J32.

51. Paul J. McGee, interview by Thomas M. Ryan, "Interview with Paul J. McGee, Platoon Leader, 3rd Platoon, G Company," August 11–12, 1988 (Kenneth Hamburger Collection), 1.

52. Colonel Edwards wrote that the last attack started at 0530, but the radio logs contradict this. The last entry for the major attack on G Company was around 0346 hours. Edwards, "The Siege of Chipyong-ni," 27; S3 Journal, 14 February, J55.

53. McGee, interview by Thomas M. Ryan, 28–29.

54. Edwards, "The Siege of Chipyong-ni," 27.

55. S3 Section, 23rd Infantry Regiment, S3 Journal, 14 February, J67.

56. Ibid., J92; Edwards, "The Siege of Chipyong-ni," 28; McGee, interview by Thomas M. Ryan, 1.

57. Headquarters, XIX Army Group, CPVF, "Chinese Critique of Tactics Employed in the First Encount." U.S. Force Korea, March 29, 1951, accessed October 5, 2014, www.usfk.mil/usfk/Uploads/120/ChineseCritiqueofTacticsEmployedintheFirst Encount.pdf, p. 299.

58. Tom Ryan, interview by Kenneth Hamburger, "Interview with Tom Ryan of Company K," n.d.; Aubrey Milbach, interview by Kenneth Hamburger, "Interview with Aubrey Milbach, Radio Operator for K Company," May 1993.

59. S3 Section, 23rd Infantry Regiment, S3 Journal, 14 February, J33, 34, 40.
60. Ibid., J65, 69; Gerald G. Epley, "General Orders Number 106, 2nd Infantry Division," Korean War Project, May 13, 1951, accessed December 2, 2014, www.koreanwar.org/html/2011_2ID_korean_war_records_go.html, p. 1; Ryan, interview by Kenneth Hamburger.
61. Gerald G. Epley, "General Orders Number 119, 2nd Infantry Division," Korean War Project, May 29, 1951, accessed August 6, 2014, www.koreanwar.org/html/2011_2ID_korean_war_records_go.html, p. 3.
62. Gerald G. Epley, "General Orders Number 128, 2nd Infantry Division," Korean War Project, June 1, 1951, accessed September 4, 2014, www.koreanwar.org/html/2011_2ID_korean_war_records_go.html, p. 3.
63. S3 Section, 23rd Infantry Regiment, S3 Journal, 14 February, J86, 98, 113; Edwards, "The Siege of Chipyong-ni," 28–29; S2 Journal, 140001 February 1951 to 152400 February 1951 (Kenneth Hamburger Collection, College Park, MD: Department of the Army, 1951).
64. Headquarters, X Corps, Daily Summary, February 14, 1951 (Kenneth Hamburger Collection, College Park, MD: Department of the Army, 1951), 1.
65. James H. Polk, Periodic Intelligence Report No. 141, Period 132100I–142100I Feb 51, X Corps (Kenneth Hamburger Collection, College Park, MD: Department of the Army, 1951), 1; Headquarters, 38th Infantry Regiment, Command Report, February 1951 (College Park, MD: Department of the Army, 1951), 9–10.
66. Donald M. Byers, interview by author, January 10, 2015.
67. S3 Section, 23rd Infantry Regiment, S3 Journal, 14 February, J100, 110.
68. S2 Section, 23rd Infantry Regiment, S2 Journal, 140001 February 1951 to 152400 February 1951; Freeman, *Wonju Through Chip'yong*, 33; James H. Polk, Periodic Intelligence Report No. 142, Period 132100I–142100I Feb 51, X Corps (Kenneth Hamburger Collection, College Park, MD: Department of the Army, 1951), 2.
69. S3 Section, 23rd Infantry Regiment, S3 Journal, 14 February, J120.
70. We do not know exactly when the mortar hit, but we can estimate it was between 0907 and 0951 hours. Freeman directly called division at 0907, which meant he was inside the command post. At 0951, the radio operator logged a report that Captain King was taking over as S2, which meant something happened to the original S2. Captain Hall, the doctor on site, maintained in his account that only Freeman and Meszar were present, while Freeman writes that all three (Shoemaker, Meszar, and Freeman) were in his tent. Freeman's account seems to be more accurate when compared to the radio logs. Hall wrote his account in 1992. Paul L. Freeman, interview by unknown, n.d. (Kenneth Hamburger Collection, Sierra Vista, AZ), 91.
71. Robert M. Hall, letter to Col. Kenneth Hamburger, October 2, 1992, Raleigh, NC (Kenneth Hamburger Collection), 2–3; S3 Journal, 14 February, J125; Freeman, *Wonju Through Chip'yong*, 34.
72. Interestingly, the logs do not mention when Chiles arrived or when Freeman left. We do know that Chiles briefed General Almond at 1600 hours on February 15; Freeman would have been gone by then. According to Almond's daily summary on February 14, Ruffner wanted to relieve Freeman, but Stewart's account contradicts this. George C. Stewart, interview by Tymothy W. Caddell, "Service in WWII & Korea," June 7, 1985, p. 19; Harold R. Martin, "The Two Terrible Nights of the 23rd," *Saturday Evening Post*, May 19, 1951: 153–59; Headquarters, X Corps, Daily Summary, February 14, 1951, pp. 1–3; Edwards, "The Siege of Chipyong-ni," 46; Paul L. Freeman, interview by James N. Ellis, April 16, 1974, p. 4.

73. Frank Meszar, interview by Kenneth Hamburger, November 17, 1992 (Kenneth Hamburger Collection).

74. Hall, letter to Col. Kenneth Hamburger, 3.

75. Marcel G. Crombez, "Command Report—1 Through 28 February 1951, 5th Cavalry Regiment" (College Park, MD: Department of the Army, 1951).

76. The log entry read 3rd Battalion, which makes no sense since 3rd Battalion was on the east side of the perimeter. The French Battalion would be the one to greet 5th Cavalry. S3 Section, 23rd Infantry Regiment, S3 Journal, 14 February, J156, 161.

77. John Collins, "'Mosquito Spirit' Leads Operation Punch through 'Dark Days,'" Kenneth Hamburger Collection, *Atlantic Flyer*, March 1988: A5; John Collins, "Flying Story Number 62; Diary of a Mosquito." *Atlantic Flyer*, September 1991: A9.

78. McGee, interview by Edward C. Williamson, 3.

79. McGee, interview by Thomas M. Ryan, 2–4; Melhorn, "Combat Information," 8; McGee, interview by Edward C. Williamson, 3–4.

80. Edwards, "The Siege of Chipyong-ni," 30–31.

81. Headquarters, XIX Army Group, CPVF, "Chinese Critique of Tactics Employed in the First Encount," 297–303.

CHAPTER 7

1. Harley E. Wilburn, interview by author, January 18, 2015.

2. S3 Section, 23rd Infantry Regiment, S3 Journal, 14 February (Kenneth Hamburger Collection, College Park, MD: Department of the Army, 1951), J153.

3. Carl F. Haberman, interview by Edward C. Williamson, "Interview with Captain Carl F. Haberman, 4th Platoon Leader, G Company, 23rd Infantry—Part of the G Company After Action Report, Chipyong-ni," October 18, 1951, p. 2.

4. Paul J. McGee, interview by Thomas M. Ryan, "Interview with Paul J. McGee, Platoon Leader, 3rd Platoon, G Company," August 11–12, 1988 (Kenneth Hamburger Collection), 5–6.

5. Paul L. Freeman, *Wonju Through Chip'yong: An Epic of Regimental Combat Team Action in Korea* (College Park, MD: Department of the Army, 1951), 34–35.

6. McGee, interview by Thomas Ryan, 6; James W. Edwards, "The Siege of Chipyong-ni," in *Staff Ride Read Ahead Packet, Battle of Chipyong-ni, 13–15 February 1951*, by U.S. Eighth Army Staff (Seoul: 2nd Infantry Division, 1990), 34.

7. S3 Section, 23rd Infantry Regiment, S3 Journal, 14 February, J157.

8. McGee, Paul J., interview by Edward C. Williamson. "Interview First Lieutenant Paul J. McGee, 3rd Platoon Leader, G Company, 23rd Infantry—Part of the G Company After Action Report, Chipyong-ni," October 18, 1951, p. 4; W. H. Melhorn, "Combat Information: Small Units in Defense, Training Bulletin #3" (Kenneth Hamburger Collection, Fort Monroe, VA: Department of the Army, April 23, 1952), 8; Gerald G. Epley, "General Orders Number 88, 2nd Infantry Division," Korean War Project, April 29, 1951, accessed August 9, 2014, www.koreanwar.org/html/2011_2ID_korean_war_records_go.html, p. 1.

9. The 503rd Field Artillery was an African-American unit. Even though President Truman had signed an executive order desegregating the Armed Forces in 1948, it was not an instantaneous process. At the time of Chipyong-ni, the 503rd was still a segregated unit with white officers and African-American enlisted soldiers. Edwards, "The Siege of Chipyong-ni," 38; Haberman, interview by Edward C. Williamson, 1;

John A. Elledge, interview by Edward C. Williamson, "Interview with Captain John A. Elledge Arty, Liaison Officer to 37th Field Artillery Battalion, Battery B, 503rd Field Artillery Battalion—Part of the G Company After Action Report, Chipyong-ni," October 31, 1951.

10. McGee, interview by Thomas M. Ryan, 8.

11. Melhorn, "Combat Information," 8; McGee, interview by Edward C. Williamson, 4; Paul J. McGee, interview by Thomas M. Ryan, "Interview with Paul J. McGee, Platoon Leader, 3rd Platoon, G Company," August 11–12, 1988 (Kenneth Hamburger Collection), 7.

12. McGee, interview by Edward C. Williamson, 5; Melhorn, "Combat Information," 9; McGee, interview by Thomas M. Ryan, 10.

13. Melhorn, "Combat Information," 9; McGee, interview by Edward C. Williamson, 5; McGee, interview by Thomas M. Ryan, 9.

14. McGee, interview by Thomas M. Ryan, 8.

15. McGee, interview by Edward C. Williamson, 8; Melhorn, "Combat Information," 10.

16. McGee, interview by Edward C. Williamson, 6.

17. Melhorn, "Combat Information," 9–10; McGee, interview by Edward C. Williamson, 6.

18. Later, McGee determined that two CPVF soldiers had sneaked up to Ottesen's hole and lobbed two grenades into it. However, no one ever found the corporal's body. Melhorn, "Combat Information," 11; McGee, interview by Edward C. Williamson, 6–7; Charles F. Heady, interview by Edward C. Williamson, "Interview with Charles F. Heady, Platoon Leader, 3rd Platoon, F Company" (Kenneth Hamburger Collection, College Park, MD: Department of the Army, October 18, 1951), 1.

19. Seymour Harris, "Return to Heartbreak Ridge," Korean War Project, February 1951, accessed February 27, 2015, www.koreanwar.org/my_html/korea010.htm; Edwards, "The Siege of Chipyong-ni," sketch 8.

20. S3 Section, 23rd Infantry Regiment, S3 Journal, 14 February, J178, 182, 187–90; S3 Section, 23rd Infantry Regiment, S3 Journal, 15 February (Kenneth Hamburger Collection, College Park, MD: Department of the Army, 1951), J15, 22; Melhorn, "Combat Information," 10.

21. Douglas Graney, *Cottonseed Easy Six* (Denver: Outskirts Press, Inc., 2010), 127–28.

22. Several accounts contradict each other. McGee's account said Bennett was hit in the head, while Bennett's account says he was hit in the leg. Obviously, I chose Bennett's version over McGee in this case. Melhorn, "Combat Information," 11–12; McGee, interview by Edward C. Williamson, 7; Kenneth C. Green, Roy F. Benoit, Donald E. Nelson, Bernard Jack, and Herbert G. Ziebell, interview by Edward C. Williamson, "G Company, 23rd Infantry—Part of the G Company After Action Report, Chipyong-ni," October 18, 1951, p. 2.

23. McGee, interview by Edward C. Williamson, 7; McGee, interview by Thomas M. Ryan, 9–10; Green, et. al., interview by Edward C. Williamson, 2; Gerald G. Epley, "General Orders Number 80, 2nd Infantry Division," Korean War Project, April 12, 1951, accessed December 22, 2014, www.koreanwar.org/html/2011_2ID_korean_war_records_go.html, p. 3; Edwards, "The Siege of Chipyong-ni," 38–39.

24. Herbert Ziebell, interview by Thomas M. Sullivan, March 1, 2006, Oshkosh, WI, 10.

25. No one knows who ordered 2nd Platoon to pull out. Lieutenant Heath died several months after Chipyong-ni, but before the Army historians interviewed him. McGee said he never knew who ordered it. McGee, interview by Thomas M. Ryan, 8, 12; McGee, interview by Edward C. Williamson, 7–8.

26. McGee, interview by Edward C. Williamson, 8; Melhorn, "Combat Information," 12; Green, et. al., interview by Edward C. Williamson, 2.

27. McGee, interview by Thomas M. Ryan, 9.

28. Gerald G. Epley, "General Orders Number 146, 2nd Infantry Division," Korean War Project, June 15, 1951, www.koreanwar.org/html/2011_2ID_korean_war_records_go.html (accessed November 28, 2014), 2; Epley, "General Orders Number 80, 2nd Infantry Division," 1; Gerald G. Epley, "General Orders Number 92, 2nd Infantry Division," Korean War Project, May 1, 1951, accessed December 23, 2014, www.koreanwar.org/html/2011_2ID_korean_war_records_go.html, pp. 1–2; Edwards, "The Siege of Chipyong-ni," 38.

29. Later, his friend, Sgt. Doyle A. Cox, received McGovern's Colt 1911 sidearm when he returned from R&R in Japan. Cox had left Chipyong-ni right before the Chinese sealed the cordon. Doyle A. Cox, interview by author, January 17, 2015; Epley, "General Orders Number 80, 2nd Infantry Division," 1.

30. Gerald G. Epley, "General Orders Number 106, 2nd Infantry Division," Korean War Project, May 13, 1951, accessed December 2, 2014, www.koreanwar.org/html/2011_2ID_korean_war_records_go.html, p. 1.

31. Gerald G. Epley, "General Orders Number 105, 2nd Infantry Division," Korean War Project, May 12, 1951, accessed December 23, 2014, www.koreanwar.org/html/2011_2ID_korean_war_records_go.html, p. 1.

32. Epley, "General Orders Number 146, 2nd Infantry Division," 3.

33. Gerald G. Epley, "General Orders Number 192, 2nd Infantry Division," Korean War Project, June 18, 1951, accessed August 9, 2014, www.koreanwar.org/html/2011_2ID_korean_war_records_go.html, p. 5.

34. Gerald G. Epley, "General Orders Number 90, 2nd Infantry Division 1951," Korean War Project, April 3, 1951, accessed September 15, 2014, www.koreanwar.org/html/2011_2ID_korean_war_records_go.html, pp. 2–3.

35. Unfortunately, the citations do not mention which platoon. I am convinced that Gilleland was probably in 1st or 2nd Platoon. Hardly anyone survived from 3rd Platoon, and I think McGee would have mentioned Gilleland's role or helped write the award. Gerald G. Epley, "General Orders Number 160, 2nd Infantry Division," Korean War Project, June 16, 1951, accessed December 23, 2014, www.koreanwar.org/html/2011_2ID_korean_war_records_go.html, p. 6.

36. Epley, "General Orders Number 88, 2nd Infantry Division," 1–2; Haberman, interview by Edward C. Williamson, 2.

37. The award citation mentioned enemy machine guns, but Halbrook told me he shot at enemy mortars, firing from a nearby cemetery. Gerald G. Epley, "General Orders Number 63, 2nd Infantry Division," Korean War Project, March 22, 1951, accessed December 23, 2014, www.koreanwar.org/html/2011_2ID_korean_war_records_go.html, p. 2; Edwards, "The Siege of Chipyong-ni," 38–39; Joe E. Halbrook, interview by author, January 20, 2015.

38. Epley, "General Orders Number 160, 2nd Infantry Division," 6.

39. Epley, "General Orders Number 80, 2nd Infantry Division," 3; Gerald G. Epley, "General Orders Number 460, 2nd Infantry Division," Korean War Project, August 18, 1951, accessed December 23, 2014, www.koreanwar.org/html/2011_2ID_korean_war_records_go.html, p. 2; Epley, "General Orders Number 88, 2nd Infantry Division," 1.

40. Earl Becker, interview by author, January 25, 2015; George Collingsworth, interview by author, January 25, 2015.

41. Collingsworth, interview by author.

42. S3 Section, 23rd Infantry Regiment, S3 Journal, 15 February, J12, 15, 29.

43. William P. Summers, "Other Views—My Words," *Orlando Sentinel*, May 29, 2000, accessed January 12, 2015, http://articles.orlandosentinel.com/2000-05-29/news/0005290160_1_medal-of-honor-honor-winner-war-ii.

44. William T. Bowers, ed., *The Line: Combat in Korea, January–February 1951* (Lexington: University Press of Kentucky, 2008), 245–56; Jay Young, "Remembering Central PA Soldiers," *Altoona Mirror*, November 11, 2008, accessed January 12, 2015, www.altoonamirror.com/page/content.detail/id/513187.html; Department of the Army, "William S. Sitman," Medal of Honor—US Army, February 1, 1952, accessed January 12, 2015, www.history.army.mil/html/moh/koreanwar.html#SITMAN.

45. Robert W. Curtis, "Chipyoung-yi," in *Staff Ride Read Ahead Packet, Battle of Chipyong-ni, 13–15 February 1951*, by U.S. Eighth Army Staff (Seoul: 2nd Infantry Division, 1990), 252–53; James W. Edwards, letter to Paul Freeman, May 7, 1951 (Kenneth Hamburger Collection, Department of the Army), 1; Emmett Fike, letter to Thomas Ryan, USFK/EUSA, March 1, 1988, Warrior, AL (Kenneth Hamburger Collection), 1.

46. The issue of rank is interesting; the records show several different ranks. According to the January 1951 command report, Curtis was a 2nd lieutenant while Heady was a 1st lieutenant in March 1951. In order for the date of rank to have been an issue, then Heath, Heady, and Curtis all had to be 2nd lieutenants or 1st lieutenants. I made a decision that they were all still 2nd lieutenants. Curtis, "Chipyoung-yi," 253–54; Heady, interview by Edward C. Williamson, 1; John H. Ramsburg, interview by unknown, "Interview with Captain John H. Ramsburg," July 2, 1951 (Kenneth Hamburger Collection), 1; S3 Journal, 15 February, J41.

47. Ramsburg, interview by unknown, 1–2; Curtis, "Chipyoung-yi," 254–55.

48. Ramsburg, interview by unknown, 1–2; Curtis, "Chipyoung-yi," 255; Wilburn, interview by author.

49. Gerald G. Epley, "General Orders Number 102, 2nd Infantry Division," Korean War Project, May 10, 1951, accessed January 9, 2015, www.koreanwar.org/html/2011_2ID_korean_war_records_go.html, p. 4.

50. McGee, interview by Thomas M. Ryan, Tape 3, 1–2.

51. Wilburn, interview by author.

52. S3 Section, 23rd Infantry Regiment, S3 Journal, 15 February, J62; Heady, interview by Edward C. Williamson, 1; Ramsburg, interview by unknown, 2; Curtis, "Chipyoung-yi," 255–57; Fike, letter to Thomas Ryan, 1.

53. Wilburn, interview by author.

54. Epley, "General Orders Number 146, 2nd Infantry Division," 9.

55. Gerald G. Eppley. "General Orders Number 114, 2nd Infantry Division," Korean War Project, May 21, 1951, accessed January 9, 2015, www.koreanwar.org/html/2011_2ID_korean_war_records_go.html, p. 3.

56. McGee, interview by Thomas M. Ryan, 16.

57. It is interesting to me that Pitlick mentioned a captain. Was it the battery commander or Captain Elledge? I do not know. According to Lieutenant Colonel
Edwards, the half-track had been there, and when Lieutenant Curtis ordered the
crew to move, the vehicle accidentally was driven off the jeep trail and abandoned,
except for one man. Kenneth Paul Pitlick, interview by Nora Worthen, April 16,
2002, Kenneth Paul Pitlick Collection, AFC/2001/001/loc.natlib.afc2001001.327,
Veterans History Project, American Folklife Center, Library of Congress; Gerald G.
Epley, "General Orders Number 161, 2nd Infantry Division," Korean War Project,
June 16, 1951, accessed January 3, 2015, www.koreanwar.org/html/2011_2ID_
korean_war_records_go.html, p. 4; Edwards, "The Siege of Chipyong-ni," 41, 43;
Arthur J. Junot, interview by Edward C. Williamson, "Interview with First
Lieutenant Arthur J. Junot, 1st Platoon Leader, Tank Company, 23rd Infantry—
Part of the G Company After Action Report, Chipyong-ni," October 16, 1951, p. 1.

58. Edwards, "The Siege of Chipyong-ni," 43; Freeman, *Wonju Through Chip'yong*, 36.

59. Curtis, "Chipyoung-yi," 257.

60. Curtis, "Chipyoung-yi," 257–60; Robert W. Curtis, interview by Kenneth
Hamburger, October 23, 1992.

61. Curtis, interview by Kenneth Hamburger; Curtis, "Chipyoung-yi," 260–62.

62. Junot, interview by Edward C. Williamson, 1–2; "Le Battalion Francais de l'ONU en
Coreé, Decembre 1950–Novembre 1953," n.d., EMAT (Kenneth Hamburger
Collection), 5; Melhorn, "Combat Information," 13–14.

63. Curtis, "Chipyoung-yi," 262–63; Curtis, interview by Kenneth Hamburger.

64. S3 Section, 23rd Infantry Regiment, S3 Journal, 15 February, J69–70, 72.

65. Haberman, interview by Edward C. Williamson, 2; Edwards, "The Siege of
Chipyong-ni," 48.

66. Edwards, "The Siege of Chipyong-ni," 48; Edwards, letter to Paul Freeman, 2. Pratt's
letter to Tom Ryan differed slightly from his interview, which became the subject of
Pratt's book. In Pratt's book, instead of saying "Piece of cake . . . " Edwards said, "The
companies' dugouts are just over the crest and all prepared. All your men have to do
is go up cautiously, then rush over the top and into the existing positions. Shouldn't
be a big order." I combined his two accounts to some degree, though the subject
matter is the same and the substance of the conversation did not change. Sherman
Pratt, letter to Tom Ryan, Command Historian EUSAK, n.d., Arlington, VA
(Kenneth Hamburger Collection), 4.

67. Matt Schudel, "Sherman W. Pratt, Army officer and lawyer," *Washington Post*,
October 14, 2013, accessed January 24, 2015, www.washingtonpost.com/local
/obituaries/sherman-w-pratt-army-officer-and-lawyer/2013/10/14/e4b34cee-31e3
-11e3-8627-c5d7de0a046b_story.html.

68. Pratt's account is interesting. There is a lot of dialogue, which he admits might not be
100 percent accurate. Despite this, it is the only in-depth account I have of these
meetings. In addition, his version does not really contradict anything else that is out
there. Edwards even admitted that he did not give Pratt detailed instructions, and
Pratt's account confirmed this. The B Company commander assumed Edwards was
lackadaisical. On the contrary, that was his command style. Edwards's other commanders attested to his style of leadership, in which the colonel tended to only provide a
task and purpose to his subordinates. Either way, I decided to include Pratt's version.
Sherman W. Pratt, *Decisive Battles of the Korean War: An Infantry Company Commander's
View of the War's Most Critical Engagements* (New York: Vantage Press, 1992), 195–98.

69. Ibid., 198.

70. Pratt, letter to Tom Ryan, 4–5; Richard S. Kotite, letter to Maj. Roy E. Appleman, December 3, 1951, Tokyo (Kenneth Hamburger Collection), 1; Edwards, letter to Paul Freeman, 2; Junot, interview by Edward C. Williamson, 2.

71. Edwards, letter to Paul Freeman, 2; Edwards, "The Siege of Chipyong-ni," 45–46; Paul L. Freeman, "Farewell Letter to the 23rd Infantry Regiment," February 26, 1951, San Francisco, CA (Kenneth Hamburger Collection).

72. Dewey R. Andersen, letter to Col. Kenneth Hamburger, December 21, 1992, Lincoln, NE (Kenneth Hamburger Collection), 3–4.

73. Gerald G. Epley, "General Orders Number 150, 2nd Infantry Division," Korean War Project, June 15, 1951, accessed January 14, 2015, www.koreanwar.org/html/2011_2ID_korean_war_records_go.html, p. 4.

74. Pratt, *Decisive Battles of the Korean War*, 199–200.

75. Kotite wrote that 2nd Platoon was under the command of a Eugene Reinhardt, not Chapman. However, Chapman's Silver Star confirmed he was there. It was hard to find because it had the wrong date. Kotite, letter to Maj. Roy E. Appleman, 2.

76. Edwards, "The Siege of Chipyong-ni," 49; Edwards, letter to Paul Freeman, 2; S3 Journal, 15 February, J103.

77. John B. Dumaine, "After Action Report Covering Operations of the 23rd Regimental Combat Team during the Period 290630 January to 152400 February 51" (College Park, MD: Department of the Army, 13 March 1951), 6; S3 Journal, 15 February, J96, 101, 104–5.

78. Nabozny did receive a posthumous Silver Star for his actions. Epley, "General Orders Number 146, 2nd Infantry Division," 1.

79. Pratt, *Decisive Battles of the Korean War*, 200–201.

80. S3 Section, 23rd Infantry Regiment, S3 Journal, 15 February, J111; Edwards, "The Siege of Chipyong-ni," 50; Edwards, letter to Paul Freeman, 2; Charles W. Hurlburt,, interview by Edward C. Williamson, "Interview First Lieutenant Charles W. Hurlburt, 4th Platoon Leader, Tank Company, 23rd Infantry—Part of the G Company After Action Report, Chipyong-ni," October 17, 1951.

81. Edwards, "The Siege of Chipyong-ni," 50–51; "General Orders Number 92, 2nd Infantry Division 4; Gerald G. Epley, "General Orders 193, 2nd Infantry Division," Korean War Project, June 18, 1951, accessed January 15, 2015, www.koreanwar.org/html/2011_2ID_korean_war_records_go.html, pp. 3–4; Gerald G. Epley, "General Orders Number 154, 2nd Infantry Division." Korean War Project, June 15, 1951, accessed September 5, 2014, www.koreanwar.org/html/2011_2ID_korean_war_records_go.html, p. 8; Epley, "General Orders Number 160, 2nd Infantry Division," 6–7.

82. Pratt, *Decisive Battles of the Korean War*, 203–4.

83. Kotite, letter to Maj. Roy E. Appleman, 2.

CHAPTER 8

1. "5th Cavalry Regiment Organizational Legacy," First Team US, 1996, accessed February 12, 2015, www.first-team.us/assigned/subunits/5th_cr.

2. Kenneth E. Hamburger, *Leadership in the Crucible: The Korean War Battles of Twin Tunnels and Chipyong-ni* (College Station: Texas A&M University Press, 2003), 196–97; Martin Blumenson, "The Controversial Task Force Crombez." *AUSA*, August 2002, accessed February 12, 2015, www.ausa.org/publications/armymagazine/archive/2002/8/Documents/Blumenson_0802.pdf, 1.

3. Arnold E. Mitchell, letter to Col. Kenneth Hamburger, February 22, 1993, Tampa, FL (Kenneth Hamburger Collection).

4. Keith M. Stewart, letter to Col. Kenneth Hamburger, January 21, 1993, Lafayette, IN (Kenneth Hamburger Collection), 2–3.

5. S3 Journal, 5th Cavalry Regiment, extract from the 5th Cavalry Regiment's S3 Journal, Part of the Task Force Crombez After Action Report (College Park, MD: Department of the Army, February 1951); Crombez, Task Force Crombez, Part of the Task Force Crombez After Action Report 1951, 1.

6. Marcel G. Crombez, "Command Report—1 Through 28 February 1951, 5th Cavalry Regiment" (College Park, MD: Department of the Army, 1951); Map of 5th Cavalry Regiment's Route to Chipyong-ni, Part of the Task Force Crombez After Action Report (College Park, MD: Department of the Army, February 1951); Headquarters, 1st Battalion, 5th Cavalry Regiment, extract from the Operations Log, 1st Battalion, 5th Cavalry Regiment, Part of the Task Force Crombez After Action Report (College Park, MD: Department of the Army, 14–15 February 1951); Charles J. Parziale, interview by Martin Blumenson, "Interview with Regimental S3, Charles J. Parziale, Part of the Task Force Crombez After Action Report," March 27, 1951, p. 1.

7. Robert A. Humphrey, interview by Martin Blumenson, "Interview with the Regimental S2, Robert A. Humphrey, Part of the Task Force Crombez After Action Report," March 27, 1951, pp. 1–2.

8. Several accounts provide different numbers of tanks in the column. Marcel G. Crombez, interview by Martin Blumeson, "Task Force Crombez, Part of the Task Force Crombez After Action Report," March 26, 1951, p. 2; Parziale, interview by Martin Blumenson, 2.

9. Crombez, interview by Martin Blumeson, 2; Parziale, interview by Martin Blumenson, 2; Crombez, "Command Report—1 Through 28 February 195110."

10. Originally, 3rd Battalion, 5th Cavalry, was 3rd Battalion, 14th Infantry, but when the Korean War began, the Department of the Army reflagged the unit so that it could become part of the 1st Cavalry Division, which was already deploying to Korea from Japan. Hamburger, *Leadership in the Crucible*, 193–95.

11. Norman F. J. Allen, letter to Victor Fox, August 17, 1979, Panama City, FL (Kenneth Hamburger Collection), 2.

12. Ibid., 2–4.

13. Norman F. J. Allen, letter to Jim Cardinal, April 27, 1984, Panama City, FL (Kenneth Hamburger Collection), 1.

14. John C. Barrett, interview by Martin Blumenson, "Interview with John C. Barrett, Part of the Task Force Crombez After Action Report," April 26, 1951, pp. 4–5; James Cardinal, letter to Col. Kenneth Hamburger, March 17, 1993, San Francisco, CA (Kenneth Hamburger Collection), 7; Carroll Gifford Everist, "Carroll Gifford Everist," Korean War Educator, February 2008, accessed February 16, 2015, www .thekwe.org/memoirs/everist_carroll/index.htm.

15. George B. Pickett, interview by Martin Blumenson, "Interview with George B. Pickett, Part of the Task Force Crombez After Action Report," April 1, 1951, pp. 1, 4.

16. Barrett, interview by Martin Blumenson, 1–2.

17. Crombez, interview by Martin Blumeson, 2; S3 Journal extract, 5th Cavalry Regiment.

18. Headquarters, 5th Cavalry Regiment, "Periodic Operations Report No 138 for period 151800/I to 161800/I Feb 51, Part of the Task Force Crombez After Action Report" (College Park, MD: Department of the Army, February 16, 1951); Crombez, interview by Martin Blumeson, 3; Joe W. Finley, interview by Martin Blumenson, "Interview with Joe W. Finley, Part of the Task Force Crombez After Action Report," March 28, 1951, p. 1.

19. Alex Leary, "Gunning for Home," *St. Petersburg Times*, July 20, 2003, accessed February 16, 2015, www.sptimes.com/2003/07/20/Korea/Gunning_for_home.shtml.

20. Homer Bassford Reed and George E. Reed, interview by Martin Blumenson, "Interview with Homer Bassford and George E. Reed, Part of the Task Force Crombez After Action Report," March 28, 1951; Paul Campbell, interview by Martin Blumenson, "Interview with Paul Campbell, Part of the Task Force Crombez After Action Report," March 27, 1951.

21. Billy R. Williams, "Witness Statement of Billy R. Williams, Part of the Task Force Crombez After Action Report" (College Park, MD: Department of the Army, February 21, 1951).

22. The platoon leader mentioned in Giddens's account was probably Lieutenant Chastaine. Jessie O. Giddens, "Witness Statement for Jessie O. Giddens, Part of the Task Force Crombez After Action Report" (College Park, MD: Department of the Army, February 21, 1951).

23. Hiram E. Cornelius, "Witness Statement of Hiram E. Cornelius, Part of the Task Force Crombez After Action Report" (College Park, MD: Department of the Army, February 20, 1951); Thomas W. Boydston, "Witness Statement of Thomas W. Boydston, Part of the Task Force Crombez After Action Report" (College Park, MD: Department of the Army, February 21, 1951).

24. Lloyd L. Jones Miller and George W. Miller, interview by Martin Blumenson, "Interview with Lloyd L. Jones and George W. Miller, Part of the Task Force Crombez After Action Report," March 28, 1951, pp. 1–4.

25. Leary, "Gunning for Home"; Headquarters, 1st Battalion, 5th Cavalry Regiment, extract from the Operations Log, 1st Battalion, 5th Cavalry Regiment, Part of the Task Force Crombez After Action Report (College Park, MD: Department of the Army, 14–15 February 1951), 2.

26. Everist, "Carroll Gifford Everist."

27. Ibid.

28. Wayne O. Kemp,, interview by Martin Blumenson, "Interview with Wayne O. Kemp, Part of the Task Force Crombez After Action Report," March 27, 1951; Russell A. Gugeler, *Combat Actions in Korea* (Washington, D.C.: Center of Military History, 1987), Chapter 9.

29. Donald F. Russell, "Witness Statement of Donald F. Russell, Part of the Task Force Crombez After Action Report" (College Park, MD: Department of the Army, March 27, 1951); Hubert M. Cobb, "Witness Statement of Hubert M. Cobb, Part of the Task Force Crombez After Action Report" (College Park, MD: Department of the Army, March 27, 1951).

30. Crombez, interview by Martin Blumeson, 3.

31. Joe Kirkland, "Statement by Master Sergeant Joe Kirkland, Company D, 6th Medium Tank Battalion, Part of the Task Force Crombez After Action Report" (College Park, MD: Department of the Army, 1951).

32. Thomas Bayes, Jr., "Witness Statement of Thomas Bayes, Jr., Part of the Task Force Crombez After Action Report" (College Park, MD: Department of the Army, 1951).

33. George C. Lee, "Witness Statement of George C. Lee, Part of the Task Force Crombez After Action Report" (College Park, MD: Department of the Army, 1951).

34. James Maxwell, "Witness Statement of James Maxwell, Part of the Task Force Crombez After Action Report" (College Park, MD: Department of the Army, 1951).

35. William R. Bierwirth, "Witness Statement of William R. Bierwirth, Part of the Task Force Crombez After Action Report" (College Park, MD: Department of the Army, 1951; Department of the Army, "3.5-inch Rocket Launchers M20 and M20B1," Korean War Online, August 1950, accessed February 23, 2015, www.koreanwar online.com/history/Bazooka/1.pdf, p. 8; Pickett, interview by Martin Blumenson, 3–4.

36. Maxwell, "Witness Statement."

37. Giddens, "Witness Statement."

38. S3 Journal extract, 5th Cavalry Regiment.

39. Martin Lee, interview by author, January 31, 2015.

40. Grant Mead, interview by author, January 31, 2015.

41. James W. Edwards, "The Siege of Chipyong-ni," in *Staff Ride Read Ahead Packet, Battle of Chipyong-ni, 13–15 February 1951*, by U.S. Eighth Army Staff (Seoul: 2nd Infantry Division, 1990), 51.

42. Ibid., 52–53; Headquarters, 5th Cavalry Regiment, "Periodic Operations Report No 138."

43. Mead, interview by author.

44. Harley E. Wilburn, interview by author, January 18, 2015.

45. Seymour Harris, "Return to Heartbreak Ridge," Korean War Project, February 1951, accessed February 27, 2015, www.koreanwar.org/my_html/korea010.htm.

46. Carroll Gifford Everist, letter to Col. Kenneth Hamburger, March 1993 (Kenneth Hamburger Collection, Sierra Vista, AZ), 4–5.

47. Allen, letter to Jim Cardinal, 1–2.

48. Cardinal, letter to Col. Kenneth Hamburger, 7.

49. Hamburger, *Leadership in the Crucible*, 216; General Headquarters Far East Command, "Awards and Citations for Marcel Gustave Crombez," Military Times Hall of Valor, January 29, 1952, accessed February 26, 2015, http://projects.militarytimes .com/citations-medals-awards/recipient.php?recipientid=7196.

50. Stewart, letter to Col. Kenneth Hamburger.

51. According to Captain Barrett, the Patton tank also contributed to the casualties. When it fired, the concussion could knock off soldiers. In addition, several incidents occurred in which traversing turrets knocked men off. Lastly, the back of the tank was too hot to stand on for extended periods. One unconscious soldier lying on the back of the Patton sustained burns to his face because of this oversight. Clarence L. Umberger, interview by Martin Blumenson, "Interview with Clarence L. Umberger, Part of the Task Force Crombez After Action Report," March 28, 1951; Crombez, interview by Martin Blumeson, 5; Barrett, interview by Martin Blumenson, 5–6.

52. Edwards, "The Siege of Chipyong-ni," 28, 55; Headquarters, 23rd Infantry Regiment, "Casualty Report of the 23rd Infantry Regiment for the Battle of Chipyong-ni for the Period 3–16 February 1951, Part of the February 1951 Command Report" (College Park, MD: Department of the Army, 1951).

53. Leo Dobbs, interview by author, January 23, 2015.

EPILOGUE

1. Peng Dehuai, "Chapter XIV: The War to Resist U.S. Aggression and Aid Korea—October 1950–July 1953," in *Memoirs of a Chinese Marshal*, edited by Sara Grimes, March 17, 2005, accessed January 18, 2015, www.paulnoll.com/Korea/War/war -Peng-Dehuai-book-07.html.

2. Unknown, "Paul Lamar Freeman," April 1988, Arlington, VA (Kenneth Hamburger Collection), 163–64; Unknown, "Paul Lamar Freeman—Biography," May 1962 (Kenneth Hamburger Collection, Sierra Vista, AZ).

3. Edme des Vollerons, "Biographie du General Monclar," General Monclar, 2013, accessed February 27, 2015, http://translate.google.com/translate?hl=en&sl=fr&tl= en&u=http%3A%2F%2Fwww.generalmonclar.fr%2Findex.php%2Fle-general-monclar %2F17-biographie-du-general-monclar&anno=2.

4. *Gaston Gazette*, "Obituary for Paul J. McGee," May 13, 2009, accessed January 15, 2015, www.legacy.com/obituaries/gastongazette/obituary.aspx?n=paul-mcgee& pid=127227102&.

5. Headquarters, XIX Army Group, CPVF, "Chinese Critique of Tactics Employed in the First Encount," U.S. Force Korea, March 29, 1951, accessed October 5, 2014, www.usfk.mil/usfk/Uploads/120/ChineseCritiqueof TacticsEmployedintheFirst Encount.pdf, p. 299.

6. Paul J. McGee, interview by Thomas M. Ryan, "Interview with Paul J. McGee, Platoon Leader, 3rd Platoon, G Company," August 11–12, 1988 (Kenneth Hamburger Collection), 10.

7. Paul L. Freeman, interview by James N. Ellis, April 16, 1974; Matt Schudel, "Sherman W. Pratt, Army officer and lawyer," *Washington Post*, October 14, 2013, accessed January 24, 2015, www.washingtonpost.com/local/obituaries/sherman-w-pratt -army-officer-and-lawyer/2013/10/14/e4b34cee-31e3-11e3-8627-c5d7de0a046b _story.html.

8. "Hubert L Lee," Military Wikia, n.d., accessed February 12, 2015, http://military .wikia.com/wiki/Hubert_L._Lee.

9. Martin Lee, interview by author, January 31, 2015.

10. Harley E. Wilburn, interview by author, January 18, 2015.

11. James W. Edwards, "The Siege of Chipyong-ni," in *Staff Ride Read Ahead Packet, Battle of Chipyong-ni, 13–15 February 1951*, by U.S. Eighth Army Staff (Seoul: 2nd Infantry Division, 1990), 60; Cavalry Outpost Publications, "5th Cavalry Regiment Decorations," First Team US, October 2009, accessed February 27, 2015, www .first-team.us/assigned/subunits/5th_cr/5crndx09.html.

BIBLIOGRAPHY

BOOKS AND ARTICLES

Appleman, Roy E. *Disaster in Korea*. College Station: Texas A&M University Military History Series, 1989.

Blumenson, Martin. "The Controversial Task Force Crombez." *AUSA*, August 2002, www.ausa.org/publications/armymagazine/archive/2002/8/Documents/Blumenson_0802.pdf (accessed February 12, 2015).

Bowers, William T., ed. *The Line: Combat in Korea, January–February 1951*. Lexington: University Press of Kentucky, 2008.

Coleman, J. D. *Wonju: The Gettysburg of the Korean War*. Washington, D.C.: Brassey's Publishing, 2000.

Collins, John. "Flying Story Number 62; Diary of a Mosquito." *Atlantic Flyer*, September 1991: A9.

———. "'Mosquito Spirit' Leads Operation Punch through 'Dark Days.'" Kenneth Hamburger Collection. *Atlantic Flyer*, March 1988: A5.

Curtis, Robert W. "Chipyong-yi." In *Staff Ride Read Ahead Packet, Battle of Chipyong-ni, 13–15 February 1951*, by U.S. Eighth Army Staff. Seoul: 2nd Infantry Division, 1990.

Dehuai, Peng. "Chapter XIV: The War to Resist U.S. Aggression and Aid Korea— October 1950–July 1953." In *Memoirs of a Chinese Marshal*, edited by Sara Grimes, March 17, 2005, www.paulnoll.com/Korea/War/war-Peng-Dehuai-book-07.html (accessed January 18, 2015).

Edwards, James W. "The Siege of Chipyong-ni." In *Staff Ride Read Ahead Packet, Battle of Chipyong-ni, 13–15 February 1951*, by U.S. Eighth Army Staff. Seoul: 2nd Infantry Division, 1990.

Gaston Gazette. "Obituary for Paul J. McGee." May 13, 2009, www.legacy.com/obituaries/gastongazette/obituary.aspx?n=paul-mcgee&pid=127227102& (accessed January 2015, 2015).

Graney, Douglas. *Cottonseed Easy Six*. Denver: Outskirts Press, Inc., 2010.

Gugeler, Russell A. *Combat Actions in Korea*. Washington, D.C.: Center of Military History, 1987.

Hamburger, Kenneth E. *Leadership in the Crucible: The Korean War Battles of Twin Tunnels and Chipyong-ni*. College Station: Texas A&M University Press, 2003.

Leary, Alex. "Gunning for Home." *St. Petersburg Times*, July 20, 2003, www.sptimes.com/ 2003/07/20/Korea/Gunning_for_home.shtml (accessed February 16, 2015).

Martin, Harold R. "The Two Terrible Nights of the 23rd." *Saturday Evening Post*, May 19, 1951: 153–59.

McMichael, Scott R. *A Historical Perspective on Light Infantry*. Fort Leavenworth, KS: Combat Studies Institute, 1987.

Millett, Allan R. *The War for Korea, 1950–1951: They Came from the North*. Lawrence: University of Kansas Press, 2010.

O'Neill, Mark. "Kim Il-Sung's Secret History." *South China Morning Post*, October 17, 2010.

Pratt, Sherman W. *Decisive Battles of the Korean War: An Infantry Company Commander's View of the War's Most Critical Engagements*. New York: Vantage Press, 1992.

Ridgway, Matthew B. *The Korean War*. New York: De Capo Press, 1967.

Sawyer, Robert K. *Military Advisors in Korea: KMAG in Peace and War*. Washington, D.C.: Center of Military History, 1988.

Schudel, Matt. "Sherman W. Pratt, Army officer and lawyer." *Washington Post*, October 14, 2013, www.washingtonpost.com/local/obituaries/sherman-w-pratt-army-officer -and-lawyer/2013/10/14/e4b34cee-31e3-11e3-8627-c5d7de0a046b_story.html (accessed January 24, 2015).

Slate, Scott. "Chipyong-ni high-water mark of the Korean War." *Indianhead*, www.2id .korea.army.mil/news/Indianhead, August 1, 2005: 9.

Stackhouse, Glenn A. "They Stood and Fired: Brothers in 37 Survivors of 600-Man Red Trap." *Knickerbocker News*, January 30, 1952: 2A.

Stokesbury, James L. *A Short History of the Korean War*. New York: Quill, 1988.

Summers, William P. "Other Views—My Words." *Orlando Sentinel*, May 29, 2000, http://articles.orlandosentinel.com/2000-05-29/news/0005290160_1_medal-of -honor-honor-winner-war-ii (accessed January 12, 2015).

Tomlin, Jimmy. "Trinity veteran's Korean War memories remain vivid." *High Point Enterprise News*, August 4, 2013, http://debug.paxton.zope.net/highpoint/life/features/ x135060486/Trinity-veterans-Korean-War-memories-remain-vivid (accessed November 22, 2014).

Young, Jay. "Remembering Central PA Soldiers." *Altoona Mirror*, November 11, 2008, www.altoonamirror.com/page/content.detail/id/513187.html (accessed January 12, 2015).

AFTER-ACTION REPORTS

Bagley, Henry, Herman L. Seabolt, Leland L. Cargle, Joseph A. Talotta, Billy M. Lloyd, Richard D. Goldsberry, and George F. Bammert, interview by John Mewha. "After Action Interview with the soldiers of L Company—Part of The Twin Tunnels After Action Report Collection," June 16, 1951.

Barenkamp, William P., interview by John Mewha. "After Action Report—Part of the Twin Tunnels After Report," May 16, 1951.

Barrett, John C., interview by Martin Blumenson. "Interview with John C. Barrett, Part of the Task Force Crombez After Action Report," April 26, 1951.

Bass, Richard M., Carl A. Spencer, William A. Shelton, Marvin J. Mueller, and Richard J. Laba, interview by John Mewha. "After Action Interview with 1st Platoon,

Company K, 23rd Infantry Regiment—Part of Twin Tunnels After Action Report," May 16, 1951.

Bayes, Thomas, Jr. "Witness Statement of Thomas Bayes, Jr., Part of the Task Force Crombez After Action Report." College Park, MD: Department of the Army, 1951.

Bierwirth, William R. "Witness Statement of William R. Bierwirth, Part of the Task Force Crombez After Action Report." College Park, MD: Department of the Army, 1951.

Boydston, Thomas W. "Witness Statement of Thomas W. Boydston, Part of the Task Force Crombez After Action Report." College Park, MD: Department of the Army, February 21, 1951.

Brooks, Willis P., interview by John Mewha. "After Action, Twin Tunnels—Part of the Twin Tunnels After Action Report," May 17, 1951.

Campbell, Paul, interview by Martin Blumenson. "Interview with Paul Campbell, Part of the Task Force Crombez After Action Report," March 27, 1951.

Cobb, Hubert M. *Witness Statement of Hubert M. Cobb, Part of the Task Force Crombez After Action Report.* College Park, MD: Department of the Army, March 27, 1951.

Cornelius, Hiram E. "Witness Statement of Hiram E. Cornelius, Part of the Task Force Crombez After Action Report." College Park, MD: Department of the Army, February 20, 1951.

Crombez, Marcel G. "Command Report—1 Through 28 February 1951, 5th Cavalry Regiment." College Park, MD: Department of the Army, 1951.

———, interview by Martin Blumeson. "Task Force Crombez, Part of the Task Force Crombez After Action Report," March 26, 1951.

Dumaine, John B. "After Action Report Covering Operations of the 23rd Regimental Combat Team during the Period 290630 January to 152400 February 51." College Park, MD: Department of the Army, 13 March 1951.

Elledge, John A., interview by Edward C. Williamson. "Interview with Captain John A. Elledge Arty, Liaison Officer to 37th Field Artillery Battalion, Battery B, 503rd Field Artillery Battalion—Part of the G Company After Action Report, Chipyong-ni," October 31, 1951.

Finley, Joe W., interview by Martin Blumenson. "Interview with Joe W. Finley, Part of the Task Force Crombez After Action Report," March 28, 1951.

Freeman, Paul L. "Periodic Operations Report 134 for Period 281800 to 291800 January 1951, 23rd Infantry Regiment." Kenneth Hamburger Collection. College Park, MD: Department of the Army, 1951.

———. *Wonju Through Chip'yong: An Epic of Regimental Combat Team Action in Korea.* Personal Report. College Park, MD: Department of the Army, 1951.

G2 Section, 2nd Infantry Division. Intelligence—Staff Section Report of the G-2, 2nd Infantry Division—Part of the Twin Tunnels After Action Report. College Park, MD: Department of the Army, February 1951.

G3 Section, X Corps. Combat Notes Number 5—Part of The Twin Tunnels After Action Report Collection. College Park, MD: Department of the Army, 1951.

———. Combat Notes Number 11—Chipyong-ni. Kenneth Hamburger Collection. College Park, MD: Department of the Army, 1951.

Giddens, Jessie O. "Witness Statement for Jessie O. Giddens, Part of the Task Force Crombez After Action Report." College Park, MD: Department of the Army, February 21, 1951.

Glassman, George H. John W. Dravecky, Dean A. Davidson, and Robert Gilbreath, interview by John Mewha. "After Action, Twin Tunnels—Part of the Twin Tunnels After Action Report," May 17, 1951.

Green, Edward L., interview by John Mewha. "After Action Interview with Edward L. Green—Part of Twin Tunnels After Action Report," May 17, 1951.

Green, Kenneth C., Roy F. Benoit, Donald E. Nelson, Bernard Jack, and Herbert G. Ziebell, interview by Edward C. Williamson. "G Company, 23rd Infantry—Part of the G Company After Action Report, Chipyong-ni," October 18, 1951.

Haberman, Carl F., interview by Edward C. Williamson. "Interview with Captain Carl F. Haberman, 4th Platoon Leader, G Company, 23rd Infantry—Part of the G Company After Action Report, Chipyong-ni," October 18, 1951.

Headquarters, 1st Battalion, 23rd Infantry. "Battle of the Tunnels," Draft After Action Report. Kenneth Hamburger Collection. College Park, MD: Department of the Army, 17 March 1951.

Headquarters, 1st Battalion, 5th Cavalry Regiment. "Extract, Operations Log, 1st Battalion, 5th Cavalry Regiment, Part of the Task Force Crombez After Action Report." College Park, MD: Department of the Army, 1951.

Headquarters, 23rd Infantry Regiment. "23rd Regimental Combat Team Perimeter Defense of Chipyong-ni," After Action Report. Kenneth Hamburger Collection. College Park, MD: Department of the Army, 1951.

———. "Casualty Report of the 23rd Infantry Regiment for the Battle of Chipyong-ni for the Period 3–16 February 1951, Part of the February 1951 Command Report." College Park, MD: Department of the Army, 1951.

Headquarters, 2nd Battalion, 23rd Infantry Regiment. Daily Journal, 29 January 1951. Kenneth Hamburger Collection College Park, MD: Department of the Army, 1951.

Headquarters, 38th Infantry Regiment. Command Report, February 1951. College Park, MD: Department of the Army, 1951.

———. "Hoengsong—Section of the Command Report for 38th Infantry Regiment, February 1951." Kenneth Hamburger Collection. College Park, MD: Department of the Army, 1951.

Headquarters, 5th Cavalry Regiment. "Periodic Operations Report No 138 for period 151800/I to 161800/I Feb 51, Part of the Task Force Crombez After Action Report." College Park, MD: Department of the Army, February 16, 1951.

Headquarters, X Corps. Command Report, X Corps, February. Kenneth Hamburger Collection. College Park, MD: Department of the Army, 1951.

———. Daily Summary, February 14, 1951. Kenneth Hamburger Collection. College Park, MD: Department of the Army, 1951.

Heady, Charles F., interview by Edward C. Williamson. "Interview with Charles F. Heady, Platoon Leader, 3rd Platoon, F Company." Kenneth Hamburger Collection. College Park, MD: Department of the Army, October 18, 1951.

Humphrey, Robert A., interview by Martin Blumenson. "Interview with the Regimental S2, Robert A. Humphrey, Part of the Task Force Crombez After Action Report," March 27, 1951.

Hurlburt, Charles W., interview by Edward C. Williamson. "Interview First Lieutenant Charles W. Hurlburt, 4th Platoon Leader, Tank Company, 23rd Infantry—Part of the G Company After Action Report, Chipyong-ni," October 17, 1951.

Junot, Arthur J., interview by Edward C. Williamson. "Interview with First Lieutenant Arthur J. Junot, 1st Platoon Leader, Tank Company, 23rd Infantry—Part of the G Company After Action Report, Chipyong-ni," October 16, 1951.

Kemp, Wayne O., interview by Martin Blumenson. "Interview with Wayne O. Kemp, Part of the Task Force Crombez After Action Report," March 27, 1951.

Kirkland, Joe. "Statement by Master Sergeant Joe Kirkland, Company D, 6th Medium Tank Battalion, Part of the Task Force Crombez After Action Report." College Park, MD: Department of the Army, 1951.

Lee, George C. "Witness Statement of George C. Lee, Part of the Task Force Crombez After Action Report." College Park, MD: Department of the Army, 1951.

Map of 5th Cavalry Regiment's Route to Chipyong-ni, Part of the Task Force Crombez After Action Report. College Park, MD: Department of the Army, February 1951.

Maxwell, James. "Witness Statement of James Maxwell, Part of the Task Force Crombez AfterAction Report." College Park, MD: Department of the Army, 1951.

McGee, Paul J., interview by Edward C. Williamson. "Interview First Lieutenant Paul J. McGee, 3rd Platoon Leader, G Company, 23rd Infantry—Part of the G Company After Action Report, Chipyong-ni," October 18, 1951.

McGee, Paul J., interview by Thomas M. Ryan. "Interview with Paul J. McGee, Platoon Leader, 3rd Platoon, G Company," August 11–12, 1988. Kenneth Hamburger Collection.

Melhorn, W. H. "Combat Information: Small Units in Defense, Training Bulletin #3." Kenneth Hamburger Collection. Fort Monroe, VA: Department of the Army, April 23, 1952.

Messinger, Edward J. Command Report, February 1951, 9th Infantry Regiment. Kenneth Hamburger Collection. College Park, MD: Department of the Army, 8 March 1951.

Mewha, John. "Narrative—Twin Tunnels, 3rd Battalion, 23rd Infantry Regiment—Part of the Twin Tunnels After Action Report." College Park, MD: Department of the Army, 1951.

Miller, Lloyd L. Jones, and George W. Miller, interview by Martin Blumenson. "Interview with Lloyd L. Jones and George W. Miller, Part of the Task Force Crombez After Action Report," March 28, 1951.

Palmer, Richard A., interview by John Mewha. "After Action Interview with Richard A. Palmer—Part of Twin Tunnels After Action Report," May 16, 1951.

Parziale, Charles J., interview by Martin Blumenson. "Interview with Regimental S3, Charles J. Parziale, Part of the Task Force Crombez After Action Report," March 27, 1951.

Pickett, George B., interview by Martin Blumenson. "Interview with George B. Pickett, Part of the Task Force Crombez After Action Report," April 1, 1951.

Quinn, William W. "Enemy Tactics and Equipment, Combat Intelligence Bulletin Number 1, G2 Section, X Corps, Ridgway Papers Box 117." Combat Intelligence Bulletin, Carlisle Barracks, PA: Department of the Army, 1951.

Reed, Homer Bassford, and George E. Reed, interview by Martin Blumenson. "Interview with Homer Bassford and George E. Reed, Part of the Task Force Crombez After Action Report," March 28, 1951.

Richardson, Beverly T. "After Action Report for Period 29 Jan to 16 Feb 51, 3rd Battalion, 23rd Infantry—Part of The Twin Tunnels After Action Report Collection." College Park, MD: Department of the Army, May 2, 1951.

Roberts, Charles H., Anthony Durante, Robert C. Whitton, Charles M. Robinson, Arland A. Lottman, James E. Jones, Junior Crayton, Major R. Ramey, Anthony T. Hardon, Charles R. McCullough, Charles B. Ellis, Alfred G. Adler, and Cecil Eide, interview by John Mewha. "After Action Report for Item Company Twin Tunnels—Part of the After Action Report Twin Tunnels," May 17, 1951.

Russell, Donald F. "Witness Statement of Donald F. Russell, Part of the Task Force Crombez After Action Report." College Park, MD: Department of the Army, March 27, 1951.

S3 Journal, 5th Cavalry Regiment. Extract from the 5th Cavalry Regiment's S3 Journal, Part of the Task Force Crombez After Action Report. College Park, MD: Department of the Army, February 1951.

Headquarters, 1st Battalion, 5th Cavalry Regiment. Extract, Operations Log, 1st Battalion, 5th Cavalry Regiment, Part of the Task Force Crombez After Action Report. College Park, MD: Department of the Army, 14–15 February 1951.

Sager, Perry A. "Periodic Operations Report 79, Headquarters, 2nd Battalion, 23rd Infantry Regiment." Kenneth Hamburger Collection. College Park, MD: Department of the Army, 30 January 1951.

Sanford, William A., interview by John Mewha. "After Action Report with William A. Sanford—Part of the Twin Tunnels After Action Report," May 17, 1951.

Stacy, James E., interview by John Mewha. "Interview with James E. Stacy, Executive Officer, 3rd Battalion, 23rd Infantry Regiment—Part of the After Action Report Twin Tunnels," May 17, 1951.

Thompson, Charles M., interview by John Mewha. "After Action, Twin Tunnels—Part of the Twin Tunnels After Action Report," May 17, 1951.

Umberger, Clarence L., interview by Martin Blumenson. "Interview with Clarence L. Umberger, Part of the Task Force Crombez After Action Report," March 28, 1951.

Unknown. "Battle of the Tunnels Area," After Action Report. Kenneth Hamburger Collection. College Park, MD: Department of the Army, 1951.

———. "Company 'F' 23rd Infantry Regiment, 'Rescue Patrol'—Part of the Twin Tunnels After Action Report." College Park, MD: Department of the Army, 1951.

Williams, Billy R. "Witness Statement of Billy R. Williams, Part of the Task Force Crombez After Action Report." College Park, MD: Department of the Army, February 21, 1951.

GENERAL ORDERS
The following General Orders for the 2nd Infantry Division can be found on the Korean War Project website, www.koreanwar.org/html/2011_2ID_korean_war_records _go.html.

Epley, Gerald G. General Orders 193, June 18, 1951.

———. General Orders Number 1, January 1, 1951.

———. General Orders Number 61, October 9, 1950.

———. General Orders Number 63, March 22, 1951.

———. General Orders Number 80, April 12, 1951.

———. General Orders Number 87, April 28, 1951.

———. General Orders Number 88, April 29, 1951.

———. General Orders Number 90, April 3, 1951.

———. General Orders Number 92, May 1, 1951.

———. General Orders Number 102, May 10, 1951.

————. General Orders Number 105, May 12, 1951.

————. General Orders Number 106, May 13, 1951.

————. General Orders Number 114, May 21, 1951.

————. General Orders Number 119, May 29, 1951.

————. General Orders Number 121, May 27, 1951.

————. General Orders Number 123, May 29, 1951.

————. General Orders Number 128, June 1, 1951.

————. General Orders Number 146, June 15, 1951.

————. General Orders Number 149, June 15, 1951.

————. General Orders Number 150, June 15, 1951.

————. General Orders Number 154, June 15, 1951.

————. General Orders Number 160, June 16, 1951.

————. General Orders Number 161, June 16, 1951.

————. General Orders Number 192, June 18, 1951.

————. General Orders Number 460, August 18, 1951.

Graves, Rupert D. General Orders Number 299, July 16, 1951.

————. General Orders Number 504, September 3, 1951.

INTELLIGENCE REPORTS, X CORPS

The following intelligence reports, written by James H. Polk, are part of the Kenneth Hamburger Collection and can be found in College Park, Maryland, at the National Archives Annex.

Periodic Intelligence Report No. 123, Period 232100I–242100I Jan 51.

Periodic Intelligence Report No. 129, Period 012100I–022100I Feb 51.

Periodic Intelligence Report No. 133, Period 052100I–062100I Feb 51.

Periodic Intelligence Report No. 134, Period 062100I–072100I Feb 51.

Periodic Intelligence Report No. 137, Period 092100I–102100I Feb 51.

Periodic Intelligence Report No. 138, Period 102100I–112100I Feb 51.

Periodic Intelligence Report No. 139, Period 112100I–122100I Feb 51.

Periodic Intelligence Report No. 140, Period 122100I–132100I Feb 51.

Periodic Intelligence Report No. 141, Period 132100I–142100I Feb 51.

Periodic Intelligence Report No. 142, Period 132100I–142100I Feb 51.

S2 SECTION, 23RD INFANTRY REGIMENT

The following journals from S2 Section, 23rd Infantry Regiment, are part of the Kenneth Hamburger Collection and can be found in College Park, Maryland, at the National Archives Annex.

S2 Journal, 100001 February 1951 to 102400 February 1951.

S2 Journal, 110001 February 1951 to 112400 February 1951.

S2 Journal, 120001 February 1951 to 132400 February 1951.

S2 Journal, 130001 February 1951 to 142400 February 1951.

S2 Journal, 140001 February 1951 to 152400 February 1951.

S2 Journal, 290001 January 1951 to 292400 January 1951.

S3 SECTION, 23RD INFANTRY REGIMENT
The following journals from S3 Section, 23rd Infantry Regiment, are part of the Kenneth Hamburger Collection and can be found in College Park, Maryland, at the National Archives Annex.
S3 Journal, 30 January 1951.
S3 Journal, 1 February, 1951.
S3 Journal, 5 February 1951.
S3 Journal, 6 February 1951.
S3 Journal, 7 February 1951.
S3 Journal, 8 February 1951.
S3 Journal, 9 February 1951.
S3 Journal, 10 February 1951.
S3 Journal, 11 February 1951.
S3 Journal, 12 February 1951.
S3 Journal, 13 February 1951.
S3 Journal, 14 February 1951.
S3 Journal, 15 February 1951.

FRENCH AWARDS AND GOVERNMENT REPORTS
Award Citation for André Bizot. Kenneth Hamburger Collection. French Army, July 1951.
Award Citation for François Couric. Kenneth Hamburger Collection. French Army, July 1951.
Award Citation for Gustave Gatoux. Kenneth Hamburger Collection. French Army, July 1951.
Award Citation for Louis Leroux. Kenneth Hamburger Collection. French Army, July 1951.
Award Citation for Moise Borst. Kenneth Hamburger Collection. French Army, July 1951.
Award Citation for Paul Amban. Kenneth Hamburger Collection. French Army, July 1951.
Award Citation for Robert Girardot. Kenneth Hamburger Collection. French Army, July 1951.
Headquarters, 3e Company. *3e Company Journal de Marche, February 1, 1951. Battle of the Twin Tunnels.* EMAT, Box 288: French Army, 31 May 1952.
Huschard, Captain, speech. Kenneth Hamburger Collection. EMAT, 1951.
"Le Battalion Francais de l'ONU en Coreé, Decembre 1950–Novembre 1953." Kenneth Hamburger Collection. EMAT, n.d.
Monclar, Raoul. "Report of the Battle of Chipyong-ni." Translated by Kenneth Hamburger. Kenneth Hamburger Collection. Vol. No. 7, Box 404. French Army, 1951.
"Rapport sur la Guerre en Corée." Kenneth Hamburger Collection. EMAT, n.d.

UNPUBLISHED MATERIAL
Allen, Norman F. J., letter to Jim Cardinal. Kenneth Hamburger Collection. Panama City, FL, April 27, 1984.
———, letter to Victor Fox. Kenneth Hamburger Collection. Panama City, FL, August 17, 1979.

————, letter to Victor Fox. Kenneth Hamburger Collection. Panama City, FL, September 18, 1979.

Andersen, Dewey R., letter to Col. Kenneth Hamburger. Kenneth Hamburger Collection. Lincoln, NE, December 21, 1992.

Barthelemy, Maurice, interview by Kenneth Hamburger, December 15, 1992.

Becker, Earl, interview by author, January 25, 2015.

Beeby, Bob, letter to Col. Kenneth Hamburger. Kenneth Hamburger Collection. Sierra Vista, AZ, November 9, 1992.

Bérerd, Serge-Louis, letter to Col. Kenneth Hamburger. Kenneth Hamburger Collection. Translated by Kenneth Hamburger. Poitiers, France, April 3, 1992.

————. "Misunderstandings in the Field." Letter to Col. Kenneth Hamburger. Poitiers, January 27, 1993.

Bolen, James, interview by author. "James Bolen Questionnaire," January 29, 2015.

Butler, Frank C., letter to Col. Kenneth Hamburger. Kenneth Hamburger Collection. New Harbor, ME, November 6, 1992.

————, letter to Col. Kenneth Hamburger. Kenneth Hamburger Collection. New Harbor, ME, January 9, 1993.

————, letter to Thomas Ryan. Kenneth Hamburger Collection. New Harbor, ME, October 13, 1987.

Byers, Donald M., interview by author, January 10, 2015.

————. "Speech at Chipyong-ni." Kenneth Hamburger Collection. Chipyong-ni, February 13, 1991.

Cardinal, James, letter to Col. Kenneth Hamburger. Kenneth Hamburger Collection. San Francisco, CA, March 17, 1993.

Collingsworth, George, interview by author, January 25, 2015.

Cox, Doyle A., interview by author, January 17, 2015.

Curtis, Robert W., interview by Kenneth Hamburger, October 23, 1992.

DeCastries, François, interview by Kenneth Hamburger, December 15, 1992.

Dobbs, Leo, interview by author, January 23, 2015.

Edwards, James W., letter to Paul Freeman. Kenneth Hamburger Collection. Department of the Army, May 7, 1951.

Evans, Morris V., letter to Col. Kenneth Hamburger. Kenneth Hamburger Collection. Marlboro, NJ, November 30, 1992.

Everist, Carroll Gifford, letter to Col. Kenneth Hamburger. Kenneth Hamburger Collection. March 1993.

Fike, Emmett, letter to Thomas Ryan, USFK/EUSA. Kenneth Hamburger Collection. Warrior, AL, March 1, 1988.

Freeman, Paul L. "Farewell Letter to the 23rd Infantry Regiment." Kenneth Hamburger Collection. San Francisco, CA, February 26, 1951.

————, interview by James N. Ellis, April 16, 1974.

————, interview by unknown. Kenneth Hamburger Collection. Date unknown.

————, letter to T. R. Fehrenbach. Kenneth Hamburger Collection. San Antonio, TX, August 31, 1966.

Gilbert, George M., interview by Kenneth Hamburger. "Interview with George M. Gilbert—Driver for Lieutenant Haire, B Battery, 82nd AAA Battalion," December 5, 1992.

Guthrie, William R., letter to Col. Kenneth Hamburger. Kenneth Hamburger Collection. Winter Haven, FL, October 16, 1992.

Halbrook, Joe E., interview by author, January 20, 2015.

Hall, Robert M., letter to Col. Kenneth Hamburger. Kenneth Hamburger Collection. Raleigh, NC, October 2, 1992.

Harris, Thomas C. "Experience in Action, Twin Tunnels, Wonju, Korea area." Kenneth Hamburger Collection. Gulfport, FL, October 15, 1992.

Hauck, Larry, letter to Col. Kenneth Hamburger. Kenneth Hamburger Collection. San Antonio, TX, July 2, 1986.

Henkel, James, interview by author, January 29, 2015.

Hoffman, Donald W., letter to Col. Kenneth Hamburger. Kenneth Hamburger Collection. Stow, OH, September 2, 1992.

Jaupart, Claude L., letter to Col. Kenneth Hamburger. Kenneth Hamburger Collection. Nice, France, December 31, 1992.

Journet, Gérard, letter to Col. Kenneth Hamburger. Kenneth Hamburger Collection. Horbourg-Wihr, France, n.d.

Judd, Ben, letter to Col. Kenneth Hamburger. Kenneth Hamburger Collection. April 1, 1993.

Kamperschroer, John, interview by author, January 20, 2015.

Kotite, Richard S., letter to Major Roy E. Appleman. Kenneth Hamburger Collection. Tokyo, December 3, 1951.

Krueger, Ralph H, letter to Col. Kenneth Hamburger. Kenneth Hamburger Collection. Sierra Vista, AZ. November 18, 1992.

Lee, Martin, interview by author, January 31, 2015.

MacGuyer, Glenn C., letter to Col. Kenneth Hamburger. Kenneth Hamburger Collection. Olympia, WA, December 29, 1992.

Mead, Grant, interview by author, January 31, 2015.

Meszar, Frank, interview by Kenneth Hamburger, November 17, 1992. Kenneth Hamburger Collection.

Metts, Albert Caswell. "Humorous and Human Interest Stories." San Antonio, n.d.

———, letter to Col. Kenneth Hamburger. Kenneth Hamburger Collection. San Antonio, Texas, 1992.

Milbach, Aubrey, interview by Kenneth Hamburger. "Interview with Aubrey Milbach, Radio Operator for K Company," May 1993.

Mitchell, Arnold E., letter to Col. Kenneth Hamburger. Kenneth Hamburger Collection. Tampa, FL, February 22, 1993.

Monclar, Rauol. Kenneth Hamburger Collection. Sierra Vista, AZ, n.d.

Pratt, Sherman, letter to Tom Ryan, Command Historian EUSAK. Kenneth Hamburger Collection. Arlington, VA, n.d.

Ramsburg, John H., interview by unknown. "Interview with Captain John H. Ramsburg," July 2, 1951. Kenneth Hamburger Collection.

Ryan, Tom, interview by Kenneth Hamburger. "Interview with Tom Ryan of Company K," n.d.

Sawyer, Bickford E., letter to Col. Kenneth Hamburger. Kenneth Hamburger Collection. Honolulu, HI, October 6, 1992.

Schutz, Peter F., letter to Col. Kenneth Hamburger. Kenneth Hamburger Collection, n.d.

Stewart, George C., interview by Tymothy W. Caddell. "Service in WWII & Korea," June 7, 1985.

Stewart, Keith M., letter to Col. Kenneth Hamburger. Kenneth Hamburger Collection. Lafayette, IN, January 21, 1993.

Tuttle, William, interview by author, January 30, 2015.

Unknown. "Paul Lamar Freeman—Biography." Kenneth Hamburger Collection. Sierra Vista, AZ, May 1962.

———. "Paul Lamar Freeman." Kenneth Hamburger Collection. Arlington, VA, April 1988.

Walker, Ansil L. "A Battle of the Forgotten War." Kenneth Hamburger Collection. Tacoma, WA, February 1990.

Wilburn, Harley E., interview by author, January 18, 2015.

Wilburn, Harley E., letter to Col. Kenneth Hamburger. Kenneth Hamburger Collection. Centralia, MO, February 20, 1993.

Ziebell, Herbert, interview by Thomas M. Sullivan, Oshkosh, WI, March 1, 2006.

OTHER SOURCES

"5th Cavalry Regiment Organizational Legacy." First Team US, 1996, www.first -team.us/assigned/subunits/5th_cr (accessed February 12, 2015).

American Battle Monuments Commission. "Clement Leonard Pietrasiewicz." American Battle Monuments Commission, January 25, 1954, www.abmc.gov/search-abmc -burials-and-memorializations/detail/Korea_25223#.U-aZpGO8Phs (accessed August 9, 2014).

Arlington National Cemetery. "Matthew Bunker Ridgway." Arlington National Cemetery, March 1993, www.arlingtoncemetery.net/ridgway.htm (accessed July 22, 2014).

Bergin, William E. "General Order Number 21, Award of the Medal of Honor to Hubert L. Lee." Medal of Honor Citation, Washington, D.C.: Department of the Army, 25 February, 1952.

Brown, Lynnita Jean. "Korean War Casualty Information—China." Korean War Educator, 2014, www.koreanwar-educator.org/topics/casualties/p_casualties_chinese.htm (accessed November 3, 2014).

———. "Korean War Casualty Information—Participating Nations." Korean War Educator, 2014, www.koreanwar-educator.org/topics/casualties/p_casualties_ participating_nations.htm (accessed November 3, 2014).

Cavalry Outpost Publications. "5th Cavalry Regiment Decorations." First Team US, October 2009, www.first-team.us/assigned/subunits/5th_cr/5crndx09.html (accessed February 27, 2015).

Central Intelligence Agency. "Daily Report." Baptism By Fire: CIA Analysis of the Korean War Overview, January 13, 1950, www.foia.cia.gov/collection/baptism-fire -cia-analysis-korean-war-overview#Daily Reports 1950 (accessed June 25, 2014).

Chiles, John H. "23rd Infantry Regiment—Command Report." Korean War Project, January 1951, www.koreanwar2.org/kwp2/usa/2id/003/USA_2ID_070015_0151 .pdf (accessed September 2014).

———. "Narrative Summary of Command and Unit Historical Report, Period 1 September–30 September 1950." Korean War Project, September 1950, www.korean war2.org/kwp2/usa/2id/003/USA_2ID_070013_0950.pdf (accessed September 2014).

Cold War Files. "Syngman Rhee." The Cold War Files: Interpreting History through Documents, 2014, legacy.wilsoncenter.org/coldwarfiles/index-33794.html (accessed June 23, 2014).

Collins, J. Lawton. "Army Department Teletype Conference ca June 1950." Truman Library, June 27, 1950, www.trumanlibrary.org/whistlestop/study_collections/ koreanwar/documents/index.php?documentdate=1950-06-00&documentid=ki -215&pagenumber=1 (accessed June 27, 2014).

Department of the Army. "3.5-inch Rocket Launchers M20 and M20B1." Korean War Online, August 1950, www.koreanwaronline.com/history/Bazooka/1.pdf (accessed February 23, 2015).

———. "William S. Sitman." Medal of Honor—US Army, February 1, 1952, www .history.army.mil/html/moh/koreanwar.html#SITMAN (accessed January 12, 2015).

Everist, Carroll Gifford. "Carroll Gifford Everist." Korean War Educator, February 2008, www.thekwe.org/memoirs/everist_carroll/index.htm (accessed February 16, 2015).

Fockler, Richard C. "Afternoon at Twin Tunnels." Patriot Files, November 17, 2002, www.patriotfiles.com/index.php?name=News&file=article&sid=344 (accessed February 8, 2014).

———. "Letter 81: Letter of Richard Fockler to Korean War Project." Korean War Project, October 29, 2006, www.koreanwar.org/html/letters_to_the_lost_from_ korea.html?set=75 (accessed August 9, 2014).

G2. Army Department Teletype Conference, June 25, 1950. Naval Aide Files, Truman Papers. Truman Library, June 25, 1950, www.trumanlibrary.org/whistlestop/study_ collections/koreanwar/documents/index.php?documentdate=1950-06-25& documentid=ki-21-11&pagenumber=1 (accessed June 27, 2014).

General Headquarters Far East Command. "Awards and Citations for Marcel Gustave Crombez." Military Times Hall of Valor, January 29, 1952, http://projects.military times.com/citations-medals-awards/recipient.php?recipientid=7196 (accessed February 26, 2015).

Harris, Seymour. "Return to Heartbreak Ridge." Korean War Project, February 1951, www.koreanwar.org/my_html/korea010.htm (accessed February 27, 2015).

Headquarters, 23rd Infantry Regiment. "23rd Infantry Regiment, February 1951." Korean War Project, February 1951, www.koreanwar2.org/kwp2/usa/2id/ 003/USA_2ID_070015_0251.pdf (accessed October 5, 2014).

———. "Command Report, Period 1–31 December 1950." Korean War Project, December 1950, www.koreanwar.org/html/2011_2ID_korean_war_records_unit .html?pid=3 (accessed July 20, 2014).

———. "Narrative Summary, Period 1–31 October 1950." Korean War Project, October 1950, www.koreanwar2.org/kwp2/usa/2id/003/USA_2ID_070014_1050.pdf (accessed July 17, 2014).

———. "Narrative Summary, Period 1–30 November 1950." Korean War Project, November 1950, www.koreanwar.org/html/2011_2ID_korean_war_records_unit .html?pid=3 (accessed July 18, 2014).

———. "War Diary, 23rd Infantry Regiment. July 1950." Korean War Project, July 1950, www.koreanwar.org/html/2011_2ID_korean_war_records_unit.html?pid=3 (accessed July 19, 2014).

Headquarters, 2nd Infantry Division. "Command Report, 2nd Infantry Division, From 1 January to 31 January 1951." Korean War Project, January 1951, www.korean war2.org/kwp2/usa/2id/003/USA_2ID_070015_0151.pdf (accessed September 2014).

————. "Command Report, From 1 December 1950 Through 31 December 1950." Korean War Project, December 1950, www.koreanwar.org/html/2011_2ID_ korean_war_records_unit.html?pid=1 (accessed July 22, 2014).

————. "War Diary, Headquarters, 2nd Infantry Division 1–30 November 1950." Korean War Project, November 1950, www.koreanwar.org/html/2011_2ID_ korean_war_records_unit.html?pid=1 (accessed July 19, 2014).

Headquarters, U.S. Eighth Army, Korea: General Orders No. 114. "Harold P. Mueller, Distinguished Service Cross." Military Times Hall of Valor, March 4, 1951, http://projects.militarytimes.com/citations-medals-awards/recipient.php?recipientid =6774 (accessed August 4, 2014).

Headquarters, U.S. Eighth Army, Korea: General Orders No. 278. "Stanley C. Tyrell, Distinguished Service Cross." Military Times Hall of Valor, May 31, 1952, http://projects.militarytimes.com/citations-medals-awards/recipient.php?recipientid= 6846 (accessed August 1, 2014).

Headquarters, French Battalion. "Compte Rendu Minute Sur le deroulement des Operations de Defense de Chipyong Ni." Kenneth Hamburger Collection. Chipyong-ni, February 1951.

————. "Le Battalion Francais de l'ONU en Coree, Decembre 1950–Novembre 153." Ministre de Defense, February 1, 1951, www.memoiredeshommes.sga.defense .gouv.fr/fr/arkotheque/inventaires/ead_ir_consult.php?ref=SHDGR_GR_7_U _287_301_jmo&fam=9 (accessed September 30, 2014).

Headquarters, XIX Army Group, CPVF. "Chinese Critique of Tactics Employed in the First Encount." U.S. Force Korea, March 29, 1951, www.usfk.mil/usfk/Uploads/ 120/ChineseCritiqueofTacticsEmployedintheFirstEncount.pdf (accessed October 5, 2014).

Heck, Marlene Elizabeth. "The Blair House. Inside the Home: The Truman Study," 1989, www.blairhouse.org/about/inside-the-home/truman-study (accessed June 30, 2014).

Historical Section, G-2, Headquarters 2nd Infantry Division. "2nd Infantry Division and the Korean Campaign: Vol. 1, 8 July 1950–31 August 1950." Korean War Project, August 1950, www.koreanwar2.org/kwp2/usa/2id/003/USA_2ID_070013_ 0850.pdf (accessed September 2014).

"Hubert L Lee." Military Wikia, n.d., http://military.wikia.com/wiki/Hubert_L._Lee (accessed February 12, 2015).

Jessup, Philip C. "Memorandum of Conversation about the Situation in Korea." Truman Library, November 21, 1950 www.trumanlibrary.org/whistlestop/study_collections/ korea/large/documents/pdfs/ki-15-11.pdf#zoom=100 (accessed July 18, 2014).

Joint Chiefs of Staff. "Army Department Message, Joint Chiefs of Staff to Douglas MacArthur, June 29, 1950." Harry S. Truman Administration File, Elsey Papers. Truman Library, June 29, 1950, www.trumanlibrary.org/whistlestop/study_ collections/koreanwar/documents/index.php?pagenumber=1&documentdate= 1950-06-29&documentid=ki-3-19 (accessed June 29, 2014).

————. "Directive to the Commander of the United Nations Forces Korea." Harry Truman Library, September 27, 1950, www.trumanlibrary.org/whistlestop/study_ collections/korea/large/documents/pdfs/ki-18-3.pdf#zoom=100 (accessed July 17, 2014).

————. "Telegram from JCS to CINCFECOM." Truman Library, November 6, 1950 (accessed July 18, 2014).

———. "Views of the Joint Chiefs of Staff." Truman Library, November 9, 1950, www.trumanlibrary.org/whistlestop/study_collections/korea/large/documents/pdf s/ci-3-6.pdf#zoom=100 (accessed July 17, 2014).

Joint Chiefs of Staff, United States. "General Order No. 1." Center for Strategic and International Studies, August 17, 1945, csis.org/files/media/csis/programs/taiwan/ timeline/sums/timeline_docs/CSI_19450902b.htm (accessed June 20, 2014).

Lay, James S., Jr. "A Report to the National Security Council by the Executive Secretary on the United States Courses of Action with Respect to Korea (NSC 81)." Truman Library, September 1, 1950, www.trumanlibrary.org/whistlestop/study_collections/ korea/large/documents/pdfs/ki-17-1.pdf#zoom=100 (accessed July 17, 2014).

———. "A Report to the National Security Council by the Executive Secretary on United States Courses of Action with Respect to Korea, NSC 81/2." Truman Library, November 14, 1950 (accessed July 18, 2014).

———. "National Security Council Policy on Korea." Truman Library, November 6, 1950 (accessed July 18, 2014).

Korean War Project. "First Lieutenant Thomas Henry Heath." Korean War Project Remembrance, 2014, www.koreanwar.org/html/korean_war_project_ remembrance.html (accessed October 10, 2014).

MacArthur, Douglas. "MacArthur Telegram to JCS." Truman Library, November 4, 1950, www.trumanlibrary.org/whistlestop/study_collections/korea/large/documents/pdfs/ ki-22-13.pdf#zoom=100 (accessed July 17, 2014).

———. "Telegram from Douglas MacArthur to the Secretary of the Army." Truman Library, November 6, 1950, www.trumanlibrary.org/whistlestop/study_ collections/korea/large/documents/pdfs/ki-22-23.pdf#zoom=100 (accessed July 18, 2014).

Meszar, Frank. "Operational Annex to Command and Unit Historical Report Period 9 July–31 July 1950, 23rd Infantry Regiment." Korean War Project, July 1950, www.koreanwar2.org/kwp2/usa/2id/003/USA_2ID_070013_0750.pdf (accessed September 2014).

Muccio, John J., interview by Jerry N. Hess. "Oral History Interview with John J. Muccio," February 10, 1971, www.trumanlibrary.org/oralhist/muccio1.htm.

National Security Council. "A Report to the President by the National Security Coun- cil on the Position of the United States with Respect to Korea." Truman Library, April 2, 1948, www.trumanlibrary.org/whistlestop/study_collections/korea/ large/documents/pdfs/kr-7-1.pdf (accessed June 24, 2013).

Pitlick, Kenneth Paul, interview by Nora Worthen. Kenneth Paul Pitlick Collection (AFC/2001/001/loc.natlib.afc2001001.327), Veterans History Project, American Folklife Center, Library of Congress, April 16, 2002.

"Rauol Monclar." Ordre de la liberation, February 21, 2006, www.ordredelaliberation .fr/fr_compagnon/686.html (accessed July 21, 2014).

Ruffner, Clark L. "2nd Infantry Division—February 1951 Command Report." Korean War Project, February 1951, www.koreanwar2.org/kwp2/usa/2id/003/USA_ 2ID_070015_0251.pdf (accessed September 2014).

Sebald, William J. "Telegram, William Sebald to Dean Acheson, June 30, 1950. Harry S. Truman Administration File, Elsey Papers." Truman Library, June 30, 1950, www.trumanlibrary.org/whistlestop/study_collections/koreanwar/documents/index .php?documentdate=1950-06-30&documentid=ki-4-1&pagenumber=1 (accessed June 29, 2014).

Truman, Harry S. Handwritten Note by Harry S. Truman, June 30, 1950. President's Sec-
    retary's Files, Truman Papers. Truman Library, June 30, 1950, www.trumanlibrary
    .org/whistlestop/study_collections/koreanwar/documents/index.php?document
    -date=1950-06-30&documentid=ma-2-2&pagenumber=1 (accessed June 30,
    2014).
United Nations Security Council. "Resolution 82 (1950) of 25 June 1950." Refworld,
    UNHCR The UN Refugee Agency, June 25, 1950, www.refworld.org/
    cgi-bin/texis/vtx/rwmain?docid=3b00f15960 (accessed June 27, 2014).
United Nations Statistics Division. "National Accounts Main Aggregates Database."
    UNSTATS, 2014, unstats.un.org/unsd/snaama/dnllist.asp (accessed November 3,
    2014).
U.S. Army Center of Military History. "23D Infantry." Lineage and Honors Information,
    March 28, 2013, www.history.army.mil/html/forcestruc/lineages/branches/inf/
    0023in.htm (accessed June 30, 2014).
Vollerons, Edme des. "Biographie du General Monclar." General Monclar, 2013,
    http://translate.google.com/translate?hl=en&sl=fr&tl=en&u=http%3A%2F%2F
    www.generalmonclar.fr%2Findex.php%2Fle-general-monclar%2F17-biographie-du
    -general-monclar&anno=2 (accessed February 27, 2015).
———. "Ansil L. Walker Recalls the Battle of Chipyong-ni During the Korean War."
    Historynet, August 21, 2006, www.historynet.com/ansil-lwalker-recalls-the-battle
    -of-chipyong-ni-during-the-korean-war.htm (accessed November 22, 2014).
White House. "Press Release, June 30, 1950. Harry S. Truman Administration File, Elsey
    Papers." Truman Library, June 30, 1950, www.trumanlibrary.org/whistlestop/study_
    collections/koreanwar/documents/index.php?documentdate=1950-06-30&
    documentid=ki-4-23&pagenumber=1 (accessed June 30, 2014).
World War II Army Enlistment Records. "Stanley C. Tyrell," 2014, http://
    wwii-army.findthebest.com/l/2120201/Stanley-C-Tyrrell (accessed August 1,
    2014).

ACKNOWLEDGMENTS

Like each of my past endeavors, this book was not the work of one man. I had a great deal of help along the way. First, I would like to thank the veterans whom I interviewed for this book: Earl Becker, James Bolen, Donald Byers, George Collingsworth, Doyle Cox, Leo Dobbs, Joe Halbrook, James Henkel, John Kamperschroer, Grant Mead, Glen Medieros, William Tuttle, and John Wilson. In addition, I would like to extend a special thank you to Harley Wilburn, his son Steven, and Martin Lee, who provided photos for the book. Most of all, I would like to thank veteran Jim Coulos, secretary of the 23rd Infantry Regiment Association; without his help, I would not have been able to contact all the other Tomahawk veterans for this book.

Next, I would like to extend my gratitude to the people who helped me plan and guide my trip to South Korea. First is Won Pak, also a Korean War veteran. Mr. Pak organized my trip, putting me in contact with several people who were instrumental in my tour of the various battlefields. These included Seoung Jeoung Lee Cathy, my tour guide and interpreter for the trip to Chipyong-ni, Col. Bill Jong-Hwan Lee, who offered wonderful hospitality and stories, and Col. William Alexander, Ret., who gave me a personal tour of the 2nd Infantry Division Museum and answered several questions about key figures in the battle.

Furthermore, I would like to acknowledge the following individuals who helped me with my research into the battles of Chipyong-ni and the Twin Tunnels: Jo Tison-Chizmar at Real War Photos, for providing me with some great photos of the battle and the Korean War; Scott Cross at the Oshkosh Public Museum for sending the Herb Ziebell letters to me; Kingston Montgomery Winget for providing photos from his father's collection; and Donald Fair and Lucy Chubb at the U.S. Army Heritage and Education Center for sending me photos from the U.S. Army Signal Corps collection.

In terms of research assistance, my biggest contributors were brothers Hal and Ted Barker, and Col. Kenneth Hamburger, Ret. Hal and Ted Barker are the founders of Korean War Project, an amazing website that is a treasure-trove of primary source material on the Korean War, specifically the 2nd Infantry Division. After I asked, they posted all the general orders from the 2nd Infantry Division online; these orders have all the award citations for the 2nd Infantry Division, and while searching through all of them, I discovered numerous award descriptions that became incredible additions to the book.

Col. Kenneth Hamburger wrote the book *Leadership in the Crucible: The Korean War Battles of Twin Tunnels and Chipyong-ni*, which served as the starting point for my study of the battles. When I asked him what he did with all the research, he told me he still had it and was willing to give it to me, provided I donated it after I was done. It was a mountain of material, source of approximately 60 percent of my research in the end. Without it, this book would have never happened. Thank you.

I would like to recognize my two agents: George Bick, and my new agent and George's former boss, Doug Grad. Gentlemen, thank you again for representing me. I also would like to thank my editor, Dave Reisch, at Stackpole Books. Thank you for taking a chance on my manuscript. The Korean War deserves a lot more attention, and you have ensured that it will not remain the Forgotten War for long.

Alas, I would be remiss if I did not mention my good friend Stanley Choy, who helped me translate several items from Korean into English. Lastly, I would like to thank my lovely wife. Without her, I would not have been able to write anything. She is my motivator and my voice of reason.

INDEX